Hearts of Sorrow
Vietnamese–American Lives

Those vicissitudes we have experienced
Cause our hearts to break.

Trải qua một cuộc bể dâu,
Những điều trông thấy mà đau đớn lòng.

(Nguyễn Du)

Hearts of Sorrow

VIETNAMESE–AMERICAN LIVES

James M. Freeman

STANFORD UNIVERSITY PRESS
Stanford, California

Stanford University Press, Stanford, California
© 1989 by the Board of Trustees of the
Leland Stanford Junior University

Original printing 1989

Last figure below indicates year of this printing:

99   98   97   96   95   94   93   92   91   90

Printed in the United States of America
CIP data appear at the end of the book

To the memory of my
father Eugene Freeman,
my greatest mentor.
Also to my mother Ann,
my wife Patricia, and
my son Karsten.

Acknowledgments

I am grateful to the following institutions for their support of the research which resulted in this book. The National Endowment for the Humanities granted me a Summer Stipend in 1982 and a Fellowship for College Teachers in 1983–1984, at which times I collected much of the biographical data on which this book is based. San Jose State University granted me a sabbatical leave in 1983–1984 and a small grant in 1985 for research and writing related to this book. During a fellowship year in 1976–1977 at the Center for Advanced Study in the Behavioral Sciences at Stanford, California, I developed an approach to the study of life histories, of which this book is one example. I am solely responsible for the conclusions and perspectives of this book, which do not necessarily reflect either the opinions or the policies of the institutions named above.

Many Vietnamese-Americans volunteered their time and efforts to ensure the completion of this project. Graduate student Rosy Tran devoted several hundred hours to many phases of the work: locating prospective narrators, working as an interpreter, analyzing the materials we collected, and evaluating the reliability and credibility of the information. Her dedication went far beyond anything that I would have expected, and it is deeply appreciated more than she might ever realize.

I am especially grateful to Dr. Quang Le, who spent many hours discussing with me topics related to Vietnamese values, customs, literature, historical events, and issues in contemporary Buddhism. From him I began to appreciate aspects of the Vietnamese experience that otherwise might have taken me many more years to discover.

Graduate student Hai Nguyen also devoted countless hours to this project, sandwiched in between his studies and his full-time job. I shall never forget his selfless efforts and excellent judgments, which influenced the directions of this book. I am grateful to Mr. Dam Bui, Mr. Ngo Ngoc Trung, Ms. Hue Le, Dr. Nguyen Long, and Dr. Chu Anh Que for the help they gave during various phases of this project. I thank Professor Fauneil Rinn for reading and commenting on an earlier draft of this book.

No words can adequately convey my admiration for the courage and the trust that the narrators showed by telling their life stories to a virtual stranger. By mutual agreement, their real names do not appear in this book; neither do most places in which they lived, except for Saigon and Hanoi. Many of the narrators were interviewed for dozens—in some cases hundreds—of hours, extended over many months. It was their dedication and concern that made this project possible. I am grateful to them for their hospitality and for their willingness to discuss past events, including painful memories.

Portions of Chapters 13, 17, and 41 appeared as "Vietnamese War Widow" in *San Jose Studies* (Vol. 14, no. 2, Spring 1988), while portions of Chapters 7, 24, 30, and 38 appeared as "Turnings in the Life of a Vietnamese Buddhist Nun," in *Betwixt and Between: Patterns of Masculine and Feminine Initiation* (Louise Carus Mahdi, Steven Foster, and Meredith Little, eds. La Salle, Ill.: Open Court Publishing Company, 1987). I am grateful to these publishers for permission to reprint these articles in modified form.

Mr. Huu Dinh Nguyen

I am indebted to Mr. Huu Dinh Nguyen in ways that go far beyond the usual acknowledgments. His high ideals, his tough-minded practicality, his compassion, his insights, his perfectionism, his gentle but powerful criticisms, his unstinting efforts on this project, and his determination that I finish this book—all influenced me most deeply.

For some six years, Mr. Huu Dinh Nguyen and I worked together on this book. His contributions to its final form were indispensable: not only was he interpreter, translator, and severe critic, he also greatly influenced both the overall theme and the structure of this book. He was a guide as I attempted to describe and convey not only the surface details but the inner spirit of the people whom we interviewed. Our viewpoints differ in many ways, but in one we were in complete agreement: our commitment to producing a document that would enable others to understand and appreciate the Vietnamese refugee experience.

For over two decades Mr. Huu Dinh Nguyen was a soldier; most of those years were spent in combat. When his people lost the war, and he and his family fled as refugees, Mr. Huu Dinh Nguyen made the decision to devote the rest of his professional life to helping refugee children, the most vulnerable and innocent of the victims of war, persecution, and unrest. His prodigious talents would have enabled him to retrain in virtually anything he had wished. It was his commitment to children that led him to earn a Master's Degree in Social Work and to become a social worker, a position far below that which he had held in his native country.

For the hundreds of volunteer hours which he spent on this project, Mr. Huu Dinh Nguyen asked nothing in return; his only wish was to see this book completed. Had he been willing, I would have listed him as a coauthor; since he declined out of modesty, I acknowledge him as my friend and mentor beyond compare.

Contents

Guide to Narrators

PART I

Hearts of Sorrow

Introduction

As she handed me the final assignment that completed her undergraduate education, I asked the young Vietnamese woman if she planned to attend her graduation ceremony. Tears came to her eyes, and she replied softly, "No, my parents are no longer alive; they died in Vietnam. My education meant so much to them. I cannot go when they are not there to celebrate."

Parent-child bonds, sadness in remembering the death of one's parents, the high value placed on education, these are certainly not unique to the Vietnamese. But the grief of that young woman derived from something more: she is a refugee who sought political asylum in the United States; she may never again see her ancestral land. Never can she celebrate without triggering memories and sadness.

This book is about the end of an era, a world lost, a way of life that exists now only in memory. It is also about people whose lives were devastated by war and the refugee experience, but who found the inner strength to struggle on and create new lives in a new cultural environment. The narratives in this book provide a glimpse into the personal lives of Vietnamese-Americans, revealing some of their deepest hopes and fears and documenting what they consider to be their successes and failures.

By its very nature, a book that recounts the experiences of refugees has political implications. In collecting and editing these life stories, my aim was not to advocate a particular political position, but to give people the opportunity to express their views, which are emphatically not neutral. Most of these people saw themselves as victimized and betrayed by the Socialist Republic of Vietnam. That is why they are refugees, and that is one of the reasons they wished to speak of their experiences. They do not represent all points of view, but they do speak for a great number of Vietnamese-Americans.

In 1980, I began the research for this book because I perceived that there was a lack of information about Vietnamese-Americans as *persons*. Although there was an increasing literature on problems of adjustment, American views of the Vietnam war, and information on general Vietnamese cultural values and customs, I saw little that conveyed the actual experiences of a people from their own points of view. Also missing were accounts of people that described the varieties of Vietnamese cultural experiences. Little attention was paid to the lives of people in their homeland and to the connections between their childhood environments, their responses to traumatic events, and their ways of adjustment in America.

This book illustrates some of those connections. It does not feature the life stories of leaders, generals, and other famous Vietnamese; these people are frequently interviewed, and their public views are well known. My interest is less with the decision makers and more with those affected by their policies, whose views are often overlooked and unheard. The life stories in this book are those of "ordinary" people, many of whom have extraordinary stories to tell. They also reveal striking insights about themselves and the new land that has adopted them.

The experience of working with many Vietnamese-Americans in the creation of this book led me to confront aspects of my own life that I had not previously considered, to examine my own childhood family experiences from new perspectives. It also caused me to realize how little I knew about my Vietnamese-American neighbors. I remember my initial surprise at hearing Vietnamese-Americans describe themselves and their culture as "sentimental," for that was certainly not my image of them. It is now. These narratives moved me to reconsider events in Vietnam, as well as American views of Vietnam, in ways that I had earlier overlooked. I remember wondering why so many Vietnamese were so virulently anti–Communist; now I know. At first I found it hard to grasp why family separations were so deeply traumatic; the narratives in this book vividly indicate why that is so. I had difficulty understanding why the American lack of discipline, whether in the family, at school, or elsewhere, was so deeply offensive to Vietnamese-Americans. Now I know why.

These life stories have enlarged my horizons concerning the Vietnamese refugee experience and have caused me to ask myself how I might have responded had I been confronted with similar crises. They have prompted me to look at my own society in new ways: family, concepts of the person, friendship, education, economic opportunities, self-sufficiency, hardship have all taken on new meanings for me as a result of this project and of the many friendships I have formed with Vietnamese-Americans. The narratives of this book reveal a commentary, not only on Vietnam and Vietnamese-Americans, but on America as well.

CHAPTER I

The Vietnamese Refugee Experience

Misconceptions and Realities

In the spring of 1975, following the fall of Vietnam, Laos, and Cambodia to the Communists, the United States and many other countries opened their doors to refugees fleeing from Indochina. The first group consisted mainly of military and government people along with their families, but as conditions worsened in Indochina, subsequent waves of refugees, tens of thousands, attempted to escape at great personal risk: at least 10 percent died en route. The Vietnamese survivors represented a wide spectrum of people, including former South Vietnamese soldiers or officials, farmers, fishermen, students, children, teachers, Catholic priests and nuns, Buddhist monks and nuns, disaffected Viet Cong and North Vietnamese soldiers and officials, doctors, lawyers, and business people. They continue to leave, a testimony to the betrayal of freedom under Communist rule, escalating pervasive corruption, and the failure of that regime to fulfill basic human needs. From Laos came thousands of highland tribal peoples such as the Iu Mien and the Hmong, many of which had faced genocide by the new Communist rulers. From Cambodia, many thousands of people fled, bringing with them accounts of atrocities of such unimaginable horror that for several years outsiders refused to believe them. By late

1987, some 847,569 Indochinese refugees, including 529,706 Vietnamese, had sought and been granted refuge in the United States (*Refugee Reports*, December 18, 1987: 10). The total number of people of Indochinese descent in America, including children born here, is probably over 900,000.

During the first five years of this human tragedy, I paid scant attention to it. I had never been in Indochina and had no interest in doing research on refugees or on life-styles that soon would be extinguished. I saw little that I could do in a practical way, for I had no special expertise with which to help them. My humanitarian and research interests at that time centered on the Untouchables of India and the sufferings to which they were subjected. I had lived for some 3½ years in India and had collected the extensive life story of an Indian Untouchable, which was published in 1979. I did not anticipate that my major research and community service commitments in the 1980s would focus on Indochinese refugees.

I live in Santa Clara county, California, which, behind Los Angeles and Orange counties, has the third-largest concentration of Indochinese refugees in the United States. In 1988, their estimated population was 90,000–100,000 people, of whom the majority, at least 75,000, were Vietnamese. By 1980 their presence was noticeable in many ways: a deteriorating downtown core around the university where I teach had begun to be transformed into a lively Vietnamese business and shopping center; increasing numbers of students from Indochina were in schools, high schools, and colleges, and were quickly affecting the character of the schools in which they were enrolled; a steady number of families from Indochina were receiving public assistance; large numbers of Indochinese adults were employed, primarily as low-level technicians, in high-tech "Silicon Valley" companies; an increasing stream of secondary migrants, people initially settled elsewhere in America, were resettling in Santa Clara county because of the weather, available jobs, and the presence of relatives who already resided here; delinquent youth gangs emerged and directed their violence and their extortion rackets primarily at people of their own ethnic background. Although the settled residents of the valley talked about how the refugees must adjust to Santa Clara county, it seemed clear that the county and its residents were affected by and would in turn have to adjust to these newcomers from Indochina. At that point, I began to take an interest in the Indochinese communities around me.

During the year 1980–1981, I explored possibilities, met people in the Indochinese communities, and consulted with specialists in the resettlement and training organizations that served these refugees. My concern was to find activities that fit my skills and that did not duplicate the work of others, but that met compelling needs others had overlooked.

To my surprise, aside from stereotypes and generalities, I found very little information on Indochinese refugees. In Santa Clara county, except for figures on the numbers of refugees receiving public assistance, there was virtually no reliable statistical information regarding these people. For example, county officials, as well as persons involved in refugee resettlement and training programs, did not know that of the refugees under their care hundreds were highland Lao tribal peoples, such as Iu Mien and Hmong, whose customs and life-styles differed vastly from those of other Indochinese refugees. These people were pushed into English classes and job training programs utterly unsuited for them. Their children, who did not understand English, did not speak in school, and in a couple of cases were labeled "mentally retarded." Because these children were from Laos, Lao-speaking interpreters were brought in to speak with them, but these people could not speak the children's highland languages (see Freeman, Nguyen, and Hartsell 1985).

I realized that, notwithstanding their increasing number and their distinctive customs and activities, much about the refugees remained invisible. Despite our long involvement in Indochina, most Americans, including me, neither understood nor appreciated the life-styles, values, and traditions of Indochinese cultures. In spite of the publication of dozens of popular works on the Vietnam war by authors variously described as "grunts," generals, peaceniks, and warmongers, these books contained virtually no understanding of the cultural patterns and character of the peoples on whose lands that war had been fought. The informed writings of Westerners who were experts on these peoples, such as Joseph Buttinger (1958, 1972), William Duiker (1981, 1983), Gerald Hickey (1964, 1982), David Marr (1971, 1981), and Douglas Pike (1978, 1986) appeared to be rarely cited or known by the wider public.

As I came to know Vietnamese refugees in the Santa Clara Valley, I heard increasing complaints that most reporting about them remained erroneous, misleading, and demeaning. They were particularly upset by media reportage that emphasized such topics as criminal gangs, which they considered wholly unrepresentative of the overwhelming majority of the Vietnamese-American people.

Although they had initiative, a work ethic, and the innovativeness which Americans have traditionally admired, Vietnamese-Americans found themselves criticized, insulted, demeaned, and drawn into conflicts with other political or ethnic groups who, without understanding them, felt threatened by their presence. Vietnamese-Americans were also dismayed to find themselves portrayed as welfare sponges or as persons who take jobs away from others. They found that people questioned their right to be in America and also accused them of receiving special treatment from the government, such as interest-free loans. Others insinuated that Indochinese refugees had used unfair means to achieve their successes. Equally invidious were the stereotypes that the Vietnamese-Americans invariably were successful, and thus had no need of special services. They were also deeply disturbed by conventional North American interpretations of the Vietnam war, which often omitted the South Vietnamese, either as participants or as victims. Communist views of the war and the postwar Socialist Republic of Vietnam were treated more sympathetically than those of the South Vietnamese government, which was allied with the Americans (see for example Gough 1978, Harrison 1983). The problem with these global views and stereotypes was that the Vietnamese as persons were overlooked.

Because of these complaints, I designed this book, in which Vietnamese-American people could express themselves in their own terms about subjects they considered important and wanted other Americans to hear. In addition, I inquired about the justification for their complaints. As I began to work with refugees, many people asked me, "Why are these Vietnamese here in America?" Others were more forthright in expressing what they really meant: "What right do they have to be here? Why are they able to get in while people from other countries are kept waiting? And what's so different about their adjustments and those of other immigrants?"

Most Americans are immigrants or the children or grandchildren of immigrants; perhaps that is why many think that they know something about the adjustments necessary to survive and prosper in America. I found, however, that people often overlooked the distinction between immigrants and refugees.

Immigrants *choose to come* to a new life, whereas refugees *are forced to flee*—often for their lives. Vietnamese refugees left their old life, not freely, but because they were persecuted or feared being persecuted on account of their ethnic, religious, or political affiliations; had they not felt threatened, they would not have left. Although the Socialist Republic of Vietnam now encourages Vietnamese refugees to visit their native land, many refuse to do so, fearing that, as happened to one boatload of returnees in 1975, they would be hustled off to reeducation camps to face starvation, overwork, and slow death. And unlike immigrants, most refugees make no real preparations for migrating. American law has recognized this distinction—specifically in the use of the presidential "parole" authority to admit aliens during emergencies and, more recently, the Refugee Act of 1980 (Loescher and Scanlon 1986).

These refugees face what sociologist Ruben Rumbaut calls a double crisis. The first is shared by all immigrants: "The oppressive *load* imposed by the sheer need to survive: to find shelter and work; to learn to speak an unknown language; and to adjust to a drastically changed environment despite the barriers of poverty, prejudice, minority status, pervasive uncertainty, and 'culture shock.'" In addition, the refugee, unlike most immigrants, must also come to terms with the *losses* of the past that include home, country, family, friends, work, social status, material possessions, and meaningful sources of identity. Rumbaut calls this double challenge a "high-demand, low-control situation that fully tests the refugee's emotional resilience and coping resources and produces severe psychological distress even among the best prepared and even under the most receptive of circumstances" (Rumbaut 1985: 435–436).

Social worker Huu Nguyen mentions a third challenge. "It is not simply that the Vietnamese must cope with 'losses of the past.' The Vietnamese aim to return to their homeland; at the same time, they realize that this may be difficult to achieve. This dream is what keeps them going; they strive to find a way, they work for this goal, even though they know it is remote" [personal communication, 1987].

The legal status of refugees is not the only area where there is misunderstanding. Another is the failure to realize that all Indochinese refugees are not alike. The "invisibility" of the highland Lao Hmong and Iu Mien tribes in San Jose is one example. Another is the variation in school performances among Vietnamese, Chinese-Vietnamese, Hmong, Lao, and Khmer students, as documented in San Diego county (Rumbaut and Ima 1987). A third example is the enormous variety of Vietnamese life-styles and traditions. The narratives in this book provide a glimpse of regional and personal variation among the Vietnamese.

Despite great variation in the responses of refugees to America, there are some commonalities of adjustment. In his comparison of refugees from Cuba, Southeast Asia (Indochina), and the Soviet Union, anthropologist David Haines observes that factors such as age and sex profoundly influence the kinds of problems that new refugees face, and that these factors may transcend cultural differences. The elderly typically find adapting to America difficult. Women in their roles as wives and mothers may remain confined at home and may be less influenced by their new society. Southeast Asians are a much younger population, with more children than Cuban or Soviet refugees, and this affects Southeast Asian employment related to meeting household financial need. Other factors also influence refugee adjustments: occupational and educational background; life experiences, values, and expectations; family and kinship; experiences in transit; and the varying receptions in America at different times and places (Haines 1985: 17–35).

Many of these factors continue to be important after the initial adjustment of about three years. Haines documents downward occupational mobility and low income of Cuban, Southeast Asian, and Soviet refugees, who often come to the United States with relatively high occupational and educational backgrounds. High-status refugees often express dissatisfaction with their jobs and their adjustment. Barriers to earning adequate household income include large families and difficulties in learning and using English. Haines views refugee families both as a help in emotional and economic adjustment and as a center for problems involving conflicts between traditional culture, represented by parents, and American culture, represented by schools, peers, and the media, with refugee children caught in the middle. He observes that many refugees who have had a traumatic exodus may suffer long-term emotional distress but that solutions to refugee mental health problems are difficult because different refugee populations have different assumptions, expectations, and understandings about such problems and how they should be dealt with (Haines 1985: 37–55; for further details on specific refugee groups see the additional articles in Haines by other writers).

Another misconception, still believed by many, is that a high percentage of refugees are on welfare. This is most emphatically not the case in Santa Clara county. According to the Department of Social Services, in July 1988 no more than 22 percent, or about 17,880 persons, two-thirds of them children (6,386 "family cases" with an average of 2.8 people per family case), received any form of public assistance: cash, food stamps, and medical or social services. This included people who received Federal Refugee Resettlement Assistance for a period of 18 months, during which time they were expected to learn how to adjust to America, learn English, learn usable job skills, and become placed in employment. After 18 months, assistance is terminated for those without children. Families with children are eligible for AFDC (Aid to Families with Dependent Children). Only 10,466 Vietnamese—only 14 percent, again two-thirds of them children—received such assistance.

Complaints about Indochinese refugees on welfare also overlook the fact that while the numbers of refugees coming into the county of Santa Clara have increased steadily, the numbers of refugees receiving public assistance have not increased proportionally. According to the Department of Social Services of Santa Clara county, in 1981, with their population at 35,000, the number of all Indochinese refugees served, including those from Cambodia and Laos, was around 19,400. In the following three years, the number fluctuated slightly: in 1985, it was around 19,600, and by 1988 it was only around 20,200 out of a greatly increased population of some 90,000–100,000. The reason is that the majority of refugees who receive welfare do so only temporarily, until they can establish themselves as economically independent and self-sufficient people. Many refugees by choice have never been on welfare. Surveys elsewhere show similar patterns of quick economic adjustment to American society (see Nguyen Manh Hung 1985: 203).

The accusations of special treatment given the Vietnamese are also unfounded. They remain, nevertheless, as widely cited pieces of folklore. Time and again people tell me, "Those Vietnamese get special treatment from the government: interest-free loans for houses and cars. Look, they drive around in new cars and live in new houses. We can't afford that." The fact is, Indochinese refugees have had an extremely difficult time securing loans in the Santa Clara valley, as well as elsewhere, because they have had no credit history in America; also many refugees at first distrusted banks. After 1981, this situation began to change as some banks pioneered in extending loans to Vietnamese businesses; by 1987, with the success of numerous businesses, loans have become a more routine part of Vietnamese business developments.

The new cars also are not a result of special privileges. At first, Vietnamese refugees bought new cars for the simple reason that they wanted to be free from the worry of car repairs. Now that many Vietnamese auto repair shops have developed (see Narrator 7), refugees have turned to acquiring second-hand cars. More significant are patterns of saving among many of the refugee groups. Most of the Vietnamese do not eat out much; they do not go on vacations if they cannot afford them; and they do not buy on credit. As a rule they do not live beyond their means. Compared with what many have endured in the Communist-orchestrated economy of food shortages, saving a portion of an American salary is easy.

To buy houses, relatives pool resources. One woman told me how relatives all over the world have helped her buy her house in the Santa Clara valley; she in turn helps them when they need it. That's what makes houses affordable, not special government help. The lesson to be learned is not the fairy tale about special privileges, but rather that, like many refugees and immigrants before them, they might teach Americans a thing or two about frugality, self-reliance, initiative, and about discovering new opportunities that the native-born peoples of this country systematically overlook.

Another scapegoating stereotype is that refugees, especially the Vietnamese, take away the jobs of other people. When used in conjunction with the myth about welfare, the refugee is put in a no-win situation. This claim, like that of welfare, is misleading, if not simply fictitious. The Vietnamese, many of whom were the elites of their country, have taken entry-level jobs that others dismiss as not good enough. After appropriate training, they also have taken skilled technician jobs in electronics companies. Often, their employers have been unable to find enough people to fill these jobs. And because many Vietnamese have been willing to work long overtime hours, they have been sought after by many companies.

Refugees, again mostly Vietnamese, also have started businesses that would not, and indeed could not, have been duplicated by others. Many Vietnamese businesses now hire people of different nationalities and ethnic groups to work in their firms. Far from taking jobs away from others, these businesses provide new job opportunities for others. This trend is seen throughout the United States.

One area where the Vietnamese do compete for jobs is in certain professional occupations, especially engineering and the health professions. To put this in perspective, however, in the first ten years that the Vietnamese and all other Indochinese refugees came to America, their total number was no more than 735,000. This was less than the average of 800,000 legal immigrants who come to America each year and probably less than the number of illegal aliens who entered America in any one year during that ten-year period. The total number of Indochinese refugees in America is a very small fraction of the total population.

The Vietnamese are dismayed at what they consider to be the highly exaggerated coverage by the popular American press of Vietnamese youth gangs. Largely unobserved in these reports is the extent to which these gangs are wholly unrepresentative of the overwhelming majority of the Vietnamese in America—and also that they often are a direct outcome of the failure of American schools to provide a place for refugee students (see Narrator 8). A 16-year-old boy, with no English skills and a couple of years of education in Vietnam, is put into an American high school because of his chronological age. He becomes discouraged and drops out onto the streets, where he meets older youths who at the age of 18 immediately lose all public assistance benefits and therefore the opportunity to finish trade school or high school. With inadequate job skills and command of English, they have great difficulty finding employment, and there are often no community service support systems which focus on the needs of Vietnamese youth. Faced with this situation, these youths turn to the only support system available to them, the street gangs. This does not justify what they do, but it explains why they do it.

As a final matter of concern, many Vietnamese believe that American portrayals of the Vietnam war seriously distort the events and omit the perspectives, not of the men who made the decisions, but of those who paid the consequences (see Banerian 1984 and his criticism of Karnow 1983; see also Nguyen Manh Hung 1985: 207). In their view, most descriptions cover the surface of events, not their deeper meanings. Many Vietnamese say they are particularly upset that the Communists are often presented idealistically, while the South Vietnamese Nationalists are described in unfavorable ways. For example, corruption and violations of human rights are overstated for the Nationalists and underrepresented for the Communists, whose excesses are downplayed. Several Vietnamese have asked me why the Western press lavished so much attention on the immolations of Buddhist monks who in 1963 protested the Diem regime, but overlooked the more numerous immolations in 1978 near Can Tho that were protests against the Communists.

Successes: A Local Example

Throughout America have come stories of the rapid successes of the Vietnamese. Within their first decade in this country, starting with little more than the shirts on their backs (and in some cases not even that), Vietnamese people made their presence felt in many positive ways. In Santa Clara county their impacts were profound and immediate: in the physical environment, through the revitalization of a deteriorating downtown core; in the workplace, where they became renowned for their efficiency, hard work, and high standards; in the schools, where many excelled and literally set new standards of achievement; in culture, where rich traditions of music, poetic recitations, and other aesthetic events were regularly performed; and in the economy, where the incomes earned by the Vietnamese, and the taxes they paid, far exceeded the welfare given to people in their group.

The first priority upon arrival in America was simply to survive through hard times; that is evident in the life stories contained in this book. The refugees came with no plans and in large numbers to a country that had made virtually no plans to receive them, especially in such numbers, and did not know how to provide informed assistance.

By 1985, the start of the second decade of Vietnamese refugees in America, a second phase of adjustments had begun: expansion from mere survival to economic strength and self-sufficiency. A survey done by Huu Nguyen in that year revealed the extent to which the Vietnamese in Santa Clara county had taken charge of their own destinies: 26 medical doctors, 17 dentists, 5 lawyers (with an additional person commuting from Los Angeles), 15 full-time real estate agents and brokers and numerous part-time brokers, 16 accountants, 24 insurance agents, over 200 engineers, over 2,000 electronics technicians, over 5,000 production workers, over 3,000 support services workers, 36 restaurants, 10 weekly, bi-weekly, or monthly Vietnamese publications, and three hours per week of Vietnamese television programming. There were an additional 242 small businesses, including groceries, tailor shops, barber shops and beauty salons, printing and graphic design, photography studios, bookstores, jewelry shops, Oriental medicine and acupuncture, pharmacies, upholstery shops, car dealerships, travel agencies, furniture stores, shoemakers, catering trucks, television sales and repair shops, grocery stores, automobile service stations, automobile body shops, and loan agents. There was an association of Vietnamese jewelry stores, an association of car dealers, an association of Vietnamese physicians, and the Vietnamese Chamber of Commerce. Perhaps never before in American history had such a large block of people faced with such overwhelming obstacles succeeded so fast in turning around their lives to become economically self-sufficient contributors to the community in which they lived.

Hearts of Sorrow

Despite their stunning successes, the Vietnamese have not adjusted to America without costs and difficulties. Not all Vietnamese are successful; some households have become welfare dependent; despite many school successes, a number of students do poorly; there are continuous reports of communal tensions and strife between Vietnamese and others who feel threatened by their presence and who blame the Vietnamese for their own difficulties. There are the well-publicized, if not overpublicized, activities of youth gangs, whose victims are mostly other refugees.

Many refugees have experienced devastating losses of relatives and friends, have personally undergone terrifying ordeals as prisoners in reeducation camps and jails or as "boat people" fleeing Vietnam; virtually all have experienced a sense of guilt at leaving behind loved ones in Vietnam whom they probably will never see again. They know that the Communists in Vietnam are deliberately dismantling society as they knew it. In America, too, they find that many of the values and social arrangements that they cherish wither when confronted with the American leveling process. Vietnamese parents have much difficulty rearing children in the permissive society of America, in which the authority of adults is undermined (see Narrators 1, 2, 4, 6). Children distance themselves from their parents. For many parents, who sacrificed greatly for their children, these changes are almost as devastating as the loss of their homeland.

No matter how successful the children are, they often seem to be unable to live up to the expectations of their parents, even if they wish to do so. The parental expectations were formed in Vietnam; the children must succeed in America, in which the contexts of parent-child relationships are different. Both parents and children often feel deep discomfort about this conflict between parental authority and children's freedom: the parents see themselves as sacrificing for their children, who abandon them; the children see themselves as performing well, yet their parents reject them because of their social behavior.

Nguyen Manh Hung suggests that two things distinguish the Vietnamese refugees from other refugees and immigrants who have come to America: "the exposure of the boat people to the horror of pirates' attacks and their perception of injustice done to their collective image." By injustice, he means that as losers in an unpopular war, their collective role "has been misinterpreted and distorted by the winner and by the mass media in the United States" (Nguyen Manh Hung 1985: 206–207).

The narratives in this book deal with these two issues, but they also reveal a third important feature of the Vietnamese refugee experience: beneath the surface of success in America lies sorrow. Refugees from other communities also experience this predicament, but what is distinctive about the Vietnamese version is its particular cultural expression. One young man said, "On the outside, I am like an American. I drive to work in my car. I eat hamburgers at lunch. But on the inside, I am Vietnamese; I cannot forget my mother, hungry in Vietnam, while I have it easy here." Others say, "Life is not at ease here." Although they are deeply grateful for the basic freedoms of America, they feel in but not of this culture, yet there is no homeland to which they can return. They realize that they represent the end of an era, a way of life that will never again be seen. The tragedy of their lives is highlighted for many in the opening verses of *The Tale of Kieu*, Vietnam's most famous literary work, by Nguyen Du, Vietnam's greatest poet.

> Those vicissitudes we have experienced
> Cause our hearts to break.
>
> Trải qua một cuộc bể dâu,
> Những điều trông thấy mà đau đớn lòng.
>
> (Translated by Huu Dinh Nguyen)

In this long narrative poem written in the early nineteenth century, the heroine Thuy-Kieu retains her chaste outlook and purity over many years while being betrayed, dishonored, and subjected to terrible ordeals and suffering. In literal translation that passage reads, "To experience the events of the mulberry-covered sea, while watching over these events, causes sorrows of the heart." The "mulberry-covered sea" refers to the time it takes for the sea to transform itself into a mulberry field and back again into the sea, a poetic expression for momentous upheavals that occur in nature or in the lives of a people, to the fate of a nation and a grief so deep that it speaks to all people, to a mourning for the sufferings endured by the Vietnamese over the centuries. (See also the translations and commentary by Huynh Sanh Thong 1973: 33, 145; 1983: 3, 169). *Hearts of Sorrow*, the title of this book, is inspired by Nguyen Du's immortal words; it is the theme that connects the life stories.

This interpretation of the story of Kieu was pointed out to me by several Vietnamese people; it is one widely accepted by elderly Vietnamese-Americans, who often are visibly moved when they hear the recitation of the opening lines of *The Tale of Kieu*. They frequently liken their own experiences to the heartbreak and suffering epitomized in Nguyen Du's narrative poem. Not all Vietnamese resonate equally to the poetic tragedy of the heroine Thuy-Kieu. Vietnamese-American youngsters, who have not grown up with *The Tale of Kieu*, show less interest in the poem and its outlook than do their parents. But for those whose formative years were spent in Vietnam, *The Tale of Kieu*, their national treasure, is part of their soul.

CHAPTER 2

Creating *Hearts of Sorrow*

In the preparation of this book, I interviewed some 40 men and women. Many were from Santa Clara county, California; others were located throughout the United States. Fourteen of these narrators, ranging in age from 16 to 80, are included in this book. They represent a wide range of occupations, levels of education, localities in Vietnam, political orientations, and religious preferences; they also represent both first-wave refugees who left in 1975 and second-wave refugees who escaped after 1975. Three persons originally scheduled for inclusion in the book changed their minds because they feared retaliation against their families or because they considered the accounts to reveal too much of their personal life. No material from their 150 hours of interviews appears in the book.

Some persons understandably wanted to convey their strong anti-Communist sentiments, to let Americans know what it meant to live under Vietnamese Communist oppression. But quite a few of the persons whom I interviewed extensively focused on topics other than politics, war, and resistance movements. When these surfaced in their accounts, they often were integrated into a larger view of the person's life as a whole. Many people spoke with nostalgia of their childhood in villages, of family life even when it involved deep conflicts between parents and children or between siblings.

Prominent in the design of this book were four features. First, refugees were not informants to be questioned, but rather participants who were consulted and who retained powers of editorial discretion and the option to withdraw at any stage of the research and writing. This book project was framed as a community effort to disseminate information about Vietnamese-American life-styles, perspectives, and adjustments, as agreed upon by the participants and myself. Second, participants received copies of the narratives they contributed. Of particular concern to many narrators was that they leave a legacy for their family and their community: the memories of a life-style, values, and traditions that are rapidly being obliterated or altered both in Vietnam and in America. Third, because of the community-service nature of this project, a portion of the royalties from the publication of these materials is to be donated in an appropriate way for the public benefit of Vietnamese-Americans or refugees. Finally, Vietnamese-American researchers were trained to carry on the research, so that eventually they could take over and maintain a continuous oral histories project.

Many narrators feared that their remarks might provoke retaliation against themselves or their families, either in the United States or in Vietnam. To allay their fears, I chose participants, not randomly, but rather through a network of Vietnamese-American contacts whom the narrators trusted. I based my selection of narrators on their different backgrounds and diverse viewpoints; I also looked for those who had something to say, were able to articulate it, and wanted to do so. The views they present are contradictory and often controversial. The interviewing process varied widely depending on the personalities of the narrators, the extent to which they needed to be prompted with specific questions, and the ways they responded to me and my researcher-interpreters, and we to them. The interviews, taped whenever the narrators were willing, ranged in length from two or three hours to over 100 hours. Some of the accounts covered the span of a person's life; others focused on a certain time period or series of events that were particularly important to the narrator.

The life stories in this book are, strictly speaking, not autobiographies, but narratives that are the product of my collaborative activities with the narrators and the researcher-interpreters. The words are those of the narrators; they are, however, a response to questions asked by me. Together, the narrators and I determined what portions of their texts would be included for publication and what would be excluded. But I alone edited these accounts, arranged them according to themes, and provided explanatory notes and interpretations. My aim was to present important aspects of Vietnamese culture, history, and personal character which influenced the adjustments of Vietnamese refugees in America.

Many of the narrators recited well-known ethical precepts, as well as proverbs and songs that they remembered from their childhood. In describing periods of crisis or conflict, some narrators recalled curses, obscenities, and insults uttered at that time. To retain the flavor of their speech, I have presented in translation such quotes and expressions as they stated them, whether or not they depart from standard meanings.

After the fall of South Vietnam, the Communists changed the name of Saigon to Ho Chi Minh City. I have followed the preferences and usage of the narrators in the naming of the city.

Although it uses biographical and historical materials, the book is not simply a collection of life stories, nor is it a conventional narrative of the Vietnam conflict. While it documents remembered childhood experiences as well as Vietnamese responses to resettlement in America, it is not strictly a psychological study nor one of social adjustment. Rather, it traces the effects that a major historical event, the fall of Vietnam to the Communists, has had on the lives of ordinary Vietnamese people who have come to America, and the ways in which they themselves view their situation. Unlike Santoli's oral histories of Vietnam refugees (1985), this book traces the connections between the life experiences of people in Vietnam and their adjustments in a foreign land.

It is no accident that the narratives are presented as fragments, not full life histories. In describing their life stories, narrators presented not a seamless, continuous chronology, but pieces of recollected incidents that they sometimes strung in chronological order.

Accounts that describe "The Vietnam War" as a totality present a view of events distant from the ways in which individual participants, such as the narrators in this book, experienced or viewed those events.

The life story of each narrator may be read in two ways: thematically and chronologically. The narrative chapters of the book are placed into five parts that follow a chronological order: Vietnam: Childhood, Youth, and Character; Vietnam: Sorrows of War; Vietnam: Sorrows of Liberation; Flight to Freedom; and America: Heartache Beneath Success. Introductions to these sections highlight the main themes or historical events that are discussed by various narrators or are implicit in their accounts.

Most chapters in each section are arranged in roughly chronological order. However, Chapter 18, "The Death Toll in My Family, 1945–1975," sums up, in a way, the effects of war over a long period. And Chapters 19–22 tell of the reeducation camp experiences of an ex-colonel in the South Vietnamese Army. The impact of these six years of starvation and labor camp punishment is best appreciated if they are presented as a continuous narrative. The colonel's additional prison experiences, related to his attempted escapes from Vietnam (Chapters 32 and 33), appear in another section of the book.

The life story of a single narrator may be found as several chapters in different sections of the book. In this way, experiences of childhood, or of the war years, or of social adjustments in America can be more easily compared. At the same time, the narrator of each chapter is identified so that his or her story can also be read chronologically; a brief editor's note at the end of each chapter lists other chapters about the same narrator (see also the Guide to Narrators on pp. xiv–xv). The opening of each chapter places the selection in context and may also summarize aspects of the narrator's life story not otherwise included, point out important themes of the narrative, and specify how the texts were collected.

PART II

Vietnam: Childhood, Youth, and Character

Introduction

For many narrators, the remembered days of childhood and youth were especially vivid. Of particular significance was the way in which the narrators drew on their childhood experiences to understand their responses to war and to domination by the Communists, and their adjustments in America. Although they idealized their childhood, often quite intentionally, many people spoke also of the hardships they endured, especially the loss of parents, famine, disruption caused by war, and extreme poverty (see also Banerian 1986, Huynh Quang Nhuong 1982, Tran Van Dien 1981).

Despite their widely different childhood experiences, most narrators mentioned several themes that they saw as the building blocks of their character. The first and most important was family and parents. Those who lost parents in childhood mourned that loss and viewed their childhood as incomplete. The death of a father meant the loss of a guiding, disciplined authority; the loss of a mother meant the lack of nurturance, sentiment, and affection.

Frequently mentioned were numerous examples of the extreme sacrifices that parents made for their children; this in turn fostered in the children a deep sense of obligation to their parents. The key to this relationship, said many narrators, was the unconditional love that their parents showed for them and their brothers and sisters. The identities of the children were forged in this environment of love and sacrifice; what was expected from them in return was unquestioned obedience to parents and obligation not only to living family members, but to those who had preceded them and those who would follow them. The enormous burden of guilt and sense of frustration that Vietnamese-Americans feel for members of their family left behind in Vietnam, especially parents, is evident in the moving stories that these narrators tell, not only of childhood, but of their adjustments in America.

Love, authority, obligation, and proper behavior, including politeness, also were fundamental values in the school environment, which complemented what children had learned at home. A favorite and widely quoted proverb was "King, Teacher, Father"—the child's obligation was obedience to these authority figures in the order listed. Other proverbs explicitly linked love and harsh discipline: "When we love our children, we give them a beating; when we hate our children, we give them sweet words." The reason for this was stated in another pithy saying: "Fish will be rotten without salt; children will always be rotten [spoiled] if they have disobeyed their parents." Implicit in this was the notion that harsh discipline and beatings did not constitute abuse of a child, but its reverse: loving care, concern, and attention. No wonder, then, that so many Vietnamese in America comment in bewilderment on what they see as undisciplined Americans, lax socialization practices, school environments that foster undisciplined independence in children, and child-protective laws that perpetuate this chaos by intruding into the home to prevent child rearing in the Vietnamese style.

A number of the narrators lived in hamlets and villages and speak of them with fond remembrance: childhood games and close friends; tending water buffalo; picking bamboo shoots in the forest; village celebrations, especially the new year season; fishing, cooking, and eating eels; and the wide variety of tasks that changed with the season. As one narrator put it, "Our life depended not on the time clock, as in America, but on the seasons. This is much more exciting and interesting than working in the city, where every day you go to work at the same time and do the same boring tasks. Our agricultural schedule was flexible, diverse, closer to nature, and enjoyable." Other words that narrators used to describe those village childhood days were "at ease" and "cozy."

Those who were reared in the cities also remember happy days. "I remember childhood as a beautiful, wonderful time," says one narrator, who lived in a large house behind one of the two stores owned by his father. "Life was so safe that we left our doors open at night."

Not only ideals but departures from them are mentioned by the narrators. Two narrators recalled that their fathers paid little attention to their families, in fact clearly neglected them. One of them, a middle child, states, "I grew up without love," and concludes that learning to adjust to this helped him to cope with other adversity when he was an adult. Another narrator describes how students were expected to exhibit unquestioning obedience in school; this did not prevent him from openly stabbing a classroom bully in the neck with a dip pen covered with purple ink.

The descriptions of childhood and youth presented by these narrators are indispensable for understanding how and why these people adjust to America in the ways they did. All narrators were asked to discuss what they considered to be important aspects of their childhood. They were clearly selective, in ways that illuminate how they view their subsequent adjustments in America, and, as is developed in Part VI of this book, what they find lacking in the American cultural environment.

CHAPTER 3

I Never Forget an Insult:
1906–1941

NARRATOR 1: ELDERLY SOUTH
VIETNAMESE CIVIL SERVANT

"Some people, when they become upset and angry, hit, shout, or swear at people. After an hour, they forget about it. But I am different. Whenever someone shouts or swears at me or speaks to me rudely, I lower myself down; I speak to that person politely; I never show anger. I still smile, but inside I never forget an insult. I will keep it with me until the day I die."

Mr. Ngon smiled slightly as he uttered these words in his frail voice. A thin, silver-haired man, he sat ramrod straight at his dining room table. Before him on the table were his notes, which he had written out in advance, and dictionaries in English, French, and Vietnamese. In the kitchen his wife was preparing tea. Sitting with us was our interpreter, a young Vietnamese university student who had been instrumental in the selection of Mr. Ngon as a narrator. Following my request, she had made inquiries to find an elderly person who was articulate and had an interesting story to tell. A local community college teacher recommended Mr. Ngon as a person with a lively sense of humor who drew on a vast array of experiences in his essays and oral presentations. At the age of 75 he had enrolled in Spanish language classes so that he could communicate more easily with many of the Spanish-speaking people in his neighborhood. Although Mr. Ngon spoke fluent French and good English, our interpreter attended most of our sessions to help explain the myriad of distinctive expressions that surfaced:

*colloquial phrases, proverbs, insults, and obscenities uttered by the charac-
ters who appeared in Mr. Ngon's life story.*

Mr. Ngon's revelation about his character appeared midway through his monumental narrative: 106 hours of taped interviews, over 200,000 words. The story is historically important: Mr. Ngon, born in 1906 of a poor family, describes daily life in South Vietnamese villages in the first decade of the twentieth century. He evokes a world and a life-style that are long gone, remaining only in the memories of elders. He describes how his mother survived as a widow by making cakes for Buddhist celebrations and by doing other jobs, including farm labor. He recollects his childhood days with vivid details that include schoolboy scuffles, cricket fighting, and the ingenious punishments that teachers devised to cow their students into absolute submission. He pokes fun at shamanic faith curers and describes how he and others unmasked fraudulent practitioners, but he also describes how a ghost once terrified him. Especially significant is his discussion not only of the ideal rules of Vietnamese society, but of the departures from these rules as they occurred in his own family as well as in others. His elder brother was a gambler who squandered his family's modest income; his grandfather's brother was a troublemaker who caused continual embarrassment to his older relatives, who had to bail him out of numerous self-made crises. Several of his own children are sources of unhappiness to him and his wife.

The workplace also receives uncomplimentary attention from Mr. Ngon. He documents corruption among French colonial officials and their Vietnamese subordinates, also among officials of the Diem and subsequent governments of the Republic of Vietnam. He describes the petty tyrannies of small officials, including their insults by gestures and words. His descriptions of the Viet Minh are equally unflattering. By contrast, his account of the Americans is surprisingly lenient; he seems more ready to forgive their transgressions than those of his own people or his own family, possibly because he is grateful for being allowed to come to America.

Historically noteworthy is Mr. Ngon's eye-opening account of how he became aligned with the French colonial government rather than the Viet Minh. Not surprisingly, he has little good to say about either side, and at one point in his narrative, he says that they are interchangeable: both killed, tortured, and terrorized civilians, burned villages, took away crops and livestock, polarized families, split villages from towns, exercised their *will by force, and disrupted the lives of everyone. Twice Mr. Ngon was a specific target for assassination by the Viet Minh, and he has a shattered arm as a memento. His first wife and his elder brother both were killed by the Viet Minh.*

Mr. Ngon's account of coping with life in America highlights the complexity of the resettlement and social adjustment process, and calls attention to the special needs of the elderly, which often go unmet and unrecognized. Some Americans say the Vietnamese are reserved, unapproachable, and hard to befriend. Mr. Ngon, by contrast, describes his efforts to befriend his American neighbors and how they rebuffed him. He notes, however, that Americans in small towns are often much friendlier than those in larger cities.

His documentation of the deterioration of Vietnamese family values and social interactions is not new, but he presents the dilemmas and heartbreak of this process, as seen by the elderly, with particular bitterness and force.

Memories of Childhood in South Vietnam

I was born in 1906 in a village of 400 people located about five kilometers from a large town in South Vietnam. My father's father was Chinese; his mother was Vietnamese. On my mother's side of the family, everyone was Vietnamese. As a child I remember that during the rice harvest, many people of the village would travel by boat to the western provinces. They would carry cane sugar and peanuts which they had cultivated. At their destination, they would make a special candy consisting of peanuts, rice paper, and sugar, which they sold to the field laborers of those provinces in exchange for rice. They also sold mortars and pestles, which were rare in the plains. Our villagers would return home with rice, which they sold in our area or kept for their own consumption.

In those days, both men and women wore long hair down to their waists. They would roll it behind their heads. This was the custom of the Chinese, and in those days we imitated them. Perhaps 5 percent of our villagers were Chinese.

Most of the people lived in houses made of wooden frames, with bamboo for walls, thatch roofs, and floors of clay. A few rich people, maybe 7 percent of the villagers, lived in houses made of wood, with red tile roofs. The village had three hamlets of about 90 houses each. The houses were separated from one another by about 50 meters, while the hamlets were about one-half to two kilometers apart. Inside, the houses were not at all like those in America. The front half of the house was a large sitting room, while the back half of the house was divided into two bedrooms separated by an altar room. We had an antique altar which stood on the mud floor. Every evening at 6:00 P.M. we burned incense; we followed the Confucian doctrine. Behind the altar was a storage space. We had a separate house for cooking, and in there we also had a space for the storage of paddy [unmilled rice]. The kitchen was separate because that's the way the old tradition was. We had no bathroom, but like the other villagers, we bathed in the river and eliminated our human wastes behind bushes. My grandparents plus the seven of us lived in that house: my parents, my elder brother, my three sisters, and me. I was the second oldest surviving child in the family; two other brothers had died.

My mother told me that when she was a young girl, her father's father was a canton chief, the head of eight villages, with many important functions. Villagers within the canton area asked him for advice on various matters such as rice agriculture and disputes among neighbors.

My mother's grandfather, the canton chief, had ten children, one of whom was my mother's father. He was a sweet and pious son who obeyed his father. But the elder son of the canton chief was disobedient, and this was a great dishonor which damaged the prestige of the canton chief and his whole family. This son, despite the objections of his parents, neglected his business as a village tax collector; he was usually in debt because he spent all his money running after petticoats and gambling on cock fighting. Debt collectors demanded payment, but he had no money.

He went to his father and said, "I cannot pay my debt; maybe I should burn my cottage and go far away from the village." People make threats like this as a last resort when they have no solution to their problems, but they do not usually follow through.

His father replied, "You see, I have been very dishonored, even more so if you burn your house and run away."

Because the situation was so serious to the family honor, the canton chief, who was not wealthy, said to his obedient son, "Go and help; pay the debt for your brother, but only this one time." So my mother's father paid the debt in rice.

This created another problem, since that was the rice he had stored for the year. If they gave it away, how would they survive the next year? As the rice was carried away, my grandmother, mother, and aunts watched, and their eyes grew moist. Everybody in the family was so upset, but they had to accept the situation. They were very sad inside, but they dared not say anything publicly because they did not want to make their elders more sad.

The next year came. The same thing happened again. Again there was no public complaint. Year after year, the disobedient son continued without thinking. He was a terrible man. And each year the family paid his debts without complaint.

One year, the family was holding the death day ceremony for one of our ancestors. Many of our relatives had gathered together that day to worship and to give offerings of cakes, fish, beef, and other things. Each person brought one dish to the altar to offer to the ancestor. The food was placed on a long table in front of the altar. Suddenly the wife of my disobedient granduncle appeared with a crying grandchild, snatched an offering of fish, divided it with chopsticks, and gave half to the child. Then she left.

All of the relatives looked around in confusion, astonishment, and anger. "She is a very bad woman," they said, for a person should never dare to do what she did. "She is very disrespectful!" they shouted.

The disobedient granduncle heard this and came running with a sickle. He waved it and threatened his mother, "This old lady dare not say anything, or I'll cut out her throat!" His mother remained silent; so did everyone else. Then he left.

When I was a young man, I returned to the village where my grandfather lived. He said to me, "The bad example of my elder brother will give an example to everyone in the future. He will be a victim of his own descendants, as Confucius has said, 'Pious submission begets pious, submissive child. Disobedient insubordination begets disobedient child.'"

And that is what happened to my disobedient granduncle, for his own sons refused to help him with food or money when he was in need. When he visited his son in the city, his son would give him no money for transportation home, so the disobedient granduncle had to walk seven hours to reach home. My own grandfather felt so sorry for him that he'd often invite him over to eat. Still, that granduncle never changed his own behavior; he always disliked my grandfather. His personality never changed. We have a proverb, "Parents give birth to the child; The Creator [Nature] creates the character."

Around 1932, my disobedient granduncle died. Normally, all the relatives and neighbors help the family during this time of need and grief. But not this time; they all went instead to my uncle's house next door. They stayed all night; they ate; they decided not to attend his funeral. The behavior of that family brought about its own bad consequences.

One day when my mother was a child, a fortune-teller came to visit my mother's grandfather, the canton chief. The fortune-teller saw my mother and said, "This young girl will have a hard life when she grows up." At that time she was about ten years old. As my mother was growing up, her grandfather remembered the fortune-teller's prediction. All of my mother's family were farmers; they worked very hard in the rice fields. When my mother reached the age of twenty, her grandparents decided to marry her to a family whose people were not farmers, so that my mother would not have to work hard. That's why they accepted the proposal from my father's family. My father was a pharmacist, not a hard job. They figured that my mother would live easily with such a husband.

But after her marriage, the life of my mother continued to be very hard. My father drank rice wine every day [was an alcoholic]. He played cards for money. His income was not enough, so my mother had to work every day. Often she complained to her mother-in-law, who would reply, "Look, he's not the only man in this hamlet who does this; almost all the other men do the same thing."

So my mother suffered a great deal. Many times she wanted to abandon my father, but her parents opposed this. They reminded her that women had to submit three times in this world, and they would recite the Confucian-influenced rule of the three submissions: "Remaining in the house [unmarried], submit to the father. Going out of the house [married], submit to the husband. Widowed, submit to the [eldest male] child."

Her mother would also quote her another proverb: "The daughter is a girl of another family. The daughter-in-law is really the one [the daughter] that parents buy and bring home." From this my mother realized that she had to live with my father until he died.

When I was six years old, my father mortgaged his land to a rich relative for the sum of 90 Vietnamese piasters. My mother feared that my father, by taking this money, would lose the land on which we lived, so she got her father to lend her money to redeem the land. My father's parents were ashamed that their daughter-in-law had saved their land, so they moved away. By that time, my father was ill with dropsy; soon he died. I was around seven years old and had begun school that year. After my father was buried, my mother came back to live with her parents, in a village about one mile from where I had been born.

My mother was very poor, a widow who had to support her two sons and three daughters by taking lots of jobs. She worked in the fields transplanting and harvesting rice; she worked as a seamstress; she made and sold cakes for Buddhist holidays; she raised chickens and pigs, and castrated the males; and though it was illegal, she distilled rice wine, as did only a small number of villagers.

At that time, my elder brother was sixteen years old, but he was not serious. Fathers have powers to control their sons, but mothers often don't. My brother showed disobedience to my mother and her parents by gambling, even when they told him not to do that. He was nine years older than me, and he followed my father's way. I followed my mother's direction, even when we lived in my father's village. She didn't teach me anything about gambling, and her side of the family never gambled; they worked on the farm.

While my mother stayed with her parents, my elder brother moved back to his father's village, where he had been born. From time to time people from that village would visit my mother and tell her, "Your son continues to play cards and lose money."

Two years later, my mother's cousin offered him a job as a train station chief, but my brother soon returned home on vacation to play cards. When he had to pawn his clothes, my mother redeemed them with her own money. Then he resigned from employment, continued to play cards, and again asked my mother for money. She did this several times, but finally she couldn't give him any more; she was so poor that she sold her cottage to a relative. My brother didn't care; he threatened that man: "If you take that house, I'll stab you!" So the man gave back the cottage. With an ax my brother then cut down over twenty areca palms that stood in my mother's yard; that's how angry he was.

My mother was extremely displeased with this, and she lost her mind, almost like a fool. She behaved like a possessed ghost. She could not sleep, she did not want to eat, she never smiled but just sat in one place from early morning until evening without speaking to anyone. She did this for one whole year. Whenever anyone told her the right thing to do, she would consider it wrong. My grandmother told her not to be upset any more, but to come along with her to the market, where she would buy her some nice food. My mother refused to move. When friends or relatives visited, she showed no expression, whether happy or not. I was very sorry about all of this, but I was very young and didn't know how to react to the situation. My elder brother didn't dare come home because he knew that his grandparents and uncle disliked him. Even though he knew of Mother's condition during that year, he did not show his face, and I did not dare to see him; I was scared of him.

I was now nine years old and attending school; to do that, I had to cross the river. But I also had to help my uncle, a farmer who was very nice to me. Sometimes I watched the buffalo; other times I guarded the paddy fields against birds. So I went to school irregularly. I didn't have any friends because no one of my age lived near me.

During the year that my mother was ill, my grandmother twice took her to a Buddhist pagoda in another village, where she got a monk to recite exorcism prayers for my mother. This did not help because my mother was not possessed by a demon.

I was unhappy in school because I was often mistreated by the teacher. Since I attended school irregularly, I did not know my multiplication tables fluently. The teacher forced me to recite them by memory, but when I missed, he'd pinch me on the inner thigh, leaving large, red bruises. He'd tell me to hold out my hand, and he'd beat me very hard on the palms ten to fourteen times with a bamboo stick one and a half feet long. Although this left red marks on my hands, I dared not cry, or he'd beat me more. I was treated just like all the other students: beaten and pinched. I was afraid of him. For more than a year I had to put up with that. I was unhappy living in the village of my maternal grandparents.

Later in the town I had a teacher who had lost one leg in an accident. He kept rocks on his table. Whenever a student talked, he'd throw rocks at them. When the rich students didn't know their lessons, they'd stand up silently, and he'd throw his rocks. Finally he became so tired of beating them that he simply told them to sit down when they couldn't answer the questions.

In those days, we learned the ethical precept "King, Teacher, Father." A man first should show respect to his king, then to his teacher, and third to his father. We learned respect.

In the village, we students often played at cricket fighting. Crickets were a kind of toy for which we did not have to spend any money. In the rainy season lots of crickets appeared, about the size of our fifth finger. Some were black, others brown. The male cricket was very bellicose; he'd live in little holes singing "Te te te te." I'd catch the crickets and put one each in a match box. If there were two in the box, they would fight. The bigger ones were very good for fighting. I'd take them to school. But we dared not take them into the schoolroom. If a cricket sang in the middle of class, the teacher would search, and when he found who brought it in, he'd beat him with rattan two or three times. We'd hide the crickets in the bushes. Sometimes other kids would steal them. But during free time, we would bring them out, tease them with thick long grass until two crickets faced each other; then they'd fight with their very sharp teeth. They'd wrestle and bite until one lost and ran away. A dozen of us would stand around watching this, betting small amounts on one or the other. Sometimes a student would egg on others: "Go ahead, bet more; if you lose, I'll pay for you." But if the bet was lost, the student would simply run away.

One of my friends did fish fighting, a much crueler sport. While crickets fought for maybe five minutes, fish might fight for up to three or four hours. The preferred fighting fish were of two types. One was about two inches long and yellow in color, while the other was three inches and blue. They cost so much money that people did not eat them. One time I heard some men at a fish fighting event behind my house that went from 9:00 A.M. until 3:00 P.M. I was not allowed to come near, but I heard their screams, "Aaaah!"

They filled a clear jar with water and dropped in two fish. It is fun to watch this. The fish bite and shake each other, pull their jaws away, swim behind, and with their sharp teeth bite and rip off the tails and fins of their opponents. Even when injured like this, a fish continues to fight until it dies. Sometimes a fish becomes exhausted and swims away, up, down, and around, while the other one chases it. Once it runs, it always loses, so the owner grabs it out. Once a fish has lost, it will never fight again, but a winning fish can be used a second time.

When I was 11, my mother suddenly became less depressed. She was cured naturally, without treatment. We then moved to another village to live by ourselves. I went to school there, but only for a month. The same as before, we were beaten, but not on the palms, and we were not pinched. For punishment we had to go and pick out grass. I remained in this village until I was 14. During that time, my mother was still poor. For two of those years we had economic crisis.

We could not sell anything. The rich people could not sell their rice, not even cheaply. People were unemployed; food was available, but people could not buy anything. My mother used to make and sell soybean cakes; no one would buy them. She had no money to buy rice for her children. We had a very hard life. We had to eat rice soup and sweet potatoes instead of meals. Also we ate a kind of big yellow wild potato that grew in the forest. We would cut it in small pieces, plunge it in a jar with salt, leave it for five days, change the water, add more salt, and leave it for another four or five days before cooking it. If we had eaten it fresh, we would have become drunk. It was soft, and not very tasty, but when you are hungry, you eat anything. We had only one meal a day, often consisting only of soup and sweet potato. Sometimes we also had bamboo shoots.

In 1920, when I was 14 years old, I went to a larger town to attend school. I remember especially one of my teachers: he was fond of women. The sister of one of his students became his lover.

This was easy to know because the student was often seen whispering to the teacher, making the arrangements for the teacher to meet his sister. The student acted proud to be given special attention.

We had about 50 students in that class. We sat in ten rows of five each. The top students, like me, were in front, so that when the principal would visit the class, the teacher could ask us questions and we would answer them. Our writing assignments were done with dip pens and purple ink.

One day, the teacher gave us a dictation. As we were writing, I put my ink jar in front of me. The student whose sister was friendly with the teacher walked up to my seat, dipped his pen in my jar without asking permission, and walked back to his seat. Throughout the dictation he went back and forth, dipping his pen in my inkwell. I dared not say anything to him because I knew his sister was the teacher's girlfriend. I did not mind that he used my ink, but after a while every time he dipped his pen he also rapped me on the head with his knuckles, in front of everybody. I didn't know whether the teacher saw it, but I couldn't say anything. The second time he did it, I became upset. It hurt me a lot. The third time, I waited silently. He never suspected. I continued to write. He hit me again, turned his back on me, and started back to his seat. I went after him, and with a very sharp pen I jabbed him hard and deep in the back of his neck. His face turned pale. It hurt him. The teacher saw, and his face also turned pale. The boy was startled but he dared not do anything. We stood still, not knowing what to do, while a purple stream, a mixture of blood and ink, dripped down.

Our teacher was very cruel. He used to punish us with kicks in the buttocks, punches to the head, and slaps in the face. After stabbing that student, I did not care whether or not the teacher punished me. I was happy for getting revenge, even if my teacher beat me. This time he was really angry. He thought for a while, then said, "You are very cruel. I want you to go home this afternoon, dismissed from class forever!"

I left after that. I did not dare to say anything. He did not bother to ask me why, did not give me any chance to speak at all. While walking home, I cried. On the way, I met my elder brother, who was going to the market. He asked me why I was crying, and I told him that my teacher had dismissed me from school. He took me to a restaurant and we discussed what to do. Finally he said, "Don't worry, I'll go and talk to your teacher and beg him to forgive you and let you return to school."

We went to the teacher's house; because I was afraid, I stayed outside while my brother talked to him. Then the teacher called me in and said that I could return to school that afternoon.

That sort of misbehavior happened often. The students from the market bullied those coming in from the village. The town boys were wealthier and had more friends to support them than did the isolated village students. One town boy carried a knife and let everyone know that if anyone passed him when we had a running race, he would stab them. The town boys often did not do well in school. They had money, so after they failed the exams, they could go back home and help in their family shops. But I was poor; I had to study very hard.

In 1924 I earned my primary school certificate, which enabled me to teach elementary school. Since I won a scholarship after the examination, I attended a teacher's college in Saigon for four years. All of the students were on a scholarship. The school provided us with clothing, food, books, a place to live, pens, pencils, paper, and even tickets for us to go home at every holiday and vacation.

This school was part of the French system of education. I came to know the French, and I found that not all French are bad. The majority are good; a few aren't. Unfortunately for us, we had a very mean and arrogant French science instructor. If a student couldn't answer her question, she spoke impolitely. "You are a donkey!" she would say. We were very afraid of her. She would punish us by writing our names in the note roll every time we could not answer her questions. Then she would not allow us out on the weekends, which made us feel very sad.

She could not remember our names, so she called us by the number we had been assigned on the class roster. There were 25 of us in the class. This would be very amazing for American instructors; they know the names of their students. It is very bad for teachers not to remember the names of their students. That's my opinion.

Even though we were scared of her, we poked fun at her. She would call roll, "Number Five?"

Number Five would quietly say, "Absent, Madam." Since she

never bothered to count, she never realized that they were ridiculing her. Almost the entire class would be there, but several absences would be recorded for the day.

She did not respect the Vietnamese, and for books on French, she picked the very hardest ones she could find. The French were afraid that the Vietnamese students would get too much education and then would resist them, so they tried to hold us back. The books used by French kids were much easier than our texts, and their exam results were lower than ours. But they got a "French" diploma, and we got a "Vietnamese" diploma. In spite of the French attempts to hold us back, we were not less intelligent, and we did better because we made a greater effort.

In 1928 I graduated with a diploma that enabled me to teach in town elementary schools.

Young Adult

My mother-in-law used to believe in shamans, but I didn't. Three times I saw them at work, but what they did looked like tricks. Once, my wife's nephew became ill, so my mother-in-law brought in a shaman to cure him. The nephew was unconscious with a high fever. The shaman burned incense and paper money made of imitation silver and gold, the kind used for dead people. He covered the eyes of his assistant with a wide red cloth to create the deception that the assistant could not see through the cloth. In fact he easily could see through it. In the meantime, hidden from the sight of the shaman, a person in the family put a flower and leaf or other items in a box. After the exorcism was complete, people then asked the shaman what was in the box. He turned to his assistant and told him to list the contents. The assistant chanted a song backwards, in which he enumerated the items; then the shaman announced that the box contained a leaf and a flower. The assistant was supposed to be possessed by the spirit during this time, but often he seemed to be faking it. If the shaman didn't know the contents of the box, he would use various cheating tricks to discover what was inside.

One time, when I was 28 years old [1934], I played a trick on a shaman. Like the women did, I went outside and picked up a flower. Instead of placing it in the box, I threw it away and substituted a handkerchief. I brought the closed box out to the shaman. He said we would find a leaf and a flower. Then he prayed and shook the box, but no sound came out. The family was quiet. After that, people believed me instead of the shaman, but they did not dare to say anything because they were afraid of the shaman.

During times of drought we used to invite shamans to pray. They would sit on a palanquin and stick skewers through their cheeks. People believe that spirits or devils come into their bodies that make them behave in strange ways. The shamans walk back and forth for about five minutes over pieces of broken glass; they do not get cut; they do not bleed.

I don't know what to think about this. I don't believe in the gods, but one time I came to visit a relative who lived about three kilometers from my house. I started back on my bicycle around 8:30 P.M., when it is neither daylight nor dark. I saw about 50 meters in front of me the form of a woman who was sliding across the road while sitting down! I didn't know whether or not it really was a ghost, but I was going to test this. I rode my cycle slowly towards her, holding onto the handlebars. Just as she crossed the road, I came up behind her. I thought of kicking her with my shoes; if I'd hear a noise, I'd know it was a real person. If no sound came, I'd know it was a ghost. That was my intent. But when I approached, I was shaking; I dared not do it! I kept on following her like that until she crossed to another side of the road and left. I didn't believe she was a ghost, because she did not vanish, but when I told the story to the villagers, they cried, "She's a ghost! We've met her many times!"

In September 1928, at the age of 22, I took my first teaching job, as the principal of a village school which had four classes. I remained there for one year; in 1929, I was transferred back to the town where I had studied between the ages of 14 and 18.

In 1930, I began to look for a wife. A former classmate of mine, who was also a teacher in the school in which I was the principal, introduced me to his granduncle, who was a matchmaker. This old man told me that if I wished to marry a particular woman, I would have to bring along my mother to meet the bride's family.

Ordinarily when people came to a young woman's house, she

would hide. If a man wanted to see a prospective bride, he had to go there unannounced so that the young woman would not be aware. My friend took me to her house on a pretext, so I saw her without her knowing that I was looking her over as a bride.

My mother went to the matchmaker's house and told him that she wanted him to set up a day for the engagement. She herself did not want to meet the bride's family or talk to them at all because she gave me freedom of choice. The matchmaker set up the engagement day three months later, and I was married a month after that.

When choosing a bride, families look for several characteristics. First, the parents of the bride and groom should be about the same age. It would not be good if one set of parents were old and the other were young. Otherwise they might have difficulty in communication. The families should be of equal status. The rich never want to marry the poor; people related to royalty never want to marry with ordinary people. Education is not considered an important feature. But the character of the family is important; so is the character of the bride and the groom.

First, a bride should be a good housekeeper, who can care for the home, cook, sew, and do child care: the perfect lady. Second, she knows how to communicate, to watch what she says, and not blurt out whatever she wants to: she should speak with respect. Third, she should show femininity, which is seen in how she walks and sits. She should be flexible and soft, she should not laugh so loud or talk loudly. She should have perfect behavior. Fourth, we also look at her personality, to see how she behaves under normal situations. We find this out by asking her relatives and friends who know her well.

We have proverbs that describe how we select a bride. "When you buy a pig, choose the sow. When you buy a girl, choose the generations." We also say, "If a bride is docile, she is a [real] girl [feminine]. If a groom is pious, he is a [real] boy." At the wedding of a bride and groom, we recite a conventional expression of good wishes, "The male and female phoenix birds [a well-matched couple] speak the same [keep the vow, or live peacefully]."

While I was teaching in the town, I had 13 Montagnard students. The French had gone into the mountains and forced a number of

these Montagnard children, about ten years old, to go to the town
to receive an education, so that they could later work for the
French. I felt sorry for these children; they looked so miserable.
Several times a number of these children escaped from the school
and tried to hide in the forest. The district police rounded them up
and returned them to the school. When asked why they ran away,
the only thing the children said was that they missed the forest.
(For a sympathetic account of Montagnards, see Condominas 1977;
for documentation of their contemporary plight, see Hickey 1982.)

French inspectors were in charge of checking the schools. They
were higher than the school principals. Some inspectors were very
mean; they expected the teachers to offer them gifts, such as
money, food, or gold, given at times such as the New Year. When
I was a principal, teachers who offered gifts to the inspector got
quicker promotions. Otherwise they might be held back for six or
seven years. The poor like me did not have money for gifts. It took
me seven years to be promoted.

One day a French inspector and his Vietnamese subordinate
came to my school. I stood up and left my desk so that the French
inspector could sit down. As he looked at my roll books, I had to
teach. Suddenly the French inspector called, "Stop! Come here!"
He was very arrogant. First he asked why the names of many students were crossed out. Then he asked why so many others were
absent. Because he had used such a severe tone, I became so angry
that I couldn't answer for a moment.

Finally I replied, "Before I answer the question, I would like to
ask the inspector a short and simple question. This is a village
school, not a town school. Right now it is harvest time. The students of this school have to stay home and help their parents harvest
sugarcane and rice. They'll remain home not a day or two, but a
month or two. Every afternoon, instead of going home at five
o'clock, I have to stay for another hour writing letters to the parents
of these absent children asking them to send their boys and girls to
school. During the weekends, I spend most of my time riding
around the village searching for the absent students, asking them
to return to school. Their parents insist that their children will attend school the next semester. That's the best I can do. I cannot get

any better result. So I'd like to ask you, what is the best technique to help the students return to school?"

The French inspector gave no answer. He told the Vietnamese subordinate to come up with an answer. The Vietnamese inspector did not know what to say either. The French inspector pointed a pencil at him and said, "You answer him! You answer him!" The Vietnamese inspector just stood there, silent.

Then the French inspector said, "Leave it aside; go back to your lesson." I wrote math word problems in Vietnamese: "What is the total cost of the polished rice?" The French inspector asked the Vietnamese inspector to translate, but he made a joke out of it by mistranslating it: "What is the total cost of the paddy?"

The Frenchman asked me in French, "Well, how much does a liter of paddy cost?"

I replied in French, "I don't know."

"Why not?" he asked.

"People don't sell paddy by the liter, but by 40–liter cans. Besides, there's no paddy in this math problem. Why did you ask about paddy?"

The French inspector realized that his Vietnamese subordinate had made fun of him, so he pointed his pencil, waved his arm, and said, "What did you say?" Such an action is impolite, but higher status people are allowed to do it when talking to those who are lower. The Vietnamese inspector was embarrassed and kept silent.

Then the Frenchman asked me, "One liter of rice, how much is it?"

I replied, "It depends on the quality." I gave the middle cost. Then the inspectors left.

Two weeks later I came to town to get my paycheck, and I visited the Vietnamese inspector's office. There I received a letter of warning; this is considered very bad. No reasons were given. I was not promoted for seven years, while others received promotions within two or three years.

Seven years later, I visited the Vietnamese inspector. He said, "What's the matter? Why have you come to see me?"

I said sarcastically, "I have just received my promotion, and I have come to *thank* you."

"How long did it take for you to get your promotion?"

"Not long; only seven years."

His face changed color, and he turned his face away in embarrassment. Then he said, "I suggested your name to the Board, but the Province Chief refused to recommend you three times."

From 1930 to 1936 I was married to my first wife, who was also a schoolteacher. In 1931 our first daughter was born; in 1933, our second child, a son, was born. Both of these children died of typhoid fever, at the ages of two and one. In 1935 we bought a house, even though a fortune-teller warned us not to buy it; he said it was haunted. We lived for only one year in that house. In 1936, the year that our third child, our second son, was born, I separated from my wife, and because I was sad, I moved away to teach in a village school. The paperwork took a long time, but we finally divorced in 1938. Our son stayed with his mother. The reason for our divorce was that we didn't have many agreements with each other. We had to ask for an application of divorce at the court house. The judge ordered me to pay 15 piasters a month for food for my son, but nothing to my wife because she had her job.

She had a particular behavior [that I didn't like]. When she had her two months of vacation, or one month for the New Year, she didn't want to go to my mother's house, since she didn't get along with my mother or sister. In Vietnam, some mothers-in-law are difficult to deal with. In this case, my mother was not that type of person. The fault was that of my ex-wife, who disliked my mother. It was my decision, though. I told my wife; she said okay.

I had a cousin who had been a classmate of mine in the town. He also married a teacher. Every year my cousin and his wife would go to his father's house on every vacation. But when I went home, my wife refused to accompany me, and all my relatives asked me, "Where's your wife?" I was very humiliated.

One time, my mother came to see me in the town. Our servant girl refused to open the door. "I am the mother of your master," my mother said. "Why don't you open the door for me?"

The servant girl replied, "My mistress ordered me not to open the door for anyone."

My mother was very angry and cried loudly and publicly: "I'll never come back here!"

When I divorced, all my relatives agreed that it was a good idea. "Your wife is stubborn," they said.

My wife continued to live in the town, and the two of us remained friendly; we just separated.

In 1946 the Viet Minh controlled Vietnam. For a while during that year, no school, no market, no activity could take place. My wife went to Saigon and asked to be reassigned to her work. The French ordered every teacher and secretary to go back to work again as before; they sent her to a village school. Those teachers who were sent to the countryside were kidnapped by the Communists [Viet Minh]. That is what happened to her. I did not find out until 1948, when I returned to the town where we had lived. Her father came to me and said, "In 1946 your ex-wife was arrested by the Viet Minh on the way to school. She was killed."

"What do you mean?" I asked.

"She disappeared and has never been seen again. Your son now lives with his uncle in Saigon."

In the years that followed, that son from time to time visited me; eventually he became an air force student pilot and studied and lived in France for about one and a half years.

After my unsuccessful first marriage, I was afraid to get married again; I didn't dare select by myself. So I did not want to marry again. But my mother and uncle pressed me to marry a second time. They said, "A man must have his own family. Rare is the man who stays single."

My second wife was my mother's choice. My mother contacted an old woman she knew who was a relative of my future wife. That old woman served as the go-between. My mother went to my wife's house to see how she was. Was she crippled or ugly? What did she look like? She asked the go-between about the personality of the girl. Was she polite? Did she know how to sew and cook? Mostly my mother cared about politeness, about a girl who was not stubborn. My mother came back with a good report. She said, "I agree to take her as your second wife. She does not have a good education, but she belongs to a good family. I persuade you to go to her house for one time. If you want to go and see her, we'll discuss that."

I asked a friend who was a carpenter to go with me by bicycle.

For several months in 1937 that carpenter had worked in the house of my future wife, and he knew her well. Suddenly I found her alone at home; her mother had left. It was not usual for young women to be alone. I went with the carpenter and listened and sat in the background. I watched the two of them talk.

She figured that I had come to see her. Three young men before me had visited, but her mother had rejected them. When a woman gets puberty and is 18 to 20 years old, the age of marriage, she knows what might happen. When a young man comes to her house, she always thinks, "This might be the man who has come to see me." Countryside girls are really embarrassed; they hesitate to speak with the young men. Because they are very shy, they run and hide when a young man comes to the house. Sometimes a man will ask a question that is a pretext to talk to his future wife: "I am looking for a carpenter. Do you know someone in this village?"

She would reply, "It might be my mother might know."

And the boys make up other questions to ask them. "Who has lots of fields in this village?"

The decision was not mine, because of my unsuccessful selection the first time. I didn't want to make the family sad. I let my mother make the decision, figuring that if the marriage didn't work out in the future, my mother could not blame me for it. She never blamed me directly for my first wife, but because of my wife's misbehavior she had lost face with her neighbors.

Thinking of all of this, when I saw my mother, I said, "She is okay." We remembered that my first wife had been educated, and that had made her very proud and stubborn. I liked the fact that my second wife did not have much education, only two years in an elementary school. She could write almost correct Vietnamese and could do simple addition, subtraction, and division; that's enough. Also, she was strong, and when asked by my mother, she agreed to live with her future husband. She was not too educated and stubborn; she could live with our family. She was a village person, yeah.

The relationship between people in the family is very important. When marriage occurs, they must select a daughter-in-law and son-in-law carefully. The relationship must be kept the same. If a new wife is impolite, it destroys the relation between the members of the family; they consider that if they have thrown away the daughter-in-law, they have lost their son. If they have thrown away the son-in-law, they have lost their daughter.

In America it is not the same way. Here you are very free; children choose their own spouse. They don't care about agreement or disagreement of their parents. But it is not that way in Vietnam. When we make a choice for a new boy or girl in the family, we must have future agreement of every relative. If a new son-in-law or daughter-in-law shows insolence or inappropriate behavior, so all the relatives no longer recognize the son or daughter who married such a person. We then have lost our daughter or our son. And this happens very often.

Two months after I met my second wife at her house, we were married at a big wedding. She was 20 years old and I was 32. Most of the time a man is older than the woman he marries, but only by one to six or seven years. For about eight months we lived in the house of my mother; then we moved near the school where I taught. In 1939 our first son was born, but he died at birth. Our second son, who now lives elsewhere in America, was born in 1941.

[See also Chapters 14, 16, and 34.]

CHAPTER 4

Youngest Daughter: 1914–1934

NARRATOR 2: SOUTH VIETNAMESE
ELDERLY RURAL WOMAN

Ba (Mrs.) That, a short, thin woman with a high, soft voice, has lived in the United States since 1975, but in dress, food, language, and social customs, she lives almost as if she had never left Vietnam. Almost always she wears the short blouse and wide black trousers traditional for her region of Vietnam; she speaks no English; she dislikes American food and rarely eats it; she defers to her husband's whims and spends much time serving him. When I visited their house on social occasions, she stayed in the background, except to show me her backyard garden, in which she grew an astounding variety of fruits, herbs, and vegetables, many of them completely unfamiliar to me.

One day I asked her if she would be willing to tell me her life story. By then I knew that she had been born in a South Vietnamese village around 1914. I was interested in interviewing her particularly because she had retained much of that village outlook in later life. At first she was quite flustered and asked permission from her husband, who said she might do so. She was quite willing to tell her life story, she said, but she did not know how to do it. Her husband and I explained to her that in a life story, she might remember and discuss events that had occurred in her childhood, youth, and later years as well as those events and persons who had been important in her life.

As a youngest child, Ba That received customary special treatment, and she describes the effects of this on her and her nine older siblings. She presents vivid images of life in a South Vietnamese village (for comparisons with other villages, see Hickey 1964, Huynh Quang Nhuong 1982, and several of the narrators in the present book). Most important is her account of what happened to her large family when it split during the war, some supporting the Communists, others the Nationalists. The death toll on both sides was great; several of her brothers and sisters were killed, along with other relatives, a grim reminder of the effects of 30 years of war on the Vietnamese people. Also significant is the way she ensured the escape of her husband and herself in 1975 during the final collapse of South Vietnam. Although she had never been more than a few miles beyond her home village and the nearby provincial town, she revealed an inner strength and an insight that prompted her to move quickly and decisively to leave her homeland forever, an act that undoubtedly saved her husband's life.

As a refugee in America, unable to learn English, ill at ease with non-Vietnamese people, and unable to adjust to American foods and life-styles, Ba That spends her time isolated at home, cleaning her house, caring for her husband, and growing vegetables in her backyard.

Childhood Memories

I am the youngest of my family, as was my father; my mother also was almost the youngest in her family. I didn't know anything about my grandparents because on both sides they were already deceased. I was born in a big South Vietnamese village with three hamlets. As I remember, lots of relatives of mine lived around one big hamlet. Everybody lived in this one place. The hamlet contained one meeting house, a shrine, and a pagoda. There was no market, and the main road was one mile away. We would walk to the road. No one had cars. To reach the main road, we had to pass over a little wooden bridge. When it rained too hard, some of that bridge would float away, and we couldn't get through. The roads in the village were cow and buffalo paths. For transporting paddy and other quality things, we used carts drawn by two buffalo; we walked alongside the carts. We also used shoulder carriers to bring boxes of goods to the market. I could carry that to the main road, and from there we took a horse carriage seven kilometers to the market town. All kinds of trees lined the road, along with bamboo.

I grew up in a very low and long house with walls made of wood and a roof made of red tile that had blackened with age. The house consisted of a front bedroom–sitting room, two rear rooms, and a storage room for rice. Next to the house was a long cottage, part buffalo shed and storage area for mortars and pestles and part kitchen. In the front bedroom–sitting room were three low wooden altars. Each evening our family would burn incense for our ancestors. In there we had lots of furniture. I remember a large round table that turned around and three wooden camp beds. My father used to sit on the edge of one of these beds next to the round table chewing betel; my mother also chewed a lot of betel.

We had a garden with banana and pineapple trees. In one corner of the garden, my father would tie our six buffalo to big trees and would leave straw for them to eat.

In front of the house on one side were betel plants and areca nut trees. Also in front was a well that supplied water for our family. To pull up the water, we placed a large container at one end of a long thick pole that was tied at the middle to a post in the ground. At the other end of the pole we placed a heavy stone or piece of wood, and this created a seesaw that lifted the water.

Because I was the youngest in the family, all the people of the family loved me very much: parents, sisters, brothers, everyone. Because my father loved me, my sisters and brothers pampered me. I remember that when I was young, the relatives and friends of my parents came to live with us so that they could help us to take care of cows and buffalo. During the day they would go out and work; later in the afternoon they would come home and carry me on their shoulders. My sisters and sister-in-law teased me. Usually I would be bathed by my sisters because they loved me.

Whenever Mother would leave the house, the others at home would tease me. I would hide myself in a corner and refuse to talk to anybody; if they'd look at me, I'd curse them, "Montagnard!" [Editor's note: She used an insulting reference to highland tribal peoples.] They'd continue to tease me, and I'd cry.

Then they'd say, "We feel sorry for our youngest; Mother's gone; that's why she feels sad and sits in the corner." I'd cry more. When Mother arrived in the large front yard, I'd cry even louder.

Then she'd say, "When I go away, you always tease my youngest child." At that time, I was six or seven years old, and my father had already passed away. They teased me just for fun. They knew that because I was the youngest, I was spoiled by my mother, so they liked to tease me.

My eighth brother, who attended school in Saigon, sometimes would visit us in the village. He'd tease me with a funny satirical folk song, which ridiculed the improper behavior of a child.

> Listen! Listen! Listen to the youngest sister's song.
> Her small mouth resembles that of the *Long Tong* fish.
> She puts on the leisured airs of her grandmother.
> Her clothes are trailing; her hips swing as she walks.
> Someone would say she resists with arrogant gestures.

At the time I was young; I didn't know anything, so everybody laughed, and I'd curse them, "Montagnard!" They kept on repeating the song, so I remembered it. When I grew up, they no longer did this to me; only when I was young. Once in a while they would tell me how they had teased me when I was a child.

In addition to pineapples and bananas, we had lots of bamboo shoots, pomegranates, plums, guava, coconut, and grapefruit. In the countryside, we cultivated corn, chili, green onions, and beans; when they were ripe, we cut them, ate them, and cultivated new ones. We didn't buy in the market, like here. We ate according to what was ripe in that season. Once in a while when we went to the market, we would buy the fat from the meat. We would render it and preserve it in a jar hung from the roof.

During the rainy season we'd catch fish in the paddy fields. In the sunny season, sellers would bring fish into our village. I would buy fish sauce in a big jar and save it to eat. We also bought a much stronger, darker fish sauce which contained the whole fish.

I don't remember at what age I began to help in the garden, maybe 13 or 14, but I do recall that I didn't do well. Most of the time I stayed home to cook, not work in the fields. Sometimes I helped in the garden, but I was not as skillful as my sisters. When I was younger, they taught me how to do things around the house. I did know how to sweep the floor and to cook. Youngsters in the countryside must know how to do everything; they are forced to help, and the work is very difficult, such as winnowing rice. In our free time, we had to baby-sit our nephews and nieces. In the countryside, we did not sit around doing nothing: we'd water the trees; we'd cook when others went to the fields; we would do things according to the season.

Everybody had a different task. Children rarely went to school; they stayed home and worked in the fields or the household. My sixth sister had to work hard washing clothes, baby-sitting, and cooking, with the help of another sister, until she got married.

Every day early in the morning, my ninth sister would take the buffalo to the fields and stay with them until sunset. I felt sorry for her, and so did my third brother. Finally came the time when my ninth sister should be married. My third brother told my mother, "Let her stay home so that she won't turn dark. She's always out in the sun guarding the buffalo. She's 16 years old; she should wear nice clothes and fix her hair." My mother let my ninth sister stay home, and my third brother, who worked in Saigon, found her a groom.

As a little girl, I sometimes played games with other girls. I played "beating the chopsticks" very well. Four of us would go to a nearby creek and pick some kind of fresh tree or bush to make the chopsticks. Our hands became messy and dirty from this. Then we'd go home. We'd sit on the floor, throw a ball up in the air, twist and turn the chopsticks about five times, and then catch the ball with our hands before it hit the ground. If you failed to catch it, the others would beat you on the heel of your foot with their chopsticks.

Boys and girls also played "throwing the handkerchief." They sat in a circle very close to each other. One person stood outside with a handkerchief. The others would watch as that person ran around the circle. He would secretly drop the handkerchief on someone and then try to run around the circle before that person discovered that the handkerchief had been dropped on him.

Our village was famous for its agriculture. We made sugar from sugarcane. We also had all kinds of bamboo shoots, and we grew those for a living. People never rested without doing anything; they earned according to the season.

After the New Year, people stayed home and enjoyed themselves for a while without working; they began agricultural work again in February and March. They would plant sugarcane; also peanuts, which took three months and ten days. They would hire neighbors who were poor to harvest them, and then we shared the peanuts with them.

When the rainy season began in April, we started our rice fields; within one to two months, rice stalks had appeared. When the time came to transplant them, the landowner hired a villager to recruit workers who knew how to do this work. They would work from early morning until noon; then the owners would serve them lunch consisting of cooked sticky rice, chicken soup, and sweet rice cake, along with tea. If the fields were close to our house, the workers went to our house; otherwise, we carried the food to them, along with a tent. It was very hard work.

At the end of the transplanting work, the workers would contribute some of their earnings to buy chicken and pork and to make rice cakes that would be offered to forsaken spirits [those who had died by accident and had left no descendants] and to spirits, who protected the laborers against illness during the working period. After that, they had a party, eating, playing a stringed instrument, singing, playing, and teasing one another. I did not attend the ceremony, so I know only what people told me about it. We had two seasons of rice growing and harvesting, one of three months, the other of six. Each transplanting worker was paid about 20 liters of rice at the time of the harvest. Each worker at the harvest earned one-sixth, one-seventh, or one-eighth of what he gathered, depending on the quality of the yield of that field. Each harvest period took two to three months.

At the end of the second harvest, around January 20, the owners and other villagers gave an offering to the [tutelary] spirit. And for about five days they had free time to prepare for the new lunar year and visit the graves of their ancestors.

On the twenty-third day of the last lunar month, we held a simple ceremony in which we said goodbye to our household god. Because we did this, he would bring his report to God about our family during the past year. We offered him cooked sweet rice and cakes. In the morning of the thirtieth day, we welcomed him back by offering him a meal. In the afternoon we offered a large meal to our ancestors and welcomed them back for four days. The god of the household stays home after that, but we say farewell to our ancestors on the fourth day of the New Year.

My sister-in-law and mother taught me how to cook for the New Year. When I was young, my mother did the cooking; when I was older, I had to cook. I did not cook a lot for the New Year, just bamboo shoots with pork, a dish of sour bean sprouts and onions soaked in water, pork sausage, and sweet rice cake. We had to offer food to our ancestors during the first three days of the New Year. On the fourth day, a final meal was offered to bid farewell to them.

In our celebration of the New Year, we would glue a piece of pretend money made of gold and silver paper on each post of the house; also on the horns of our buffalo. This paper money was the kind which we give to dead people to accompany them on their journey.

To prevent devils from coming and eating our food during this New Year period, we used to scare them by hanging a charm on some bamboo planted in front of our house. Others would hang charms on their doorways. The charm was the printed Chinese character of a ferocious tiger. We would also tie the charm to a packet of areca nuts and betel leaves. In the old days, we placed poles not only in the front, but in the back, at the storehouse, and near the well. To each of these we tied charms, betel leaves, and areca nuts. In recent years, we stopped doing this.

On the first day of the New Year, we would visit relatives; grandchildren would visit their grandparents; brothers- and sisters-in-law would buy food and offer it to the ancestors of their wives or husbands. Relatives would burn incense at the altars of others and would go back and forth to visit.

We would make new dresses for the New Year. I remember that when I was young, my sister made them for me. When I grew up, I had to make them myself by hand, not by machine. The New Year was a very happy day, a time to celebrate.

We did not have movies or theaters in my village, but I remember once when I was young that my third elder brother brought a singing machine [record player] into the village. It was a square machine with a round place for a disc [record], a needle, and a thing to wind up the singing machine. There was a modern theater opera that first started in the town of My Tho. People would sing and talk like in the theater. The first theater group of actors and actresses that established the modern theater made records of their performances. My third brother, who lived in Saigon, knew about this, so he bought the singing machine and the record.

My house was the only one in the village with a record player, so everybody came to my house; it was like a theater. People stood outside and listened; it was very crowded. Every time we'd turn it on, people would tell each other and gather to listen. They'd stay until we turned it off. They would say, "It's strange: where did you get that?" And they asked, "How could this machine talk? Does it have a voice in it?"

Father

My father worked like other farmers in Vietnam. In March, the family moved out to the rice fields, which were far away from the house, and built small cottages. In April, at the beginning of the rainy season, Father first made a nursery of rice. Then he plowed the rice fields. Throughout April and sometimes May, they plowed the fields with his buffalo. When the men became tired, they rested in the cottage. And they ate lunch there: usually rice and fish, sometimes pork and bamboo shoots collected from the nearby forest, and also some vegetables that grew in the rice fields.

In June, we transplanted the rice, and Father constructed banks and dikes to keep in the water. When it rained, the water rose, and fish swam into the flooded fields. Often they would be caught in a tightly woven bamboo basket which had been planted below the ground. My father would catch many fish in the rainy season, which my mother would cook and bring to the hamlet to sell. Often Father would catch eels, which he would carry home in a large basket fastened to his back with rattan straps. We had enough fish to eat every day and to sell. Also, he would throw some in the front yard to give to his daughters. They'd take the fish, pry open their mouths with a small piece of bamboo, scrape off the scales, wash the fish, and cook them to eat.

I remember that my father wore two sashes of silk, one green and one red, both four inches wide. We did not have belts in those days; he used to fold one of these to carry betel; then he'd wrap it several times around his waist like a belt.

My father was a man of the countryside, a peasant. He rarely came to the city. One time, he visited his nephew in Saigon. His nephew, a young teacher, was an orphan whom my mother and father had helped, so he loved our family very much. But when Father, his uncle, visited him in the city, the young man felt very ashamed because Father was not civilized, but rustic. In the city, the young men wore French clothes, but my father wore black cotton village trousers with a long wide sash made of green or red silk, into which he would put a small packet of betel and tobacco. He wore his hair in a bun tied in the back; he chewed betel all the time, and he spoke in the way of a rustic man. When he saw something new, like the electric tramway or a house with many stories, he stood and stared at it. His nephew felt ashamed to accompany him around the city. Often he would hurry my father back to the house. Father said to his nephew, "I want to look at the new things in the city. Why do you hurry me home?" His nephew pretended to be tired.

In later years, after my father had died, his Saigon nephew, my cousin, bought an automobile. Then he regretted too much how he had behaved. "If my uncle were still alive, I could bring him to many areas to look." My cousin told me of these things many years later.

Because he was a peasant, Father liked to marry his daughters to men living near the forest who were hunters like himself. He did not want to marry his daughters to city people. There was another reason. The first time he came to visit his son and his nephew living in Saigon city, he needed to go to the toilet. He opened the water closet, smelled the very bad odor, immediately picked up his umbrella, and returned home to the countryside, where, when people needed to defecate, they went behind a tree or bush. He said, "In the city, it's easy to eat but difficult to defecate; in the country, it's difficult to eat but easy to defecate." He did not like the city but loved the countryside. "Living as a farmer is happy because the family has everything." He meant that they had rice and sugar all year round, peanuts and green beans, much fish during the rainy season, and when he had free time, he could hunt wild deer, fox, and other animals in the forest.

Father also used to catch eels in the rice field. Most people scraped off the mucus of the eels using the outside skin of rice stalks. But Father didn't do that. One time he caught an eel, beat it to death, and then stuck a forked bamboo pin up and down along the length of the eel. Because nobody else was home, he barbecued it and gave it to me to eat, along with some big crystals of salt. The eel was not cooked; it was so rare that when I ate, blood came out. Just at that time, my fourth sister-in-law came home and saw blood dripping from my mouth. She checked the eel, saw that it was rare and bloody, and told me gently so as not to hurt Father's feelings, "Don't eat this eel; it's not cooked yet. Wait for me and I'll cook it more for you."

But I said, "No, no, my father told me that it's good."

Sister-in-law took it and re-barbecued it for me. I was about four years old.

In the countryside, we don't eat at the table. We sit on a big, flat bed of wood and eat, with our food on a wooden platter made from a big flat tree. We would eat three times a day: morning, noon, and afternoon. During the harvest, most of the people worked in the fields, and they ate very early in the morning, around 5:00 A.M. Then they'd walk to the fields carrying some rice wrapped in an areca leaf from which the flower arose. They'd work until late and then eat late in the evening. So meals were not exactly on schedule, but depended on the season.

My father passed away when I was five or six. Father came down with a fever; he fell unconscious for several days; then he passed away. I don't know exactly what caused it.

While Father was still unconscious, Mother went to a shaman. Before he agreed to help, the shaman required a payment of a coin which was a big amount of money at that time. On one side of the coin was a number, on the other the figure of a lady. The person requesting help was supposed to put money in a plate on the table, whatever amount they wished to give. The head of the lady on the coin would point in a direction. When the shaman saw in what direction, he picked up the plate with the coin, placed it in front of the altar, and described the cause of the illness or misfortune.

The shaman said that he knew the cause of my father's death. Father had gone to a rice field and was returning home late in the evening. He passed by a big shellac-oil tree, where a transvestite Montagnard shaman once had had an altar. That Montagnard shaman was deceased, but the spirits of the shaman still remained around the tree. Father used to pass by that tree early in the morning and late in the evening, and the spirits of that deceased shaman possessed him. Normally, noontime is when it is most easy to be possessed by a spirit, but also 6:00 A.M. and 6:00 P.M. In the early morning and the early evening, it is half dark, half light. Any time like that is dangerous. The noon hour is dangerous because the sun is in the middle.

Father passed away at home. Because I was so young, I didn't know. I ran into the room and took a look. In the countryside, when someone passed away, the relatives used to cover his face with three pieces of red paper and a piece of red cloth material too. They would bundle three pieces of steamed rice balls on top of his head, along with a burned candle. I don't know why this was done; I just know that's the way it was. I heard that when you burned the candle, the dead person would be able to see where to go.

When I was young, I didn't know how to be afraid. I uncovered the piece of paper to take a look. My cousins, standing in the kitchen, saw what I did and asked, "Where did you go?"

"I went to visit my father," I said.

"Honey, 'Uncle' passed away; don't go there."

"No, 'Uncle' is not dead; he's sleeping."

"No," my cousin said, "he's passed away. Go away."

I said, "No, I'm not afraid." I ran to my cousin's house to visit my sick brother.

My brother said to me, "You should not visit your father during the time he is dead. I'm afraid you'll get the heat from Father and transmit it to me." In the countryside, people believe that when a person dies, his heat still remains, and that it can make others ill.

I ran back home. Then someone in the family went to the district town to send the news by telegram to another brother in Saigon.

Father's body remained three days at home; then he was buried. I didn't know anything, so I didn't cry. Mother cried a lot and wailed, "My husband passed away and left me with many children."

On the third day after the death of my father, as others did, my mother invited a Buddhist monk to conduct a ceremony. The monk cut banana leaves to make a small ladder which he placed on the grave, along with sweet soup. He also gave the deceased an offering of sweet rice. People believed that the ladder enabled the deceased person's soul to climb out of the grave on the third day after he had been buried.

The monk then walked around the grave three times reciting the canon. We wore white mourning clothes as we followed him. We also carried a live rooster or hen around the grave, then let it go freely. The buffalo boys loved to catch the chicken when we set it free because they believed that the hen would be very fertile. This third day ceremony was like opening the grave to set the deceased free. I have heard of the forty-ninth day ceremony, but we did not give offerings or celebrate it.

One hundred days after my father's death, my mother invited three monks to recite the Buddhist canon. They wore saffron-yellow and multicolored robes, along with monks' hats of the same colors: red, white, and yellow stripes. We offered vegetarian food for the deceased. The monks took turns reciting the canon. They started at seven in the evening and continued until the next day at 10:00 A.M. People wore white clothes for mourning.

The master monk carried a bell with him as he walked around an area in the front yard. We followed him. He read the scriptures and hit the metal bell. After making three circles around the place, he bowed to the altar; so did we. The food offerings in the front yard were given away to the children of neighbors.

Mother

I felt closer to my father. My mother was a little bit of a miser. If the children wanted something, she'd give just a little, not much. If I wanted a new dress, Mother would bring me one, but it would be less expensive, not the prettiest. If my mother taught me something, and I did not do it skillfully, she yelled at me.

After her wedding, my sixth sister lived somewhere else. Every time she came to visit us and didn't do something right, Mother yelled at her. When Father was alive, Sister would come and visit him because she missed him. My mother told me this.

My mother taught me everything: cooking, cleaning, rice husking. When I grew up, I helped. I would store rice in a big loft. She taught me how to water the plants and how to carry water. This was very hard work when I was young. Mother used to beat me very hard when I did something wrong. She had a very hot temper; she even beat my older brother. She'd tell him to lie down, and then she'd beat him with rattan. When Father was still alive, if my brothers made mistakes, he'd tell them to lie down on a cot, one, two, three, all in an orderly line. Then he'd use rattan on them. The first strike hurt them more than the others. They were beaten with rattan if they broke a porcelain rice bowl or argued against elders. The girls were not beaten with rattan, but were slapped with a hand anywhere, on the back or butt, and whenever. This happened up to the age of about eleven or twelve.

When I got older, Mother used to yell at me a lot because of that hot temper of hers, but she no longer beat me. I don't remember all the reasons, but there were lots of them. If I went to visit my brother's house and didn't come home in time to cook dinner or if I got home late, she yelled at me. When I was young, I would start cooking a pot of rice on the stove and then forget about it; my cousins would remind me, or something else would happen. I would take off somewhere and return home to find the rice burned. Then Mother yelled at me, and I had to cook all over again. I didn't cry when she yelled, only when she beat me. In the countryside, we never received rewards for good behavior. For the New Year, we would receive a new dress, not black pants. The two colors were white and black, that's all.

I started school at the age of seven. My mother had to take me to school every time we had a flood; then she'd come to bring me home, a distance of about three kilometers. Whenever we came to a muddy spot, she'd put me on her shoulders and carry me across.

I studied very little, only a few years until the age of eleven or twelve. I learned how to read and write well enough. In my class I did not dare to fight in school. I had male teachers, including my cousin, who taught there.

Mother loved me very much when Father passed away; she was very brave after that time. I remember that Mother used to wear mourning clothes after the death of my father. She'd sit near the altar and cry by herself. And at night she burned a kerosene lamp, sat, and cried by herself. Every night she did like that, I don't remember exactly for how long.

Children had to listen to their parents. I remember a phrase, "A dress cannot be worn over the head." It meant that a child could not argue with her parents but must listen to them. If a girl wanted to talk to boys, she had to talk seriously; she could not flirt around. My mother usually said like this, "Those who still remain with the old traditional customs are afraid that girls will go away with boys [live together without being married]." If that happened to a particular family, they would lose respect. People respect those families who have children married in a ceremony. I grew up hearing people say, "In a girl's life, a solemn wedding is a very happy moment."

In my village there was a family in which all the girls followed men without marrying them. My mother always reminded us of that family.

The elder sister was considered a mirror for the younger ones to follow. This was taught to us just by talking, whenever things turned wrong. My parents were not very strict, but they would not let their children go over the limit. You know, girls always like boys, but I cannot talk to them if I like them. That's what my mother said, and that's what happened to most of us.

Once in a while we'd leave our village and go to the district market. Often the Chinese hawkers would carry their goods to our village, where they would call out, "Vai eeee." When we heard that long sound, we knew they had come to sell us their materials. We'd call them into the house with their goods, and everybody from the village would come, look, and bargain. There was no fixed price. The Chinese would go through the village and buy empty bottles which they would later sell back to others.

When I was young, Mother used to scare me by saying, "You

are the daughter of Chu Lo!" He was a Chinese man who used to buy empty bottles or exchange cake for them. Whenever he came to our house, he would hang his clothes on the deer heads we had hung on the wall. He wanted to buy the deer heads. My mother refused. One time she also said, "My daughter's eyes always fill full of tears, which always drip from her eyes." And that has been a problem all my life. The Chinese man brought some medicine and offered to exchange it for a deer's head. Again my mother refused, so old Chu Lo gave it to my mother for free. We mixed the medicine with rainwater and put it on my eyes. This helped stop the dripping of my tears. Therefore, Mother used to say to me, "He gave the medicine to us because you are his daughter!" Because of this, every time I saw him, I ran and hid. Mother did this to tease me, but also to make me afraid.

Young Adult

In the village, people would wake up early in the morning, but the exact time depended on the season. Most people woke up around 6:00 or 7:00 A.M., but my mother would wake me about 5:30 during the cold seasons of November, December, and January. She usually would get some dead leaves to burn to get some heat. After this, we would pull water from the well. From eight to nine in the morning, we would water the fruit trees and cook rice. Everyone ate around 9:00 A.M. This was the first of two meals; the other was at 4:00 P.M.

During the dry season we had to go and buy fish. My mother and I would walk a couple of kilometers to the main road to meet the fish sellers who had bought from the boatmen.

At that time, there were no rice mills in our village, so we removed the rice husks by using a hand paddy-mill. This was a sort of grinder made of bamboo, wood, and clay. We'd throw the rice in an upper bin, pull a revolving lever, grind off the husk, and gather the husked rice which fell out of the openings. The heavy lever required two people to turn it.

We also removed the bran using a very heavy log with a knob at the end. This was like a pestle. One man or two women could operate it. We'd lift the log and let the end with the knob fall into the hole of a wooden mortar set in the ground; this removed the bran from the rice. Sometimes we also used a mortar on which we pounded the rice.

Usually I used the grinding husker and then a mortar; after that, I'd winnow the rice. The winnower consisted of a bin with a handle attached to four wooden blades. When I turned the handle, the blades moved and made a strong wind. The lighter husk fell first into one basket placed below the winnower; the heavier paddy fell afterwards into another basket. Then I'd pound it again for an hour or more with a mortar to take off the bran. Sometimes I'd pound the rice alone; at other times, my mother, sister-in-law, or niece would help me, and from time to time, our neighbors, young peasant girls, would come over with their rice. We would exchange labor. They used to sing love songs while pounding rice, and when they saw a young man passing by, they'd sing verses to him; he would then reply with a verse of his own. In my family, we would not sing songs like that because it was not proper. A girl from the easy life has got to have a serious attitude.

[See also Chapters 18, 28, and 35.]

CHAPTER 5

I Grew Up Without Love:
1925-1937

*"When the Communists came, I cringed. It was like living in a shell."
With these words, Mr. Chung summarized his response to living for 26
years in Communist-controlled North Vietnam. A Chinese native of Hanoi, in his late fifties when I interviewed him, this slight, soft-spoken man
and his family twice chose to remain in the North rather than leave. The
first time was in 1954, when many Northerners opted for the South; the
second was in 1978, when many Vietnamese people of Chinese ancestry
were expelled from Vietnam. In 1980, government authorities threatened
to persecute Mr. Chung if he remained; only then did he and his family
depart.*

*Because of his reluctance to leave North Vietnam, Mr. Chung's narra-
tive is particularly significant. Here is no boat person fleeing oppression,
but rather a man who chose to accommodate to the Communist life-style.
His account leaves no doubt of his antipathy towards the Communists.
Nevertheless, he remained under their control without any external show
of resistance. In fact, he was selected to be a discussion leader for Communist reeducation classes, in which people were made to "confess" their
"capitalistic sins." The pervasive effects of this instruction are evident both
in his outlook and in the vocabulary he uses to express his views.*

*What is it like to live under a totalitarian regime in which those in
power try to control not only a person's behavior, but his thoughts? What*

kinds of adaptations must people make to survive under these conditions, and at what psychological cost? To what extent is such control maintained by physical force?

Mr. Chung observes that the threat of physical force was ever present, but only rarely used. Most people were kept in line by other means. Mr. Chung gives us a vivid description of several mechanisms of social control used with great effectiveness by the North Vietnamese Communists, and he concludes that, given the way they had been conditioned, the North Vietnamese could never have been defeated by the Americans short of total annihilation. His account of Communist social control corroborates that of former Viet Minh official Hoang Van Chi (1964), whose book has been an embarrassment to the Communists and a frequent object of their attacks.

Barrington Moore (1978) has suggested that when confronted with extreme oppression from which there appears to be no escape, most people most of the time, as a means of adaptation, come to accept the moral authority of their oppressor. Although Moore possibly overstates his case (see Freeman 1986), Mr. Chung describes one way in which at least partial acceptance occurs: to survive, he "turned off his mind" and repeated without thinking whatever he was told to do or say. The fact that for many years he remained in Vietnam in this situation is a consequence not only of the nature of the oppression that he encountered, but also of his early childhood experiences, which in his view stamped his character as one which accepts authority without question.

Similar questions of why people obey or resist oppressive authority arise in the accounts of Narrators 12 (Ex-ARVN Colonel) and 13 (Ex-ARVN Captain), who "voluntarily" showed up to be incarcerated in reeducation camps, in which they were subjected to indoctrination of Communist ideology, hard labor, and starvation.

Many Vietnamese have exclaimed that it is difficult to convey to Americans the experience of living in an environment of pervasive, continuous, and long-term oppression. Mr. Chung's account describes a life of intimidation made all the more remarkable by the ordinary, nonresistant daily activities that make up his life story. His views of Communist society, based on his many years of residence in Hanoi, may be contrasted with Kathleen Gough's idealistic portrayal of the Socialist Republic of Vietnam (Gough 1978).

Mr. Chung and I met through a mutual acquaintance, who told him that I was looking to interview an ordinary person who had lived his entire life in North Vietnam. At first, Mr. Chung had reservations about telling his story. Because he was a North Vietnamese who had never fled to the South, many other refugees distrusted him. He was afraid of being identified both by the Communists and by those who had escaped from them. He decided nevertheless to talk of his life because he considered it his responsibility to do so.

"My contribution is a small one, but it is my way of expressing my gratitude to the American people. When I was forced to leave Vietnam, I had no idea where I would go. To come to America was unimaginable; it is really a privilege. At first I thought that only the intelligentsia could be admitted. I was allowed in because I have an in-law who came here six months before I did."

Mr. Chung wants Americans to realize the vicissitudes his countrymen have endured; he hopes that his life story will help others understand the Vietnamese experience. He concluded his narrative with a statement reminiscent of Nguyen Du's "Hearts of Sorrow" passage:

"There is a sorrow of the Vietnamese people. Actually they didn't want to leave their homeland, but they had to because of the regime under which they could no longer live. I think the Vietnamese are the most unfortunate people in history. They were born in the wrong century, at an inappropriate time. If only they had been born a century earlier or later, they would not have had so many bad events happen to them. Even after 30 years of war they could not live in peace, but had to leave their country. They are no different from any other people, so why did they have to suffer so much? If we have to cry for the Vietnamese people, only an ocean can contain all the tears."

At Mr. Chung's request, I took notes but did not tape the seven interview sessions (about 20 hours of narration), which took place, according to his wishes, at an office during the fall of 1984.

I was born in Hanoi in a well-off family of Chinese descent. We had a traditional cloth-selling business which my father operated out of our house, a long brick building with a tile roof. It was not divided into rooms; patios separated the different parts of the house used for business. We also owned a French car.

My father didn't care much about the family; he spent a lot of money on girls and other enjoyments of life. Because he was usually out of the house, I rarely saw him, and I don't remember much about him. He never took care of us. Like some families that were rich, we children were cared for by housemaids. My main memory of my father was his death.

When I was about ten, my father developed an abscess on his bottom. He was treated by one hospital after another, but the abscess remained for over a year. My mother rented a house for him in a resort area, and we used to visit him there. Because penicillin was not available, his problem did not go away. Then his body swelled up, and he couldn't be cured. I just came and looked at the body of my father and was scared; I didn't dare come near.

One morning, Grandma awakened me and said, "Your father passed away." My mother cried, and I followed her in crying. Many relatives pitied my mother because of the early death of her husband, who was in his thirties. I was about 12 years old.

Mother now sold our house to move to the countryside, actually a suburb about four kilometers from the city. The new house we rented, of mud, bamboo, and thatch, was not as valuable as our old one. Mother took over the business of selling wool clothes and underwear. When business was good, we bought the country house and expanded trade to include weaving. After about one year, we moved back to the city and bought another store.

My mother was sometimes taciturn, but also kind and compassionate. She loved her poor relatives and gave them money. I loved my mother; without her support, my life would have been worse. She was very gentle; she rarely scolded her children. But I did not have her love and affection. She only loved the youngest child; this is common among the Vietnamese. I was well fed, but as the third of four children, I received no caresses, hugging, or pampering; I never knew affection in my childhood.

I felt a bit of pity for myself, but I was not sad. I accepted it, for our Vietnamese custom was to love the youngest. Anyway, my younger brother was more handsome than I; that's why he was loved more.

I grew up without love, and that's why I became such a shy person; I had ambition, but I never had the aggressiveness to take a chance and follow out my interests. I had a friend who was a journalist and very energetic in his opposition against the Communists.

They destroyed his office with a bomb. I wanted to follow him, but I did not dare, because I was scared.

My shyness was due to the fact that when I was very small, I was handed over to my aunt [mother's sister] and uncle [mother's brother]. [He did not explain why this happened; possibly it occurred after the death of his father.] These two relatives, who were single, lived together in a different house. I cried often, and my aunt couldn't stop me. My uncle would scare me by putting a dark blanket over himself. We had no electricity at that time, just oil lamps, so I was terribly frightened. I think it had a great influence on my shyness.

Also, I was not loved by other members of the family. I remember grandfather [father's father] sitting and smoking opium while we children played and ran around him. Suddenly I slipped and broke his long tobacco pipe. I was really scared; I ran to a neighbor's house to hide. I was around ten years old. He didn't beat me because I was so scared and ran away.

In the family, the children gave Grandfather the highest respect, then Grandmother, and after them our parents. Later on, Grandfather became even more strict: whenever a housemaid passed by him, she was not allowed to look at him straight. If she did, he would reprimand her with harsh words of criticism, swearing, and with insults referring to genitalia. Opium smoking was not considered bad. Only the rich families could afford the habit, and it was nothing to be ashamed of; under French rule, opium smoking was encouraged. Grandfather got angry at the housemaids probably because he was getting older, could no longer run the business, and so handed it over to his wife and his daughter-in-law, my mother, since his son was already ill. But the two women didn't have any business skills, and so Grandfather saw his business going down.

Grandfather didn't pay much attention to me. For example, if he cut an orange into pieces for us four children, my younger brother got the biggest, and I got the smallest. That was why I could endure under different stresses and difficulties later in my life. I had learned endurance; I had become used to that. When I entered adult life, I had an inferiority complex. For example, when I meet or accompany someone who speaks better English than I, then I am unable to speak English. I have great respect for intellectuals, for people with high degrees.

When I was a child, the back door of my house looked out onto a great banyan tree. Many women would pass by it, bow, and put the palms of their hands together in a greeting of respect. My mother, a fervent Buddhist, told me to stoop when I passed the tree, and not to look at it because it was a sacred thing. [This was a folk belief, not part of formal Buddhist tradition.]

When I grew up, I learned that such things as statues of the Buddha or the cross are symbols to be respected, but not to be feared. I can say that I do not believe in any religion, I do not have any faith. Probably the banyan tree was considered sacred because of ignorance; people couldn't explain natural phenomena such as lightning. This happened in the old days, not now, for people no longer respect such things. But I remember as a child lowering my head and bowing when I passed by one of the Buddhist temples in the Chinatown section of Hanoi. I remember bowing before big statues of Chinese saints in the Quang Thanh temple. I would only look at the first line of statues at the altar. The many other lines always looked mysterious and scary; I didn't dare to look at them.

As a child usually I'd be awakened at 7:00 A.M., and I'd begin to prepare to go to school. I did this on my own; no one ever told me about school or encouraged me to go. I usually ate some bread, then hurried to school, which began at eight. When I was young, I was shy, and quite afraid of my teacher. When I woke up in the morning, I cried for fear that I would be late for school. The teacher often praised me for being a good student. I was only beaten once. One day, many of us could not remember our lessons. One by one the teacher asked us questions, and when we could not answer, he hit us on the hand with the ruler.

Because there was not enough room for all the students, we took turns attending half-day classes. After I was finished for the day, I went home, ate a meal, and did some studying. My favorite foods were fried meat, hot rice, shrimp fried in flour batter, French bread, and pâté. I also liked to read books and newspapers.

I especially remember my fifth-grade teacher. He used to praise me because I was good at French grammar. I wasn't so good at math, though. I especially loved that teacher because I also enjoyed reading Vietnamese literature, and my teacher was a novelist. He paid a lot of attention to me not only because of my French grammar and dictation, but also because I was the only student with a Chinese name in our class of 60; he rarely had Chinese students.

Even after the Communists took over, I used to see him from time to time. Many students used to go to his house, which was near the school. With his students, he remained reserved, for he never knew if they were Communist Party members or security police. He feared that he might say something not in line with the Communist regime. So his countenance reflected his worries about life. He looked really old and worried; his wife had just passed away, his two children were about to enter the university, and he had to do his own cooking. His retirement benefits were insufficient, so he had to teach French to live. The difficulties of life in Vietnam make people taciturn, gloomy, not smiling. My old teacher was happy and proud only in his past knowledge, not in the things he could learn under the new regime.

[See also Chapters 15, 17, and 39.]

CHAPTER 6

Make Friends with Equals: 1927–1940

On the morning of August 8, 1976, Phuong Hoang, his wife, and four children, dressed only in bathing suits, set out for a Sunday sea ride in their small bamboo raft. They made their way to a 40-foot fishing boat anchored offshore. Phuong Hoang quickly pushed them aboard, told them to lie down, and then said, "We are leaving our country." Only then did his family discover that they would never be returning to Vietnam.

For nearly one year, Phuong Hoang had prepared secretly for this moment, telling no one in his family, for fear that they might inadvertently disclose the carefully planned escape. With no seafaring experience and no navigational aids but the stars and a toy compass, this man set out on a 1,500-kilometer journey to Manila.

I asked him, "What did your family say when you told them they were leaving their homeland forever?"

"Nothing," he replied. "They were too seasick."

We were sitting in his apartment where, over the course of ten interviews and 25 hours, I was to collect a detailed and lively account of the life of a conservative, middle-class teacher. What came to interest me especially was not only his dramatic escape, but his motivations. Unlike many of the narrators whom I interviewed, Phuong Hoang was not singled out for persecution; he was not sent to reeducation camps. What then would prompt a 49-year-old teacher to risk not only his own life but that of his entire family,

*to leave behind forever other relatives and friends and a familiar culture for
an improbable, heroic journey and an unknown, uncertain future? This is
a culture in which people quote the proverb, "Going away in a far direction; seeking food." In other words, only those searching for food leave
home. Never before in the long history of this civilization has there been a
mass exodus of persons fleeing the country; neither war nor famine, both
of which have occurred in the twentieth century, have dislodged the Vietnamese from their homeland. But the Communists have.*

*"Better to die than to live another day under Communist rule," replied
Phuong Hoang, and die he almost did, along with his family, on their
dangerous voyage to Manila.*

*In America, his life has been especially hard; his wife has been unable
to learn English and, like many older Vietnamese women, is isolated and
home-bound. Phuong Hoang has taken a succession of temporary jobs that
are much lower in status than those he held in Vietnam. He continually
faces the threat of unemployment. He and his wife have been subject to
anti-Vietnamese discrimination. They do not feel welcome in America,
but they can never return to Vietnam because of the fear of retaliation.
Despite his difficulties, Phuong Hoang adamantly insists that he made
the right choice, for in his view, conditions in Vietnam are intolerable.
By that he does not mean simply economic hardship, for he is used to that,
both in Vietnam and in America. Rather he cites the suppression of basic
freedoms, direct and conscious political oppression. Like many Vietnamese-
Americans, Phuong Hoang becomes deeply offended when he hears Americans say that Vietnamese refugees have come to America simply to get
secure jobs, for they see themselves not as immigrants, but as refugees,
victims fleeing the political oppression of an entire people. For Phuong
Hoang, life in America is not better than in Vietnam except in one crucial
respect: he is free from Communist rule.*

I remember childhood as a beautiful, wonderful time. My father
owned two stores in our town in which he sold canned food, bev-
erages, cigarettes, and liquors from France, England, Scotland, and
Germany. They also sold many sets of china. My parents were
quite rich; they sent me to a French school in the town.

In those days [the 1930s], people lived with no trouble under the
French. We had no thieves; life was so safe that we left our doors

open at night. We lived behind one of our stores, in a five-room brick house with a red tile roof. I had three brothers and seven sisters.

Childhood was a happy time; I did not worry about the future. My earliest memory is returning home from school when I was about six years old. I'd go to the beach and swim and fish. I had lots of fun.

Each morning I would eat steamed meat inside fried white flour. Then my brothers and sisters and I would go to school together. At school, we spoke French; in addition to arithmetic, we learned about French politics, geography, and history. We received very little instruction about the Vietnamese language or history. We studied for four hours in the morning; then we went home for lunch, and returned at two in the afternoon. After school we would go swimming, or go to the fields for cricket fighting, which was lots of fun. We also did this during our school breaks.

We respected our teacher like our father. We had to sit straight on a hard chair, remain quiet, and listen. When our teacher arrived, we had to stand up silently until he told us to sit down. Our job was to obey, not like some American children, who do not show respect; they lean over, put their feet up, and do not pay attention.

My father, like others, did not show his love to his children, but felt it in his mind. My mother showed love to us. She would pick us up when we were small, sing to us, and try to make us happy. Father was not supposed to do that; he would buy us clothing, and because we attended a French school, he also bought us shoes. Most children simply went barefoot.

Our parents and teachers expected discipline and obedience from us. We grew up hearing proverbs that reminded us of our obligations: "Fish without salt smells bad [becomes rotten] and is inedible; children who refuse everything [disobey their parents] become bad." To remember the role of our parents, we heard, "When drinking water, remember its source." When we become successful, we should remember our parents, who made that success possible.

Because of this emphasis, our education was quite different from that in America. In addition to the usual subjects of mathematics, history, science, geography, and so on, we had an important unit of instruction on how to live in society as good citizens: how to respect parents, teachers, old people, brothers, and sisters. Ours was an education based on custom. We learned how citizens should pay taxes to the government, rules of politeness and respect, and the proper rules of relationship between young men and women, who should never touch or shake hands. If a man wanted to marry a particular woman, his parents should find an old friend or relative of the woman to serve as a mediator.

As we grew older, we came to learn that it is best to make friends with equals and to marry people of our own social level. Sometimes this was based on wealth, and often on education, but most importantly on the character and moral reputation of the family. The parents generally made these decisions because they could judge better than their children. The match needed to be appropriate, and when there was a mismatch, we expressed this by saying, "A round pot fits a round lid; a misshapen pot fits a misshapen lid."

Of course, our horoscopes also had to match; otherwise we'd have bad luck: early death, no children, loss of wealth, or some other tragedy. We were really concerned about bad luck, not only from horoscopes, but also from the placement of the main doors of our houses. If they faced a neighbor's roof shaped like an inverted V, or at the end of a street that formed the middle of a T, that was terrible! We could not live in such a house without suffering a terrible illness or other catastrophe. If the door of a store faced a roof or a road like that, no one would enter the store. It was with these beliefs that I grew up, and they are still important in my life.

[See also Chapters 29 and 36.]

CHAPTER 7

Predestined for the Religious Life: 1932-1952

NARRATOR 5: NORTH VIETNAMESE BUDDHIST NUN

The first time I saw the Vietnamese nun, in the spring of 1982, she was performing a ceremony at her pagoda, located in a predominantly Hispanic neighborhood in a West Coast American city. The small lawn in front of the pagoda was festooned with brightly colored Buddhist flags; the exterior walls were covered with paintings and decorations, transforming what had once been a modest five-room house into a miniature island of Vietnamese culture. Throughout the day, the transformative image was perpetuated by the hollow, measured beats of the wooden bell; the drone of chanting; the super-sweet smell of burning incense; the subtle flavors of specially prepared rice cakes and other delicacies; and the kaleidoscope of dazzling yellow, green, and blue women's tunics, contrasted with the drab-colored suits of the men. Older women, wearing subdued browns, spoke to each other with animation; they smiled widely, revealing red-and-blackened betel-stained teeth.

Most striking of all was a slight, youthful-looking woman with a shaven head who wore a plain brown robe—the nun. Only later would I learn that she was over 50 years old. Somehow, through simplicity, she projected a commanding presence, at once both lively and dignified, personal yet distant, an individual with whom each follower could identify in his or her own way: the nun was a mother-figure for children, a counselor for troubled adults, a mentor for older women, a ritualist for those celebrating weddings or funerals, a spiritual master for those wishing to enter the monastic life, and a narrator for the anthropologist.

When we met, I told her of my project, and she said she would be happy to tell me about the Buddhist way and her own experiences as a nun in Vietnam and America (see also Freeman 1987). Our sessions began around seven in the evening, and lasted from three to five hours. One of my Vietnamese friends helped as an interpreter, but also participated as a third discussant. While talking, we drank tea and occasionally ate oranges, persimmons, or other fruits and snacks donated to the pagoda. I taped the interviews and also wrote notes throughout the evening. On occasion, other persons stopped by to visit the pagoda or the nun. Often she would leave to attend to these persons, but sometimes they joined us and expressed their views of the Buddhist way.

The direction of the interviews was structured, yet flexible; interwoven with the details of her life story is the nun's own exposition of the principles of Buddhism, along with her interpretation of some of the formative events of contemporary Vietnamese history.

The interviews began in October 1982 and continued almost weekly until May 1983. After a three-month break, we met for the final time in September 1983. Earlier I had told her that for our final session I wanted her to discuss how her masters had influenced her life. I figured that this was an appropriate way to culminate our 64 hours of interviews. With vivid anecdotes, the nun described how her master both taught and lived the Buddhist way. Her greatest master was Dam Soan, whom she described as "successful in all respects." Then she concluded, "She was no less than others," a designation which I believe aptly fits the nun herself.

As we were parting, the nun said, "When we began this evening, I had no idea what I would say; not until I heard your questions did I know what to say; it just came out of my unconscious."

I replied, "My questions, too, came from the same source; I had no idea what to ask you until I heard you speak; then I just let it flow. If we do something in a natural way, it is much better."

She nodded, "Yes, much better."

The position of a nun in Vietnamese society is an ambivalent one. Parents often object to and try to dissuade a son or daughter who wishes to choose the monastic life, for it removes them from family ties and commit-

ments. At the same time, Buddhist monks and nuns are given great respect for developing those very traits that enable them to disengage from ordinary society.

In many respects, the life story of the nun highlights the opposition between religious and secular spheres in Vietnamese society. The Buddhist monastic life chosen by the nun is aimed to prepare a person for a new mode of being, achievement of enlightenment. This reverses the principles and life-styles of ordinary, hierarchical, secular society. Ordinary social identities are removed. A monk or nun is known only by the religious names conferred upon them by their religious masters, and later by the names of the pagodas in which they temporarily reside. A novice is shorn of hair, given plain food and garments, and taught to devalue personal attachments. At the same time the novice is enjoined to be compassionate, knowledgeable, and involved for the betterment of other people, all of whom should be treated equally.

In this chapter, the nun describes how she was drawn to the monastic life at the age of five and how the simple lessons she learned while a child remained with her as the foundation of her faith.

I was born in 1932 in a village of about 400 people located in a province of North Vietnam. My father was a farmer and a seller of oriental medicines. My mother took care of my father, my elder sister, and myself.

My earliest memory is that of going to our village pagoda with my parents. I remember that I felt so comfortable there; the pagoda attracted me, I cannot explain why. I now realize that I was predestined for the pagoda. When I was five years old, I told my parents that I wanted to go and live in the pagoda. This was an unusual request from one who was so young, but they did not resent or resist my going there. They figured that I was too young to know what I was doing, and that I'd soon get tired of it. I never returned home again.

When I was young, my daily tasks at the pagoda, which housed six nuns, consisted of house chores such as sweeping and cleaning the house, watering the vegetables, and watching the water buffalo to keep it from eating the rice. At the evening service, I would listen to the nuns reciting the Buddhist prayers. In this way, when I was very young, I learned it by heart.

At the pagoda, we awakened around 4:30 or 5:00 A.M. After breakfast, most of us worked in the rice fields. During the dry season, we cultivated sweet potato and peanuts, while the master remained at the pagoda and cleaned it.

Between the ages of six and twelve, I attended school, where I learned Chinese characters with Vietnamese meanings. While at school, I played with other children, but I had no attachments to them. After school, I'd simply return to the pagoda to do my chores.

One day, when I was still very young, I came from school and found that lunch was unappetizing. A nun said to me, "I'll give you an additional dish; it's a very special one for the master."

I replied, "If I have the right to eat it, give it; if you are doing me a favor, don't." I didn't eat.

Three hours later, the nun took away the special food, saying, "You didn't want the food, so now go hungry." That night I went to bed without food.

That incident taught me a lesson that has stayed with me all my life. I had become angry at first because the nun hadn't served the special dish, then resentful when she brought it as a favor. It was an insignificant event, yet I attached too much importance to it. I failed to keep an even outlook, and the result was that I suffered for it. What I learned from this was never to be angry, nor disappointed; I use that lesson to teach others.

In 1944, when I was 12 years old, I moved with my master to another pagoda. For the next six years we were frequently on the move because of war. I saw the flooding of Hadong city in 1945, and the Japanese invasion of North Vietnam, when they dragged French soldiers through the streets to humiliate them.

But my most vivid memory of that time was the terrible starvation of the people. [See also Chapter 11.] I saw many people die in the villages. The Japanese were losing the war, so they didn't let people cultivate rice, and they threw the rice from storehouses in the river. People streamed into the cities looking for food, stealing whatever they could find, even taking it out of the hands of other people. Ravenous people overate and died of indigestion; the

Japanese executed others for stealing, but many simply died of starvation.

When we traveled during these days of turmoil, I was afraid, but my master reassured me, "If something happens, accept fate, but not passively. If there is danger, we should try to escape."

After the defeat of the Japanese in 1945, the Viet Minh and the French fought for control of the country. Again for safety we had to move from one village to another. Finally in 1948, we walked to Hanoi, passing right through the Viet Minh into French-controlled territory. We settled in a large pagoda.

In those troubled days, my master taught me one important lesson. "If you can do something of benefit for others," she said, "try to do your best not only for yourself but for them. Don't be disappointed if you fail; don't be overjoyed if you are successful, for success or failure depends on many circumstances. You may succeed because you are lucky. If you fail, don't feel bad. The main thing is devotion. Failure or success is of no importance."

When I was ten years old, I received my religious name. My master conferred it on me when I participated in the first of three ceremonies that we call "Acceptance of Restraints." At the first or lowest level, we are received as novices. In the ceremony, we commit ourselves to sacrifice things, to follow the rules, to study the Buddha-teachings and canon every day, to wear Buddhist dress, to hold no property, to eat no meat but only vegetables, and to devote our lives for the benefit of others, with an attitude of disinterest, or rather, without self-interest. In other words, we develop less ties for self-attachment, but greater concern for others. For example, if I have a child, I must love it, but since I have no child, I can love my neighbor's child without attachment.

For the same reason, we don't eat meat. The Buddha-teaching is that of cause and effect. If we do harm to somebody, it causes harm to us; we are responsible for our own actions. If we eat meat, we have lost love for the animals. We should show love; the more we eat meat, the more we destroy our love.

So we are taught to consider the seat of love. Our expression has two parts. The first means to bring happiness to somebody other than yourself, while the second refers to the relief of suffering of somebody else. This is a Buddha-expression, the combination of both. If somebody drives me downtown, it makes me happy, since it saves me from walking, so that is happiness and the relief of suffering for the person who offers it.

Before I went through this first-stage ceremony, I was given formal preparation. I had to learn a prayer that I recited when washing my hands, "I use water to wash my hands. I pray for everybody to have clean hands and to understand the Buddha-teachings." When I washed my face, I uttered a different prayer, and so on.

Then I was subjected to a review and tests, not formal tests as in school, but observations through our normal routine. I had to learn the Buddhist canon and rules, but in addition, the master watched my behavior, and tested me to see how I would react. Once, she left a certain amount of money nearby when I was sweeping the floor. She wanted to see if I would keep it or return it, indicating that I was not attracted to desire. She watched to see if I took fruit from the trees in front of the pagoda. Sometimes she would create an incident such as accusing me of making a mistake and would observe my reaction. She also evaluated how I conversed with other people, in a normal way or with flattery to make them happy.

When my master decided I was ready, she announced, "My disciple deserves to be raised to a higher rank. I am responsible for her." The other nuns and monks didn't examine me directly, but they had observed my behavior. They had to approve me unanimously, or I would not be raised to a higher status.

The first-stage ceremony marked my official entrance into the Buddhist religious community. It was a big ceremony presided over by three senior monks.

At the age of 20, I went through the second-stage ceremony, which raised us to a new level. At this stage, monks had to observe 250 rules, while nuns had to follow 348 rules. [Editor's note: Some monks say that the required number of rules for nuns is 290.] Ten senior monks conducted this ceremony for some 15 to 20 other new nuns drawn from many pagodas. It was a big event attended by hundreds of people. The monks, dressed in saffron robes, conducted a ceremony, and the superior monk delivered a sermon on the meaning of the ceremony as well as the ten major rules we had to observe. The description of each rule was ten words long, and consisted of prohibitions such as not to lie, steal, or have lewd ideas. Then we made our vows.

After this ceremony, I was sent to a nun-training school in Hanoi. This was a more formal, detailed, and advanced training than I had received before. In my earlier training, I learned the everyday activities, such as cleaning rooms, prayer, washing hands, and all of the regular services, plus elementary reading and learning of the canon. But at the school we went more in detail, more in depth with the study and explanation of the canon. The first half of the day basically was for myself. I studied for my own improvement, knowledge, and personality. The second half of the day was devoted to economic activities for the self-support of the pagoda. These included handicrafts such as knitting sweaters, making mats, operating hand looms for cotton cloth, all sold to people, and working in the rice fields.

Each year, we also went into a period of retreat for three months. To hold a retreat, at least four nuns or monks agreed to attend. This was an even more intense period for religious activity, with an even stricter regimen than our ordinary routine. On the retreats, we slept only five and a half hours a night. Unlike our ordinary routine, we spent more time in study and prayer, less time in work. Particularly if we went to large pagodas for our retreats, we became involved in a much more intense experience for religion, for we came into contact with people who were much more advanced, and that inspired us to learn more.

From this training, I have learned to distinguish superstitions and obsessions from Buddha-nature. Dreams, for example, reflect our obsessions. If we want to have a car, we dream about that car. This has no significance. I don't believe in the interpretation of dreams. Similarly, a lot of people say that some days are good days, and others are bad, or unlucky. But according to the Buddha, all days are good days, for it depends on us. A lot of people follow the superstition of lucky or unlucky days. Others believe in those ideas which come from Taoism, not Buddhist teaching.

We are responsible for our own deeds; nobody can be responsible for our own deeds but ourselves. The Buddha cannot make us good or bad; he can advise or show us, but then it is our own choice. If a medical doctor gives you a prescription and you throw it away, how can the doctor cure the illness? The Buddha is like a guide; if he shows the way and you don't follow it, the fault is not his, but yours. He cannot make us good, but he can help us. He loves people equally, and gives all people the same opportunity to use, to apply his help. Then it is up to the person, female or male, to develop their Buddha-nature.

That is why in our Buddhist tradition, unlike that of the Catholics, a nun can fulfill all the responsibilities of a monk. I can offer any kind of service, worship, or teaching of the Buddha to people, anything that a monk can do, except for one thing. At the second level of the "Acceptance of Restraints" ceremony, a monk can give exams to other monks, but a nun requires the participation of a monk.

In order simply to preserve harmony, we have eight rules for the social behavior of nuns with monks. These are basically rules of respect and deference, and avoidance of conflict and criticisms of monks.

Feminists in the West have found the teachings of the Buddha easy to criticize, particularly that men should have some control over the behavior of women. But the feminist criticisms greatly misunderstand us. A nun should be restrained simply to avoid disruption. But likewise, the monk must treat the nun with respect. The eight rules are created to assure a harmonious relationship between monks and nuns. This does not mean that monks are superior to nuns. In religious activities, both are equal, just as they are equal in spirit, soul, and capability. [Editor's note: This is the nun's personal interpretation of the rules, even though many of them explicitly require nuns to defer to monks without any alteration or distortion of the regulations. (See Narada Maha Thera 1982: 166–167.)]

[See also Chapters 24, 30, and 38.]

CHAPTER 8

Growing Up in a Catholic Village: 1942–1966

NARRATOR 6: CENTRAL VIETNAMESE FISHERMAN / BUSINESSMAN

With a firm handshake and a nod, Mr. Liem invited us into the living room of the modest house he rented in a small farming town. His wife placed a pot of jasmine tea on the low coffee table in front of the couch. On the walls were prints of Jesus and Mary; on the mantelpiece stood a small Catholic altar and photos of deceased relatives. The aroma of imperial rolls frying in oil came from the kitchen, where Mr. Liem's 13-year-old daughter was preparing our lunch. I had traveled to Mr. Liem's town with a Vietnamese acquaintance, who was assisting me in this interview. We would stay at the Liem household for several hours before returning home.

My acquaintance knew that I was looking to interview an ordinary working man, preferably a villager. He had previously spoken at length with Mr. Liem about my biographies project and had set up our interview. As a respected and trusted man in the Vietnamese Catholic community, my acquaintance provided not only translation help, but also assurances that Mr. Liem's confidentiality would be protected and that his views would be accurately represented.

As soon as the interview began, I realized that Mr. Liem had a special quality about him. Although not highly educated, he was articulate, clear, and direct. Most surprising and impressive was the self-assured, commanding presence of this solidly built man of medium height. He exuded the genuine confidence and optimism of a pragmatic, take-charge sort of person who sees himself in control of his own destiny. He was forthright but not arrogant, polite but not self-effacing, friendly and open but not familiar. His strength, I found, came not only from his own inner resources, but from his upbringing in a devout Catholic household in Central Vietnam run by his strong-willed, independent, entrepreneurial mother.

Because our time was short, I had Mr. Liem first give me a brief overview of his life story; then we focused on some of the central events he mentioned. His narration of his life experiences in Vietnam flowed in a coherent linear direction with little or no prompting from me or my Vietnamese acquaintance. However, when we discussed adjustments in America, focusing on present conditions rather than past events, I found myself asking many more questions: "Explain more about the phrase 'feeling at ease.' What changes have occurred in your family as a result of being in America? Tell me about your friends in America. What are your easiest and most difficult adjustments in America? What have you learned from Americans, and what might Americans learn from the Vietnamese? What expectations do you have for you and your family? Now that you are in America, what are your thoughts and nostalgia about Vietnam?"

To all but one question, Mr. Liem replied without hesitation. When I asked him what Americans might learn from the Vietnamese, he gave a hearty laugh and said, "I do not want to say what Americans can learn from the Vietnamese."

Nevertheless, his account leaves no doubt that Americans could learn something of the opportunities that exist in America, even for persons who arrive on our shores without technical skills, high education, and knowledge of English or of the customs of our land. Mr. Liem's story highlights one of the ways in which Vietnamese refugees succeed in America. The ingredients for success involve hard work, adaptability in facing new challenges, a willingness to undergo personal sacrifices, and an extremely high motivation to provide economic security for their families in America and their relatives in Vietnam.

I was born in 1942 in a Central Vietnamese Catholic village. My father died when I was very young, but my mother is still alive. I was the seventh of eight children, five boys and three girls.

For the first eight years of my life, I lived in that fishing village. The sea and a beach lay on one side of the village. On the other side, a river flowed by in the shape of an L. During the summer and the fish season, the villagers were very active. I remember especially that each year, because we were Catholics, we celebrated "Fish-Catching Day." The boat which caught the most fish on that day became Number One. The leader or owner of the boat received congratulations, in cash. Then he gave this money to the Church. We held a big celebration, like Christmas. At night people went out in the boats, lit candles, and had a procession on the sea. This was in honor of God and St. Mary. During the years we lived in that village, I did not attend school. Not until I was ten years old was I sent to school in a coastal town.

In 1950, when I was eight years old, my mother moved the family a little south to a small town near the beach. We continued to work as fishermen. Then in 1954 we moved to another Catholic village which remained our home until 1975. It was situated on a foothill. Thanks to God and St. Mary, that small village became bigger and bigger. The sea was on one side of the village, and a river on the other. Because sand silted up at the sea, the land became bigger, and so more people came to live in the village.

There are so many beautiful things that as a Vietnamese I remember, very sentimental. We had very good relations with our neighbors. We visited each other almost daily. When we had good things to eat, we would offer them to our neighbors, and they did that for us. We were not relatives, but we liked each other; we were like relatives. We were so close that we maintained our ties by mutual marriages.

That village became very prosperous, and bigger day by day, until November 1963. After the overthrow of President Diem, our village became a sharp thorn for the new regime, which considered us to be from the old regime because we were Catholics. They connected us with the political party of one of President Diem's brothers. Angry students came into our village and burned it. We escaped by boats, and for the next month, we lived on a small island occupied by the Vietnamese Navy. Then we came back to our village and rebuilt it.

Within two to three years, our village was more beautiful than before. We constructed our houses of brick and stone. Later, the government gave us compensation, a certain amount of money.

We lived there, each of us in the family, until 1975, when we dispersed. Each of us went our ways, some abroad. The village is still prosperous.

As I grew up, I did not see my father. I am very unhappy about that. My mother and brothers told me that my father died early when I was very young. Mother did not remarry, so she went through many years of difficult times, like 1945, when we had the hunger year [famine and starvation in North Vietnam caused by the Japanese; see Chapter 11].

My mother brought her eight children from one city to another to get what we needed. She worked very hard to raise us, and finally we came to a fishing village. My mother is feminine, but she has the spirit of a man; she can do everything, and she's resourceful. Also, she had good social manners; that's why a lot of people like her. She had a boat. During 20 years in that village, she became the owner of the Number One fishing boat. Although she was a widow, she led her family to a good degree of prosperity.

After the Communists took over and I decided to escape from Vietnam, I discussed this with my mother many times, but she decided not to go with me. "I am old already," she said. "Three of my children are now in the U.S.A., but five are in Vietnam. If you leave, then four will be in America. Life is happier in America. I don't want to go with the happy children; I've decided to stay with the ones who had miserable hardship. When every child of mine lives in America, then I'll go." That is the kind of sacrifice she will make for her children.

All of us children loved her because she did not remarry. She stayed as she was and raised us. She is still loving and healthy, so every month we collect some money and send it to her. It is very little to do compared with what she has done for us.

[See also Chapters 25 and 37.]

CHAPTER 9

Childhood in North and South Vietnam: 1946–1968

NARRATOR 7: NORTH VIETNAMESE AUTOMOBILE MECHANIC

Trac was born in 1946 in a Catholic village of 1,000 persons in North Vietnam. He is now the successful co-owner of an automotive repair shop in a West Coast city. In 1954, at the age of eight, he, his family, and most of his fellow villagers left their home forever and relocated to South Vietnam to avoid the Communist persecution of Catholics. Nevertheless, Trac remains a North Vietnamese villager at heart. His life story describes in vivid and concrete detail, in the distinctive expressions of his region, what it was like to experience childhood in a community that is now just a memory. True, many of his relatives still live there, but after more than three decades of Communist rule not much is left of life as Trac knew it. Indeed, Trac left Vietnam because, as he expresses it, "The Communists controlled too much of the life of the people, who had no freedom to do anything, even basic freedoms. There is no freedom even to travel around from the countryside to the city or the city to the countryside. To travel, everyone needs a pass from the government. And it is difficult to get it."

After his move to South Vietnam in 1954, he and his family moved to several locations. He describes a later childhood of constant uprooting as his family searched for jobs and kept on the move to avoid the authorities, who were after them for making wine without a license. They learned tobacco farming. During the Tet Offensive of 1968, their house was destroyed by shells. He was subsequently drafted into the army, worked in the military police for several years, and tried but failed to escape at the time of the fall of Saigon. He went into the jungle, looking to join up with resistance fighters, but finding none, he returned home. He later escaped by boat, was eventually resettled in America, and became an automobile mechanic and co-owner of a repair shop.

Of his adjustments to America, he says, "My body is in America; my heart and mind are in Vietnam. Adjustment to America is not impossible, but you lose something. Americans have no heart. They have no sense of helping others. They lack humanness."

He related how in Vietnam, if a person saw someone having difficulties, even a complete stranger, a person would go to his or her aid. "If someone had a stalled car," he observed, "I'd help them out; I'd not ask for payment. If I did a job for someone and he couldn't pay me, I'd tell them to pay me when they could. There's a friendly bond that links even strangers. You might meet someone on an intercity bus, start talking, become friendly, and ask that person to come home for dinner. You just can't do that in America. If you try to be friendly here, to help people, they'll rip you off. If I helped someone by fixing their car free, they'd drive off insulting me, 'Go back home to your country.' That has happened to me.

"A few weeks ago, someone parked in such a way as to block the only entrance to our auto repair shop. My partner asked the man to move on, which he did. But a few minutes later he returned with a huge iron bar; he bashed it on my partner's head. I took my partner to the hospital. You can't trust Americans. If I see someone whom I think cannot pay, I give a ridiculously high estimate to get them out of my shop. In Vietnam, I'd have helped such a person; here I protect myself."

Trac's wife was listening to his discussion. She added, "At work, I've been snubbed by Americans. All the Vietnamese women work on one line. One time, we tried to be friendly, to open conversation, and to give gifts to lines of women of other groups. They ignored us; they did not reply, but turned their backs on us. They acted as if we do not exist. Our neighbors, who come from many different groups, are friendlier to us, not like the workers."

To survive in America, Trac and his wife have found it necessary to create a protective shell around themselves. They cope with Americans by shutting them out. If they appear inscrutable and not too friendly, it's not because of their Vietnamese socialization, but because of the negative ex-

periences of their American socialization, and they generalize this when they say, "We have learned to become Americans."

Trac is a person rooted in a tradition that he will always carry with him, no matter what hardships befall him, no matter where he goes. Despite all that he and his family have gone through, the disruption and the wrenching of their lives out of their village foundation, Trac remains a happy man, a centered man whose security in a turbulent, disintegrating world was forged in a family, village, and religious environment that sustains him.

In 1946 I was born in a village near a branch of the Red River in North Vietnam. We lived about a half day's walk from a town. My village, which contained about 1,000 people, was surrounded by bamboo trees. Most of the houses of the village were of mud and thatch. In our compound, however, our main building was made of red brick. Inside we had a central altar for the worship of ancestors, and partitioned places where the family slept. Our mud and thatch storage hut was used also as a school, for my older brother was the teacher. We also had a separated kitchen, a barn for our buffalo, a large rice-threshing yard, and a great pool for catching rain water. Our family had some land which we used for irrigated rice cultivation.

I was the youngest of six children, and because of this I received special attention. I was taken everywhere by my parents, and if they didn't take me, they brought back gifts of cake or candy. I was favored as the proverb says, "Rich youngest child benefits; poor youngest child suffers." In other words, whether rich or poor, everything will be for the youngest.

At the same time, I was expected to show absolute obedience to my parents. This was unquestioned for a child, whether at home or at school. We were taught to obey first: we learned how to obey parents, how to show respect to older people, how to cross our arms and bow whenever we saw an older person, how to obey our older brothers, sisters, and parents. And we learned how to speak in a special respectful way to them, giving a respectful "yes" when called, and using another form of respectful "yes" when obeying a command. We learned the proverb, "First study politeness [good behavior], next study literature." We were also taught the proverb, "Fish will be rotten without salt; children will always be rotten [spoiled] if they have disobeyed their parents."

Each week, either my parents or teacher would recite, "Father's deeds [done for the child] are as big as the Thai Son Mountain; Mother's devotedness is like the incessant spring from the source." From this we learned of the obligation with love of parents for their children.

My parents expected me to do some small chores at home, such as watching the chickens to see that they did not eat the rice. In addition, I was required to go to school, go to church twice a day, and to attend Bible class every night. We had a special section for confession. I began Bible training at the age of five through oral lessons. After I had finished my Bible training, I was allowed to go out and play.

As a child, I awakened around five in the morning. After going to church, I would return home for breakfast that consisted of rice, yams, and corn. Then I watched chickens for a couple of hours. Around ten in the morning, school began in our mud storage house. My elder brother was the teacher. During class, if I saw the chickens eating our rice, I was expected to jump up and chase them away. By the time I left North Vietnam at the age of eight, I could read and write simple Vietnamese, spell pretty well, and do elementary mathematics.

All the students sat and kneeled on a big mat on the floor. We used pens made of bamboo sticks, and ink on bad paper. The teacher sat at a desk, with a blackboard behind him. If we students did not do our lessons correctly, he beat us on our bottoms with a stick, or he hit us on the palms of our hands with a ruler. I was very afraid, even if he was my elder brother.

Around noon, we stopped for our lunch break, which lasted until 2:00 P.M. My parents wanted me to nap, but usually I went swimming, or caught fish and snails. We returned to school for two hours, then were released for the day. Then I did my homework, along with feeding the chickens. Usually I would eat something, then about 5:00 I would go to church, then to Bible class until about

8:00. After this, I would eat roasted yam, boiled peanut, and roasted corn, then go to bed.

Our daily routine changed during our times of celebration. During the New Year celebration, we went to my paternal grandfather's house, located one mile away. The preparations there took two weeks, as different people cooked rice cakes and other foods. For one month we celebrated; people say that January is the month for eating, playing, and enjoyment. People played cards and gambled, the older men participated in wrestling contests, people sang, and they watched traditional Vietnamese drama productions.

In addition to Christmas and Easter, we also had a big celebration for St. Jean, our main village saint. On that day there was no work or school. The church was cleaned by a man whom we called the Public Announcer. He was the poorest person of the village and came from our lowest class. His father and grandfather had also done this job. He beat a drum while making an announcement throughout the village. After Mass, some of the men who knew how to cook killed pigs, cows, and chickens for the entire village. The rich people donated these animals.

I really liked living in the village; it was comfortable, I felt at ease there, and no worries. Our life depended, not on the time clock as in America, but on the seasons. This is much more exciting and interesting than working in the city, where every day you go to work at the same time and do the same boring tasks. Our agricultural schedule was flexible, diverse, closer to nature, and enjoyable.

When I was a small child, I took care of our family's big water buffalo. After school, I would lead it to green fields to graze. While it went back and forth by itself, I'd play with my friends. In one of my favorite games, we divided into two teams which threw mud at one another. When a boy was hit, he became a prisoner of the other side. I also enjoyed cricket fighting. I and my friends would carry large crickets to school in match boxes. During recess time, we would set them to fight.

From time to time I watched buffalo fights. Each village had its own land. The buffalo fought to gain grazing fields for a couple of days or weeks. For this event, we would choose the strongest buffalo of our village. On summer days, we enjoyed flying huge five-foot kites with bamboo frames, covered with oiled paper, with wings and a tail like a bird. When it flew, the whistle put on it made a terrific sound.

When I was six or seven years old, French troops would come into the village during the day. My friends and I would wave and shout "Bonjour!" A few children would run after the soldiers, who gave them bread and canned fish. I stayed away because my family was so rich at that time, and the French officers would stop at my house for a meal of fried chicken. I saw them there. Sometimes they gave me something to play with, like the shell of a spent bullet. At night, they would go back to the city where they stayed. Then the Communists [Viet Minh] would appear and try to convert us. They would teach us with a dance, melody, and words to sing. They were very good with children but not with adults. I still remember the song [Trac danced as he sang]:

> Here is the forest; here is the rice field,
> Life is so free.

The Viet Minh were mostly young men and women in their twenties. They would tell us to fight against the French, that the Vietnamese should fight for independence, and not among themselves. They taught us how to make mock wooden guns and how to shoot, and they would divide us into two teams, one the French, the other the Communists. The Communists always won. Sometimes they gathered the adults of the village together for propaganda; then we were not allowed to attend. But the adults did because they were forced to.

But what did I know about these things? I was a child. I didn't know much about Communists. When they came at night, I played games with them; it was funny. Then the next day I would wave to the French and say "Bonjour!" The French by day, the Communists by night.

I am lucky that I was born and grew up in a village. I liked it. Even after we departed for the South, I lived at first in another village, then later in Saigon. So I know both village and city life.

One day Father said, "Pack some clothes; we are going to the South."

I had no idea where I would be going; I did not know North or South. I hid some of my playthings and a fishing pole, figuring I would have them when I returned to my village.

The day before we left, Father and Mother sold our buffalo, cow, and all of our properties to some non-Catholic people who planned to settle in our village. My parents knew that they could not live under Communist control, so they sold everything they could in order to leave as soon as possible. They did this without showing any feeling. From then on my big memory of childhood would be our constant moving from place to place, for our family would no longer be stable in any one community.

We set out from the village and walked for one day until we arrived at a town. From there we took a train to the harbor. We boarded an American ship, which took us to South Vietnam, where we were placed in a refugee camp: rows of yellow tents located in the middle of a rubber forest, flooded with rainwater and full of mosquitoes. We had no nets, so we suffered. That first night, a rumor circulated through the camp that we refugees were to be used as fertilizer for the rubber trees! We built a village right in that forest; the government let us cultivate as much land near the forest as we could handle by ourselves.

I noticed many differences between the North and the South. I could not understand the way the Southerners talked; it seemed to me that they spoke too fast. They could understand me only if I spoke very slowly. The Southerners dressed in a more fashionable and neater way. Schools were different: in the North, students of all classes studied in the same room; in the South, each class had a separate teacher.

But the biggest difference was in cultivation: corn in the South, rice in the North. We used buffalo and irrigation in the North; in the South, the rains were sufficient. In the South, we began new jobs such as chopping wood and selling it in the new village. Our life in one way was easier in the South because the government gave us fertilizer, kerosene, agricultural tools, and cash. In other ways, we encountered lots of difficulties. There were no jobs, no way to earn money except farming in an unfamiliar way, where we had to wait for people to supply us with food and money. Water was very scarce; wells were twelve and thirteen meters deep and still did not supply enough. Also, we heard rumors that the Communists would kill us and put us under the rubber trees.

After six months, we moved to the town that was located about five kilometers from our new village. This enabled my elder brother to resume work as a schoolteacher and also to work as a male nurse. Because of this, we had more money. The rest of the family turned to making soybean curds. Mother often would send me to the bazaar to buy things. I enjoyed this because I got extra money, which I spent on candy and on the lottery. A man would have a small table which he had placed on his bicycle. He would spin an arrow; sometimes I won a little bit of "pulling candy" or peanuts.

I remember also seeing a shamanistic curer hypnotize a young man, who walked on hot coals, about two feet square. The young man had some kind of mental disorientation in which he would frequently strike his mother and father. To cure him, the shaman told him to walk over the coals. The young man was afraid and refused. The shaman coerced him until finally he walked on the coals and stayed on them for about ten minutes. But this did not cure him. A couple of days later, he returned to attacking his parents.

We remained in the town for two years; then, when I was about 11 years old, we moved to Saigon because my brother-in-law said that living there was better. I had never seen a city like that, with its big buildings, comfortable schools, airplanes, and lots of cars. It was much more crowded than the small town.

In the next ten years my family moved three more times around the suburbs of Saigon. We had to keep on the run because we got into making illegal wine, without a license. The process of getting a license was simple, but we didn't understand it, so we moved a lot. We supplemented our income by gardening and raising pigs and chickens. In 1965 we learned how to cultivate tobacco, and we did that for three years. This earned us a big income.

During the years that I attended school, I learned about the Communists and what they did. I also heard from my father how when we lived in the North, the Communists had jailed him three times to try to get him to join with them. He was an influential man of the village, who could convince the villagers to join with the Communists. When he refused to cooperate, they released him. When he saw the opportunity to escape in 1954, he took all of us to the South. Some of his friends who remained behind were later arrested and killed.

At the time of the Tet Offensive of 1968, we were living in a house right outside a strategic hamlet [a special fortified hamlet created for the protection of villagers]. The Viet Cong surrounded the hamlet, but were unable to enter because the villagers, most of whom were Catholic, fought back. During the battle, my family moved into a cousin's home within the hamlet, and we remained there for one week. When the South Vietnamese Army (ARVN) counterattacked and dropped bombs, many houses outside the hamlet were destroyed, and ours was one of them. Everything of ours was destroyed; again we had nothing. There was no reason to stay, and so we moved to a community where my elder brother lived. There we started an ice cream business and built a house. Five months later, I was drafted into the Army of the Republic of Vietnam. My days of childhood and youth were over.

CHAPTER 10

Not to Beat Is Not to Love: 1963–1979

NARRATOR 8: SOUTH VIETNAMESE YOUNG POET

In 1979, Trung, a 16-year-old boy from a fishing village on a southern island, along with several other friends of his own age, were reported to the Communist authorities for passing out anti-Communist leaflets which they had printed. Only a few weeks before, one of their friends, 14 years old, had been sent off to jail for six months. His crime: ridicule of Uncle Ho at an Independence Day meeting.

How much more serious was the crime of Trung and his friends with their leaflets. Knowing that they would be arrested if they remained, they stole a boat owned by an old lady who had cheated many people: she would offer to help people escape from Vietnam, pocket their gold, and then do nothing.

Once away from the shore, the youths sang and cursed the Communists, and they stopped to swim and to fish. Then they ran out of oil, and their engine burned out on the high seas. They ran low on food and water. Trung was scared, but he believed in fate. So they sang and told jokes. Many boats passed but would not stop, even when the youths swam over to them. After seven days, one without food or water, they landed in Thailand and were taken to a camp. After several months they arrived in America.

For this youth, America has hardly been easier than Vietnam. He is what is termed an "unaccompanied minor," a youth who has arrived here without close family. When I met him, he was living in a shambles of a slum apartment with four other young men hardly older than himself. One of them, his brother-in-law, had sponsored him but then virtually abandoned him. Trung, like many unaccompanied minors, was passing his adolescent years without parental guidance or the emotional warmth of or bonds with a caring adult. As Jeanne Nidorf rightly notes (1985: 413–419), "such youths often experience intense feelings of loneliness, homesickness, and a longing for parental nurturance. They are vulnerable to feelings of confusion, shame, and generalized despair," since lack of family brings self-denigration through the feeling of being an outcast. Nidorf believes that such youths are at significantly higher risk for suicide than their peers because of their lack of a well-defined family structure to provide guidance. Finally, she claims that unaccompanied minors are also at higher risk for gang activity, which may serve as a substitute "family."

Trung's school experience in America made him an especially likely candidate for recruitment into gangs. Because of his chronological age, he was placed in a high school grade far beyond the education he had completed in Vietnam. Although he was ahead of his American counterparts in math, he could not keep up in other subjects; his English was halting; he was taught few useful job skills, and he became discouraged, without family, living in a strange land where no one cared about him.

One day, while leaving school, Trung was attacked and stabbed by a gang of four youths, who told him to get out of America. When I asked Trung what he thought about the incident, Trung said that at first he felt angry, but later he simply wanted to forget about the event. "I don't want revenge now," he said. "It's a foolish thing."

To an American outsider, Trung appears to be a youth headed for trouble, unable to speak English well, with no prospects or training to help him cope when, at the age of 18, his public assistance is terminated. But his Vietnamese friends know him in quite another light, as an outstanding guitarist and as a poet of extraordinary power and depth. He could not speak articulately, but his creative expressions revealed unexpected dimensions of understanding of his own conditions of loneliness and despair.

I did not know of Trung's talents until the fifth of our seven interview sessions, which occurred between November 1981 and January 1982, during which he narrated a text of some 10,000 words. In an offhand way, he mentioned that he sometimes wrote poetry; would I be interested in seeing it? When I assured him of my considerable interest, he pulled out some of his poems and read them to me. I was struck by their eloquent simplicity.

I said to him, "Have you told your social worker about your poems? I think he would be very impressed with them." The youth said he had not ever mentioned them to the Vietnamese social worker but would do so if I recommended it. The social worker was stunned when he read Trung's poems, for he had had no inkling of the talents of this semieducated youth.

Trung's genius indeed is seen in his poetry, which describes his memories of his homeland, his loneliness in a strange land, his frustrations in doing mathematics. He told me, "I write when I am lonely or when I am especially happy." His friends come to him for love poems, which he writes and gives them, and which they then recite to impress their girlfriends. But his most powerful poems are those of loneliness. Examples are found in Chapter 40, in which Trung describes his adjustments in America.

Trung's poetry also reveals a humorous side. One evening, frustrated with a mathematics homework assignment, he wrote "Sick of Math." Trung also has written sarcastic poems about "Girls Who Think They Are Too High and Mighty to Pay Attention to You." These poems follow strict rules of Vietnamese poetry.

Trung, who calls himself "The Sorrowful Hero," says, "I remember crying twice in my life. The first time was when my father hit me; the second was when I left my country."

Trung's story has a happy ending. As a result of the strenuous efforts of the Vietnamese social worker, Trung was placed in a job-training program that prepared him for employment; he subsequently moved to the Midwest, received job offers, and took one of them. His employability has enabled him to cope with adjustments in America in a way that otherwise he could never have done.

My first recollection is that of my father. He as well as his parents had been born on our island. With my father's salary from his government job and the little land we had, we were a middle-income family. Then in 1975 the Communists took over; we lost our land and my father became a fisherman.

At the age of seven I started school. The building was made of cement block walls, with a tile roof, and a different room for each of the five grades. Next to this school was a different one for the sixth through twelfth grades. My home was only 150 feet from these schools. It was a square, five-room, two-story house painted white, with a red tile roof and a garden in the back. In the house we had tables, chairs, wooden beds, electric lights, and a radio, but we had no water at the house. We had to buy water for drinking. We also shared a well far from the house with several other families; this water, which we carried home by cart, we used for bathing and washing clothes.

I had a room to myself, as did my older brother and older sister. Another brother lived in a separate house, and so did another married sister. It did not matter whether we lived in the house or outside; we could be independent or dependent, whatever we wanted. My two brothers worked as elementary-school teachers, while my sister at home was a housekeeper.

As a child, I remember swimming and fighting. This would happen with friends at school; we'd get in trouble and fight. We used to play a game in which a boy would run up to a spot, touch it, and then run back while making the sound "uuuu," while the others would try to stop him from crossing the line from which he had started. We also played a form of hopscotch. We liked to climb trees, to go fishing, and to play a form of battle with sling shots and wooden weapons.

Each day I'd get up around 7:00 A.M. My mother would give me money to go to the market to buy breakfast: sticky rice or vermicelli soup. Along the way to the school and at work sites, people also sold these foods, along with fish. Since my home was near the school, many friends came by and we'd all walk together along the road. When we heard the teacher beat her drum, we'd enter the class.

Our teacher was about 50 years old and very strict. We treated her with great respect. After entering the classroom, we'd stand until the teacher arrived and gave us permission to sit down. As a mark of respect, we crossed our arms on our chests, and when she spoke to us, we responded by saying, "Respected Teacher."

Six days a week, Mondays through Saturdays, from eight to noon, we were in class. At midday we went home for a large lunch of rice, fish, green vegetables, pork, and fruit. Usually the whole family was there. Then we'd go swimming or play games until 6:00

P.M., when we had dinner. It was like lunch. We all sat at a table and ate at one time. The dishes were in the center. We waited for my father to take the dishes first; then we could share from the dishes.

We had total submission to our father; we listened to what he said, and we had to obey what he said. If we were playing and Father came home, we quit playing; we went home when called, and we always did it. Well, sometimes I misbehaved, but Father taught me to be correct. The first two times he'd talk to me, but the third time, he'd beat my bottom with a stick. We Vietnamese say that not to beat is not to love the child. We have a proverb, "When we love our children, we give them a beating; when we hate our children, we give them sweet treatment." When we saw our father, we looked down out of respect, but also because we were scared of him.

Since I was the youngest son, the seventh of nine children in the family, Father showed a lot of affection to me, so it was easier for me than for the other children. My mother was very permissive; while she scolded me, she never beat me. Mother would give me money. Often Father gave the money to Mother, who would give it to me, but Father never gave me the money directly. I had more contact with Mother than with Father; I feel more attached to her, and I miss her most of all.

I was also especially close to my number six sister. I confided in her on all things: study, play, trips. She was the person who always blamed me. She'd scold me; this showed me that she was interested in me and cared for me. When I did something wrong, like fighting at school, or if I took something, she blamed me. Once when I was about 13 or 14 years old, I stole food from a neighbor. Boys didn't steal that much, but lots of them cut school. There were a number of big farms where people cultivated all sorts of fruit. We'd sneak in and take mangoes and jackfruit. When my sister found out, she'd say, "You should not do that. Next time if they catch you, they'll cut your hand off!"

She'd blame me for being lazy at home. She'd tell me to do something such as getting water from the well, and I'd call out, "I won't do it!" Then I'd run away.

She'd call out, "Brother, come back!"

Not all of the children in our family went to school; my younger sisters didn't. All in my house were not smart. I was the brightest, but lazy. I always cut class, went fishing, went to the pagoda to consult the monks who worked as fortune-tellers. I wanted to know about my future. The fortune-tellers would say something funny. I never believed them. "If you study hard, you will get your high school diploma." Of course it happens if you study; so what? "You will have a girlfriend in September." Another favorite was "You will live a long life." I don't believe it. I didn't pay the fortune-tellers because I was a student, so it was free. Then I'd go fishing. The people who went to the pagoda were simple people. Mostly it was women who believed in the fortune-tellers. My mother believed in them, but I never saw her consult them.

At home I was called by number. In the South, the first child is called "Number Two," the second is "Number Three;" since I was the seventh, I was called "Number Eight." [Editor's note: The elder son is considered precious, and parents fear that a jealous demon might try to kill the son. Parents call him "Two" so that he does not appear to be so valuable.] I also had a funny nickname, but I don't want to mention it. My brothers and sisters had no funny names, but some of the people at school did have names that might relate to the character or the physical condition of the person. A student named Hung was called "Scabies Hung"; another fellow, whose name was Dung, was known as "Obese Dung." A third boy, Tam, was called "Rash Tam," while Hai was known as "Braggart Hai." A woman who cries easily, or who is disappointed because her children do not listen to her, is called "Wet Jackfruit" because after six months this fruit falls easily from the tree, like tears falling easily. Sometimes a mother gives her child a bad or vulgar name such as "Penis" to protect him from the envious gods. In English it sounds dirty, but not in Vietnamese, and it was commonly given to boys.

When I was about 11 years old, I developed a strange spirit sickness. I could not move; I just stayed in bed. I had a headache and a high temperature, but not too high, and loss of energy. There is no real name for this; I was not really sick, but also not well. I went to a doctor many times, but he could not cure me. My mother's mother used some old medicine made of an herb. The point of the leaf is white while the leaf becomes darker at the stem. My grand-mother cut the leaf, dried it, boiled it, and made me drink it. The leaf had a very sour flavor. She also steamed some of the leaves, then covered a blanket over my head for 15 or 20 minutes, and had me breathe the vapors. She also gave me "wind rubbings" [vigor-ous rubbings of a coin on various parts of the body] several times during the illness. After two weeks of this, I was cured. This inci-dent was the basis of the nickname I gave myself when I grew older and wrote for my school newspaper. My family used to complain, "You are sick all the time." So I called myself "Permanently Sick Trung."

My grandparents used to tell me that "permanently sick" or "spirit sickness" was caused by a devil that possessed the patient, but I didn't believe that; I just cannot accept that. One time I saw a shamanic curer. To show his ability, he stuck a metal pin through his cheeks. Later that day the shaman prepared some burning coals about fifteen feet in length. He said that those who walk on those coals will be safe for the entire year. First he threw a talisman of paper on the coals to see if it burned. That was to protect us so that we would not be burned. Two friends and I, as a joke, ran across the coals before the shaman threw down the talisman. We weren't burned. The shaman was so angry he ran after us with a knife, but he could not catch us.

A happy time for us was the celebration at the New Year. At that time all of my uncles, aunts, and grandparents gave me lots of money. We played lots of games. Although I frequently misbe-haved at other times, I behaved well during the New Year; my father never blamed me because it was the New Year. I got new clothes; I would visit the houses of my relatives to worship their ancestors. A person should never do anything bad at that time be-cause if they do, bad luck will be carried on throughout the year. After taking the money from my uncles and aunts, I counted it; then I'd play with it. This was a free day. For three days everything stopped. We played cards, we set off firecrackers in the streets, we drank a little rice wine, and sometimes some beer. Children did this too out of curiosity. Even the poor celebrated. They'd borrow money to buy pork and other things. Even if poor, they wanted to start the new year with plenty of food. Usually they could not entertain, but at this one time of year they did so; they bought food and new clothes; they went to the movies. This was the only time of the year that they had things. Materially and spiritually they'd have their fill for the year.

I believed in all these things about the New Year when I was young, not now. I changed my mind because I know how to think now. If you do something bad to someone, some day that person will do bad to you. This is not magical.

Those were happy days. Sad days were when Father or Mother scolded me. That happened when I would not obey an order to do something, when I was lazy and procrastinated. From time to time I ran errands for my parents; I'd go to the market and return home immediately. Often I played late, then came home too late to study well. Then my parents were angry. I was not a good student.

When I was in the tenth grade, boys and girls were in the same class. We were putting on a drama in which I was supposed to hit a girl with a broom. She was supposed to grab it and push me back. She pushed me as I stepped back, and I fell and hit my head on the corner of the table. Lots of blood came out, and the teachers were called to stop the bleeding and apply a bandage. Then they took me to the hospital.

That year, our theatrical performance won the district competition, so we were chosen to give performances in a large city on the mainland. For the first time in my life I left my island.

[See also Chapters 26 and 40.]

PART III

Vietnam: Sorrows of War

Introduction

The incidents reported in this part of the book cover the years 1945 to 1980 and include topics such as the great famine of North Vietnam at the end of World War II, Viet Minh resistance activities against the French colonialists, activities of the French against the Viet Minh and of the South Vietnamese government against the Viet Cong, civilian life in Communist North Vietnam, and the effects of war on families.

My aim is not to present a chronology nor even a conventional history of these turbulent years, for that has been done, with varying viewpoints, in many recent books. Rather, the accounts here present personal vignettes of incidents that had particular significance in the lives of the narrators. Some individuals did give accounts of well-known events or persons. I did not include them in the book unless the narrator knew these people personally, was a direct participant in the events, or discussed how these events or people specifically affected them.

For those who lived in the North, the two events most frequently mentioned were the famine of 1945 and the relocation to the South, which occurred in 1954. The famine took an estimated two million lives, some 20 percent of the population (Karnow 1983: 144; Tran Van Mai in Ngo Vinh Long 1973: 221). It was caused by the Japanese occupying Vietnam, who forced peasants to grow cash crops, stored rice for their own troops, and destroyed much of it at the time of their defeat. Some Vietnamese also place partial blame for this disaster on the French. Starving peasants streamed into towns seeking any source of food; many died on the streets, despite efforts to help them. Many of the narrators described the Japanese as the most cruel of their colonial rulers.

The massive movement of nearly one million people from North to South Vietnam in 1954, a result of the Geneva Accords, was a traumatic event especially for those narrators who were children at the time. As one person observed, he had to learn new customs and a new way of speaking; it prepared him for his second refugee experience after the Communist victory in the South. The majority of those who left the North were Catholics who feared Communist repression against their religious community. Many spoke of their fathers who were singled out for assassination; others told of the pain of leaving not only their ancestral homes, but relatives who chose to remain behind and with whom contact was lost for years.

The victims of three decades of war were not all on one side; neither were families. The tragedy for many was that the war split their families into factions supporting opposing causes, and on both sides relatives were killed, including innocent bystanders. A number of narrators tell of the effects that this had on their families.

Most of the time, the narrators of these life stories were not involved in armed conflict, but they lived with the threat of war every day. At any moment, the war might explode into their lives with devastating consequences. Imprisonment and torture, the murder of a husband by the French and of a wife by the Viet Minh, the violent deaths of numerous relatives by both sides, the burning of villages, the bombing of Hanoi, attempted assassinations, living in fear and uncertainty, the enforced separation of families: all are found in these narratives.

CHAPTER 11

Famine: 1945

NARRATOR 9: NORTH VIETNAMESE CATHOLIC PRIEST

A Vietnamese Catholic elder led me up the winding wooden steps of a century-old Victorian house to the cramped room occupied by Father An-Phong. Light streamed through the front window, illuminating the sparse furnishings: bed, small couch, table, chair, and small wooden case of books. Father An-Phong, a slight man in his middle forties, rose to greet us. He already knew about my project and that I was looking to talk with a Vietnamese Catholic priest who had lived under Communist rule. He agreed to be interviewed provided that all specific personal and place names be omitted from his narrative. He claimed that he would be blunt about many topics, and during our seven hours of interviews, held on four days, he did not hesitate to criticize the American intervention in Vietnam, although his most vehement condemnations were for the Japanese, the French, and the Communists in Vietnam.

Whatever their political outlook may be, virtually all North Vietnamese born before 1940 speak with considerable bitterness about the Japanese occupation of Vietnam and the Japanese role in causing the great famine of North Vietnam. Father An-Phong, born in a North Vietnamese delta village, describes how his family managed to survive during those terrible days. He recalls the conflict between the French and the Viet Minh and how it affected him and his family. With many other Northerners he came to the South in 1954. After completing his seminary training, he became a priest in 1965, and subsequently served as a military chaplain. After the fall of Saigon in 1975, the Communists refused to allow military chaplains and those who worked for the Thieu regime to continue to serve their parishioners; the older ones were told to stay with the archbishop, while the younger priests were told, "Go back home and marry." After five years of imprisonment, starvation, political indoctrination, and forced labor in several Communist reeducation camps in South Central Vietnam, Father An-Phong was released. He claims that many prisoners were released because their wives or relatives bribed camp guards. Other Vietnamese deny this, saying that release depended on higher officials; bribes to guards were used to smuggle in goods and to have easier access to prisoners.

Back home, cadres would come to the houses of former prisoners and threaten to rearrest them unless their families offered bribes. Because of this, many former prisoners attempted to flee the country. The Catholic priests and Buddhist monks released from reeducation camps were under particularly tight control. They were prohibited from preaching religion, and they had to live under the control of the bishop or a head monk, who would have to report to the police. In 1981, Father An-Phong escaped from Vietnam to Thailand in a 10-meter boat that contained 60 people. For two of the three weeks that they were on the seas, they had no food and very little water. In that same year, Father An-Phong came to the United States, where he has continued his studies while serving as a parish priest.

In his view, the Americans, like the French before them, did not understand Vietnam and its history, and they completely failed to comprehend the Communists; that's why, although well-intentioned, the Americans not only were unsuccessful, but actually interfered with the South Vietnamese resistance to Communism. He emphasized that to understand Vietnamese people, Americans would have to know three points about Vietnam that he considered quite important. (For other views on the French and American failures in Vietnam and reasons for Communist successes, see Fitzgerald 1973, Harrison 1982, and Pike 1986.)

Why the French and the Americans Lost

First, not many people know that the Vietnamese people as a whole won the war against the French, not the Communists alone. Americans often say that the Communists won that war, as if, at that time, the Communists were a single dominant force, but that was not so: all of the Vietnamese people wanted to remove French colonialism, and so they participated actively with any group that fought the French. Also, in the beginning, most of the Vietnamese people did not know that the Viet Minh and Ho Chi Minh were Communists; that is why many of the seminary students left to fight with Ho against the French. Many people who joined the Viet Minh were not Communists; they viewed themselves as patriots. Later, they found that they could not escape. Some of them eventually became high officers in the Communist army, even though they were not Communists. One of our former seminarians became a general.

Second, the failure of the French in Vietnam was not political but psychological. They did not know the Vietnamese people; they did not understand their psychology. The French thought that they could use force to defeat the Communists. At first, a lot of people who knew about the Communists preferred the French. They did not like the French; rather they disliked the Communists more. The Communists used this to advantage. For example, a few guerrillas would shoot at French planes from the tower of a church; their aim was not so much to shoot down the plane as it was to create the illusion that they had control, and that the area was a Communist stronghold. The French then would destroy the church. The Communists also wanted the church destroyed, but they tricked the French into doing it for them. By doing so, they caused people to hate the French troops, who used ferocious force against the Vietnamese people. This was not an intelligent military or psychological strategy, for force can never win over the spirit of a people; rather, it pushed them to fight in a nationalist cause against the French. Many good Catholics, Buddhists, and Protestants in the 1940s and 1950s found themselves caught in the middle of an impossible situation. They could not join the Communists, who were antireligious, particularly anti–Catholic, and they could not support the French, whose troops were destroying their churches, burning their villages, and raping their women. I witnessed this in North Vietnam. That's why many people remained neutral. The French defeated themselves.

Finally, the Americans failed in Vietnam for the same reason as the French; they could not understand the psychology of another country. Had they come to Vietnam to serve as advisors in high technology or modern medicine, they would have succeeded, but they could not be advisors on the psychology of the Vietnamese people, and that is what they did. When they came to Vietnam, they were very proud; they thought they understood everything. We were civilized, but they who knew nothing thought that they could teach us about our country and our customs. Outsiders cannot teach people their own customs. Many Vietnamese military officers knew exactly the strategy of the Communist troops, and they told their American advisors what to do to beat the Communists. We were Vietnamese; we knew each other very well; whether Communist or Nationalist, we knew each other's tricks. The Americans didn't, and they refused to pay attention to the advice of the Vietnamese officers. Rather, they forced the Vietnamese military to fight Communists the "American way." So many operations were defeated by the Communists, and many Vietnamese Nationalists were ambushed and killed conducting operations according to the will of the Americans, after the Americans had been told that their way was wrong. We knew that if we followed American advice, we would be defeated by the Communists. In many operations, it was not the Communists who defeated us, but American advisors. Our troops coming back from the field would be chewed out by a rearguard American officer for having dirty clothes; they'd send our men into mined fields insisting that they were safe or prevent them from going into unmined fields, insisting that they were dangerous. They'd say that one area had a lot of Communists when it had none, and that another area had no Communists when it had many. They couldn't tell the difference.

The Americans were naive. If a Vietnamese person spoke English well, the Americans trusted him, so the Communists sent infiltrators who spoke excellent English; the Americans believed these people more than the loyal Vietnamese who worked for them but whose English wasn't so good. We knew who were Communists posing as Nationalists and who were truly loyal. We told our American advisors; they ignored us. Because of my position in the military, many high officers, including generals, confided to me the names of Communist infiltrators; after 1975, many of the people they named became heads of provinces, districts, and hamlets. And many of them were the highly trusted "friends" of the Americans. The Vietnamese security men knew exactly who were the Viet Cong living in Saigon, pretending to be Nationalists, and they informed the Americans, who didn't believe them. In the town where I was stationed, the Americans constructed some buildings. I heard that many employees were Viet Cong cadres, and our security men knew this very well, since they had overheard the workers talking to one another about Viet Cong activities. But again, the Americans refused to believe us, since the men we accused spoke good English, worked very hard in the construction of the buildings, and pleased their American supervisors. Everywhere the Americans went, they were served by the Viet Cong, and never knew it: their barbers, their bartenders, their prostitutes. Americans are gullible; in Vietnam they completely underestimated the Communists, who were cunning and quite skillful in tricking and misleading the Americans.

Famine

I am a Catholic priest, and I should tell you first about religion in Vietnam, about what it means to be a Vietnamese Catholic. Many Westerners think that all Vietnamese are either Catholic or Buddhist. This is incorrect, for the Vietnamese also follow other religions such as Protestant, Hoa Hao, and Cao Dai. Westerners also often think that the religions they hear about in Vietnam are opposed to each other, that if a person is a Buddhist or a Confucian, he cannot be a Catholic. This is not so. The Vietnamese are open-minded with any religion. As a Catholic priest, I very much like Confucian and Buddhist thought. I can be a Buddhist Catholic. All Vietnamese people worship their ancestors; we all accept the theory of Confucianism. At the same time, they can follow Lao Tsu, Cao Dai [a syncretic twentieth century religion of Vietnam], the Buddha, the gospel of the Christians, Catholic or Protestant. Our minds are not closed to other ways of worship. As Catholics, we must be baptized and must go to church on Sundays, but at the same time, we accept all good things in any religion.

For example, I kept a Buddhist statue in my chaplain's office; I used a calendar with a Buddhist temple on it; and in Vietnam I used to go to the pagoda. When we held a solemn Mass in church, we also invited Cao Dai, Buddhists, and Confucians, and they came to our church; Catholics also were invited sometimes to go to pagodas to attend Buddhist services. In the Vietnamese countryside, village, or city, we lived very close to one another.

I was born in a Northern Vietnamese delta village consisting of two hamlets and about 1,000 people. Surrounding the village was a bamboo fence. My family used bamboo not only for protection, but for items such as beds, tables, chairs, baskets, and fish traps. Even our houses were made of bamboo, along with mud and leaves, with wooden columns, and thatch or tile roofs. Our principal product, on which we lived, was rice. We often ate fish caught from a nearby pond. My family was not rich, but middle class. I was the youngest of six sons and two daughters, of whom two died in childhood. My mother, like every mother in Vietnam, was a housewife who cared for children, went to the market, and cooked meals. My father, a farmer, had studied Chinese characters; he determined that my brothers and I would study Vietnamese history and French language. I learned that the Vietnamese had resisted the Chinese for 1,000 years, during which there had been many revolts. Vietnam also had been under French colonial rule, and more recently under control by the Japanese. We always had a dissatisfaction against foreign invaders.

When I was six years old, the big event of my childhood occurred, the great famine of 1945. (See also Ngo Vinh Long 1973: 219–276.) When I was older I found out that the Vietnamese put up a great resistance against the French colonialists. Because of this the French confiscated much rice in the North. This was our staple food. I was told that the French threw rice in the sea; the whole country went hungry and had no strength to fight.

What I did see was what the French did to my own family. They came to our house, checked our stored rice, and confiscated it. Father was silent, but mother cried a lot.

Another reason for the famine was that the Japanese defeated the French, and refused to let us grow rice; the Vietnamese were told to grow jute, so most people didn't have enough food. My family concealed rice in a secret place. We placed husked rice in clay jars and buried them in the ground. Each jar contained 80–100 kilograms of rice. We covered the jars with soil and grew grass over them. A month's supply of food could be placed in a couple of jars. This just gave my family enough to live on through the famine. Many people were too hungry and weak to steal our concealed rice, even if they found it. When everybody was hungry, we helped one another in the hamlet. Some people came to my house, and my mother gave them rice and fish sauce. Everybody was hungry, but because we shared, only five or six people died of starvation in my hamlet and village.

We delta people did not die, but in other areas it was much worse. The people who lived near the sea could catch fish, but they had no rice. They became so hungry that they had no strength to catch fish. So they streamed into the towns, starving.

I remember that when I went to school every day each student was required to bring a match box filled with rice. We would put the rice in soup, and we would distribute it to the hungry.

The starving people went here and there, from one village to the next, all day long, searching for food. They would eat any vegetables or herbs they could find, anything to live. But most of them died of starvation, especially in the very cold winter, when they did not have enough strength to fight against the hunger and the cold. On the way to school, I saw them die.

I think that if the Japanese had not been defeated, more people would have died. With their defeat came anarchy, and the Viet Minh stepped in. Now we could grow food; no one stopped us or confiscated it. Around the house, we cultivated vegetables that had a short growing season. So we had enough food after the Vietnamese New Year, 1946. In January we sowed seeds, and in May we harvested rice. Then some people died from overeating.

The French government tried to use the famine to destroy and repress the revolutionary movement of the Vietnamese. They did not achieve that goal, because after the famine, the revolution roared throughout the country. The Communists took advantage of that situation to build up the hatred of the nation against the French. Many people followed the Communist movement. At first, Ho Chi Minh didn't show himself as a Communist, but rather as a patriot against the French colonialists. Many people, especially Catholics, helped him. Many seminarians left their religious lives to follow the revolutionary movement of Ho, and later some of them became Communist leaders.

Between the French and the Viet Minh

At that time, we hated the French and loved the Viet Minh. One of my brothers, who was fairly well educated, taught us the Viet Minh songs. Now I realize that they had been influenced by Communist ideas. The Viet Minh informed us about the French. They would use our leisure time, talking about nationalist issues. Under the French, many villagers were illiterate, and this was a deliberate policy of the French. The Viet Minh forced us to learn to read so that we could read Viet Minh newspapers, slogans, and books. Many people liked the Viet Minh movement because through it they were taught to read. My brother was their teacher; everybody had to learn to read and write, even old men and women. When they went to the market, they would have to pass through a gate. To enter the market, they had to show that they could read and write. The Viet Minh taught us about the bad behavior of King Bao Dai and his royal family, and they taught us to hate them. When we went to the bathroom, we said that we were going to the house of Bao Dai. Similarly, nowadays Vietnamese people tell each other, "I'm going to visit Ho Chi Minh's tomb!" History always repeats itself!

The Viet Minh also helped people to farm more effectively. That way, they would have more rice to redistribute. They always used good appearance to cover their bad real intent.

From the Viet Minh, we also learned how to shoot guns as well as self-defense fighting. And they taught us new songs, plays, patriotic poems, everything influenced by Communist theories.

They also arrested some villagers, particularly those who were rich, educated, or who belonged to the National Party. In my village more than ten people were taken away by the Viet Minh and were never seen again. I was told that they were killed secretly.

In 1946, the French reoccupied Vietnam, but only in the big cities. Those of us in the countryside lived with the Viet Minh, especially at night. I belonged to the Viet Minh youth movement federation, and I sang songs praising Ho Chi Minh and the Viet Minh. At night most of our villages were under the control of the Viet Minh, but during the day, the French made many forays into the villages chasing Viet Minh guerrillas. The problem was that they did not know who was Viet Minh and who was not. When French troops came to a place, the villagers would flee to avoid arrest and torture. The French grabbed anybody they suspected to be Viet Minh; in reality, some of the people they arrested were against the Viet Minh.

When I was ten years old, my brother and I were arrested, along with three females and ten other males. The soldiers led us to the military post. They forced us to push little bamboo boats for them that seated three or four soldiers. I was up to my chest and shoulders in the water. On the way, they beat me on the head with poles, and they put burning cigarettes on our cheeks. This was a favorite torture that they inflicted especially on the young women, and later they also raped them. The men who did this were from the French Foreign Legion, tall and strong Muslim men from North Africa. I was very afraid. At the post, a translator told us that the Communists were quite dangerous. They told us to abandon the Viet Minh and come to town to live under their protection. And they told the older men to join their army. Because we were so young, my brother and I were released, and we returned to the village. The other prisoners we never saw again.

Because of such behaviors, we villagers did not have a good feeling for the French. When they came to a village, the French did not distinguish between Communists and simple villagers. When they were fired at by guerrillas, the French would go to the village, burn down all the houses, arrest all of the villagers they found, and torture and kill some of them. But the guerrillas were rarely killed; they had fired the shots, then left the village. The Viet Minh were able to manipulate the French in this way to ensure that the villagers hated them.

About once a week, the French would sweep through our village looking for Viet Minh. We children, along with our mothers, would hide in the pagoda or in the church, for these were strong buildings that could withstand rifle shots. The men usually hid in the bushes, or in underground drains, or in secret shelters which had underwater doors in our ponds.

One day in 1952, the French shelled our village; my eldest brother and his two daughters were killed, my brother's wife lost an arm, and our family house was burned to the ground. After that, my family left the village for the nearby town. Even though we did not support the French, we realized that we could not follow the Viet Minh because of their hostility towards religion, especially Catholicism. In 1953, my family moved to Hanoi, and I entered a minor seminary. By 1954, Ho Chi Minh and his people showed themselves to be Communists, especially after they occupied North Vietnam. When the Northerners saw this, many of them left for the South, and we were among them. We traveled on a large Swedish commercial boat. Because we were in Hanoi, we did not have any difficulty getting out, but for many people in the villages, the Viet Minh interfered with their attempts to leave: refusing to give them passes, blocking the main roads, trying in many ways to discourage their flight, and interrupting the efforts of the United Nations to help people leave.

They had good reason to leave. In 1952 the Viet Minh had introduced the policy of denunciation in a public trial, which led to the elimination of certain types of people: the wealthy, landlords, well-educated teachers, and especially religious people such as Catholic priests and Buddhist monks. It was a horrible action which had previously been practiced by the Chinese. Many people were killed, often by their own relatives. Sons and daughters had, in effect, to kill their parents by denouncing them in popular courts. Servants, sons-in-law, and daughters-in-law especially were forced to make these accusations. There were three levels of denunciation: words, beating, execution. All of these occurred in my home village. The Viet Minh trained the poor to accuse the wealthy. Those who were slated for execution were confined during the day, then at night led to a common place in the village where, after they kneeled, they would be accused. This might go on for three or four nights, but in some cases lasted a couple of months. Finally they were led off and shot at the village cemetery. Four people in my village died in this manner. The purpose of these public trials and executions was to crush any resistance against the Viet Minh. After that movement, the Viet Minh showed themselves as Communists. Great fear spread through North Vietnam, because nobody could resist them. These public trials and executions lasted until around 1956, by which time we had already fled to Saigon.

CHAPTER 12

Jailed by the French: 1945-1948

NARRATOR 10: EX – VIET MINH RESISTANCE WORKER

In the spring of 1982 I met a vigorous Vietnamese elder, Mr. Nguyen Long Giang, who claimed to have been involved in the resistance movement against the Socialist Republic of Vietnam. As we sat in the spotless living room of his new condominium, decorated with Vietnamese calendars and photographs, he told me he had been invited to visit the camp of the resistance movement somewhere near Vietnam; he had remained with them for several days. Because he was 64 years old, he was not involved in fighting, but in recording their activities. To reach them, he was led by guides through jungles and over hills for several days. He told me about the ideals of the resistance movement, their continual moving around, their hardships in securing food, and that while they posed no significant military threat, they remained as a symbol of opposition to Communism. He showed me a videotape he had taken, which included a speech by one of the resistance leaders.

Initially, I wished to interview Mr. Giang because of his visit with the resistance movement. But as I heard his narration, conducted in English during two sessions of about two hours each, I realized that his entire life had been devoted to resistance against various forms of oppression. As a young man from North Vietnam, he participated in the resistance against the French, was caught and imprisoned by them, and was tortured on five occasions. On each of his wrists is a band of scar tissue one inch wide as a

*result of his being hung for many hours with his arms tied behind his back.
In prison, Huynh Tan Phat, his Viet Minh leader, who later became a
prominent figure in the Socialist Republic of Vietnam (vice-chairman of
the Council of State in 1987), was able to organize prisoners to resist the
French. Although Mr. Giang subsequently became disillusioned with the
Viet Minh and broke with them, he praises Huynh Tan Phat, whom he
admired for his great powers of persuasion and leadership. Mr. Giang's
prison experience is especially significant in showing how the Communists
were able to gain popular support for their cause. (On the rise of Nationalist and Communist movements from differing perspectives, see also Duiker
1981, 1983; Harrison 1983; Hoang Van Chi 1964; Marr 1971, 1981; Ngo
Vinh Long 1973; and Pike 1978. For accounts of those who became disillusioned with the Communists, see Doan Van Toai and Chanoff 1986;
Nguyen Long 1981; Scholl-Latour 1985; and Truong Nhu Tang 1985.)
The narrative that follows is based on my interviews with Mr. Giang,
and on a portion of his memoir, "I Contributed to My Beloved Country's
Independence."*

I was born in a town in North Vietnam in 1918. I was the third
of six children, four boys and two girls. We lived on a crowded boulevard where my father ran a shop selling and repairing watches.
Like other children, we lived in a very strict family. As a child, I
went to school, sometimes watched cinema, but I really liked sports
and was very good at soccer. Even today I am very athletic and
continue to play tennis.

After completing high school, I attended college in Hanoi, but I
did not complete my studies. In 1944, at the age of 26, I traveled to
Saigon, where I met a friend who asked me to participate in a clandestine organization against the French. In those days, everyone
hated the French. After 86 years of French rule, everyone wanted
to rise against them. So when my friend asked, I said, "Okay, fine."

Each week we would meet at a very remote temple, and listen
to Huynh Tan Phat, a man who later became an important leader
of the Viet Cong and a prominent person in the Socialist Republic
of Vietnam. At the time, we did not realize that he was a Communist; we found that out much later. He would analyze the events of
the war and tell us how it would end. After the nuclear bombs were

dropped on Hiroshima and Nagasaki, he held a special meeting in which he urged us to rise up against the French. The time to strike, he said, had now come.

We moved to a nearby province to run our resistance activities. Our group consisted of about one thousand people, including men, women, and young kids too. All were fighting. At first our weapons consisted of sharpened poles; those who had weapons went first; those who had no weapons followed. Later, we acquired guns and ammunition for use against the French.

Our fighting mostly consisted of guerrilla ambush. We would sabotage with mines, or we would throw grenades into crowds at restaurants full of French soldiers. I did not throw grenades, but rather participated in the propaganda activities of the movement. Huynh Tan Phat selected me for this because of my education. For six months he trained me; then I would go around and whisper to my friends about how we should resist the French. I educated them in the spirit of resistance. I would talk about how the French had come to Vietnam, invaded our country, forced their government on us, imposed heavy taxes on our people, built more prisons than schools, prohibited our people from sending their children abroad, and made our lives difficult. I showed how the French protected just a few Vietnamese people who obeyed their commands to put the yoke on the necks of our people. When I said these things, I found that everyone wanted to fight the French. So we organized the Vanguard Youth. This was something like the Boy Scouts, but we trained them as soldiers, with the encouragement of the Japanese.

In 1945 the Japanese overran the French in Vietnam and put them in prison. The Japanese claimed to be our friends, but we realized that they were making us a colony, just like the French had. Many Vietnamese were anti-Japanese, but our leaders told us to support the Japanese, so that we could use their help in throwing out the French. At any cost, we had to get rid of the French. During the time that the French were in prison, we openly trained our Vanguard Youth. Then when the Japanese lost the war and abandoned their barracks, we grabbed their weapons and ammunition to use against the French.

After the Japanese surrender, the British troops, under the command of General Gracey, were assigned to disarm the Japanese in South Vietnam. With the backing of the British, the French colonialists took this opportunity to try to put the yoke of slavery back on the necks of the Vietnamese people. They disguised themselves and mingled with the British. Their first target was to take back Saigon and use it as a base to invade other areas. We all knew about their plots, and we prepared everything. When the first shot was fired, the People's Central Committee of South Vietnam released an emergency order to sabotage all strategic and economic installations in and around Saigon; then we withdrew our forces into the surrounding countryside villages and nearby cities, where we organized a guerrilla war against the French enemies.

Because of my duties, I was one of the last to leave the city. Disguised as a peasant, I rode a bicycle to Bien Hoa city, 30 kilometers northeast of Saigon. The first thing I did was to present myself to Mr. D.B.M., who had proclaimed himself the "Special General Controller of the East Zone." Later I realized that he was simply a kind of warlord.

For two days I waited to meet him. Finally he saw me for two minutes. As soon as I told him that I was a member of the People's Committee of T.B. Province, he shouted angrily that I was simply an ugly coward who dared not to stay resisting with others against the enemies. I tried to explain, but instead of listening, he pushed the bell on his desk. Immediately a young fellow came in and led me to a nearby room, where I was interrogated by a skinny, unlettered guy. After an hour, I was released.

The next day, while searching for my comrades along a busy, noisy street, I recognized a Vanguard Youth member, a boy 15 years old who had been a sentinel at the headquarters where I worked. With him was a young woman whose husband had been captured when our headquarters had been attacked by two truck loads of French soldiers. The rumor was that her husband had been executed the following day behind the Saigon Cathedral. The youth and the woman were so happy to meet me; they insisted on going with me everywhere.

The next day, the people of Bien Hoa were thrown into a panic. Loudspeakers mounted on cars and horse-drawn carts announced that the enemy was at the suburbs and then blared the slogan,

"Empty houses, bare gardens." We were told to destroy everything and then leave the city to participate in the general resistance.

The three of us rode on the same bicycle, rushed along with the incredible mob. Five kilometers from the city, our front tire went flat. We threw away the bicycle, and I tried to hitchhike. No cars stopped. Then my pretty young companion made a sign, and a black Citroen abruptly stopped. Two men wearing black pajamas sat in the rear; a driver sat alone in the front. One of the men in the rear told the boy and me to sit in the front and motioned for the young woman to sit in the back with them. As soon as the car started, that man asked me what I was doing and where we were headed. After I told him, he asked if we recognized the man sitting next to him. Without waiting for a reply, he said, "This man is P.T.D., the supreme leader of the Binh Xuyen forces," and he introduced himself as B.N., commander of the Binh Xuyen army. He claimed that he had killed thousands of people, including the French and their henchmen. I was a little scared; I knew that he intentionally was trying to frighten me, figuring that I was the husband of that young woman.

I knew of the Binh Xuyen. During peace time, under French domination, they were a criminal gang named for the village they lived in, which was located near Cholon, the Chinese section of Saigon. They were famous for robbing from the rich and sharing with the poor. With their money, they bought lots of ammunition from the defeated Japanese and organized an army to fight the French. While they used this "resistance mask," in fact they remained simply gangsters who lived outside of the law.

When we arrived at Suoi Cut village, the commander ordered me and the boy to get out of the car. When the young woman started to leave, he pointed a pistol at her head. The terrified boy snatched my hand and pulled me out. The car proceeded to a nearby compound of elaborate two-story buildings which once belonged to French rubber-plantation owners. The boy and I walked along the road congested with people, animals, carts, and cars. It was dark when we reached Xuan Loc district. Thousands of people had sought shelter in a small hall at the market.

Suddenly I realized that I had left my precious bag in the black Citroen; all of my money and my important documents were in that bag. The boy and I planned to take a train to the North. Without the money, we couldn't do anything; I had to recover that bag at all costs. The next day I told the boy to wait for me around the market; I returned to Suoi Cut village.

I arrived at the front gate of the compound at dusk. Behind the sentinel booth stood a barbed wire gate at which everybody had to stop. When I announced that I wanted to meet B.N., the Binh Xuyen commander, two men in guerrilla attire immediately pulled out their pistols and pointed them at my waist; a third guard pointed a submachine gun at my back. When I asked why they were doing this, they gave no answer, but just pushed me forward. We reached a building in which many people were going in and out. The three men pushed me inside and indicated that I should sit under a large staircase, next to two men and a woman. They were blindfolded, and their wrists were tied tightly behind their backs. They uttered not one sound. The man on the end, a Eurasian with a blood-soaked shirt, lay dying in a pool of his own blood and urine; the smell was disgusting!

As I sat there, people passed by, ignoring our fate. Then two young fellows stopped in front of me and joked that they were happy to see that more people would be going by "direct train," a slang expression for going to "another world"! One of them said, "The more people we kill, the more successful our revolution will be; without killings, the revolution has no meaning!" To show off to his friend that he was a real historian of revolution, he announced, "After the Bastille was liberated, hundreds of thousands of French traitors were killed!"

After they left, I was not only scared, but sad. Not long ago, I had been teaching the cadres about the French Revolution, as well as others. Now they applied these lessons on me! I remembered the remarks of Charles Dickens in *A Tale of Two Cities*, and I realized that all revolutions were more or less similar. Human life was worth nothing during a revolution. I knew that my life was in great danger. I remembered that when I was at home, my mother used to tell us that when we faced danger, we should pray for protection to Quan The Am, the Buddhist "saint." I did not know whether or not it would be effective, but when we were in a real panic, it was natural that everybody would cling to something in the hopes that they would be rescued. That's why I closed my eyes and whispered prayers to Quan The Am. When I opened my eyes, to my surprise, I recognized a man walking down the corridor. Kim, "that damned mechanic" as I called him, used to take care of our cars at headquarters. He was renowned as one of the most courageous guerrilla fighters; he had successfully thrown grenades and set fire to installations of the enemy around Saigon and Cholon, causing heavy damage. I called out to him.

With great astonishment, he asked why I was sitting in the spot reserved for criminals who would be executed that night in the backyard. Without wasting a minute, I told him the whole story, from my ride in the black Citroen to my arrest. He explained that B.N. had used the "resistance cover" to hide his criminal deeds: he had robbed, raped, and slaughtered many innocent people. B.N. had been sentenced to capital punishment, along with his gang and all other people involved with him. No wonder I had been scheduled for execution when I had asked for him at the gate.

My friend Kim escorted me to his boss, who was none other than the man who claimed to be the "Commander of the East Guerrilla War Zone." I was startled to discover that I recognized him. He had changed a little since I had last seen him: now he sported a mustache and a Japanese-style military uniform complete with sword and pistol. He looked at me as if he had never met me. In fact, not long before the revolution, I had been a coconut oil supplier, and he a contractor for a Japanese firm in Saigon. We used to meet once a month in his Japanese office. Although neither of us knew the other was doing so, both of us had worked with the Japanese for the same reason, to get information about them that we could supply to our comrades. Never did he tell me that he had been trained in any clandestine military school. Now suddenly I found that he was a commander. I remembered that he had money, and that he could buy weapons from the Japanese to organize an army of which he was the commander.

My friend Kim explained to the commander that I was innocent. I don't know whether it was because of his position or because we knew each other pretty well; the commander just shook hands with me and left. I was free.

After retrieving my bag, I asked Kim about the fate of the young woman. He smiled and whispered, "If you don't want any more trouble, just forget her. Don't worry about her. She now has a comfortable life; lots of people take care of her." I understood what he meant.

I continued in our independence struggle against the French. One time the Vanguard Youth reported that French troops were trying to cross the Cau Kieu Bridge nearby. I was ordered to go and take a look. When I arrived, I found heaps of furniture on the street forming a long barricade to block the French from proceeding further. I met with a French officer, and we discussed the best way to avoid fighting and casualties. I agreed that if his troops withdrew beyond the bridge, I would tell my people to clear the road. But when the people saw the French withdrawing, people on both sides of the street shouted happily; instead of clearing away the furniture, they threw additional pieces on the road. The French returned and opened fire on us. I ran into an alley which ran along a canal. A French soldier took aim and fired at me, but I dodged his bullets, slid into the canal, and escaped.

I was able to elude the French as long as I was in the hinterlands. From time to time I would go into Saigon, and it was on one of those trips that the French finally caught me. Suddenly they made a raid in which they systematically checked house by house. I destroyed all of my documents. When they demanded to see my papers, I had none to show them. They took me as well as others to a police station. Under interrogation, another prisoner told them that I was a high-ranking officer of the Viet Minh.

As a result of this, I was taken to prison, without a trial, where I remained for 18 months. Five times they tortured me. They forced me to lie down; then they poured water mixed with soap in my mouth. When my belly was full of water, they jumped on it; the soapy water ran out of my ears and nose. Because I was a high-ranking official, they wanted to extort information. They tied my wrists behind my back, and they hung me, suspended by my wrists, from the ceiling. For hours and hours I hung there. After that I could not hold chopsticks in my fingers for more than three months. They tied an electric wire around my neck and body. And my nose, the blood came out of my nose.

After they were done with me, they threw me in the prison with the common criminals. The jail consisted of two long cells, with an alleyway in between. About 200 prisoners were placed in each cell. The moment the cell door closed behind me, a man came up to me. His back and arms were completely covered with tattoos. He punched me in the face. I was in no condition to resist. He forced me to take off my clothes, and he took those and my mat. He lay down, and he ordered me and the other prisoners to massage him and to use our mats like fans to keep him cool. We had to pull those mats day and night like slaves.

This man was a senior prisoner, convicted of raping and killing people, and sentenced to life imprisonment. He controlled the prison from within, along with a small number of common criminals who were his followers. Those of us who were political prisoners, about one hundred men, secretly decided to organize a revolution. We wrote to our relatives and asked them to send us, not food, but cigarettes. At lunch and dinner, we gave those cigarettes to the Chinese man who brought food to our cell. In return, we asked him to supply us with small pieces of iron. At night, we sharpened these into knives.

When our force was strong enough we told our relatives to send us more food. The senior prisoner would demand all of our food. One day, when he demanded that food, we refused to give it to him. He shouted to his disciples to attack us. We pulled out our knives, and in the battle that followed, four of his men were killed.

Suddenly we heard the voice of the prison director. "If you don't stop fighting, we will open fire and kill all of you!" We looked up to see machine guns aimed at our cell. The common thieves did not speak French as did the political prisoners. We replied, "We [political prisoners] know that if we make mistakes, the law will punish us, but in this cell, those fellows do not know that."

The director asked us to point out those guys, and we pointed to them. From that time on, the political prisoners controlled the prison. We organized the prison as a tiny government. We wrote general laws which we called the "Prisoners' Constitution"; more than 3,000 prisoners were expected to respect and enforce these rules. For the first time, a historical democratic era had begun in a Vietnamese prison. We formed a commission, with an executive committee guided by a chairman. We organized a Vietnamese Prisoner's League; each month, a representative of that league contacted the prison to demand reforms, such as rations of beef or fresh fish, things like that. Ordinarily, each day we ate dried fish, cheap red rice, and sometimes boiled egg, but very seldom did we receive vegetables and never any fruit. From time to time I would organize hunger strikes to demand improvements in our treatment. In this I was following the orders of Huynh Tan Phat, the leader of our secret movement, who also had been captured.

From now on, we were organized. At five in the morning, the bell from the cathedral sounded and we awoke. Three of our men went around with megaphones and chanted a wake-up song, and we cleaned up our cells. Then we formed a line to go to the basin to wash and clean our teeth. After that, we all prepared for resistance. We sang patriotic songs. Then we taught the prisoners about the military, how to hide, advance, fight, and everything like that. Other groups learned how to read and write in Vietnamese, or they studied French or English. We didn't have chalk, so we used a brick and wrote on the floor.

We founded a newspaper, called *Prisoner's Voice*, and I became the editor. I wrote a drama so that we could act out our teachings. In my articles I wrote about marching with the revolution, to encourage people to fight the French. There was only one copy of the article. To communicate with other cells, we had to go to the infirmary and fold the material into our waistbands.

One day, a guard at the door discovered that I was carrying an anti-French cartoon drawing. For this he put me in a cell with my feet chained to a bar. The cell was so low that a man could not stand up in it. Once a day the guard would leave me a small bowl of rice and a very small amount of water. I remained chained in that cell for one month. Really! One month for carrying that cartoon.

Our commission organized protests when prisoners were about to be executed. We had a mat on which we wrote protest signs, "Against Execution." Our lawyer had smuggled us a red powder from which we made paint. We wrote the letters with a Chinese pen.

One day, after 17 months in prison, the guard led me out of my cell and into a room. A French lieutenant was sitting at a table. The moment I arrived, he hit his fist on the table and shouted, "Tell the truth!"

I replied to this hot-tempered man, "Okay, if you want me to tell the truth, please be calm; it will take me a couple of minutes. If you don't want to listen to me, then you can base your judgment on the confession they forced me to sign under torture, or you can kill me, or you can send me anywhere."

He said, "Okay, talk."

I said, "We are patriots. You didn't want France being ruled by the Germans. We are the same; we don't want to be ruled by you. I have not done any killing. My activities have been political. I think I have the right to do that."

He wrote down everything I said. Then a guard took me back to my cell.

One month later, my lawyer came to me and told me I had been released. I thought he meant that I was being transferred to Poulo Condor Island, where political prisoners are sent, but he said no; I was now free.

After that, my mother sent me a ticket, and a family friend came to accompany me back to the North. When I returned home, I found that my stepfather had been killed by the Communists. Because he had refused to attend Communist meetings, they kidnapped him one night, stabbed him to death, and threw his body in the river.

For a while I ran the jewelry and watch repair shop; then I went into other ventures: an ice-making business and a large French restaurant. My relatives had the knowledge to manage both of these enterprises.

By that time, I had begun to stay away from the resistance movements against the French. I read lots of Communist materials, and a friend who had been fighting with the Communists told me the truth about them, that they advocated no family sentiment. When a person joined the Communist Party, he should quit his family, no longer recognize father or mother, and even kill them if necessary. The people who joined such a movement often were the poor and the illiterate; they were indoctrinated; they were told, "We have to kill all the rich landowners to be happy." They were encouraged to denounce the rich, claiming that they had been ill-treated, and if it were not true, they were encouraged to make up denunciations. My family was a small business family; in our home village about 50 miles from the town, my stepfather had rice fields. Everyone who had rice fields was considered an enemy of the people, and they were kidnapped and killed. Lots were, so many, millions. The aim of the Communists was to make people poor, then in North Vietnam, and now in the South. After seven years of "independence" after 1975 [the interviews were conducted in 1982], the whole country is miserable; people do not have enough to eat; they must mix 10 percent rice with 90 percent manioc, or with the fodder we use to feed the animals. You see, they turn people into animals, so that all they think about is food, not politics or resistance against them. That's their aim, their purpose.

By 1950, when I was married, I realized that I must oppose the Communists. Still, I worked at my three businesses until 1954, when the people of the North were given six months to move to the South. Within one month we had made the move. My wife, two children, brother, sister, and mother all cried; they were so unhappy because we had to relinquish everything in order to leave. But we knew we had to go. We never again set foot in the North.

My eldest sister and her family remained behind. And since that time, we have never set eyes on one another. We have seen just her picture. In 1975, we fled to the United States. My eldest sister is now very old and ill; I send medicines to her by means of a friend in Paris. When my sister writes, it is always to report misery: shortages of food, cloth, medicine, everything. She dare not say anything else. But those forlorn letters are the only connection we have, for we know we shall never again be able to see one another.

CHAPTER 13

The Execution of My Husband: 1946

NARRATOR 11: SOUTH VIETNAMESE SCHOOLTEACHER

In 1984 I came to hear of a 73-year-old woman named Ba (Mrs.) Tam who was scheduled to arrive in America through the Orderly Departure Program. This program, designed to discourage the continuing flight of "boat people," enables a small number of Vietnamese people to emigrate to America. To be eligible, they must have a parent or child living in America. Only a fraction of those who have applied to leave have been allowed to do so; thousands are waiting. Those most likely to be released have been the elderly and those who are too ill to be economically self-sufficient. These people are not classified as refugees, and they receive no refugee assistance; their relatives in the United States must agree to sponsor them and provide all care and maintenance for the first three years that they live in America. Ba Tam would go to live with her daughter.

Ba Tam was a widow; her husband had been killed in 1946 during the Viet Minh revolution. From that time, she had, as a single mother, reared her children, supporting them by working as a schoolteacher. When I met her, she readily agreed to tell her story.

My interest in the Vietnam war is less on its heroes than its victims, the effects that the many years of intermittent conflict had on ordinary Vietnamese people. The tragedy that befell Ba Tam, her husband, and their children was one repeated tens of thousands of times throughout Vietnam, on both sides of the conflict: villages burned; civilian hostages taken and shot;

in one fateful day a tranquil farming community devastated; lives shattered. I wanted to know how Ba Tam had responded to the atrocity that left her a widow. What effects did this event have on her throughout her life? What aspects of her personal outlook and character helped her to cope with this and other hardships? What values did she instill in her children as she reared them alone?

These were for me not merely academic questions. My own mother, who is one year younger than Ba Tam, had as a young child been a victim of war, her house occupied by enemy troops, her father missing in action for seven years, her family traumatized. By some miracle, her father, who had been captured and sent to a Siberian labor camp, escaped, made his way back to his own home country and village, and subsequently brought his family to America. But those war years had a lasting effect on my mother's outlook on the world and the way in which she reared my brother and me. Despite their cultural differences, I saw in Ba Tam and my mother a common tragedy set in the wartime disruption of their families.

I also saw in Ba Tam's narrative the opportunity to compare Communist Vietnam with my own country. How are the elderly treated in the Socialist Republic of Vietnam, and how does this compare with the treatment of the elderly Vietnamese in America? What are the expectations of newly arrived elderly Vietnamese immigrants: how quickly and in what ways do they change their views and their life-styles? How do they view the prospect of living out their days far from their native land?

During the month of June 1984, I met with Ba Tam for four interviews that lasted a total of nine and one-half hours. Ba Tam, short, sharp-featured, and alert, with sparkling eyes, spoke and acted with a vigor usually seen in women many years younger, a trait she shared with my mother. She took great interest in telling her story. Her account of the death of her husband was one of the most moving and emotionally draining interviews I have ever conducted, for as she told it, she relived the experience: the terror, the uncertainty, the discovery of the awful truth that her husband would never return. With my own eyes misty, I told her that she need not go on; she replied that she must, to honor his memory.

She explained, eloquently and articulately, the early problems of adjustment that she encountered in America. I was amazed at how quickly she sized up, with uncanny accuracy, the plight of the Vietnamese elderly in America: the forgotten people, left at home while their children go to work and their grandchildren attend school; isolated, without the ability to travel about town as they did in Vietnam; unable to speak English and, if educated like Ba Tam, unable to find French-speaking Americans; feeling abandoned; unable to visit churches or Buddhist pagodas; and finding out that they are no longer obeyed or given the respect that they had associated with being elderly. Ba Tam had been in America less than one month; already she was disillusioned, and she chafed at her enforced idleness. "At their house I do nothing," she said. "My daughter won't let me do anything because she thinks everything is strange for me. She tells me to rest. But I cannot stay doing nothing." She is very happy to be in America, to see her grandchildren, to be free of the Communists, to live the easy life of Americans, but she already realizes that the Vietnamese concept of what it means to be an elderly person does not fit easily into American life-styles. She faces an uncertain future in that the guidelines and values upon which she built her life now must be adjusted to survive in an alien environment for which, despite her education, she was not prepared.

I was born in 1911, the youngest of four children of a poor family that lived in a town in the Mekong delta. We lived in a thatch and bamboo house close to the market and the elementary school. When I was three years old, my father died, and my mother supported the family by selling oranges, jackfruit, and bananas in the market. In the afternoon, when students passed by, she'd sell them candies and cookies in front of our house. I had to help my mother.

I started first grade when I was nine years old. At the end of the fifth grade, I won a four-year scholarship to study in a girl's school in Saigon. I went on to become a schoolteacher.

In 1932 I married a man five years older than me, and in 1933 we moved to Saigon. Both of us worked as schoolteachers. The following years were the happiest of my life. During that period I gave birth to four children, the first in 1934 and the last in 1946. My three sons and one daughter got along well. During those years, my husband and I worked. We had an easy life, and we often took vacations at the seaside resort of Vung Tau.

In 1945, while we were in Saigon, the Japanese occupied Vietnam for a short time. I remember that every morning for one hour the Japanese forced us to attend Japanese language classes. They were not polite to us. When they came to Vietnam, they burned all the rice stalks, also materials and clothing; people starved to death. Life was really hard for a few months. Then the Americans dropped their atomic bomb in Japan, the war ended, and the French returned to control the country. Even though we were under their domination, the French were much better than the Japanese, who were quite cruel: they would cut off the hands of thieves or sometimes beat people to death. We were so afraid during those days!

Later in 1945 the Viet Minh revolution came to Saigon. The Viet Minh mixed secretly with students and persuaded them to demonstrate. Also, people listened to them. Then Vietnamese soldiers of the French Army shot some demonstrators, after which the Viet Minh ordered all schools to be closed and told the people to evacuate the cities and return to the countryside.

My husband and I, along with our three children (the fourth was born in 1946), went back to my husband's home village and lived in the house of my in-laws. There we had rice and chickens. My husband spent his time husking paddy; I cultivated a vegetable garden and cooked meals: boiled vegetables dipped in fish sauce; fresh lemon grass salted and fried. We also ate salted shrimp sauce with boiled bamboo shoots which we collected in the forest. We remained in that village until February 1946. At that time I was six months pregnant.

In those days, the Viet Minh lived in the forest, so I did not know any of them. But one of their leaders took a room from my in-laws' house; he'd come only late at night and would leave well before dawn. I saw him briefly only once. The Viet Minh tried to recruit the villagers to their cause; because I was well educated and could speak easily, one of their people asked me to join their women's organization that carried information to the Viet Minh. I was able to refuse because I was pregnant at that time. They were very polite in trying to persuade us, and they treated people very nicely. Because of this, the countryside people often helped the Viet Minh.

Now we know their cruel nature. From north to south everybody knows that they tell lies. Even in the countryside people now hate them. The villagers remember how they helped the Viet Minh and later the Viet Cong; now they see that the Communist government tells people to cultivate rice; then at harvest time, they take most of it away, and so the villagers do not have enough money to buy materials for clothing. The officials are no longer polite. One time I heard an old woman yell, "In the old days, we helped and nurtured you; why then do you make such difficulties for us now?"

Because the Viet Minh lived in the forest, the French Army could not find them, so they attacked and burned all the villages where they assumed the Viet Minh lived. In our district, as well as the next one, the French destroyed every single village. One day in February 1946, around 8:00 A.M., Vietnamese soldiers of the French Army came up the river to our village. For about 30 minutes they fired mortars. My husband and I were at home; we were afraid, so we and our three children hid in our basement cellar, located in our garden. Every house in the village had one of these. The soldiers started to burn the houses. Then I heard a French soldier say, "Let's throw the grenade in the basement to kill everybody; I've searched and see nobody in the house."

We climbed out of the cellar, and one of the soldiers asked, "Is there anybody else in this family?"

Since my husband was afraid to speak, I replied, "No, this is our family."

"Where are the Viet Minh?" he asked.

I replied in French, "I don't know anything about the Viet Minh; they order us to stay inside our houses at night and not look outside."

The French officer asked with surprise, "How come you speak French? What is your occupation?"

"I am a teacher; that's how I learned French."

"You lie!" he shouted. "You can speak French, you remain in the village, so you must be helping the Viet Minh!" He ordered us to march to a field, and his men set fire to our house. At the field the soldiers separated the men from the women and children. Then they led my husband away. I never saw him again. Later I heard from other villagers that the soldiers had shot him down by the river. I was never even able to have a funeral for him.

From the field I watched my house burn; late in the afternoon it collapsed. I did not know what to feel. Then I heard that my husband had been killed, but the French would not let me search for him. Some men who were witnesses told me that the soldiers took them and my husband to a military post along the river. There they questioned him, "Where are the Viet Minh?"

He said, "I don't know."

But then one of my husband's relatives who worked for the French said, "A Viet Minh leader has been living in that man's house."

My husband said, "Yes, but if we did not let him stay, he'd kill us."

After that, the soldiers shot my husband and six other men. The relative who informed on him was later arrested by the Viet Minh and beheaded in the village.

My husband was gone, the village was burned to the ground, my children and I had nothing with us but the clothes we wore. The soldiers ordered us to go somewhere else, so we walked to a nearby village and stayed overnight with relatives. The following morning we walked to a town, where some other relatives gave us enough money to return to Saigon.

[See also Chapters 27 and 41.]

CHAPTER 14

Viet Minh and French:
1945–1956

NARRATOR 1: ELDERLY SOUTH
VIETNAMESE CIVIL SERVANT

In this chapter, Mr. Ngon describes how he and his family were terrorized both by the Viet Minh and by the French. He saw himself as caught between the two, whom he viewed as interchangeable. Eventually the French forced him to help them; as a result, he became a target for assassination by the Viet Minh, who nearly succeeded in killing him. In unrelated incidents, they did execute his first wife and his elder brother. He also documents corrupt practices of French officials and their Vietnamese subordinates.

Viet Minh Coercion

I remember when the Japanese soldiers arrived in our village in 1945. We feared them because they were much meaner and more courageous than the French. If a Japanese soldier heard a shot 100 meters away, he'd immediately jump up and go towards it; he was always willing to attack and would not try to avoid situations like French soldiers, who were not very good at fighting. The Japanese stood with guns ready to fight. On sentry duty, a Japanese soldier always would point their guns at any passersby. Every day at 5:00 A.M. the Japanese would run about three or four kilometers without their shirts; then they would do bayonet practice in the yard of their camp. When we saw this, we were scared.

The Japanese were really savage; they meant what they said. The Japanese would punish people publicly, beating them on the street. The French were much more afraid of the Japanese than they were of the Viet Minh.

During Japanese rule, all civil servants worked under their military government. After the Japanese lost the war, the French tried to return, but the Viet Minh claimed the country. In July 1945 the Viet Minh announced that all houses made of wood and brick and covered with red tile had to be burned down; these were the houses of wealthier people. They burned the houses and buildings next to my mother's house. Then they ordered her house to be burned. To save the house, my brother-in-law with some four other workers dismantled it so that the Viet Minh could not burn it. My mother went to live with my sister.

In September 1945, to disrupt French rule, the Viet Minh arrested, imprisoned, and replaced all the district chiefs with their men. They closed all markets, schools, and transportation; this was an order. If you did not obey, they would kill you.

My family had only a small cottage in which to live. At the moment, the French colonial government was not there, and I was not a follower of the Viet Minh rebellion. I was not a farmer; I did not have any rice fields. I did not know how to find work to live, since the Viet Minh had closed all the schools. My mother was poor, and my second wife did not have any job. I worried whether I should follow the rebellion of the Viet Minh or fly away to the town and hide from them. The French were returning and would control the province towns. But the Viet Minh controlled the villages.

Once I saw the Viet Minh execute people, after they had attacked a nearby city one night. I remember seeing the fires in the city that burned all over the place. The next day, I came to visit my rented apartment located at the district center where I taught. A messenger told people to assemble to visit wounded Viet Minh soldiers. We were led to a pagoda. The Viet Minh threw out the monk of that temple and tossed away his Buddha statues. Then they brought in the wounded soldiers and used the pagoda as a hospital. We were forced to visit them. I felt very frustrated when I saw that happen.

Later in the afternoon we were told that we must attend the execution of people who had been arrested in the battle of the city. We were led to a large district sports field that soldiers used for exercise and war training. Some 400–500 of us were forced to sit in a circle while two Viet Minh leaders, one of them later killed by the French, walked back and forth. Standing five feet behind us were Viet Minh soldiers wearing black uniforms of long pants and long shirt sleeves, and sandals made of tires. They pointed their guns at the frightened villagers.

One of the arrested men was under 40 years old. They forced him to kneel in the center of the circle. A Viet Minh soldier announced why this man was being punished. He had climbed up a tree and thrown grenades at the Viet Minh soldiers. After they caught him, they must have beaten him, for his face was quite swollen. Another Viet Minh soldier with a long Japanese sword swung once and cut off the victim's head.

Then they brought out a woman who was under 30 years of age. Her face too was swollen from beatings. She too was accused of betraying the Viet Minh by throwing grenades. The spectators were silent. They were prevented from saying anything, except when a soldier called out, "Who wants to behead the woman?" A Viet Minh woman volunteered, but she was weak. When the first blow struck, the head remained; also the second, and the third time: still the head was not severed. Then a man replaced her, struck once, and the head fell.

In my district, the Viet Minh arrested our district chief and two of his secretaries, and took them off to the forest. Then they told the principal of the elementary school to list the names of all the teachers who worked with him. I had to go back to my fruit garden to live temporarily. In that first month, the Viet Minh called back all the teachers of the district. We were forced to go with them to make propaganda in each village. I never dared to say anything. I would take my bicycle and a Viet Minh man would accompany me. What they said sounded very stupid, but we did not contradict them. Since we were afraid that they might kill us, we traveled with them silently and let them say whatever they wanted.

First the Viet Minh man would gather everybody into a group. *Everybody had to be there.* This was done by force. People were scared, and so they went. People would sit on the floor or on chairs in the meeting house. The men, women, and children of each family would sit together. And they had to remain quiet. The Viet Minh speaker would discuss the time in history when the Chinese dominated Vietnam, and also would remind us of the domination of the French. The people did whatever they had to do. The meeting took place whenever we got there, sometimes at noon, sometimes in the morning, sometimes in the afternoon, depending on the distance of the village. The meetings lasted for two or three hours. They propagated their ideas like reading a story of history. They were stupid, but we had to listen; we could not escape.

For accompanying the Viet Minh, the monthly payment for the entire group of 13 teachers was one 500 piaster bill. We were supposed to break up the bill. Since no stores would change such a large bill, we had to ride along without salary. We'd eat at home, just cooked rice and sometimes fish sauce, although it was very difficult to get at that time. I did this for about two weeks. Since I had no other way to earn my living, I did the illegal thing: I bought and sold untaxed tobacco. Every two weeks, I'd go to the district town, buy minced dry tobacco from peasants nearby, carry it to my village, and sell it there. From September 1945 to February 1946, that's how I earned some money.

French Coercion

Our lives consisted of running first from the Viet Minh and then from the French. Whenever either of them came, I'd run into the forest. Then at night I'd return to my house.

One morning, I saw five French soldiers walking through the village carrying long guns. I remembered the Viet Minh warning that they would kill anyone who had anything to do with the French. But the French soldiers had spotted us. I told my friends to be quiet and stand still or the soldiers would shoot us. We wondered what would happen to us.

In that village, everybody had escaped except my family. One French soldier stood outside with me and my friends while the other four soldiers went inside. They found some bananas and seemed really happy with that. They took those and the duck too. Then they whistled loudly and told me and my friends to go out to the road, near a banana grove. There we found another 25 soldiers who had come out of hiding when they heard the whistle. I was scared. They ordered me to go through the hamlet. I didn't dare say anything but did whatever they asked. I figured that if they knew I spoke French, they'd make me a translator for their Viet Minh captives and that would jeopardize my life.

The French ordered us around with gestures and whistles, since they spoke no Vietnamese. They assumed we were Viet Minh, and they decided that one of my friends, who was better dressed than the rest of us, was our chief. Although they did not realize it, I understood the soldiers when they spoke in French, "We'll keep that last man." In other words, they'll kill the rest of us! I pretended not to understand. I was so scared, but I continued walking, figuring that at any moment they'd shoot. When we reached the edge of the hamlet, the French spotted a buffalo boy and called him over. He showed fear until he saw me; then his face lit up in recognition. He begged, "Tell them in French that I have a personal tax card [license]." He thought they were looking for the tax paper.

"Shut up!" I replied. But the terrified buffalo boy kept on talking. All the soldiers looked at me. So in the end I had to speak French. "This boy has a tax paper; he wants you to know that." When they heard me speak French, the soldiers suddenly paid more attention to me.

"What do you do in the village?" one of them asked.

"I live in my cottage. You came and picked me up. But I forgot my license card in my house. I don't have it with me like the buffalo boy."

"Okay, we don't need that! I need to ask you something. You live here; please tell us how many people are living in the village."

"I don't know because I'm not an officer of the village; I'm just a teacher in the village school."

"Approximately how many?" the soldier asked.

"About 700 people."

"Please count how many people are on the road here."

I answered, "Five."

"Where are the rest of them?"

I replied, "They all ran away into the forest and away to the north."

"Why?"

"They are very afraid of the Viet Minh. If they don't run away, the Viet Minh will kill them."

"Are they afraid of the French troops?"

I said, "Yes, but less than the Viet Minh."

The soldier said, "We believe you tell the truth. Don't be afraid now. Please tell all these people on the road to go back to their homes, take a meal, and then go to the blown-up wooden bridge near your house, and work to rebuild it."

I was so happy: I was not going to be killed! I told my friends what the French had said. Three of them ran off and hid. Now only two of us were left.

After working on the bridge, I accompanied the French soldiers as they visited several villages. I was their interpreter. On the third day, the soldiers ordered me to go with them to the city. They allowed my family to accompany me.

In the city, I noticed that all the government secretaries had run away. All the markets were closed, as were the shops and schools; all the daily activities had ceased. This was in response to the Viet Minh order to close down everything and run to the forest. All the main streets were blocked with bricks.

The French sent me back to the district to work as a secretary for the French official. He needed a translator. I didn't want to do this job because it was very dangerous. But I had no choice; I was ordered to do it.

Corruption and Terrorism

I spent 11 months working for the French district chief and a Vietnamese man, a canton chief who also served as an interpreter. I typed unimportant letters and papers. All of the important things were done by the canton chief. My family remained in the city. About once a month I'd travel by train to visit them, and I wrote to them often. I rented a small room near the market. After work, I went home, closed my door, and went to sleep. I dared not go anywhere else because of the Viet Minh.

The dishonest canton chief was unpleasant. He was very proud of himself because of his power over several villages. Everybody hated him. He misused his power. Sometimes he would point at someone and accuse him of being Viet Minh; he would order that man to be arrested. Then he would conduct the investigation, after which he would send the victim to the French soldiers, who would take that man into the forest and shoot him.

From time to time a French captain would arrest people suspected of being Viet Minh. The canton chief would interrogate them. Every time I saw his manner, I hated it. In one case he simply ordered his men to remove a lumberman's cart and many buffalo to the district headquarters and stalled without returning them when the rightful owner provided verifiable proof of ownership.

When a prisoner was brought in, the canton chief would put his hands in his pockets, pace back and forth, look everywhere, and scowl. For him, people were nothing; he never respected them and never acknowledged them. If he thought they were Viet Minh, he'd beat them on the stomach, back, shoulders, all parts of the body with a dried bull's penis, half as wide as a man's wrist and two feet long. When dried in the sun, it becomes quite hard, yet flexible like a string; it never breaks. Gangsters use this a lot; respectable people do not. The canton chief beat both men and women until they were unconscious. I heard them screaming in pain as he whipped them. After about 15 minutes, he'd stop and ask them again. Then he beat them until they lost consciousness. Three or four times I saw him beat people. That's why I was scared of him.

He would direct people to do anything. He'd tell them, "I am the district chief. Sure, there's a French district chief, but he's new and doesn't know anything. I've been here many years and I know all the people. I am the *Vietnamese* district chief!" And people before him would clasp their hands, bow their heads, and say with respect, "Big Minister!"

The French district chief was also dishonest, and both he and his wife were opium takers. He would submit false reports of damage to a public building and then request money from the province headquarters. He would supply fictitious lists of work done and fictitious names of employees. He would make a cross or sign on the paper that they had received wages for that work. We had to certify as witnesses that we had seen him pay these people. Then he took the money for himself. He treated me very badly, for he refused to let me go back to the city, even though my job was supposed to be a temporary one for three or four months.

The French district chief also went along with a scheme developed by the canton chief to cheat rice sellers who were passing through the town. This happened to a Chinese friend of mine. He was stopped and asked to show his permit. There were two kinds of rice selling permits: those issued by the Economics Department and those issued by the Army. My friend had taken a permit from the Army because the rice they sold was better. The canton chief refused to let him pass through, saying his permit was not appropriate, since our district was associated with the Economics Department, not the Army.

My friend came to me and asked me what to do. I told him to deposit his rice at my place, go to his next location, buy fish, and bring it back to Saigon. At his next location, he was arrested because he presented a permit to transport rice from Saigon to that location, but he had no rice in the car. They thought he might have sold the rice to the Viet Minh in the forest. He explained to the chief of that district how he got into this difficulty, and that official tried to help him by sending a telegram to our district asking why this rice seller had been refused permission to carry rice.

Our canton chief denied that he had ever stopped the rice seller and told our French district chief not to answer. When my Chinese friend came back through our district, he asked me, "What can I do now?"

I had heard through gossip that the canton chief would give permission for anyone to sell rice if they sold it to his wife. I told this to my Chinese friend, and he sold the rice in this way. She wrote him a note; he presented it to her husband, and he gave permission. With the note, my Chinese friend was able to clear himself of charges of helping the Viet Minh. So he lost half the price of the rice, and the only gain he got was a note of certification. This is what the canton chief did to everybody who had an Army permit to transport and sell rice.

The canton chief stole truckloads of coffee and sold the contents in the city; he forced the tax collector to give him thousands of piasters and refused to write receipts. This man had many schemes to make money.

Once a month I would go to the city. There I would talk with the French official who had assigned me to my present job. I would remind him that it was supposed to be a temporary three-month job, and I would tell him about the corruption. "You told me to go and work like an honest man, but over there they cheat people. They are greedy for money. I cannot tell them to stop, so it is hard for me to work there." I also told him that if I complained too much, they would accuse me of being a Viet Minh.

The official instructed me to write out my complaints, and I did this. When I returned to the district town, I told my friends that there might be an investigation and that, if called, they should tell the truth. There was an investigation, but it occurred only after the French district chief had gone back to France. Complaints mounted against the canton chief. Finally the French province chief ordered the canton chief to remain confined to his quarters and be ready to answer to the charges against him. At that point, he resigned.

The other staff of the district office respected me very much. But the people outside the office defied all of us. They considered us to be working for the French, and not the Vietnamese. They didn't care if we were good or bad; they considered us all bad, and they would tell us nothing. You couldn't ask anything of them outside the office. They'd just say "Hello" in a superficial way, and refuse to give any information.

In the villages, people heard many rumors that the French killed people. That's why villagers ran away when they saw the French. But the villagers feared the Viet Minh even more—their killing and kidnapping.

My eldest brother, the gambler, was kidnapped and killed by the Viet Minh. They ordered all of the villagers to hide in the forest. They ordered my brother to report on all the villagers who fled to join the French. But the French appointed him to be a member of the village committee to report to them all the people who had fled into the forest with the Viet Minh. So he was doomed, caught between the two. He reported to the French. The Viet Minh then kidnapped him, and he disappeared forever. I think they killed him. The Viet Minh lied to my family. They said that my brother still survived but had to do some kind of mission for them. We found this out about a year after he had disappeared. The Viet Minh women's organization came to my mother's house in her village. They asked my sister to help them with making cakes for Viet Minh soldiers. In fact they were trying to detect whether she was sad or happy due to the fact that her eldest brother was missing. So they said, "Your eldest brother was arrested. Do you miss him? Do you love him?"

My sister realized that they would report what she said, so to survive she replied, "I don't care; I don't love him; I don't miss him. What he did, he has to suffer for it."

My mother had sad feelings inside just as did my sister. My mother loved her son, but outside she pretended. Despite this, my mother refused to move. This was her property, her house. "I have the right to live in my house and garden," she would say. "I did not do anything wrong."

Viet Minh Assassins

With the resignation of the canton chief, the people of the area had to elect another official to take his place. The members of the village committee asked me to submit my name. I refused, saying that the elected officer should be someone among themselves. But when the votes were counted, I had received 32 of the 35 votes; two of the remaining three votes were cast for the previous canton chief.

No one really wanted that position, for they greatly feared the old canton chief. And they were right. He sent his brother-in-law into the forest to contact the Viet Minh and spread the propaganda that I had deprived the canton chief of his position. The Viet Minh sent two assassins out of the forest to shoot me. I found out about this the hard way. [Editor's note: Here Mr. Ngon rolled up his sleeve and showed me a shattered arm.]

One day around 4:30 P.M., I left my office. I stopped at a blacksmith's shop to pick up an axe I had ordered. I used it to chop wood. I was carrying the axe and had almost reached home when I realized that something was wrong. I became suspicious, wary. The market did not look the same as on ordinary days. On the veranda of the barber shop two young men sat down. The barbers, however, cut hair inside the shop, not on the veranda. My suspicions increased when I noticed that a coffee shop had its doors closed; always before they had been open. Someone in that shop pushed open the door, peeked out, and then closed the door.

Clearly something was wrong, but I felt secure because I was armed with an axe. I thought, "If they shoot me, I cut them." I felt ready to take on the two men at the barber shop. When I reached the veranda, the two men stood up and marched down the steps. One guy's shirt and mine scratched together. Now I suspected. He bumped my arm, so I walked faster and faster. They followed me, one on each side of me. I carried my axe in my right arm. While one man followed along with me, the other ran ahead quickly to my apartment. I took five quick steps. Suddenly I stopped. The man at my side stopped too, and turned. The barrel of his gun bulged from his pants pocket.

Five or six shots burst from his automatic gun; the sparks went right past my stomach. One bullet hit me in the right forearm, shattering my bone. That bullet wound is why today I have a four-inch scar and a hand that is twisted.

At that time I was very courageous, even though blood was spreading all over my body and clothes. The axe fell down, so I ran, not to my apartment, but the office. As I ran, I cried, "Help! Viet Minh!"

Some French soldiers were drinking coffee at a nearby shop. When they heard the shots, they ran away from the shooting. They were unarmed and too scared to fight. When I passed by the French headquarters, 50 meters down the road, some men helped me into a truck and wrapped my arm.

That night, about 20 French soldiers went to the place where I was shot. I was taken to the hospital in the city. The next day they did surgery on my arm. I remained in the hospital for three months, then was assigned to a job in the city.

I found out that the man who shot me was the man at my side.

When I began to run and scream, and the soldiers shouted and ran out of the coffee shop, the assassin at my side panicked and ran towards my apartment. He was between me and the second assassin, who continued shooting. The bullets missed me, but one of them hit his companion, who collapsed with his intestines hanging out. The second assassin picked up the wounded man and carried him on his shoulders into the bamboo forest.

Two years after this incident, I was told that the Viet Minh had arrested the former canton chief. A friend of his who owned a rubber plantation told him that if he could persuade a Viet Minh battalion to surrender, the French administration would award him 30 million francs, and the battalion itself would receive even more money. The canton chief sent a message to the Viet Minh informing them and offering to meet with them. He was led into the forest for a meeting, but instead of discussing the offer, they kept him in the forest and probably killed him.

He disappeared. His wife, his concubine, and his girlfriends never saw him again. Every girl who sold rattan and bamboo in Saigon had had to sleep with this man. They had to pass through our district town; that's when he got hold of them, and they could not escape. The people were pleased when he disappeared because of so many things: his pride, his greed, his lust, his cruelty.

French and Viet Minh: I See No Difference

When I think about the French and the Viet Minh, I see no difference. They did the same thing, and people were very scared of both sides. Both the French and the Viet Minh killed people in my wife's family. In my family the Viet Minh killed my first wife and my eldest brother. And I have described a Viet Minh execution.

I also know of many cases of the French shooting and killing people. I saw them shoot two prisoners with a machine gun. I have described how the canton chief used to beat people unconscious. In every military post, the way the French investigated people was through suffering. They would mix soap with water, force a large quantity of this detergent down a prisoner's throat until he or she fell unconscious. Then the soldiers, wearing military boots, would step on the stomach of the prisoner until he vomited. From this, people would become afraid and would say anything, true or false. They did this to men and women. Both the French and the Vietnamese working for the French did these things. They beat people with big wooden rice beaters.

My own uncle had been unsure whether to support the Viet Minh or the French. The Viet Minh had told all people to stay away from their jobs, but the French had dropped leaflets from airplanes ordering people to return to work. Since his son was a former employee of the French and his daughter-in-law was a teacher, I told them to go with the French; the Viet Minh would kill them because of their occupations. So they joined the French side, and in turn they destroyed my uncle.

Village people like to hang education certificates of their children on the walls of their houses. The French saw lots of certificates in my uncle's house, so they knew that people in his house could speak French. The soldiers really liked that family. But one month later, the French burned all of the houses in two cantons, no exceptions, for that was the order.

For more than one month, they held my uncle in a military post, gave him only a little food and water, and beat him a great deal. Then they let him go. He complained that the French behaved very badly by destroying rice, killing the buffalo to eat them, and burning the houses of the people, and that this was a good way for the French actions to benefit the Viet Minh. The Viet Minh said to him, "You see what the French did to you?" One month after his beating, my uncle died from the tortures.

The French also killed a former classmate of mine who used to work as a teacher. In 1952 a Vietnamese soldier working for the French severely beat my wife's brother-in-law, who came to the city with two buffalo after a typhoon and flooding had hit his village. The French held him for less than a month, but beat him to get him to give up the buffalo. After the beating, his legs were so swollen that it took him many months to recover.

Because of these behaviors, neutral Vietnamese disliked both the French and the Vietnamese soldiers of the French army. They also disliked the police and the lawyers, as well as secretaries for the French. And they hated those who were living in the towns or cities. Such people were considered enemies. This came from the propaganda that all people living in the cities were followers of the French.

This happened to me too. From the time I was captured by the French and left my village, I dared not return to see my mother, for the Viet Minh would have arrested me. The only time I was able to visit her was in two years, 1954 and 1956, during times of truce. From 1946 to 1953, I could not visit her, nor in 1955. And she dared not visit me in town, for if she did, the Viet Minh would arrest her when she returned to her village. There was no contact between my mother and myself, not even letters. This is not simply because she was illiterate. I was afraid that the Viet Minh would catch us if I wrote to her. In 1956 my mother and sister came to live in the city where my family stayed, but most of our relatives remained in the villages.

The Viet Minh war, and the later war with the Viet Cong, affected everybody terribly, not just a few. Normally our relatives would visit back and forth with each other. But when the French arrived in 1945 [returned after World War II], half of the Vietnamese people lived in the cities and towns, and half lived in the hamlets. They separated; they could no longer go back and forth freely because the Viet Minh soldiers would not permit this. You had to stay where you lived.

That propaganda spread out; it made people become suspicious of each other. The propaganda lie was very successful. Somehow the Viet Minh created rumors of events in a way to make people believe that they had happened when they had not. The Viet Minh claimed that they had destroyed the roads and bridges, so that cars could not use them any more. I believed that, so for several months I did not travel on the roads; I believed that the Viet Minh might easily stop me and arrest me. I was quite surprised one afternoon when French jeeps drove right into my hamlet. How could they have done that?

The Viet Minh also told people that they had already encircled and invaded Saigon, and that the North Vietnamese army was already in Central Vietnam. But the troops were not there; nothing was there. Rumors like this were spread all the time.

Later, the Viet Minh closed the shops, schools, and businesses, and burned down houses. People wondered what they should do, where they should live, where they should hide their buffalo and cows. They wondered how they could survive.

I would have followed the Viet Minh if they had provided us with food when we were starving. If they had done that, they could have told me to do anything they wanted. What they gave were "Viet Minh orders," which meant, "Nothing left in the garden, empty house." We had to destroy all our fruit trees and houses to make it difficult for the French.

From 1945 until 1975 the war kept going back and forth, first with the Viet Minh, later with the Viet Cong. Psychologically, the people in the villages lost their self-confidence; they dared not visit their relatives in the towns, and those in towns dared not visit their village relatives. Each dressed differently.

The split between village and city members of our family was great. In 1971 a relative of my wife died in a village next to the district town. My wife went back and attended the funeral. A woman who was related to my wife saw her at the funeral. Instead of talking, this woman turned her back on my wife and ignored her as if they had never met before. She did this because she had lived in the countryside, under the control of the Viet Minh and later the Viet Cong, from 1945 to 1971, a period of 26 years. The widow at that funeral called to that woman, pointed at my wife, and said, "Sister, don't you know this woman?"

Without turning her face, the other woman replied, "Why shouldn't I know?" She pretended to ignore my wife completely.

My wife felt very uncomfortable and wanted to go home immediately. She was disappointed that her relative had acted like that. But the reason for it was that others from the village might have watched her relative's behavior and reported on her. It was very unusual for my wife to have made that journey to a Viet Cong village under any circumstances. The village was only five miles away from the city where she lived, but the relatives had not met in *26 years*!

[See also Chapters 3, 16, and 34.]

CHAPTER 15

Memories of Communist
Hanoi: 1945–1966

NARRATOR 3: NORTH VIETNAMESE
CHINESE-VIETNAMESE ELDER

*This chapter documents the very effective means that the Communists used
to "reeducate" the urban citizens of Hanoi. The narrator explains why he
and others had to "confess" to imaginary crimes of capitalist exploitation
of the people, and he tells how people were coerced to vote in elections for
preselected candidates.*

"Liberation" and Reeducation

Before the Communists took over in 1945, there was a very terrible famine. Even the farmers were among the hungriest. When
they saw people eating, they tried to rob them of food. I was in
Hanoi at the time. People were told to leave some food for the
hungry. A youth movement arose to collect rice for the starving,
but this couldn't solve the problem. Finally so many people were
so hungry that they dragged along the streets. In the morning when
I opened the house, I saw dead people lying on the streets. Others
were so hungry that they'd snatch food from the hands of those
who bought food. The food robbers would be beaten, but they just
kept on eating. The Japanese, who were in control at that time,
beheaded some people as examples. The people blamed the famine
both on the Japanese and on the French, who forced farmers to

grow jute instead of rice. I saw many, many people die; bodies were carried away by oxcarts. About two million people died, mostly village people, including farmers. City people had money, so they didn't starve. Our housemaids used to buy the food for us. Occasionally someone would snatch food from them, but that never happened to people in my family. The famine lasted about a half-year.

I was a young man in Hanoi when the Communists first came to power in the August Revolution of 1945. Two days before the August 17 Revolution, there was a meeting of government employees at the municipal theater. The Communists turned it into a demonstration and mobilized the people to rise up to support their cause. They didn't say they were Communists, only that they were patriots helping to gain independence. They always hid their identity like that to mobilize the people.

I didn't participate in the demonstration. I saw a great flow of people support the Viet Minh to gain independence. At that time as a youth my spirit was also lifted; my heart also burned. But that was the happiness of a person looking on, not participating.

On August 19, they used the support of the people to topple the pro-Japanese government. The Japanese had just been defeated in World War II, so they didn't care. The weapons of the Communists were nothing: a few grenades, rifles, swords, and sticks, but there was no bloodshed. The Communists profited by using the fundamental principle of choosing the right time for an uprising, utilizing the power of the people. Then they collected gold during the "Week of Gold," in which everyone had to donate something. With this wealth, they bought weapons from the Nationalist Chinese, who came to disarm the Japanese.

The war of resistance against the French began in 1946. From that year until 1954, the French controlled Hanoi, while the Viet Minh controlled the countryside. During those years, I wrote for a newspaper and wrote three or four books, mainly on politics. When I look back on those writings of my youth, I realize they weren't very good. I threw away all of my writings when the Communists came, for I dared not keep them.

Not until 1954 did we in the city come under Communist control. Our life-style was quite different from that of the Communists who lived in the villages. In their view, I was urban, liberated by the peasants, the Communists. Urban people were those who followed traditional ways of life for many years. We were the people who struggled to improve our lives in a free-enterprise, capitalistic system: not big entrepreneurs, but workers in small businesses who might try to develop a better life. We were not like America, with big cities, big industries, and big shops. The economy of Vietnam was that of small towns one-twentieth the size of those in America. Even our sidewalks were only one-third as large. What we had was small industries, manual labor, and shops which often were in the house of the owner.

When the Communists liberated North Vietnam, they wanted to introduce a life-style totally different from the traditional one, to change even the roots of society, to reorganize its infrastructure. Their aim was to turn people into the means of attaining their objectives. The Communists limited the dreams and the improvements of both employers and workers. Under the old regime we could study as much as possible, and we could earn as many degrees as possible. Under the Communists, you could study for one degree; then you had to go to work. Instead of freedom, people had to follow the government's indications, which limited their activities. You could not open a publishing house or printing shop, for the Communists put tight controls on the ideas of people. Newspapers, books, radio, even typewriters were Communist-government controlled. The means of propaganda were controlled by the government. Without new ideas, you cannot make improvements. The Communists did not allow new ideas that deviated from Communist thoughts. They claimed that their ideas were the new, innovative ones, and that every country in the world would progress towards Communism.

The Communists began land reform in 1953, even when North Vietnam was not liberated yet. City people did not know much about the peasants. But when the Communists took over the cities in 1954, all means of propaganda through newspapers and radio were used to publicize the new ideas. We were bombarded day and night with propaganda until gradually our stand was changed to the side of the peasants. We realized that this land reform was best for the peasants. How true it was to have land reform. Our thoughts were changed.

No one dared to express other opinions; no one dared to be different; we were afraid of being branded "reactionary." So all of us expressed the same viewpoint.

From 1953 to 1956, the fight was for land reform; from 1957 to 1959, the struggle was against capitalists. (See also Hoang Van Chi 1964 on land reform and thought reform.) The Communists said that this was the time of the workers, who will take power and be leaders; the capitalists no longer had any role in the history of Vietnam.

They wrote a new history according to their own ideas showing that over the past 40 years the capitalists had made no achievements. Capitalists were branded as opportunists who would sacrifice anything, even their wives, to become rich.

The Communists confiscated our property. First, the cadres came to each house, asking people's views, just to see if people showed any signs of disagreement with the Communists or expressed different ideas. If so, the Communists arrested them right away. At first we didn't realize this; later we did.

When they passed through my house, they saw that I read books all the time, especially books on Communism, so they said, "You are a progressive element; in the next few days, you will close your shop and become a group discussion leader for the classes you will attend."

I refused, saying, "I'm afraid I can't do the job; I don't know much."

One of the cadres responded, "That's all right, because I'll be behind you; I'll guide you. Don't worry." But I did worry. They only planned to use me as a means. I would seem to be leading the discussion, but actually would be a puppet pulled by strings.

For three months we had to attend classes, morning and afternoon, for eight hours a day. We were told that we were the obstacles to the new society. We had large meetings, held in a movie house, attended by 600–700 of us capitalists and entrepreneurs. We took notes like at a lecture. Most of the speakers were males, city people with some education. They were articulate. They had been selected to show enthusiasm and vigor; they wanted to show the truth of Communism.

I remember one lecture in which a man said, "I could die for the cause, sacrifice my life for the Communist cause." I had the feeling that these speakers would talk on and on until they would get sick because of talking, just to prove the truth of the revolutionaries, that Communism was the only way, that it was the truth, and that all of us should follow it. They were extremists, fanatics, talking and talking. Never in my life have I seen such enthusiasm for Communism, such lecturers!

After these talks, we broke up into small discussion groups of 15 persons, headed by a Communist cadre, but with people like me as discussion leaders. We were supposed to relate the topics we had heard in lecture to our own real situation. We had to confess how we exploited the people. Husbands and wives were always split into different groups. The Communists then tried to find if there were any discrepancies in what they said, and after each session they'd go to our houses to check up on us and find out the truth about such things as our possessions or where our profits went or why husband and wife gave different statements of profits. I didn't know much about our business since my wife used to run it, so the Communists directed questions at her. Because of this, we showed no discrepancies. My parents had been rich, but by the time we took over the business, it was very small, with goods worth only 5,000 piasters. Even so, the Communists branded us capitalists.

Never did we joke or show resistance at these sessions, never! We were very afraid! It was a solemn atmosphere, and we attended the classes with fear, never knowing who would denounce us. Our children also had to attend classes for the young, where they were instructed to go home and spy on their parents—us. They were taught to act against their parents, to brand them "exploiters," and to show others where their parents had hidden their property. And if the children of capitalists could not make successful denunciations of their parents, then the Communists used their neighbors, one capitalist against another. Before denouncing that person, they'd tell his past history, that he has not made any confession, and that it now was time for other capitalists to denounce him. The Communists would threaten to arrest one of them, and so the denunciations would begin:

"You are the capitalist who is against revolutionaries! You collaborated with the enemy! You had dealings with other capitalists to make profits, to exploit people! Was it right?"

You had to admit your guilt, even if the charges were false. *You had to admit!* This didn't happen to me because I was a very small capitalist, in business only a few years. But I was the discussion leader who urged the members of the group to answer questions about the lecture. If no one could answer them satisfactorily, the cadre gave an explanation. We all sat around a table, with the cadre in the middle, prodding discussion.

"What are the tricks of exploitation of the capitalists during French colonialism? What is the role of the working class in this revolutionary period? Why do we have to eliminate capitalism?"

After each session, all of us had to write a report describing our business, and how we had exploited people. Later, we had to read this aloud for everyone to hear. I remember I told them a true story: "Under French rule, I wanted to work for the Information Office. I knew a writer working in that office, but before giving me the job, he wanted a bribe. Then I realized how corrupt he and the government were. I decided I didn't want to work there, but live using my own business."

In discussion, I was told to leave the room for a while. When I returned, the group asked me questions, especially about my intention to work in the Information Office. "How much wrong to have intent to work in the Information Office, because it would be against the Revolution!"

Then they asked me if there were any differences between the administration of the old and the new government. I replied, "I saw some black-toothed women [peasants chewing betel] working in the new government."

The whole group jumped on me for that, "You have antirevolutionary, antiparty ideas!"

I was really afraid of the frank way they accused me, for black-toothed women, illiterate peasants, were the proletariat, the new ruling class. But the real reason they forced us to attend these meetings was to confiscate our property. Since my shop was a small one, they closed it and turned it into a house. Since I used to live at the shop, the Communists said, "Go to live in your father-in-law's house; your shop is small; it will belong to the government." He had a lot of rooms. They also confiscated his shop.

After telling me this at a meeting, they came to my house to do the inventory. They wrote down all the things used for business and those for personal use. And they put a value on the property. Then they told me to sign the report of my stock. They confiscated these things and sold them in government shops. We handed over our sewing machines, cash, and goods. We shopowners were turned into employees of government shops. My wife received 50 piasters per month, plus an additional 25 piasters as interest on our confiscated capital. We continued to get that interest for about 20 years. I tried to find people to rent some of our rooms, but rainwater leaked into the rooms, so I gave up.

We lived on the income of my wife; also, my mother hid money and didn't tell me. She knew I was a frank person and feared I would tell the Communists. We also had to sell antiques to live: vases, tea cabinets, sofas, chairs. All were sold for 200–300 piasters apiece, not much. The buyers were peasants, for at that time they were rich. They had rice, and they wanted antiques.

Also, after our meetings, the Communists would watch us to see what kinds of foods we bought, and from that they could infer if we had exceeded our allotment of money, for if we did, it meant that we had hidden savings. I felt sad. My life was at a new turning point and I couldn't tell what my life would be. I didn't confide in anyone. I dared not. I knew that my mother and wife were feeling the same tensions, so I didn't say anything.

In 1954 I had the intention to move to the South. From books I already knew something about Communism. I asked the opinion of my family. They did not want to leave. Because of the emotion and the family sentiments, I stayed with them. My family was a big one. I had long been living under the protection of my mother. Also, I had a timid nature. I miss my family when I am far from them: my parents, grandparents, brother, sisters, I miss them all, even now. I'm a sentimental person, rich in sentiments.

I remember one time when I had to go away from Hanoi for one month. I missed Hanoi and everyone so much, I could embrace everyone when I returned. I don't want to move; I don't like the idea; even moving furniture in my house disturbs me. But once I make the move and live for a long time, as in America, I get used to that spot and don't want to move. But if 20 years from now Vietnam would be liberated, I'd go back. I still miss the place where I was born and lived for such a long time.

A couple of weeks before I was forced to leave Vietnam in 1980, one of my cousins was forced to go. I went to see him off. He left his homeland. For a moment I wished I could go with him; life was too miserable, too hard. I felt sad when he went. But I did not go. Why? Because I was not forced to go. I didn't want to leave because of language problems. Also, I had held only one job for the past 17 years. I didn't think I could get employment. I wanted to stay and live with my retirement, my memories, and my friends. I was no longer young; I was not an active person. How could I survive abroad if I went? So before leaving, I lived through bewildering days.

Censorship and Control in North Vietnam

In North Vietnam, people are supposed to idolize the political leaders because they represent the party of the proletariat. It is easy for such a person to lead because when he gives orders, everyone has to follow. The Party decides everything; the government must carry out its orders. We have a congress, but when it meets, it is not to discuss matters but to carry out decisions already made. Discussion is only for matters already decided upon. Anyone can register to run for the position of congressman, but if he isn't approved by the Party, he won't be elected.

Before casting votes, people already know who will be elected. The Communists try to make that day a festival. The election is usually held at a large house, and it normally begins at 7:00 A.M. By 9:00 A.M., 90 percent of the votes have been cast. The reason is that the head of each neighborhood comes to each house to urge people to vote. He controls those people; he's responsible for them. He knows the number of voters per household, and whether or not they have voted, so it's hard for people not to go to the polls, really hard to avoid it. Before they vote, the group leader has already given them a list of seven names, of whom they must vote for five.

One time, I didn't feel like voting for five, only four. But I feared that I'd be discovered and get troubles. Someone would ask, "Why didn't you follow the instructions?" Maybe he would brand me a "suspected reactionary." Who is really elected? It is hard to check the votes, for they can put more votes in boxes for the candidates they prefer.

These elections are based on a climate of fear. I don't even confide in anyone else. If I don't like a candidate, I still must vote for him. That's why elections are finished fast. Even if you are sick, you can't get out of voting, for the group leader instructs someone to carry the voting box to you.

Newspapers are rigged just like elections. Their purpose is propaganda through mass media. The goal of North Vietnamese propaganda is to educate the population to realize, to understand that politics is the most important thing. This is the function of newspapers, radio, and, since 1975, television. The policy of the propaganda is to show the important role of the proletariat, in other words, the role of the Party, which is emphasized the most.

Newspapers belong to the Party, not to any individual. The Party determined that each group should have its newspaper: workers, farmers, youth, and others. So the Party selected those with ability in journalism and appointed them to run the various newspapers. The Constitution of the Vietnamese Communists, written in 1946, indicates freedom of speech, with no censorship. But the editor of the magazine or newspaper must be totally responsible for the magazine, so someone has already done the censorship: the editor. Every day he has to send a copy of his publication to the Office of Propaganda Education. Each day it is read. It may be acceptable, or the editor may be told to correct minor errors. If he has made a serious mistake, he is forced to resign. This is dealt with internally, so it's often difficult to know. Each week the Office of Propaganda and Education meets to scrutinize every word written. That's why it is so difficult to write under Communism. And if an editor is called to a meeting and he sees all the people dressed up, indicating that this is an important occasion, he becomes terrified, for he knows trouble lies ahead.

The front page is always reserved for the meeting of the Party's Central Committee. Sometimes speeches at the Party Convention take up the whole eight pages of the newspaper, nothing else. Five years after the liberation of 1954, there were only three newspapers. They were almost identical, with editorial columns always written by a Party leader. They were always the same, and very dry.

The one exception was a private newspaper, the *New Times*. It was allowed to exist to give the false impression that the North had freedom of press. In fact, a Party member had been sent to control the newspaper.

A certain amount of criticism was allowed, as long as it was directed at an individual not related to any party or government organization. We had the right to criticize such a person as one who slowed down the advancement of the Party. A writer was not authorized to criticize a cadre who, for example, did not weigh rice correctly, because to do so was to criticize the regime.

An author writing a book had to follow the guidelines of the Party: research, literature, all followed the Party line. I remember once when President Ho Chi Minh visited an exhibition of paintings. He made some comments about them. A few days later, the painter told his colleagues that the comments of Ho Chi Minh were not correct. "No!" the others replied. "You criticize the leader; you are not satisfied with the leader. The leader is right with his golden rule." The name of that painter was never heard again. He wasn't taken away; his paintings simply were never shown again in exhibitions. That is why professors, researchers, scholars, and artists always use the words of Ho Chi Minh and other leaders. That is why there is never anything new.

I just followed the new regime. I had no reactions to it because I'm not courageous. I'm just a coward; I try to keep a very low profile, and I follow whatever directions I'm given. I didn't call attention to myself, so people didn't bother me. I did not think. I tried to adjust, not to oppose, because resistance was impossible.

Sometimes I had to learn articles by heart. If I had to take an exam, for example, for admission to the university, I had to know and use *political subjects*, because those were the most important topics. If I would not write clearly on these subjects, I would be denied higher education, and I would be punished. If the correct

view is, "Now the Party will lead the entire population to Socialism," and a student writes, "The move to Socialism is now too
early," that's a mistake. His punishment is that he is denied further
education. Because of this, he will be unable to earn a higher salary:
he will live a miserable life.

After several years of living like this under Communism, I came
to America. When local authorities here tell me to do something, I
do it without thinking: that's the way I have been shaped. For example, I received a letter from the Department of Social Services
informing me that Health and Human Services is cutting my benefits ten dollars a month. It said that if I was *not satisfied* with this, I
could file a complaint. It never comes to my mind to file a complaint: it's ridiculous. Once the higher authorities have decided,
how can I complain? I just have to learn to live with ten dollars less.

It never came to my mind to protest against the Communist regime. Those who participated clandestinely in the resistance against
the French were considered great heroes after 1954. If they said it
was too soon to move to Socialism, even these heroes were eliminated. So what could a poor person like me do?

The Communists have a definite plan for the control of people.
For example, in North Vietnam, many intellectuals didn't want to
join the Communists. In order to show the world they had freedom, the Communists allowed the development of a democratic
party. Then they assigned their own people to join and become
leaders so that they controlled it as well as the Communist party.

Communist policy also requires control of people. In villages
they use plainclothes police who do not carry arms. They must
know people personally to identify them. Eight hours a day, starting at eight in the morning, they just visit every family. They know
all of the people and their activities; they control them very strictly.
They know the identities through three generations, who supports
the Party, who doesn't, and who is in the middle. Two families live
in a single room like this of 10 by 18 feet, and the door is always
open; the police can always enter to perform their duty of visiting
families.

In the city, one house usually has five to six families, and that
forms a cell, with a group leader. He controls everybody; he knows
who is working and who isn't; he knows which family had a friend

from outside the area visit overnight, since the host family must inform the group leader, who reports this to the police. The cells form a larger block with its representative. In this way, people are controlled.

With my friends, I'd talk about anything except politics, *never* about politics. Even during the time of the heavy American bombardment, we kept silent. One day we were ordered to eat no breakfast—ordered! I was hungry; I couldn't find anything to eat except guava. Later I met a friend. Out of anger I said, "What's happening? It appears to be a failure of Socialism!" I dared not go further. My friend's response was silence. But if he had said yes, I'd have feared that he was a spy who would report me.

There was always an air of suspicion surrounding everybody, and that helped the Communists to consolidate their regime. If you had a loose tongue, someone would report that you were speaking against the regime. Every word was controlled.

[See also Chapters 5, 17, and 39.]

CHAPTER 16

Viet Cong and Americans: 1956–1969

NARRATOR I: ELDERLY SOUTH VIETNAMESE CIVIL SERVANT

The narrator continues his account of the war years. In this part, Mr. Ngon describes his participation in activities intended to control not only the Communists, but other groups as well (see West 1985 for a military account of American and South Vietnamese efforts against the Viet Cong). He gives his opinions on why the Viet Cong successfully controlled villages through their use of propaganda, while the Nationalists often failed because of corruption (see also Tran Van Don 1978 on corruption in the Thieu regime). He describes the Tet (New Year) Offensive of 1968 (see also Oberdorfer 1984) and tells of an election in which he ran for office.

Mr. Ngon, like many South Vietnamese, used the term "Viet Cong" to refer to Communists of both North and South Vietnam. In contrast, many Americans used the term "Viet Cong" to refer only to Communists in the South. By "Viet Minh," the narrator had in mind first the resistance against the French, which included both Communists and other groups; second, he referred to the Communist movement against the South Vietnamese government in the 1950s.

Diem Years

In 1956 I was appointed chief of a district about 30 miles from the province town. The political situation at that time was not quiet. Vietnam had been divided into North and South. Ngo Dinh Diem, the president in the South, was confronted with rival political parties, the vegetarian Cao Dai, the Hoa Hao Buddhists, and the criminal Binh Xuyen, run by that gangster Bay Vien. And in addition, President Diem had to deal with the Viet Minh.

Most of my activities were directed to control of the Binh Xuyen. After some time, I was transferred to another province. Here I was put in charge of administrative details in two districts that were very dangerous because of the Viet Minh threat. They would hide in the bushes and try to blow up cars on the road. They were after guns. About once a month, they managed to kill someone this way. They were not very successful because they were not well organized.

During the time of the election of President Diem, I had to go around telling people about the election and showing them how to prepare to vote. I traveled with a lieutenant. We divided up the villages that we visited. On this one day, I took a village on the left; he took a village on the right that was up a crooked, hilly road. I met with a canton chief, and after about 15 minutes he and I went looking for the lieutenant. We found him in his jeep with his chest blown away. I returned home immediately.

One time, the Viet Minh in that province blew up a small bridge that connected two of the hamlets of a village. For weeks, the two hamlets lost contact with one another. The people who lived in those hamlets requested the province to construct another bridge for them. The officials figured that if they rebuilt the bridge, the Viet Minh would simply destroy it again. The officials offered to supply the materials, but told the villagers to do the construction, so that the villagers would realize the difficulty of the job. The Viet Minh told the people in the hamlets that the officials were simply making excuses to get the people of the hamlet to build the bridge so that the government could send troops into the villages.

President Diem had developed an organization of Civic Action workers who were sent to various villages and hamlets to befriend the people, help them, live with them, and get them to inform on the Viet Minh so that the government could drive them out. Twelve such men were under my control. I sent four of them to

four of the hamlets of that troubled village. Their job was to get
the hamlet leaders to keep a list of names of men and women ranging from 20 to 50 years of age. Five days later, I would go to those
hamlets to get the list.

When I arrived, I called a meeting. Everyone was there, including the people whose names were on the list. I told them, "Today I
want to discuss the construction of that bridge. All of you may
freely tell me whatever is in your mind about that matter."

The young men started to talk first. This was wrong, and very
unusual; the leaders must speak first. A youth said, "We wonder
why you want the bridge to be built. It is supposed to be used to
let people travel from one village to another. The bridge is going
to be built by the people in the hamlets. It is supposed to be for
them only. But in the meantime, the military will use that road too.
So why don't they build it themselves?"

These people had been strongly influenced by the Viet Minh, so
it was really hard to work with them. I had to be very firm, very
strong. Sometimes we had to cheat them, design new intelligent
ideas to handle them. I lied to the people at that meeting, "We have
received orders from the province chief to build that bridge. If you
people do not build it, others will. Now, you've asked enough
questions; from now on you answer my questions." I turned to the
hamlet leaders and said, "Is building a bridge an advantage or a
disadvantage for you?"

They said, "It has to be an advantage."

Then some elders said the same thing.

"Now," I said, "I want the younger people to say whether it's an
advantage or a disadvantage."

The younger people tried to avoid answering; they spoke indirectly. The youth who had first spoken now said, "I've got T.B. I
cannot do that work." He looked very strong and healthy.

Another youth stood and said, "During the week I have to work
far away from this village. I can only work on weekends."

A third young man said, "I cannot forget my work in the fields."

Each of them had an excuse, so who of them would build the
bridge? If I weren't firm with them, I'd lose them. I told them, "I
don't care about your excuses. I just need to know if building the

bridge has more advantages for people. Whoever will build the bridge, I don't want to know. If you all refuse to build it, there will be a bridge built anyway. In my book I've got the list of all the people in these hamlets. I'll ask each hamlet chief about every name on the list. He'll tell me if they want to work or not. I'll write down the answer, yes or no."

The first young man seemed to think a lot when he heard that. I looked at him. "Well, yes or no?"

He was frightened. He answered softly, "Yes, I accept to work."

I called on others. Most of them accepted. Nobody dared to say no because I had their names on a list, and they feared that I would report them and they would be arrested as suspected Viet Minh. As a group they were willing to refuse; when called individually, they accepted my orders. They built a good bridge because they knew it was for themselves.

I worked in many different districts from 1946–1963. Many times I found that some district chiefs were involved in corruption, and their wives would interfere with the jobs of their husbands in order to make money. This would happen when people applied for permits to build a factory or a new house: often the applicant would give gifts in money to the official's wife.

The corruption of the South Vietnamese officials affected very heavily the ability of the South to resist the Communists. The Viet Cong really liked government corruption because it got people really upset and therefore the more easily attracted to the Viet Cong. "See, it's easier to live with us than with the government," they would say. Many officials like me were not corrupt; we strongly opposed it.

The Viet Cong would go to villages. They were very sweet with the villagers, the way they spoke; they were trained to do that. When they came to a house, they'd call out, "Mom, how are you? Where is Dad?" They would ask if they could stay overnight. In the morning, they would go into the garden, cut the grass, cultivate sweet potatoes and manioc, or they would sweep the yard for the people, or fill up the water pots. They would stay until late afternoon; then they would leave. So you see, if a person did like that, wouldn't you like it?

Working for the Americans

In December 1963, I was retired from the Nationalist government [Mr. Ngon frequently uses this term to refer to the government of South Vietnam]. I had been allowed to stay on for two years beyond the mandatory retirement age of 55, but only because I had made a special request. For nearly two years I stayed retired, but it was difficult because of my low pension of only 15,000 piasters a month. My regular salary had been only 20,000 piasters.

In March of 1965, my mother passed away. In October of the same year, I received a call from a province chief whom I knew. He asked me to meet with him, and he introduced me to an American. They wanted me to work with the two of them in a new project which the American called the Census Grievance Center [a literal translation of the Vietnamese would be People Opinion Center]. The salary of 12,500 piasters a month, along with my pension, provided a good income. The project seemed to me to be very important, for it was an attempt to stamp out the Viet Cong.

The Americans had asked the South Vietnamese to set up this project because they realized during the war that they did not know the wishes of the Vietnamese people on various things. In the forest were the Viet Cong, but outside was the South Vietnamese government. At night the Communists came into the villages to make propaganda; during the daytime the South Vietnamese government sent people to make propaganda. Therefore the people were in the middle and did not know which way to follow. They were confused. So this organization developed in order to understand what people wished to know. It was funded by the Americans.

For three months I was given training in a suburb of Saigon. The Frenchman who trained us was a former rubber plantation landlord who spoke French, English, and some Vietnamese. The Communists had killed his son and taken his plantation. We planned to counter the Communists by placing cadres of our own in each hamlet or village. It was my job to teach them what to do. They would make a census of the place where they lived. We printed a paper like an identity card on which would be put a person's name, date and place of birth, the names of his parents, and his place of residence. Everybody living in the hamlet would be on the list held by the cadre. If anybody new came into the hamlet, he would have to declare his identity to the cadre to receive a new identity card. Every time a person left his house for some time, the cadre must know where he is going and what he does.

Every event that happened in the hamlet or village had to be reported to the Center, and every month each villager had to report to the cadre office with his identity card to get a monthly visa. The people complained that this disturbed them too much, but it helped the South Vietnamese government because we knew exactly where people were living and what they did.

Anytime the cadre learned of something new happening in the forest, the cadre had to report it immediately. Often the Viet Cong persuaded men living in the town to buy things for them, mostly medicine and clothes, but also sugar, salt, fish sauce, and coffee. From time to time they would meet in the forest. When the cadre learned of this, he came to my office and informed me; I would then write a secret report to the province chief, and he got the military to bombard the area. (For a military account of attempts to control the Viet Cong in another area of Vietnam, see West 1985.)

Our activities bothered not only the Viet Cong, but also the district chiefs, because it interfered with their greedy bribe taking. When our cadres learned of the bribes, they also reported that to our center. Of five district chiefs in my area, one was honest. His district was the most successful in clearing out the Viet Cong.

In Vietnam, corruption was the usual thing, and it made the Viet Cong look good. In the cities there was much corruption. The Viet Cong were hypocrites; they pretended to help people and they were polite. But when the Nationalist soldiers came into the villages, they did not have the same conduct. They'd take chickens, ducks, and pigs without paying for them, so the villagers hated them, and this was widely known. I received complaints from villagers when I worked for the government. Sometimes the stories were true; at other times rumors were spread. In the meantime, the Viet Cong flattered and pleased people.

One day I received a secret request from the province chief. He wanted a secret investigation of a Catholic North Vietnamese refugee who had been accumulating a big and illegal quantity of rice.

Someone had sent an anonymous note accusing him of supplying rice to the Communists. The man accused was also the tax collector and the security chief for the village, with about 35 guards who patrolled day and night. The Catholic priest of the hamlet might favor and protect the rice merchant because in return he gave financial support to him and his church.

Many North Vietnamese refugees worked under my supervision. One particularly loyal cadre was sent into that village disguised as a peasant. He bought some rice from that merchant, discovered that the accusation was true, and reported it to my office. Other rice merchants, jealous of this one merchant's profits, had sent the anonymous accusations. Based on my cadre's report, I informed the province chief, who sent police into the village. They confiscated the merchant's stores of rice and informed him that he had been dismissed from his appointed positions, which would now be taken over by the police.

One week later, my secret agent was shot and killed. I went to visit his wife, and she told me what had happened. He had been shot, not by the Communists, but by the rice merchant and his guards. Communists would have come at night; these killers came from the village hamlet at sunset. Everybody saw them. When they reached his house, they called out his name. He was scared, so he hid under the bed. Countryside houses are not made of concrete, but of bamboo and wood, with wide spaces in between, through which people can see. They used a flashlight to locate him, then shot him from up close three times. They made sure he was dead before they left. All of the neighbors stayed away. His wife, who was terrified, dared not scream for fear that they would kill her. When I heard about this, I arranged that his widow receive a year's salary from the center.

Between 1966 and 1969, I worked at the Census Grievance Center. The people who were pro-Communist did not like me. One night three men suddenly entered my yard wearing military uniforms and carrying long rifles. Just at that time, by accident, my daughter opened the door and went outside to urinate. A soldier entered my wife's bedroom. She was very afraid! She shrieked loudly. The man searched the bedroom. When he did not find me, he came out, swore rudely, and shouted, "He's run away already!"

These men mistakenly thought that I was sleeping in the same bed-room with my wife. But at that time I was in another room with my son, the pilot, who had come to visit me from Saigon.

Our house was divided into three sections: a large front portion that was rented by an American; a middle portion that contained a storeroom, our kitchen, and my wife's bedroom; and the back sec-tion of three bedrooms, separated from the rest of the house, where I was staying. One of the soldiers had run into the middle section of the house, a second stayed between the two buildings, and the third remained outside on the driveway area on the right side of the compound.

I looked through the shutters and I could see the two men who were outside. Our dogs were barking; my wife was screaming, "Why! Why!" She had tried to close the door, but the man had not let her. He had said, "I want to find someone." Then she had fainted and lay on the ground unconscious. For 15 minutes the third man searched inside the middle building. In the meantime, my son prepared his small pistol. Within the room we both remained si-lent. I also had a pistol which I kept in the closet, and I figured to grab it if they knocked. But they didn't come over to check the third building. Apparently they figured that it was rented by some-one else.

Tet 1968

In 1968 I was in charge of propaganda through the Census Grievance Center. We were just preparing for the New Year when one of the cadres told me that a large Catholic village near a forest area had been attacked by the Viet Cong. I was still calm, but later in the day I heard that the Communists had attacked the railway station in our city. I was at home, which was right across the street from a lot of American warehouses. I heard gunshots and we went to take a look, along with a couple of guards who stayed with me. About a mile from where I lived people were fighting. We watched. I was not afraid because at that time the Communists were using only pistols, no dynamite. Also, nearby we had a military camp used not for regular fighting, but to keep order and guard the city.

They now were ordered to fight the Viet Cong, but since they were not really fighting men, these guards were kind of scared.

The market was closed for the New Year. I found out that the Viet Cong started their attack early in the morning by shooting into the police stations and military camps. Later, helicopters chased after the V.C., who hid around the houses and shot back. The helicopters shot at the V.C. with big machine guns. Houses were burned, and many V.C. were killed, but so were the inhabitants of the houses. One of my friends whose house was burned escaped with one child, but his wife and another child died, along with three V.C. The fighting around the houses lasted for a couple of hours.

The next day, one of my American employers took me to see up close what had happened. In one section, I saw six houses that had been burned to the ground. Inside were about 25 V.C., with their partially burned bodies bloated a lot and smelling terrible; also lying there were a couple of cows, three pigs, and a number of chickens and ducks.

That afternoon, we traveled out to the Catholic village that had been attacked the day before. We were taken to a large ditch about 400 meters from the main road. About 40 bloated stinking bodies lay there, in their black uniforms with high collars. Because of the stench, I did not go too close, but I saw that they had been shot, not burned as in the city. They were not teen-agers, but young men in their twenties and thirties. Because of the smell, the Americans said they couldn't cover up the bodies with soil; they preferred to blow up the area with a bomb. Others brought soil and filled the ditch.

The village itself suffered no damage, and none of its inhabitants were killed. The South Vietnamese Army had ordered people not to shoot off firecrackers during the New Year celebrations because they did not want the sounds to be confused with gunshots. The people did not listen. Many of the soldiers joined their families during the celebrations. Only a few men remained at their posts. Even so, the V.C. could not win when they attacked.

In the North, the Communists cheated their soldiers and the common people with propaganda claiming that the people of the

South were waiting for them to come, especially at the New Year time. Everybody in the North believed this; all they had to do was to go to the South for a celebration, to join their relatives, not to fight. Because of this, young children, 13 to 15 years of age, volunteered. They did not know anything when they were armed with guns. They were not well trained, and in the confusion of the battle, many of these youngsters got separated and lost. They would go to the main road and ask people which way to go. The people recognized that they were from the North, and they arrested them. Guns were not needed; they were children and did not resist. I myself did not see these children, but many villagers told me about this. They felt sorry for the children, for they saw them as cheated by the Communists.

Later everything settled down and I found out about the attacks in other places: in Hue, where the Communists executed and buried thousands of people; in Saigon, where they attacked the American embassy and other important places too. In these attacks, the V.C. always wanted to win, but they didn't care about the people they used. They felt no regret for the bodies they left behind. I felt so sorry for the people above the seventeenth parallel, who believed the lies that had been told to them, that the South was poor, that we needed their financial help, and that we would join with them for liberation against the government of the South. I've heard stories of old men from the North after the 1975 Communist victory bringing a couple of china bowls and a pair of chopsticks to their sons in the South, only to find, in disbelief, that their sons owned two-story houses and large automobiles, possessions beyond the wildest dreams of their poor duped fathers.

During my days in the Census Grievance Center, I became involved as a candidate for election to congress. In our area there were 31 candidates for four positions. As the head of the Census Grievance Center, I had much support from many cadres and staff people, and I thought that I had a good chance to win, since many people approved of my activities. I ran because I was from a poor family, and I wanted to earn the 50,000 piasters a month salary. It was a gamble; in the end I spent 100,000 piasters on the election.

One of the leading candidates opposed me specifically because of my position on the Census Grievance Center; he used it as a target to attack me and tried in many ways to discredit me. One time he announced that the Center had been canceled, that it was no longer in service. This man also printed personal cards that falsely claimed he had held a number of important posts. At one debate among the candidates, a man from one of those organizations stood up and asked, "I have been the secretary of that organization for several years. How come I have never met you? What years were you there?" The candidate turned pale and said he didn't remember.

During the month of campaigning, I traveled to various locations. I explained to people how to vote. "At this time, there are many candidates from many parties," I said. "But you, the villagers, do not know how to distinguish the good people from those who are not. If you don't weigh your vote carefully, you will make a big mistake, and it will be very harmful for you and all the country. Now we have in front of us the Communists, who are very dangerous. If we are not powerful enough, the Communists will invade our country."

"We have something to ask you," they would say. "Why does the American Army spread the powder [defoliants] to dry our gardens?"

I would reply, "The Americans do not spread that everywhere, only on the sides of the road where the Communists ambush people or live, because the Communists hide under the thick bushes. This helps to chase away the Communists. After there is damage from defoliation, the Americans will pay back the farmer. They are ordered to check the damage and repay you. Now I ask you something. You have enough sewers and bridges, but at night the Communists come to your hamlet and order all people to dig up the road. You dare not oppose them. You work without pay for them. You destroy the road, the bridge, the sewers, and you lack these things for your daily use. Did you claim these with them?"

They would keep silent.

I thought I ran a good campaign, but when the votes came in, I was sixth; only four were elected. My big rival also lost; he came in fifth. Of the four who won, three were Catholics who were supported by Catholic voters. The top candidate was an outstanding lawyer.

At the end of 1969 the military province chief in my area was replaced by a new man. By the way he spoke, I realized that the new chief didn't want to continue the Census Grievance Center. I resigned and took another position as a warehouse security chief employed by the Americans.

Many province and district chiefs were corrupt. The staff of the Census Grievance Center put their lives on the line; their primary aims were to stop the Viet Cong and to uncover corruption.

[See also Chapters 3, 14, and 34.]

CHAPTER 17

War with the Americans and Life After: 1965–1980

NARRATOR 3: NORTH VIETNAMESE CHINESE–VIETNAMESE ELDER

The narrator describes how the citizens of Hanoi survived the war years. Mr. Chung tells of food shortages, propaganda techniques to instill hatred of the Americans, and the most terrifying event of that period, the 1972 American Christmas bombing of Hanoi. After the war, he observes that the enthusiasm of people declined for Communist holidays and celebrations. As a long-time resident of Hanoi, his negative views of Communist society differ from the sympathetic accounts of many Western writers, such as Gough 1978, and mesh more closely with those of Western and Vietnamese writers, such as Scholl-Latour 1985, Truong Nhu Tang 1985, and Nguyen Long 1981, who have become disillusioned with the Socialist Republic of Vietnam.

War with the Americans

During my entire time in Hanoi under the Communist regime, I did not see anybody die of starvation, but we had lots of food shortages, lack of nutrition, and malnutrition. If we had no rice, we ate manioc and sweet potatoes; we had something to fill our stomachs, but that's all.

Before 1965 we had enough rice to eat. During the war with the Americans, we had shortages of food. Those who worked at heavy labor received 20 kilograms of rice a month; white collar and office workers got 13 kilos. If we wanted more because a friend visited us or for ourselves, the ration was not enough. Then we could buy from the black market, where the price was triple. Small businesses operated simultaneously with the black market, which we called the "free market." It was like a safety valve. People who could save some of their harvest could sell it for more. This was forbidden, but officials closed their eyes, turned the other way.

A small seller would bring a toothbrush, toothpaste, and some soap on a tray. If a customer wanted to buy something which he didn't see, he'd ask, "Do you have talc powder?" The seller would look at the buyer to try to determine whether or not he was a disguised policeman. If he thought it safe, he'd say, "Yes, but at home. Wait, I'll get it." He'd return in a couple of minutes with the item.

There were not enough goods in the government shops, so whenever people heard that, say, shirts would be sold, they'd wait in long lines. People who had good connections with those inside bought without waiting, at a higher price. For example, if I'm the salesman, someone asks me for some shirts. I sell him 20; he sells them for three times the government price and gives me a cut. When the people waiting in line reach me, I say, "No more." Normally the state store is almost always empty.

One winter, I wanted to buy a coat. I went to the state store: nothing; already sold; wait till next year. The next year, the same thing. I contacted the saleslady. I knew she wanted to go to the theater, so I gave her a gift of a ticket. I told her I wanted to buy a coat. The next time the coats came in, she set one aside for me, and I bought it.

During the war against the Americans, Communist propaganda was so perfect that they made people believe they were fighting for a just cause, their own freedom versus the American invader, who was not just. We were told that the South was part of our country. At first we feared the Americans; we thought they were strong. But after some encounters with them, our military forces said that they were not unbeatable. We believed we'd win because we had a just cause.

My only doubts came during the 12-day bombardment in the North. I was so afraid. Except for those times, all of us believed that in the final stage of the struggle we would win. Militarily the Americans could win the war, but to control the population would be impossible.

In their propaganda, the Communists used the Americans as the scapegoat for all their failures. If a construction project failed, it was the fault of the Americans; economic failure was caused by the Americans. Wherever in the world there was disaster, destruction, and death, the Americans did it; they were the reason for struggles for independence in all places. I have described the people's opinion, not mine.

When the Communists write history, they see everything they do as correct; everyone else is wrong. And if history doesn't fit their view, they rewrite history. According to the Communists, the Japanese surrender in 1945 came not because America dropped two atomic bombs on them, but because Russia invaded Northern Japan. That's history prepared by the North Vietnamese; that's what they teach children in school.

But no propaganda could keep away my fear during the 12-day bombardment of 1972. Because we had been at war for a long time, the people of Hanoi and the nearby countryside were very alert to air raids. When they occurred, the people headed for the concrete and brick air raid shelters. These were underground a few steps, not too deep. Up to 30 people could fit into the big ones, and some were even outfitted with lights. There were many shelters throughout the city. The big ones were placed where there was space; individual one-person shelters with concrete lids were buried in front of houses, about 20 for every 30 houses. In a critical situation, two people could jump into the same individual shelter. Because I had lived in Hanoi a long time, I knew where to find shelters quickly, especially those in my neighborhood. I could draw a map of them.

For several months Hanoi had lived peacefully without incidents. Suddenly about eight in the evening, alarms sounded. I was on my bicycle, going to see a friend who lived about 30 kilometers outside of Hanoi. I was scared; I hurried inside a shelter. I remember the long rumbling. For two minutes everything trembled. I realized right away that we were being attacked by B-52s, the bombers that really scared us. I have never heard that kind of noise, never experienced such a bombing during the war.

The following day, Hanoi was evacuated. Many people moved to the countryside; they went everywhere, to the houses of relatives, or other places, and they did it without assistance. The villagers were not really happy to see such large numbers of city people, but since the order to evacuate was the policy of the Communist regime, they had to let the people stay. In Hanoi, only those on duty stayed behind, along with those who wanted to remain: they were allowed to if they wished. My mother and mother-in-law moved out, but my wife and I remained because we had a good shelter located in our house.

I helped my mother and daughter move to the countryside, where bombing was more scattered, and then I returned to Hanoi. My mother was affected by the bombardment. She became scared, and as a result a blood vessel broke and she became paralyzed. I brought her to a relative's house outside of Hanoi. She survived those days and lived until 1978 when, at over the age of 80, she died in bed.

In Hanoi, the air defense battery was so near the civilian area that civilians could not avoid being hit during bombings. Every time civilian targets were hit by chance, the Communists made quite a fuss about it; their purpose was to cause hatred. Many people were killed during the 12-day bombardment, especially in one area. I saw a row of houses turn into ashes during this period. The purpose of the bombing was to force the Communists to the conference table.

At first we were really scared of the bombings; later we got used to it. All through the night the terrible bombardment continued. When we heard the alarm, my family and my wife's brothers and sisters would climb immediately into the shelter. I'd get in fast, but my wife was much braver than I; she'd get in slower. Every night we'd hear a mixture of terrible noises: the B-52s, the bombs, the trembling of the house, the sounds of guns. Militiamen with small guns were stationed on the roofs of four-story buildings. They were taught to aim directly at planes as they came in toward them, and not to aim at the side. When the bombing was done by jet planes, the people were not so scared, and many would get out of the shelters to watch. When they saw the jets hit, they clapped, "It's down!" Even though people told me to go up and watch, I never dared to do that. I never saw any of the captured pilots, except in newspapers. Since I am afraid, I never looked for that.

During the day, I went to work as usual, and there I was assigned by my superiors for special duties. We were all supposed to comfort those who were injured. I did not work directly with the injured; I came to get information and reports. Mostly I attended meetings, collected information on casualties, and gave advice to people on how to leave the city. I told them that at this time it was too dangerous to remain and showed them where to go when the police forced them to move out of destroyed areas. I worked for a government organization, but many other agencies did the same emergency work.

Even though the air raids were horrible, I thought that they couldn't force the people to surrender. A troop landing would have to be made. Even if 50,000 American soldiers had attacked, it would not have been enough to make the North Vietnamese surrender. People thought that they had never experienced such an odd war. They could predict *when* places would be hit: first Nghe An, then Ninh Binh, then Hanoi. It was strange: why didn't the Americans strike Hanoi, the headquarters, first? Why did they strike the southern part of North Vietnam first and then move slowly upward? The Americans might have ended the war in Vietnam if they could have shaken hands with China; they were afraid of Chinese intervention.

America came as an army of pride, a proud army that had never been defeated before. The Americans could not defeat the North Vietnamese because they couldn't see beyond themselves and failed to understand the North Vietnamese. Before the Communist takeover, the majority of people were illiterate, and they blindly followed the Communist propaganda that they were Number One. They were so ignorant about other countries and things. They were like kids who are told what to do, with no chance to know, read books, and compare. They were taught that they were the best. They could not make analyses. They were like a horse with blindfolds: if you read only one book, you know only one, so you think it's the best. If you can read many, you can make comparisons, and see that one is not the best.

The Communists are afraid of people knowing too much, afraid of the intellectuals, whom they consider to be a knife with a two-edged blade: they know too much; they seem to yield on the surface, but in fact think in a different way.

Ninety percent of the North Vietnamese are poorly educated; they are fanatics. If they met a force so powerful that they couldn't deal with it head-on, they would fight guerrilla warfare. The people of the countryside were trained by the Communists so that they could survive a long war. The peasants were more easily mobilized. They were the poor people who were given some help by the Communist government. The peasants could not be swayed. Only the city people wanted the American liberation because they knew that their lives were so miserable.

Life After the War

Our most important festival is National Day, on the second of September. Each National Day, employees had to participate in the demonstrations. This meant they had to get up at 4:00 to 5:00 A.M. Everyone was afraid; all had to join. Each group and department head had a list of all participants. When the group head gave orders, people followed. They remembered what the Communists had done. They had cleared the streets of cheaters, gamblers, and prostitutes. There used to be lots of beggars, but none later! They were arrested by the police. They gave a very bad image to the new regime; everyone had to work. This was not an improvement; they worked because of fear. Afterwards, we could not see any beggars on the street anymore. They were all "reeducated," and people on the street were hungrier than ever! The standard of living of the people was not raised, only the fear. We cannot use the word "improvement" because the Communists are the poorer people. How can you improve the lives of the rich? How can you use the word "improvement"? We are the rich, not the proletariat. When the Americans came to South Vietnam, there were improvements because the standard of living of the people was uplifted; this changed life in South Vietnam. Many Vietnamese became rich, and they were grateful to the Americans.

It might be true in the case of the peasants that life improved, especially after land reform. But it was not true for the city people. We were taught to be grateful to the Party when we were made *poorer*. But people dared not say anything. It was only between relatives and good friends that we could confide in each other. Publicly everyone had to talk in the Communist way, showing that they had learned the Communist lessons: their country became independent; they should be grateful to the Party; every country in the world soon would be on the way to Communism; and the Party had led to great victories, which made the people proud. Such ideas.

By 6:00 A.M. on National Day, the demonstrations had begun, and they lasted until 9:00 or 9:30. The army, then the civilians passed by the reviewing stands, and then marched through the streets to various parts of the city. We were well dressed, with clean shirts and trousers. We walked in rows, raised our hands, and chanted. One year it was, "Down with Ngo Dinh Diem!" In other years we chanted other things. Everyone had to raise their hand and chant; otherwise they would be accused of being reactionary. During wartime, such demonstrations were limited because of the fear of bombardment. During those years we held only meetings at certain squares or in big halls.

When the Communists took over South Vietnam, the people of North Vietnam did not participate in demonstrations, for they had become sick of them. They did not oppose the Communists directly, but passively. The government knew a lot about the people, realized they were resistant, and so they organized only small demonstrations in the squares, not on the streets.

As I marched on National Day, I had no thoughts. I was only a small part of a big engine that is going. I had no reactions. I just followed orders automatically, like a machine, for when we think, we can realize what is right and wrong. On account of threats of arrest, we dared not be against them.

Around 9:30 A.M. we usually ended up at some square. After that, we marched through the streets to different parts of the city. Around noon we disbanded.

In the afternoon, we participated in many activities: watching soccer games, boating on Hoan Kiem Lake, going to the movies, and music in the evenings. I liked the soccer games.

After 20 years under Communism, I noticed that the speeches at the reviewing stand on National Day had become shorter and shorter. In the early years, the speeches of the Communists had been long; the people had listened patiently, for they didn't know Communism. But after 20 years of living with them, the people were sick of them, so the Communists made shorter speeches, just propaganda about the achievements of the past year. The speakers, all members of the Politburo, were very good at delivering speeches. The only thing, though, was that the leaders were so old that they delivered speeches slowly. Over the 20 years or more that the Communists were in power, I heard many of their leaders, mostly on the radio or, since most North Vietnamese did not have radios, over loudspeakers, which broadcast their words. I was annoyed a lot by the loudspeakers; they blasted all day into my ears, and I couldn't take a nap. The loudspeakers would be used when something important needed to be said.

Occasionally we had to participate in demonstrations to oppose things. For example, we marched to support the Buddhist movement in the South [1963], or to oppose the propagation of certain rules in the South, which we called "Fascist Rules." These were minor demonstrations which were held because the government put a high value on politics and wanted all people to be politically minded. I never attended the demonstrations against the American prisoners of war, but I saw pictures of them being marched around Hoan Kiem Lake while people threw rocks at them. This was to show antagonism to them and to denounce them as war criminals. The Communists arranged such things. Who would throw rocks? Not the people, but the Communist organizers. They assigned who would throw the rocks, who would do the chanting and denouncing, "Down with the American imperialists!" This hatred could only be carried out among people affected by the bombardment, but not everyone. The Communists tried to instigate hatred in that way. No hatred could be provoked in me. I knew it was just a staged drama.

[See also Chapters 5, 15, and 39.]

CHAPTER 18

The Death Toll in My Family: 1945-1975

NARRATOR 2: SOUTH VIETNAMESE ELDERLY RURAL WOMAN

This chapter is a sobering reminder of the devastation that war in Vietnam brought to many families. Ba That explains why her relatives split their support, some of them supporting the Communists, and others the Nationalists. On both sides, members of her family were killed as a result of this conflict. War disrupted the lives of virtually everyone in her family.

I remember the time I was staying at my mother's house. She had passed away about one month earlier, in May 1945. Her house was in a hamlet on one side of a small river. My fourth brother and his family had come to live in a hamlet downstream on the other side of the river. The two hamlets were joined by a bridge. The Japanese were losing the war, so the revolution of the Viet Minh had begun. One day, someone came to us and said that my fourth brother wanted us to visit him. Because my fourth brother worked as a police officer for the French, the Viet Minh had arrested him, along with some other suspects. We were told that he was at the meeting house near the bridge. My husband, another brother, and I went to see him and found that he had been placed in stocks located behind the meeting house. Some people like my brother had one foot locked in the stocks; others whose crimes were more severe had both feet fastened. The Viet Minh would not let us speak to him. They were in doubt about the new people whom they had arrested. We were afraid; I did not dare to say anything for fear that they would arrest me too!

The Viet Minh were very severe. They didn't say anything to us. They just imprisoned my brother there for a few days, then led him off to a very large forest. He remained with them for nearly two years. Then they released him, and he joined the police force in a nearby provincial capital city.

During the time of his confinement, the Viet Minh fed him twice a day with a handful or two of rice and a few pieces of salt. I don't know what he did in the forest. But he said they had no houses. They lived under the trees and hid. When they heard airplanes, they'd push all the prisoners underground in very big holes. Those who had a very serious crime were pushed into the hole with their hands tied. If spotted, the airplane shot them, but the Viet Minh ran and hid elsewhere.

My fourth brother had two sons, twins. When their father was taken by the Viet Minh, they were very sad. They both decided to join the Viet Minh in the hope that this would help to get their father released. The eldest twin, who like his father had been a policeman, joined the propaganda program for the Viet Minh. The younger one joined their army. He later said to his elder brother, "You can do whatever you want, but I'm never coming back to work with the French, even if Father is released." And that's what happened. The elder brother had a fiancee in the provincial city. He wanted to return to her. So later he secretly left the forest and rejoined the police with his father. By that time, his fiancee had already married another man, so he married someone else. They had three children, two boys and a girl. The younger twin stayed with the Viet Minh.

My two nephews, the sons of my fourth brother, loved each other. Even though they fought on opposite sides of the war, this did not affect their family; this is obligated. They said to each other, "Now each of us is going our separate way, but we pray that we never have to see each other because we fear we might shoot each other."

One time before going into the forest with the other Viet Minh troops, the younger twin nephew visited me in my upstream hamlet. He carried a very long rifle, and he wore a soldier's uniform that was between yellow and brown in color. He said, "Our troops are in the hamlet, so I came to visit you, Auntie, for a little while." At that time, the troops did not have enough food, so they had given him two boiled duck eggs. He had put them in his pocket to save for food. Then he said, "I've been eating too many boiled duck eggs, and they're giving me indigestion." He pulled them out of his pocket and offered them to my children.

I said, "I'm afraid of guns."

He laughed, "There's nothing to be afraid of with the gun." He pointed the gun to the floor and pretended to pull the trigger.

I screamed with terror, "Don't do that! It might explode!"

He laughed. "There's nothing for you to be afraid of." He seemed so happy, even though he had to go and fight.

At that point I heard the dogs bark, so I tried to hurry him, "Let's go."

"That's all right, Auntie, I'm just visiting you for a little while; then I'll go."

That was the last time I saw him alive. He did not come home to take any food at all.

In 1954, two months before the war stopped for a temporary armistice, as he was riding a bicycle into a hamlet in the late afternoon, the French opened fire and killed him. About a year later, his brother was killed in a jeep accident.

When my mother passed away, her lands were divided among all of her children, as she had wished. But since my fourth brother had joined the police force, the Viet Minh seized his property.

My ninth sister got really upset. She couldn't say anything while she remained in the village. The villagers competed with one another over our property, complaining, "Some have more, some have less." When her son, ten years old, climbed the coconut tree in his grandmother's yard to pick coconuts, some of the villagers who supported the Viet Minh, and who were also our distant relatives, pointed at him and threatened, "If you continue to climb, we'll tie you up when you get down. We'll arrest you!"

My ninth sister replied, "It's the property of my parents, but they want to arrest and tie us!"

My ninth sister told the Viet Minh that she wanted the property for the fourth brother's son, who was in the Viet Minh Army. Because of this, the Viet Minh left that property in the care of my ninth sister. When that young man was killed, the Viet Minh took back the property; in fact they took all of our property except that belonging to my ninth, tenth, and sixth sisters.

My fourth brother had both a legal wife and a concubine who had a son and a daughter by him. The son joined a commando unit run by a Vietnamese French citizen; when they caught Viet Minh soldiers, they gave them the choice of joining the commando unit or being shot. They protected many people from the Viet Minh. They would also capture Viet Minh couriers and collectors of money. Because they recruited the Viet Minh to turn against their own group, the commandos could identify the Viet Minh and often found out where they stayed in the forest. In 1954, the French and Viet Minh signed an armistice, but the terrorism continued. This commando son of my fourth brother was killed by the Viet Minh in 1956. So all three sons of my fourth brother were killed: two in the forest, and one in a traffic accident.

That was not the end of misfortune for my fourth brother. In 1957 he was appointed a notable of his home village. He was stationed at a village and military post close to his home village. He lived in the third village on the other side of the river. To get to work every morning, he would ride his bicycle to the river and use a ferryboat to get to the other side.

The Viet Minh watched his travel routine and organized a trap to kill him. One day a distant relative of his invited him to participate in a ceremony and feast in memory of the death of a relative. The ceremony would be held in my brother's home village. When my brother went to the ceremony, the people delayed the feast; it did not end until 4:00 P.M. Then someone hid his sun helmet. He spent about 30 minutes looking for it, then left without it. By the time he reached the ferry, it was 6:00 P.M. In our country, that is quite late; by that time, we do not see the sun; it is dark. The ferryman helped the Viet Minh terrorists. My brother got on his bicycle. When he went about 100 yards, the terrorists stopped him and tried to tie him up to carry him into the forest. He resisted by putting the bicycle between himself and them, so they cut him into pieces with an ax.

He was killed on Friday. Not until Sunday did his wife and concubine find out what happened to him. They were informed by pedestrians who found pieces of the corpse on the road. His concubine told my husband, who informed the District Chief. This man spoke angrily, "Why did this man dare to go deeply into the hamlet? He knew it was dangerous."

The District Chief sent soldiers to the spot. They gathered the pieces and buried him in the village where he had been living. At that time we were living in the provincial capital. When I was told how my fourth brother died, I thought the Viet Minh were cruel. Even relatives: they set up the trap and killed him. I knew the two brothers who did this, and why they betrayed my fourth brother.

Due to the war, relatives don't love each other any more. I had an aunt. She had a daughter who in turn had three sons. All of these people lived in our home village under Communist control. The mother of the three boys used to go to the market in the provincial capital to buy fish sauce, dry fish, dry salted fish, and medicine, which she sold regularly to the Viet Minh. This was in 1948, when people were allowed to go back and forth. One day, she took her two youngest boys with her to the market. While coming back, they walked through a large field. The French Army from a nearby post was waiting there secretly for people. They shot and killed her, along with her youngest son, who was 10 years old. Her second son, 11 years old, was wounded. Her oldest son came and brought his dead brother home. One of my husband's sisters-in-law was killed by the French in the same way.

From then on, these two boys hated the French very much. They hated whoever followed the French Army. I knew from people telling me that part of the reason that my fourth brother was killed was that he had joined the French Army, and part was a result of these two brothers, our relatives, who hated him for this.

At a later time, I met those two sons, and they talked to me in a very distasteful, disrespectful, and unfriendly way, indicating that they hated me.

They too were killed. The first was carrying a mine to put on the road when he was surprised by a French soldier who shot and killed him, tied his foot behind a truck, dragged him 300 meters into a village and left him there. That young man was about 30 years old and not educated. His brother organized a meeting in a village, the French found out, and that night they opened fire with cannon. Many people were killed, along with my relative.

In the beginning, all of the villagers joined the Viet Minh and many died in fighting against the French. I had another nephew who worked for the Viet Minh, but they suspected that he worked for both sides. One night the Viet Minh came and pulled him out of his house. He was afraid; he held onto his child. They told him they had come to shoot him but not his child. He put down the child, and they shot him right there.

They also arrested his wife and took her into the forest. Her three children were left behind, in the care of their old stepgrandmother. The Viet Minh told the mother that they had to imprison her longer. She must appear happy while a prisoner. If she appeared sad, it meant she still hated them, and she could not be released. For several months, she laughed when they laughed, smiled when they smiled. Then they released her. She and her children are still in Vietnam.

My seventh brother, a security man, married a woman who lived in a remote area far from his native village. Because he had a shotgun, the Viet Minh tried to take it away, but his wife, who was clever, hid it in a clump of bamboo near the river. Later, the Viet Minh sent another cadre, a relative of my brother's wife, to arrest and kill him. We assumed this because usually the cadres were ordered to arrest people, get them out of the village, and then kill them along the way. The quick-witted wife begged the cadre to hold her husband to speak with a Viet Minh leader. In the meantime, she was able to get a friend of hers to convince the Viet Minh leader to save her husband's life. When my seventh brother died in 1961, his wife carried his corpse back to her remote village for burial.

My eighth brother was shot and killed by French troops because they suspected that he was a Viet Minh. He lived in a village, and so he knew the Viet Minh who passed through there at night, but he was not one of them.

The ninth in the family was a sister. She did not live in the city. She had a low education and married a farmer. They had three sons and two daughters, all of whom remained in our home village during the Viet Minh period [1945–1954]. In 1954 she came to the provincial capital with all of her children. She remained there until 1975, when she returned to our home village, where all of her children knew how to cultivate, and where she had inherited some of the rice fields of our parents.

Because she had lived away from the village for many years, and because her third, fourth, and seventh brothers and one brother-in-law had worked for the French or the South Vietnamese government, she was given some trouble. Even so, she was able to claim and inherit her share, since she had written documents to prove her rights.

My third brother fought in the French Army in World War I. His eldest son worked secretly for the Viet Cong, while three of his brothers worked for the Nationalists. Two of them disappeared after 1975 and are presumed to be dead. The third was sent to a re-education camp until he became seriously ill.

Some of the people of my family wanted to join the Viet Cong. If they wanted to, it was up to them, and the family could not stop them. They had their own ideas. I think the oldest ones who are in Vietnam had to join the Viet Cong in order to survive. If they didn't, they might have been arrested. Others lived in the villages, and there they were pressured by the Communists.

Because my husband and I went to live in the city, we automatically were associated with the French. Because of this, all of our relatives who remained in the villages hated us as the enemy. The war separated everyone.

[See also Chapters 4, 28, and 35.]

Vietnam: Sorrows of Liberation

Introduction

The chapters in Part IV describe the fall of the South Vietnamese government to the Communists in 1975 and the consequences of this event in the lives of the narrators. The accounts include recollections of the collapse of Ban Me Thuot in the Central Highlands, the take-over of Saigon, life under the Communists in South Vietnam, the effects of Communist rule on Buddhists, and the reeducation camp experiences of two ex-officers of the defeated Army of the Republic of Vietnam.

Those Vietnamese who had lived in the North, who had already experienced life under Communist rule and who in 1954 had fled as refugees to the South, were particularly adamant in their opposition to the Communists, and were less inclined to believe the promises of the North, that the liberation of the country and its reunification would bring freedom. Most of these people made strenuous efforts to escape either at the fall of Saigon in 1975 or in later years.

The narrators who came from the South and those portions of Central Vietnam that were under Southern control viewed the fall of South Vietnam in 1975 as the central public event of their lives. Many of them claimed that they did not realize what would happen to them; since they were not prominent military or civilian officials, they assumed that they would be allowed to resume their lives without significant disruption. That is what the North Vietnamese had proclaimed, and they believed it. They were relieved that 30 years of warfare had ended, and they could now resume peacetime lives. When their social, religious, and political freedoms were removed, relatives, friends, or themselves sent off to reeducation camps, their private lives scrutinized, their currency abolished, much of their property confiscated, and their food reduced to survival rations while corruption increased, the narrators felt that they had been betrayed.

Particularly striking to me were the statements made by many narrators that they were prepared to accommodate to the Communist life-style until they saw that they were being treated not as brothers and sisters under one flag but as a conquered people looted and terrorized for the benefit of their new rulers. They were particularly outraged at the treatment meted to those persons taken away for reeducation, which they saw as little more than punishment and revenge. That is why those who fled Vietnam become so emotional about Communism, which they view not as a liberating force but its antithesis; the denial of freedom has a special significance for these people because of what they have experienced in Vietnam.

The narrators claim that virtually all Vietnamese people, except those specifically in power, would leave Vietnam if they could, given its present conditions. In fact, probably less than two percent have done so. Still, that adds up to well over one million people who fled, often at great personal risk to themselves, with the threat of possible retribution to their relatives left behind. This is the first time in the history of Vietnamese civilization that an exodus such as this has occurred. It has involved people in all stations of life and from different regions. They claim that they have been betrayed and that their human rights and freedoms have been violated. Both their number and their diversity indicate that they cannot be dismissed simply as a small group of disgruntled ex-elites; rather they represent a wide range of people who have found conditions in Vietnam to be intolerable. Their stories tell why this is so.

CHAPTER 19

Saigon Falls: 1975

NARRATOR 12: EX-ARVN COLONEL

In June 1975, tens of thousands of officers of the defeated Army of the Republic of Vietnam turned themselves in for what their North Vietnamese captors billed a ten-day political study period. The men were told to bring food to last them during this period. But, to their astonishment and despair, instead of being released after ten days, they were subjected to months and years of starvation, degradation, body-numbing physical labor, endless indoctrination sessions, and forced confessions designed to crush their spirits. Some prisoners resisted; others committed suicide; a few became informers for the Communists, for which they received extra food and privileges. As the years went by, other prisoners were sent to these "reeducation" camps: officials of the old administration, Catholic priests, Buddhist monks and nuns, writers, many professional people, and men or women who resisted or spoke out against the new regime. Virtually all of these people were held without trial for indefinite periods. Untold numbers of prisoners died; others were sent home, ravaged by disease and often near death. Some 5,000 prisoners have never been released.

Vietnamese Communist reeducation camps are not new; published accounts in Vietnamese describe camp life since before 1954 and up through the 1980s, providing documentation of continuous persecution of political prisoners, most of whom were never given a trial. (In English, see Doan

Van Toai and Chanoff 1986, Nguyen Ngoc Ngan and Richey 1982, Nguyen Van Canh 1983, and Sagan and Denney 1983.) Most accounts describe conditions of incarceration in South Vietnam, where the treatment of prisoners, however terrible, was milder than in Central and North Vietnam.

This narrative follows the life of a colonel who was sent first to the southern camps, but later to the harsher camps of North and Central Vietnam, reserved for high officers and difficult resistance cases. The colonel, born in 1927 and reared in Laos, speaks six languages: Vietnamese, Lao, Thai, Chinese, French, and English. After completing his university degree in Literature in 1948 at the University of Hanoi, he worked for some five years as a teacher in Vientiane and as a businessman in Bangkok. From 1953 to 1956 he was a member of the French Army; in 1956 he became a member of the South Vietnamese Army. In 1963, he was one of a number of young officers who participated in the overthrow of the Diem government. To disperse the power of these men, they were subsequently sent to posts outside of Saigon; for two years the colonel was stationed as a military attaché in another Asian country. In 1966 he returned to Saigon as an intelligence officer in the Ministry of Defense, where he gained increasingly higher positions until the fall of Saigon in 1975. In June 1975 he began his six years of incarceration in Communist reeducation camps.

In North and Central Vietnam, the colonel received unusually harsh treatment, especially in those camps run by the brutal guards of the Public Security Agency. He describes starvation, horrible conditions of crowding, and punishment by isolation in cells with no light. Twice the colonel tried to commit suicide, but a close friend and fellow prisoner provided him with the spiritual guidance that enabled him to endure. After six years he was released, but only because he was so ill that his captors figured he would die; by sending him away, his anticipated death would not be attributed to the reeducation camp. Later, while attempting to escape from Vietnam, he and his son were captured and jailed for nearly a year in a South Vietnamese town. On his sixth attempt to escape, the colonel left Vietnam through Cambodia to Thailand, where he was placed in a refugee detention camp that was in some respects as terrible as the Vietnamese camps and jails in which he had been incarcerated.

The colonel's account is significant for several reasons. His is a rare detailed description published in English of the horrors of the northern and the central camps. Because of his language background, the colonel was able to talk with people in a wide variety of settings in which he found himself. These included the Lao-speaking Tay tribe peoples of North Vietnam, who tried to help the prisoners, and large numbers of prisoners. The colonel's army intelligence background prepared him to be an exceptionally acute observer and recorder of detail. Particularly unusual is his analysis of his own emotional states throughout his ordeals, including his indecision during the days preceding the fall of Saigon. When he and his family were unable to escape, his wife blamed him for his mistake, and this contributed to his deep depression as a reeducation camp prisoner. Also unparalleled is his insider's description of Vietnamese jails.

While in the far north, the colonel met and talked with people who have been held prisoners by the Communists since the early 1950s, including Vietnamese Catholics involved in the Quynh Luu revolt of 1953 and Vietnamese soldiers of the French Army who chose to remain in the North in 1954, but who are now relocated near the border. The colonel realized that he, just as they, had been sent to languish and die in the camps.

Several months before the colonel came to America, a lifelong friend of his told me about him and his impending arrival. I thought that the colonel would have a significant story to tell and remarkable abilities to tell it. I considered it especially important to talk with him soon after his arrival in America, when his memories were still fresh.

Within about three weeks of coming to America, the colonel visited his friend, who had previously informed him of my project. Because the colonel was on his way to a job interview in another part of the United States, he recommended that we conduct lengthy intensive interviews. Over a period of three days, we met for a total of 28 hours, which I taped. He has since supplemented those materials with some written accounts which are also included in this narrative.

During his years as a prisoner, the colonel's body weight dropped by almost one-half, from 75 to about 40 kilograms. The ravages of his experience showed in his gaunt face, deep sunken eyes, prematurely gray hair, and in his slow speech and weary movements. Despite the pain it brought, he insisted on recalling his experiences in detail so that Americans will know of the ordeal of the reeducation camp prisoners.

Since the time of our interviews, the colonel has taken a job as an employment and adjustment counselor for Indochinese refugees.

As dawn broke on April 30, 1975, the last American helicopters took off from the top roof of the U.S. Embassy on Thong Nhat Boulevard. They flew up and off towards the southeast, the seaside, carrying with them the last American rear guard, leaving behind an unknown number of people, Americans as well as Vietnamese, who had been authorized to enter the U.S. Embassy compound in preparation to depart. They had waited their turn since the night before. Now the deadline was over. My family and I were among those left behind. (For other accounts see Butler 1985, Isaacs 1984, Snepp 1978, and Terzani 1976.)

As the helicopters disappeared in the distance, there was some scattered small-arms firing at them from the ground, and the reverberation as they returned the fire. Then everything sank into a strange silence. On various streets, small groups of exhausted people reeled under the weight of shoulder packs and handbags; others dropped their heavy belongings on the street and rested their weary bodies. They had criss-crossed the city to and from the evacuation in futile attempts to escape. Usually the streets bustled with vehicles and with busy trade; not now.

Around 10:00 A.M., from many routes, North Vietnamese soldiers marched into the capital city of Saigon. First came dispersed infantry squads or platoons in long lines heading to the heart of the Capital. Near noon, tanks rumbled through the streets headed for the Independence Palace. Late in the afternoon, more tanks appeared, preceding columns of trucks transporting troops and towing long guns. They positioned themselves at important intersections.

There was no trace of the Army of the Republic of Vietnam (ARVN) which just the day before, as it had for decades, dominated the city. Now all that remained was their military gear strewn along the streets: new olive fatigues with rank insignia, unit badges, intact name plates, well-polished leather military boots, helmets, dismantled M-16 rifles; even jeeps with radios and long antennas which revealed that their past owners had been high-ranking officers. On some streets, entire retreating units had left such enormous piles of gear and boots that the streets came to be known as "Highway of Boots." Young recruits had cast off their uniforms;

embarrassed, they straggled along the streets in their underwear until the inhabitants of the street, taking pity on them, threw down clothes from their balconies. The ARVN was no more.

I had not tried to escape until the last few days, when it was too late. Only then did I come to realize the enormity of my errors of judgment. During those last few days of the Republic, I spent most of my time in my office at the Ministry of Defense. For a few minutes each day I'd go five or six blocks to take a meal with my family, who lived in a comfortable studio in the building of a factory where my wife worked as a co-manager. On April 29, the Assistant Defense Minister and the general who was Director General of Manpower gathered their families on the ground floor of the Ministry of Defense. Then they climbed into military jeeps and, escorted by military police, they made their way to Nha Be to catch a navy ship for evacuation. I don't know what they felt inside as they and their families boarded jeeps while all of their soldiers at the Ministry looked on.

That night, under cover of darkness, I proceeded to desert my subordinates too. Escorted by my NCO aide, my NCO driver took me to the American Embassy, ten blocks away, while my family followed in our Volkswagen microbus. Each person carried a compact handbag. As we parked our vehicles, we saw a sea of refugees inside and outside the compound. I pushed my way towards the fence of the U.S. Embassy while my family followed close behind for fear that we would become separated in the turmoil of jostling, shoving bodies. Thanks to my military uniform, I was able to push through and reach the fence. I carried with me an old letter written by an American Lieutenant General who formerly had been the Deputy Chief of Staff for Intelligence, U.S. Army. The letter carried his three-star flag. I showed it to the Marine guard on duty and asked him to let me in along with my family. He took the letter inside the Embassy. When he returned, he told me to go around and try to get in by the rear gate. It was unreachable. For several hours we went around the Embassy in vain attempts to push through the densely packed crowd. To keep together, my wife, my children, and my other relatives walked in a queue, each clutching the flap-end garments of the person in front of them. Finally we gave up and made our way back to our vehicles, only to find that, as if by magic, all of our luggage and handbags had disappeared. Our situation could have been worse. At least the wheels on our jeeps had not disappeared, as happened to many cars. We drove back home, and I returned to the Ministry.

Later on I learned that Dr. Ho Van Cham, the Minister of Information, tried that night to climb the Embassy fence. His reward was a bleeding head, courtesy of a Marine guard on duty, who bashed him with the butt end of a gun. I think that Ho Van Cham keeps this dearly in memory as he lives out the rest of his days in reeducation camps.

Almost all of the personnel of the Ministry of Defense were left behind during the evacuation. The only ones who escaped were the Assistant Minister of Defense, two generals, and one colonel who was the last director of the cabinet. Except for me, everyone else is still in reeducation camps or jails, where they have the rest of their lives to "appreciate" the Americans and their own generals and politicians who abandoned them. I am the only one who has escaped from the country, but only after seven years of detention in eight jails: Long Giao, Tan Hiep, Yen Bai, Nghe An, Ca Mau, Ba Ria, Bien Hoa, and Sikhiu in Thailand.

By the morning of April 30, all of us at the Ministry of Defense realized that we were at the moment of collapse. Around 8:00 A.M., we agreed to melt away. One colonel volunteered to stay to make the transfer of command to the Communists. We changed into civilian clothes and, in mournful silence, stepped out of the Ministry forever. I left behind my pistol, my military gear, my personal belongings, and also my lacquered name plate inlaid with mother-of-pearl. Sadly, heavily, I strode over the paved stones, through deserted streets, until I reached home.

My wife greeted me coldly. During these last hectic days she had called me many times on the telephone urging me to let her and the children leave by the navy ship docked right at the waterfront, just a few steps from our house, but I had refused. I had been slow-minded in solving the emergency evacuation. I had figured we had a way out. I had failed to think clearly of one important fact: the Americans who knew me best were no longer in Vietnam.

How can I ever forget April 30, which began as our last faint hope for escape faded, as the world we had known ended. Faced with my wife's stony silence, I went alone into my room at the studio and listened for several hours to the Radio Saigon broadcast of the last political event of the country. I became very nervous and depressed.

The end of the Republic came at noon, at the Independence Palace, when a senior North Vietnamese officer told President Minh, "You have nothing to transfer to us; we come here to accept your surrender." These words were prophetic, for as we were soon to learn, we would be treated as a conquered people, in servitude to our Communist masters.

I went outside and watched the arrival of Communist troops in endless columns of artillery towed by trucks. Soldiers sat in the trucks and also on tanks that rumbled into the city.

The Communist soldiers looked stunned as they stared at the large crowds of civilians, with not a single ARVN soldier to be seen. Maybe they were astonished to see that the Southerners were so well fed, well clothed, and well-bred in appearance, that they rode in such luxurious cars and motorcycles. They had never seen anything like this before in North Vietnam or in the jungle where they had lived and fought all of their life.

The people of Saigon also stared and were stunned. They did not realize that the North Vietnamese had such a large army, or that they were so heavily armed with tanks and guns. Was this a "liberating" army, as they claimed, or an invading one? Just the day before, the people of Saigon had heard scare stories about how the North Vietnamese were bloodthirsty killers who would bring a bloodbath to Saigon. But what did we see? Passing before us were beardless teenagers looking so docile, peaceful, naive, dwarfed by their pith helmets, carrying rifles taller than themselves. They looked like bogus soldiers. How could they have beaten us? Each of us looked at the other with suspicion.

During the next 45 days, which were the last before my detention, my wife and I were at odds. We avoided talking to each other lest we fall into hot dispute. At lunch or dinner, we sat at the table in silence, as if we were in a house of mourning. We withdrew into our separate rooms and sank into silent, sorrowful moods and deep meditation. I understood that she was resentful about my passive attitude during the evacuation of the previous days. Many of our neighbors had succeeded in leaving Vietnam; now it was too late to take any action. I would have to break apart my family of six and let each member try to escape separately or in small groups whenever they had the opportunity. No longer could we move together.

In the days that followed, my children helped me to destroy all papers, documents, and books which we judged unfavorable for us under the new regime. This included many pictures that had recorded our good times in the diplomatic corps when we had met with high-ranking persons of the Free World. We also burned our correspondence with high dignitaries. One of my three sons and I began to till a piece of land next to our house. I dug a pond and grew corn and manioc. My wife was displeased to see me and our sons tilling the land under sun and rain. It reminded her of the old times, when she was still a girl living under Communist rule in the North, when the boors and illiterates treated intellectuals roughly. We waited uneasily for what an uncertain future would bring.

[See also Chapters 20, 21, 22, 32, and 33.]

CHAPTER 20

Prisoner Without Trial:
1975–1976

NARRATOR 12: EX-ARVN COLONEL

In this chapter, the colonel describes his first year as a reeducation camp prisoner. He recalls his initial shock as he and others are treated, not with the respect they are accustomed to, but as prisoners, and their belated realization that they have been betrayed. He describes the rotten and inadequate rations, misunderstandings between the guards and the prisoners, punishments, indoctrination sessions, and limited attempts at resistance by the prisoners. Of particular interest is how quickly, easily, and effectively the Communists were able to round up and control their prisoners. The remarkable fact is not that there was resistance, but that it was so muted: the prisoners-to-be docilely reported as ordered and were then transported to reeducation camps; they were controlled by a handful of guards and cadres; in most camps they cultivated the very crops that supported the camps: in effect, the prisoners and their families paid for their own imprisonment.

In mid-June 1975 I heard the announcement that former military officers were required to go for ten days of political study. We were told to bring just enough money and clothes to cover that period.

Close to midnight some 2,000 to 3,000 of us were called to a schoolyard and separated into groups of 40 to 50 men. Most of them were doctors, engineers, and teachers who had been in the

Army of the Republic of Vietnam. Also among us was a chef from a famous restaurant in Cholon, the Chinese section of Saigon. Because of this, I thought we were going to get VIP treatment. Now I realize that this was to lull us into unsuspecting complacency.

Around 2:00 A.M., Chinese military trucks arrived. We were loaded into them and canvas coverings were placed completely over us so that we could not see outside. We sat for hours unable to move or even turn in that crowded, suffocating space, while the loading continued. Some men needed to urinate; the guards would not let them off the truck, so the men urinated into empty bottles or nylon bags and kept it. All of us were unhappy. Some of us realized that our darkest days were coming. I felt insecure about what was to become of us.

Around 5:00 A.M. the convoy moved. People who sat near the corners of the canvas opened it a little to look out and report to the rest of us where we were going. The smokers among us were very obstinate. Despite the strong objections of others, they tried by any means to smoke, even though we were in a confined space. With this began a split between officers in the same truck: they became strangers to each other.

For seven hours we traveled nonstop. We were hungry, thirsty, and very unhappy. Finally we came to an abandoned military camp which we recognized to be Long Thanh, the rear base of the 18th Division of the ARVN. The two guards in our truck, youngsters about 18 years old, called to us to step down, stand in rows, and wait until our names were called and checked. The words they used were a shocking insult to us. They called us "Elder Brothers," but we who were in our forties and fifties were not used to such informality and familiarity from kids. As former officers and officials, we expected to be able to relax and be comfortable, not to be treated as army privates, told to line up and follow the orders of a youngster. It was a deep shock for us.

Some of us needed to urinate. Our guards refused permission categorically until all the prisoners had been checked to see that none were missing. All of us were thirsty, for we had not expected that we would need to bring water. We had figured we'd be having a feast cooked by that Chinese chef! Since they were illiterate, the PAVN (People's Army of Vietnam) did not know how to write our names correctly or form a list. They were unaccustomed to command. With their Northern accent, they mispronounced our names. As they messed things up, they got angry and shouted at us. We too became angry. Others cannot realize how we felt. Just yesterday, we had been commanding officers; now we were subordinate to illiterate youngsters. We were used to commanding such people, not to obeying them. Some of our group became very aggressive. Others, including me, feared that this would make the guards angry, and we suggested to our angry officers that they be more modest. Right from the first day, we had division and loud verbal disputes among us.

While we stood there, the commandant of the camp proceeded to give us a harangue, our first political lesson. All of us became upset. The cadre wanted to show us that he was someone important, but he didn't have rank bars on his shirt. He had reason not to wear them. All of us were very high-ranking, while he was maybe a first or second lieutenant.

The older and higher-ranking officers among us were more calm. The younger ones were more restive and tried to evade the rules. Because of them, we received more threatening treatment. The Vietnamese cadres spoke in the language of the North. At first that made us laugh, but after a while it also became boring to hear. Some of our impatient younger officers showed conceit and insolence by pulling out the hairs of their own beards. When the cadre saw this, he became furious. After making us listen to a long, rambling speech, he assigned us to various houses and finally asked if we had any questions. One man asked a question in an insulting way, using dialect that the cadre did not understand.

For lunch we were handed some rotten rice, originally from a U.S. food aid program. It had been sitting in bags in the jungle and had turned green. There were no pans or firewood; we were told to collect what we could and cook our own food. In addition, we were given a small bag of instant noodles and told to cook it in a big pan of boiling water; this would be soup. Ordinarily one person would consume that bag of noodles; now it had to be distributed to 50 or 60 people. Every one of us was discouraged. While in the field, all combat officers of the ARVN from captain on up had an orderly who had taken care of cooking, washing clothes, and other tasks. Now we ourselves had to cook rotten rice. Thus began our lives as reeducation prisoners.

We were short of everything: water, food, tobacco, drink, and other things. Because we thought we would be gone only ten days, and that we would remain in Saigon during that time, many prisoners did not bring mosquito nets, and this was the worst of all. We sat through a long night of darkness without light. Some men told funny stories to dispel the gloom; others lost their morale.

The Communist cadres did not need to prompt us; we all began to insult President Thieu, Vice-President Ky, and other officials of the former Republic of Vietnam who had flown off and left us behind. We began cursing them that first day; we still curse them.

After a few days of settling in, some prisoners were able to persuade the guards to buy them cigarettes, food, sweets, and even to send some letters to family and friends in Saigon. Some of them bribed the guards so generously that they received supplies from their families quite regularly and lived royally. This really split us apart. They never shared with us, never, and we suspected that they were antennae working for the Communists. Just a few succeeded in having their families come to visit them; the rest of us suspected them because of that. Those who were poor had no supplies at all. We'd gather and speak indirectly and sarcastically at those rich people. We'd invent stories that seemed to be about someone else, but actually were about the man right next to us. And we told stories that insinuated without directly accusing them.

Some prisoners were so *vile* that they became the servant orderlies of the rich officers, attending to their every want, washing their clothes, cooking, bringing water for the bath. For this they received food, tobacco, and other things.

Because at Long Thanh we were at a rear base, there was room for 10,000 prisoners, and that's about what we had. The guards were outside the fence; we were on the inside. Each day we had to provide a squad or platoon to do labor work at the headquarters of the Communist cadres outside our enclosure. We rotated the men who did this. To get there, we had to pass by the guards, and whenever we were outside, we had to keep in line under a leader chosen by us.

Most of us were older officers who had to wear spectacles. These were quite new and strange for the guards. North Vietnam is poor; never had these guards seen spectacles until they saw us with them. When our leader came to the gate, he had to stop and shout, "Everyone stand at attention!" Then we gave a military salute to the guard. He was very proud of this moment and not in a hurry for us to move on.

One day, the guard said angrily, "All of you take off your hats, but you *never* take off your spectacles! You are not polite to me. All of you must take off your spectacles!" He was a man from the countryside, the sort that wants to show off but makes the wrong criticism in trying to appear sophisticated.

We stood at attention and took off our spectacles while he shouted. When he finished, our group leader shouted out his report: "Honor to report, Mr. Cadre. Cell Number Three has ten persons going to labor work." Our leader then had to continue by calling out the names of the workers; to do this, he had a piece of paper with their names written on it. Instinctively he put on his spectacles to read.

The Communist private soldier stopped him and ordered, "Take off your spectacles!" Our leader did so, but he could not read the paper, so we simply stood there. Such incidents happened many times.

Each morning, around 6:00 to 6:30 A.M. we heard the beating on a piece of metal that indicated the lifting of our nightly curfew. Thousands of us were inside the fence, but our latrines were outside. We were not allowed to use them until the curfew was lifted. Also, each section of one thousand men had only two or three rows of latrines, and they were very old and quite dirty. Each morning, men would arise at 4:00 or 5:00 A.M. and wait in line for the signal to use the latrines. Some of the men had stomachaches, not so much from dysentery, which is common in the North, but from colic.

From 6:00 to 7:30 A.M. we went to the latrine, boiled water, and if we had food saved from our dinner, we ate it. Those whose families had given them supplies ate some food and coffee or tea. No breakfast was given. Some prisoners stole food from others. Because we had no room on the floor, those with extra food had to hide it somewhere else. They'd look for an empty sandbag or rice bag, hide food in it, and hang it from the corrugated iron roof.

Because of the subtropical climate, the food spoiled quickly; if the owners didn't eat it, others would steal it.

Everyone was selfish for many reasons. When our families sent supplies to us, usually they included money and a message. My wife sent me dried bananas. Inside each one she rolled a banknote that was so thin it looked like a stick. In the bottom of a bottle of meat cooked in fish sauce, she put a message wrapped in nylon. Sometimes we shared or exchanged food; if someone found money, he usually kept it, but if he found a letter, he gave it to its rightful owner. The letters were dangerous, for we never knew when a prisoner might inform the cadres. We had a few informers. We found out when the rest of us were sent North; they remained in the South.

Around 7:30 A.M. we had to study and discuss political lessons at our quarters under the supervision of the cadre; he was in charge of about 60 of us. Some of the cadres were lazy, but they also had an inferiority complex and were afraid of showing up because we would embarrass them. In discussion we might raise questions not sincerely, but with the intent to insinuate jokes and insult them. Still, the Communists were able to destroy any resistance by us or even planning for resistance because they rotated and mixed our units every three to six months.

Our lessons continued until noon, when we cooked and ate our noon meal of soup and rice so rotten it smelled when cooked. When possible, we relied on the supplies from our families.

In the afternoon, we had no discussion. Instead, we were supposed to participate in meditation, in which we thought over the lessons of the morning. In fact, we used this time to gamble, wander around, and make homemade knives, musical instruments, and domino sets. From time to time, the guards would confiscate these.

Dinner was cooked in a common kitchen for the whole subdivision, but this kind of meal most of us could not eat: rotten rice, some vegetable soup with no meat or fat but just salted water cooked with spoiled vegetables. Only the poor could eat that. Although it was forbidden, most of us cooked in our quarters using special stoves we fashioned out of milk-powder cans. With its top, we used it as a pot for cooking, but when needed, it became our stove. For fuel, we collected nylon bags in which families had sent food supplies. These bags were an efficient fuel. We cooked in the corner, with a blanket or mat covering the outside and a guard to watch for cadres.

If we were caught, we were sent into the connex, a type of big metal storage box left by the U.S. units in Vietnam. They were high enough to stand in and they had a door. Minor infractions of camp rules, such as gambling, fighting, cooking, or stealing, brought four days to a week in the connex.

For serious misbehavior such as resistance to political discussion or to cadres, our heads were shaved, we were given only one-half ration of food, and a small, half-size milk can of water a day. The shaved head was the mark of a person who had resisted a cadre's order. This was a corporal punishment: for Asian people, this is a very grave insult. Some of our officers were very proud of themselves. They saw themselves as high-ranking versus the low cadres. When they passed one another, our officers didn't salute the cadre; they'd turn aside, or they'd dare to spit in the cadre's presence. This was a big insult, a very serious one for North or South, Communist or Nationalist. When called to headquarters for criticism, these officers argued back, giving insinuating insults to the cadres or even to Communism. This earned them shaved heads.

In the connex, a prisoner could move, but he was not comfortable. In the daytime there was no air: the sun, the heat of the other men, sometimes a whole gambling party of ten prisoners crowded into the connex, made the atmosphere suffocating. At night it was cold; also, we had no bathing, and we were not allowed to leave to use the latrine. We had to urinate and defecate in improvised containers left inside the connex. Once a day the guards rotated and checked us. If the guard was friendly, he might leave the door open for a while, or even throw in a half-smoked cigarette.

For very serious punishment, a prisoner might be left in the connex for an indefinite period of time. Because he had made a political insult during our political discussion classes, one man was left inside the connex for two months. He became so seriously ill that they put him in a hospital for prisoners. For a long time we heard no news about him, for the Communists try to keep information from us. Later while working outside the compound, we met other prisoners and exchanged information on various people. From that we heard that he had been transferred to another unit.

In my group no one attempted to escape, but in others they did. After we had been in the camp for some time, some of the young men were recruited to cut firewood. Three young officers tried to escape and were immediately caught. They were beaten a few times with rifle butts. The following day the guards selected one prisoner from each subdivision to dig three graves. The Communists did this intentionally so that when the gravediggers returned to their groups, they would spread rumors that someone was dead or dying. At this point we did not know what was happening, since the events were half secret, half public. This made us worry, put us in a state of uncertainty, which is what the Communists wanted.

The next morning we were told to stay at home; there would be no political meetings, no labor. Loudspeakers were set up in every subdivision of the camp. At 7:30 A.M. the loudspeakers blared, informing us to listen to the tribunal for judging the three officers who tried to escape.

The tribunal lasted for five hours. Then came the announcement, very solemn, intended to intimidate everyone: the three evaders were convicted; all three were sentenced to death by firing squad. We had to listen to the loudspeaker until the shots rang out.

This had a big impact on us. For about three days we felt very sad. Many prisoners made comments and speculated about this event. The cadres held a special political session to discuss the incident; then we were supposed to comment on our own feelings and impressions of the event. And certainly everyone lied. But this event had a very powerful effect on us; no one else in our camp attempted to escape. Elsewhere they did. My nephew-in-law Lieutenant Chien was shot and killed while attempting to escape from Hoc Mon Camp.

In the camp I didn't notice that the prisoners had sexual desires. The food was so little and so bad that it weakened our sex appetites. Some of the younger men talked about obscene stories of sexual appetite and so on. But most of the time we concentrated on studying something. Our electrical engineer would exchange his knowledge for training in other subjects. Most of the time, due to our hunger, we talked about cooking and exchanged recipes.

When we had some leisure during the day, we'd go out to pick herbs or various kinds of wild vegetables which we supposed were edible: we ate anything. It was forbidden, but we did it anyway. Others stole bits of barbed wire to make into mouse traps, actually traps for rats as big as a man's forearm. Those who caught them were very happy to host their friends to a lunch or dinner of rat: very horrible! All these rats were dirty from living in the latrines.

Some of the prisoners caught swallows with fishing line. These birds also were dirty, for they ate the larvae in the latrines. The eaters of rats began to act very strangely. They'd catch chameleons and crickets. To steal food in the kitchen became a usual pastime for them. When we'd cook rice in large amounts, there would be a layer of burnt rice at the bottom. In the beginning, nobody liked it. After a while, when everybody was hungry, we came to an agreement that there should be an equal ration of that rice for everyone. But the hungry ones would steal it from the kitchen before it was distributed to every unit.

In the camp we rotated jobs: kitchen, latrine, collecting fuel, house repairs, medical staff, and so on. Three or four prisoners, sometimes more, would go to the kitchen to collect rotten garbage to eat. They managed like this: let's say that tomorrow would be my day to cook in the kitchen. I'd make an arrangement with my friend to find a way to throw a good cabbage in the garbage. My friend would collect it and take it to the barracks. Later he would divide it with me. Salt was strictly forbidden to store, for the Communists assumed that we would keep it in preparation to escape. Anyone caught with salt was punished. Whenever we were in the kitchen, we found a way to steal some salt, not for escape, but for immediate use. We were really in need of salt.

Although they were supposed to call us "Elder Brother," some of the guards privately addressed me with the more respectful "Uncle" [Father's Elder Brother]. They were strictly instructed not to do this. We were supposed to call them "Brotherly Soldier," but actually, informally, they wanted us to call them "Cadre," and if they could get away with it, "Respected Cadre."

We noticed quickly that they responded differently depending on how we addressed them. If we said "Brotherly Soldier," they immediately looked for ways to criticize us: our clothing, our manner of standing, or other things. We had been given a session on the regulations of the camp and the reasons why we were required to obey them. But in fact the rules were only an ideal and not actually followed. We had to learn the regulations by heart, for at any moment, a cadre might challenge us to recite Regulation Number 7 or Number 4. I am sure that they did not know the regulations but they ordered us to recite them by heart.

Our Communist camp medic was a noncommissioned officer. We were told to call him "Mr. Surgeon," even though he knew nothing. He was a man who boasted, so he was an object of our ridicule. We'd egg him on with farcical questions, "Are there big buildings in the North?"

He would reply, "Quite a lot, and everywhere!"

We knew in advance there was nothing in the North, but he boasted. So we asked, "Are there many refrigerators on the streets of North Vietnam?"

He didn't know what a refrigerator was. Because he thought they were some sort of vehicle, he replied, "Oh, there are lots of refrigerators on the streets in North Vietnam!"

When we all laughed loudly, he realized he had made a false step.

But when we were sick, we came to him, flattered him, and showed ourselves to be humble before him. This was the only way we could expect to get medicine, in other words, pills of some unknown sort which did not kill our diseases at all. We had colic from unsuitable food, intoxicating food, rice kept for many days, which was inedible, but we had to eat it. We had scabies because we were short of water for bathing, and that which we had was contaminated and dirty. Especially since the conflict with China, Vietnam received no more aid from them; this led to serious shortages of medicines and medical equipment. We had to turn to various kinds of herbs. Most of the time when we had colic, our young "surgeon" prescribed young buds of guava. For toothaches, he directed us to take kitchen salt. Because we lived in crowded, unsanitary conditions, and most of the prisoners smoked and shared the water pipe, colds were frequent. Our "surgeon" prescribed crushed garlic juice diluted in water and injected into our nostrils. This was very bad! The odor! And it made us sneeze. But at the time we thought it helped somehow. So did the salt on the toothache and the guava for colic. I have to admit it was good because of its tannin.

The Communists pretended that they had a new civilization and culture. They charged that Western civilization was debauched. Later, when we received medicine from our families, the cadres confiscated it, saying that they were keeping it in the dispensary for common use. Actually, the "surgeon" abused it for the use of himself and the cadres. They were very hypocritical.

The biggest serious disease we had was beriberi, caused by our deficiency of vitamin B-1. In many instances, this turned out to be very serious. Some of the prisoners were almost paralyzed; many who were older and obese like me could not use their feet anymore. I was among the 20 percent who came down with beriberi. Acupuncture, Zen, and calisthenics helped. Later, I received vitamin B-1 from my family. I hid it so that it would not be taken away. We all lost quite a lot of weight. I went from 75 to 40 kilograms, and others lost weight like this. A few people had injuries that came from their labor of clearing fields. One was killed and several injured by exploding mines. The total dead whom I knew about were the three who were executed, the officer blown up by the mine, and one colonel who died of hypertension. None of these men were in my unit.

Resistance among our group was very rare because as high-ranking officers we were older and more moderate. We showed no open resistance, but often adopted a noncooperation and nonresistance mood. According to regulations, we were supposed to respect government property. In fact, we tried to sabotage whatever we could lay our hands on. For example, the guards distributed to us some machetes, saws, picks, and agricultural tools: we found ways to destroy them. Instead of cutting wood with the machete, we'd hit it on iron, steel, or stone. We damaged the teeth of saws in the same way. Whenever possible we'd leave or throw away a pick or agricultural tool. When we were in the manioc fields, we weeded not only the grass, but the manioc. We'd pull it out and then leave it standing, and when possible eat it raw while we stood in the fields because we were so hungry. We could not carry it back, for when we returned, we were subjected to very strict body checks. We'd consume so much raw manioc that we became intoxicated.

When we had to clear the peanut fields and the peanuts were in a very young stage, we were instructed to be very careful to preserve the roots of the plant. We'd pull on the plant just enough to tear out the roots so that they didn't grip the earth. A few days later they would die. We had no overt leaders in these activities because we were very skeptical and distrustful of one another. But a few close friends might suggest to each other to sabotage something.

We not only ridiculed the cadres during the political discussions, indirectly of course, but we also made fun of Communist mottos. They taught us to say, "The more we work, the more we are rewarded; the less we work, the less we are rewarded." We reversed the motto: "They give us less to eat, so we must work less; no reward, no work."

We had to learn a lot of Communist songs, along with the myth of Ho Chi Minh. Among these songs was one translated from the Chinese which chanted about solidarity spirit. Whenever we had disputes or fighting among us, the others would sing this song loudly to remind us indirectly, especially those who were fighting, that we had to have solidarity, that we should use the Communist purpose for our own purpose. Our use of this song in this way occurred instinctively. We simply understood this because of the way we used it.

We were supposed to live by the phrase, "Labor is glorious." The Communists intended to have all of our units working in the fields or cutting firewood. But the fields were small and the prisoners many, so numerous that the Communists had to select us. Work became a *symbol*, a *ritual* act. In six months my unit was sent out only three or four times.

The commander of the camp was a lieutenant colonel from North Vietnam. Under him were many deputies of logistics, political efforts, planning and operations, and other areas such as security. Most of these people were cadres chosen by the Viet Minh to move to the North in 1954 during the 300-day period specified by the Geneva Agreements in which people were allowed to move in either direction. Below the deputies were the camp staff for each of the subdivisions. Each subdivision commander had many cadres, each of whom was responsible for the political reeducation of one unit of from 70 to 90 prisoners. Parallel to the cadres were the guards. Like the cadres, they were from North Vietnam. They were not under the control of the cadres but received direct orders from a separate officer at camp staff. The guards and the cadres distrusted one another, and each tried to control the other. In addition, one prisoner from each unit was selected to have contact with civilians outside the camp. These outsiders sold us fresh vegetables, salt, and some foods, along with cigarettes, tobacco, sugar, and toothpaste. They also passed along information about the outside world, and sometimes took letters to send to our relatives.

Some of our prisoners became leaders, based on their past background and their abilities to speak eloquently. I was not one of them. I stayed in the background, following instead the Chinese proverb, "Softness wins over rigidity; weakness wins over power." I tried to survive, not by resistance, but by flowing with the forces passing over me.

During the six months that we stayed in the southern camps, the Communists used political study sessions, with confessions for each lesson, and informers mingled among us to sort us into different categories of acceptance or resistance to reeducation. Those whom they considered dangerous were sent to the North.

The confessions went along with about ten political lessons. I don't remember much about them except some of the titles. One lesson commented about the extent of our crimes, our so-called crimes against the nation and people of Vietnam. All of these crimes were imaginary and exaggerated. During study and discussion sessions, the cadre in charge of our unit would try by all means to force every one of us to speak, to give an account of past activities in the army. He did not hesitate to press those who could present a good account of their lives. As many crimes as we could relate, the cadre pressed further, and suggested that the others had to imitate those examples and not hide anything from their past activities.

Quite a few of the prisoners were innocent enough to report officially during this kind of discussion every kind of crime they were supposed to have committed in the past. While the cadre directed the discussion as chairman, two secretaries recorded every word of the confessions. One former province chief announced that he had two roles, one civilian, and one as chief military officer of his sector, through which he had conducted many operations. He listed the number of Communists killed, houses burned, and villages destroyed. Everyone had to confess his own past activities in one way or another.

Some of us who were older and more experienced tried to avoid confessing. We did this by choosing our words so that in the end it was not a confession at all. We said that what we did was done for particular reasons. If we had been more inhuman we would have been more destructive to human populations. When we got orders to destroy a hamlet, we called our artillery to fire into the forest, burning it instead.

I told the cadre that I was an artillery man. Like air and navy men, those in the artillery were considered the most wicked because their power of destruction through technology was tremendous. I confessed the truth, but tried to minimize my crime. "I commanded artillery, but during this time there was no war, so I just trained my soldiers. There was no fighting, so I did not commit any crime at all. When war flared, I was sent for training in the U.S.A.; then I was transferred to staff, so I didn't harm anyone. I just surveyed. I also participated in the overthrow of the Diem regime. Then I was sent into exile as a military attaché, where I just performed ceremonial functions that did not harm anyone. When I returned to Vietnam, I served as a liaison officer in charge of protocol, so I think that with such activities I did not commit any crime at all."

The cadre was not at all pleased with my confession. He said, "Even a surgeon, a doctor in a military unit, commits a crime. It is not necessary to hold a weapon to commit a crime. The contribution of any kind of effort is also a crime. Your crimes are so many that they could be compared to the leaves of the trees in the jungle, or the stars in the sky!"

What the cadre wanted was for us to say certain conventional things. Then he would say, "I am very pleased that every one of you used the same expression to condemn yourselves."

The Communists were very smart. They'd use these confessions to categorize us. Also, they made us confess, not privately, but publicly. This created a kind of emulation encouraging each of us to confess the best of himself, which meant the worst for himself. And the informers among us tried to be friendly. If by mistake we gave them too much in confidences, they gave this information to the Communists.

At that time in the South, all of us expected to be returned home in a short time. The cadre insisted always that the length of time of our reeducation depended solely on ourselves, not on anyone else. We ourselves were to blame if we were not released. If we behaved correctly during our time of reeducation, if we made serious confessions, if we cooperated with the cadres efficiently, which meant if we denounced the next fellow, then we would have great hope to go home sooner than anyone else. All the time, this was the only story the cadre preached. And we believed him.

[See also Chapters 19, 21, 22, 32, and 33.]

CHAPTER 21

Sent North to Die:
1976–1979

This and the following chapter constitute the first detailed account in English of the harsher reeducation camps of North and Central Vietnam. The colonel tells of the uncertainty and despair of the prisoners as they were transported to the North by ship; of unbearable cold; of famished men who ate whatever they could find, even if it poisoned them; and of the dangers associated with the hard labor to which they were subjected.

Journey to the North

From time to time, groups of men were taken away from our camp. We heard rumors, but we did not really know what had happened to them. One day we were issued dinner somewhat early, and by this we suspected that something unusual was about to happen. Around 4:00 P.M. we were suddenly told to bring our luggage, gather in a large yard with our units, and await orders. We were caught completely by surprise. All we knew was that we were going to be moved somewhere.

Some new cadres appeared and told us to spread out our luggage for inspection. We had sleeping mats, our own clothing, some books and foodstuffs supplied by our families, warm blankets, and some ARVN camouflage fatigues that the guards had given us a few weeks before. During our six months in the South, a number of us had made some handicrafts: wooden images of Jesus or the Buddha carved from ammunition cases, engraved water pipes made from aluminum tubes, aluminum cups made from war materials, art boxes, knives, and fine tools, all very beautiful. We also treasured lots of rifle ammunition containers, neat, safe, heavy metal boxes that were very convenient for placing our personal belongings. This gave the guards a good opportunity to loot us; they especially liked the ammunition boxes.

Some of the men cherished their souvenir objects so much that they implored the guards to give these things back; others objected indignantly, but either way we did not get back any of those things, not even the cooking pots and pans that we had made. Some of the men tried to hold the pots, but the guards tore them from us, threw them away, and threatened us. They put our art objects in a bag, but we knew it was for themselves. Later, we realized why they would not authorize us to carry very much: in store for us was a long and hard voyage by sea.

The checking of luggage lasted six hours. During that time, we sat, but we were forbidden to move, except to go to the latrine. After I had been checked through, and my pan-broiler had been thrown away, I raised my hand and asked permission to go out to urinate. I retrieved a pot, hid it in my clothes, and placed it back in my luggage.

Sometime after 10:00 P.M. we were ordered to move to the main gate, where we found many military trucks waiting for us. As before, about 50 of us were loaded into each truck, and canvas was placed over us. The slow checking and loading continued until about 4:00 A.M. We waited for hours in the suffocating atmosphere of the closed, crowded trucks. Past experience had taught us to be careful to carry water for emergency. Each of us had a one-gallon nylon container of water.

When the truck convoy finally began to move, we were quite surprised to find that we were traveling in the direction of Saigon. We became optimistic, for we hoped to be sent back home soon. On the way, we saw North Vietnamese soldiers dressed in war gear, standing about 15 meters apart on both sides of the road. They stretched down the road for about one kilometer. This was a very impressive show of force.

We reached the outskirts of Saigon, and our spirits soared. Then the convoy suddenly turned to the Saigon New Port, actually a former U.S. naval base used for unloading war equipment. When we saw the ships, we realized our destination, and a feeling of terror came over us. Joking and talking ceased; we seemed to turn inward. A heavy silence pervaded the truck as we thought of the violated promise of the return to our families. No one had told us, but we all knew that we headed north. Most of us had our heads hidden. Like me they were probably weeping silently.

Then again we experienced a long wait as each truck discharged its load and the prisoners one by one climbed up a rope ladder to the ship. It was really frightening to climb with a heavy shoulder load which counterbalanced our center of gravity and continually threatened to hurl us into the deep waters off the wharf. As I climbed onto the deck of the ship, I saw a North Vietnamese soldier standing next to a mountain of small packages wrapped in used newspapers. As I passed him, he handed me one of them. When I hesitated, he shouted, "Take it!" His eyes were threatening. The packet would be my rations for the journey. Next to him, another soldier with his rifle in a position of attack ordered each of us to climb down inside the ship. This was more frightening than climbing up because it was deeper, right to the bottom of the ship. I was almost the last one to descend, so when I arrived, there was a dispute over where to lie down. A real depression hit us all, and continued during all the days we were on the ship.

Around 9:00 A.M. the ship began to move. As I looked around the ship, I saw about 500 prisoners on the bottom platform for cargo, about 20 meters wide and 40 meters long, an area too small to allow us to move. High above us on the deck stood the North Vietnamese Communist guards. From time to time they looked down to control us. Because we were in an open space, we tried to locate shadows projected by the sun in order to determine the direction taken by the ship. We argued on where we were being taken. After hearing several suggested destinations, one of the prisoners joked, "All of you are wrong. I am 100 percent confident that we are going to Siberia!" We all laughed. At least for a while he raised our morale.

For the first time in six months, we were far away from the cadres and guards. We cursed them and said, "They have deported us to the North, fellows!" Our humble, modest attitude full of hope changed to aggression, anger, threats. We now understood the meaning of that show of force along the road, a demonstration of their power to prevent our resistance. Many prisoners now tried to throw away as many of their possessions as they could, figuring that they would be too heavy to carry.

By the second day, we all suffered from hunger and thirst. Like the others, I had carried with me a gallon of water. I stopped using it in order to conserve it safely in the coming days. We looked for food and water anywhere else. We shouted up to the guards asking for food and water, also for medical help and for toilet facilities. Once a day they would point a water pipe at us and spray us down below, as if they were bathing cattle. At that point we realized that there was no human treatment between them and us. Although some of the prisoners complained of colic, headache, and fever, we received no medical aid. Some of us joked, "Why don't we use our own KP-cillin?" "KP" referred to a Communist-coined phrase, "Overcome adversity," in other words, the absence of medicine.

The food ration issued to us was the Chinese military food ration consisting of green bean, sugar, vitamins of all kinds, and wheat flour mixed and compressed into the shape of a cigarette package. It was so nourishing and delicious for us who were desperately hungry for sugar and food. We had to have more! We called up to the guards on the pretext that they had made a wrong body count, and that some people had been asleep when the ration had been distributed. The guards tossed a few more packets down the hold. Many prisoners scrambled to grab this plunder, and they pulled the packets from one another. I did not go after them, for such actions were so unworthy of our personality, so intolerable for a French-trained officer such as myself.

Two gasoline barrels served as latrine facilities for 500 men. They were installed on the deck next to the ladder leading to the hold. To use them, we had to climb up to the deck and somehow balance ourselves. By the second day, both barrels were overflowing. When the ship swayed, these dirty things splashed onto our trousers and legs. Even though we had to go, we couldn't; it made us lose the feeling. We could stand for hours over the barrel and not be able to go. From below the deck, we shouted loudly to the cadres, protesting the overflow on us. Finally they let some volunteers empty the contents of the barrels into the sea.

Late on the evening of the fifth day, long after sunlight had left, the ship docked somewhere. Around 1:00 A.M. loudspeakers blared that we were to climb up to the deck one by one. When we reached the deck, we saw North Vietnamese soldiers. Through loudspeakers they shouted at us to climb down a gangplank, not a rope ladder as we had used before. We saw electric lights everywhere, and something stranger also. In the South, the soldiers who guarded us wore green uniforms. Here, in addition to those soldiers, we saw for the first time men in the yellow-khaki uniforms of the Public Security Agency.

Here again, they had given us a real show of force: tanks, soldiers in war gear, combined with military dogs and Public Security Agency guards everywhere, hurrying us along.

In groups of 30 or so, we proceeded to a sanitary cordon, where we received injections, probably against tetanus. Then we bathed in a small, dirty pond and brushed our teeth. We had been five days without a bath. Next, we declared our names, identities, and other information. After this, the guards loaded us onto another convoy. All of this was done in a great rush. We were driven to a railway station, where we remained and rested for several days in empty warehouses.

Very late one evening, a train rolled up with black cattle and merchandise wagons. Standing on each wagon were two or three North Vietnamese soldiers. They ordered us to climb onto the wagons and receive a food ration consisting of dry flaked pork, along with a very bad loaf of French-style bread made with rice flour and tough as rubber. About 100 of us were pushed into each black, airless, windowless wagon. Then the North Vietnamese soldiers locked the doors. Because many units had been mixed, the prisoners found themselves next to people whom they didn't know. Disputes broke out for places to sit. Again we had the problem of having to defecate and urinate into nylon bags. Imagine how suffocated we were with all those bad smells! In another wagon, my friend Lieutenant Colonel Hung suffocated and died.

The journey was long and bad, made worse by the ancient French-built wagons, whose wheels screeching on the rails made an unbearable noise. The wagons shook terribly. The train stopped frequently with a terrific jolt, throwing us into the person next to us. It felt like the wagon would overturn.

For three days we suffered without water. Our dry food ration only made us more thirsty. Then the train derailed on a curve, and the North Vietnamese took almost another full day to make the repairs. We saw nothing and we knew nothing; we simply felt the train move up on the grade, then stop. We had been traveling from the port of Haiphong to Hanoi and then to the northern part of North Vietnam. Later, some of the prisoners recognized that we had come to the railway station at Yen Bai, the capital town of Hoang Lien Son province, a mountainous area close to China. Near there is Fan Si Pan Heights, some 3,542 meters high, known as the Roof of Vietnam. This is an uninhabited region.

We were unloaded at Yen Bai, transported by truck, then put on a river boat, and sent upstream past the Thac Ba power station. We landed in a sparsely inhabited area. North Vietnamese cadres gathered us in rows of 900, then led us about five kilometers to a glade, our new home. We looked at each other silently. The cadre of our unit explained that from now on, we had to organize our own survival, and he chose a prisoner to be our temporary leader. All contact with the cadre had to be through this leader, who instructed us to organize our sleeping quarters in the cold open air and to build an improvised kitchen and oven. Everybody had an assignment. Some collected firewood, others carried water. Since I was the oldest, I was given the easiest job, collecting firewood. The harshest was cooking rice because no one knew how to cook without a kitchen. Unlike the South, here we had nothing. This was to be my home for the next three years.

Yen Bai

For the first few days, we were allowed to rest. Then we were assigned to go to the mountains and jungle to cut lumber and bamboo for house construction and elephant grass for thatch. How hard it was for us to construct our own houses in the middle of the jungle! We had only a small number of machetes, two-man saws, pickaxes, and mattocks, so our work went slowly. A group of five people would be assigned to cut lumber in the jungle, but they would be issued only one machete. Each task had its own quotas and rules for the measurement of items to be brought in. Wood was supposed to be cut five meters long and about one foot in diameter. One man could not do this without a machete. But a five-man group had only the one tool. Their work was very dangerous. When they cut the tree, it might fall on them. Also, the men had to strip the many branches from the tree to make it ready to move from the mountain to the road. Sometimes they preferred to float the tree across a lake rather than carry it. They tied the logs together and made a raft. This saved effort and conserved the strength of the men, and this was important because they had so little food. But a number of men drowned in the lake. While traveling on the raft, some of the men caught fish, until the local inhabitants reported them to the cadres.

Cutting bamboo was more dangerous. If we cut it too high, sharp points of branches and stalks cut our stomachs. When the top fell, the branches also cut us. We had to climb up high to cut entangled branches. Then when they were on the ground we had to drag them down steep slopes to the road. We also faced problems with jungle leeches: horrible one-centimeter creatures that would crawl up our clothes, into our armpits, infiltrate right inside our bodies, consume a lot of blood, and inflate into big balls the size of lichee fruit. Then they were very harmful. We would take them off, but they were in so deep that we continued to bleed. If we had a dozen or so in us, we lost lots of blood. With our poor nutrition, the loss of blood endangered our survival.

We also encountered snakes. But the most dangerous enemy of all was hunger. We were ravenous *every day*. By one way or another, we tried to find any kind of food that we judged edible for humans. And some of us got poisoned by trying unknown fruits. The most common disease we got was constipation, the result of eating wild banana. It has so much tannin in it that it causes constipation at first, and later leads to dysentery, which killed many of the prisoners.

In my own unit, four men died from dysentery, for which we had no medicine to cure them. We also had beriberi and malaria, and another strange disease that probably was from the poison of unknown fruits and food. It made a man's liver swell, but it was not hepatitis. Very quickly, within weeks, the sick person's belly became bigger and bigger, like that of a pregnant woman; then suddenly he died. Most of the deaths were caused by that disease because we ate anything that we could find. The color and form of the fruits and vegetables in the jungle were so tempting that we ate them. Twelve men who did this in our camp of 500 died from this disease. There were five or six camps, each about 12 kilometers from the next. There was one hospital to serve these 3,000 men. The North Vietnamese brought us to the North with a definite aim: to clear uninhabited areas in the highlands and to build a strategic road there. For three years, 1976–1979, I remained at Yen Bai in Camp Number Nine, which was part of Intergroup Camp Number Six in Yen Binh District. [Yen Bai is one of several names used by prisoners who were in a large complex of camps. See Sagan and Denney 1983: 35.] During that time, I didn't see many men die at camp. I found out later that they were taken to the hospital to die.

One time I was shifted from weaving bamboo baskets to tending water buffalo. I was delighted, for I could leave camp and walk for long, lonely distances. Several times I led the buffalo up to the isolated cemetery for Camp Number Nine. I counted 30 tombs. Later, I myself buried two of my friends in that cemetery. Both died of dysentery.

One of them, Lieutenant Colonel Sang, died an especially horrible death. In the last three days of his life he passed stool 20 to 30 times a day, until he was completely dehydrated. When he could no longer walk, he crawled; when he could no longer crawl, he dirtied his own bed-platform. We were afraid of him because we had to look out for ourselves. At first, we tried to help him, but later we stopped, for we could not stay up all night. He did not say anything during his last moments. All of us felt a responsibility for writing down the hour, day, and the lunar and solar month of his death, to hand over to his family. We Vietnamese are superstitious. The family should keep that date for ceremonial rites. We believe that the soul of the dead goes around somewhere in the camp when a person suffers an unjust death.

I myself learned of the death of Quoi, my second friend, in a supernatural way. I was asleep when around 4:00 A.M. I felt someone pulling my leg to wake up. I sat up, but there was no one there. By coincidence my friend died right at that time in the hospital, one-half kilometer from our camp. A few others had similar experiences. It was not a dream that we experienced, but it looked like a dream, having someone pull your leg at the same time that they died. So we concluded that my friend suffered the unjust death of an innocent, that his soul was wandering around this area, and that he came back and awakened us to ask us for food because he was so hungry. He was an extremely tall man; he always ate everything, but never found enough.

I remember one day when I was walking with Quoi and a few others. We found a mouse's nest built in a bamboo hole. He was so happy to discover four or five newly born, still-red mice. He picked them up, stuck them on an improvised stick of bamboo, and ate them raw right there.

I am allergic to every kind of food which is not usual to me. I found it bad. Most of the men ate what they could find, such as small frogs the size of your thumb. When the men saw these in the field, they showed their happiness by catching them, pulling out their entrails, tearing off their skin, and eating them raw. They also ate live crickets, first pulling off their spiny legs, then popping the crickets in their mouths.

The most usual thing they collected was cigarette butts. This was really unworthy. It occurred particularly when we were in prisons with civilian criminals. Whenever we left the camp, we had to march in line. If a prisoner saw a butt on the ground a few meters ahead, he would rush over to it before somebody else grabbed it. For the cigarette snatchers, we invented a new expression: "catching a cricket." The cause of Quoi's death was that he ate everything he saw.

Whenever we left for work outside the camp, we tried to bring with us a new shirt or trousers to exchange for food. If we were caught trading with civilians, the cadres made us do self-criticism, or we'd be put in "jail," a stone cave that became very cold at night. Our food and water ration would be cut in half.

One night, a young helicopter pilot climbed over the fence to steal manioc from a nearby field. Unfortunately for him, the guards saw him, opened fire, and wounded him in the leg, which later was amputated without anesthesia, with no pain killer at all. He survived, but the camp commander made an example of him: all of us were required to study his case and comment on it. He was charged with trying to escape, but actually all he ever intended to do was steal a little manioc to stave off starvation.

Another time, the Communists led us by three men who had their hands tied behind their backs. All of their belongings were hanging on their necks, while on their chests were pieces of paper on which were written the words "Escaping the camp." Their faces were bruised and swollen; they looked very tired as they walked while guards pushed them from behind with bayonets. We never learned the fate of these prisoners.

The residents of the area, the ethnic people of the Lao-speaking Tay tribe, were very sincere and hospitable. They freely gave us salt, rice, sugar, and sometimes even alcohol, which was forbidden in the camp. Sometimes they exchanged these things for clothing, which was so precious for them. Since the Tay people do not cooperate with the Communists, the Communists have adopted a policy to win them over. One of the most important lieutenants of Ho Chi Minh was General Chu Van Tan, a leader of the Tho tribe, who are like the Tay. He was recently stripped of all of his functions because of his association with Hoang Van Hoan, now out of favor, who fled to China.

Some time after we had settled in the mountains of North Vietnam, our families sent us so many good warm clothes that the Communist authorities in the camp envied us. The rules strictly prohibited them from touching our clothing. On our side, we were so hungry that whenever we were assigned to leave the camp for labor, we would put on our warmer clothes under our prison uniforms. When the opportunity came, we would bargain and sell these to the Tay people for food, sugar, cigarettes, and tobacco. I didn't smoke, but the great majority did. The Communist authorities of the camp were very embarrassed because our trading activities were an opportunity for us to indirectly tell the truth to the civilian population of the area that we were hungry and badly mistreated. The area residents also learned that we were very rich men of the South with opulent South Vietnamese clothing which Northerners had never seen in their life.

Our camp was located on the land that belonged to the chief of the Tay village. When the Communists decided to enlarge the camp, they ordered his house and all of his property to be dismantled and moved away by some of the prisoners, especially those with carpentry skills. The chief was furious. In the old days, he told us, he was the respected king of the area. Since the coming of the Communists, he had lost his title, power, and all of his properties. Two of his sons had gone south to fight as soldiers of the North Vietnamese Army. Because of this, he was considered a "revolutionary family." Since he was of the new class of nobility, he had the right to insult and curse; he was not afraid of bringing trouble on himself. We, who dared not make any criticisms, were very happy to listen to his curses: "Those pirates plundered my rice fields," he said in the peculiar accent of the Tay people when they spoke Vietnamese. "My two sons are soldiers in the South. I am not afraid of them." I was able to communicate with him easily because as a child I was reared in Laos and could speak to him in Lao.

The house that we dismantled was made of wood and built of stilts higher than a man's head. Cattle lived underneath. While he supervised our work, many of us talked with him in such a way as to evoke his criticism of all the bad things of the Communists. He was proud of himself. From time to time he would put on the clothes that reflected his former authority: trousers, Vietnamese-style clothes, and a very good conical hat. He still had two horses. He would ride around with his special clothes, behaving like a landlord to show how he had been before. Because we flattered him, he was very generous to us: he would give us all the food he had in his house, green tea, and those who wanted to could smoke freely. Whenever the cadre or guard came, we were all silent. The dismantling, relocation, and rebuilding of the house on a new site took several weeks, especially since we had the tendency to work slowly.

All the time, we traded our clothes for food, to the embarrassment of the Communist cadres.

We continued these exchanges happily until one day we received a brisk order: "Do not go to work today; bring all of your belongings to the big yard for checking and control." Because the cadres distrusted one another, they were assigned to check units other than their own. They allowed us to keep clothing that was authorized for daily use. The rest were wrapped, labeled, and consigned to a rice warehouse, which was locked. There was no rice anyway; the whole country was hungry. Instead, they stored our valuable clothing. Not long after, while working in the fields, we found the wrappings of our packages with our names on them, and some of our clothing strewn about. We reported that our clothing had been stolen. The cadre waited several days before reporting it to camp headquarters. The cadre told us that an investigation committee had been formed to determine which prisoners were to blame for the thefts. Through other sources we heard that the guards who had stolen our packages had been discovered, but they were allowed to keep what they had taken.

Our camp, located on a mountain slope, was a long oval of one kilometer long and 300–400 meters wide, all surrounded by barbed wire. One third of the camp was reserved for the living quarters of the cadres and guards. The main gate led to this section. Another third of the camp was the prisoner section, all with chicken coops and latrines. We had our own prisoner's gate. The middle of the camp, separated by barbed wire, contained a pond, a buffalo shade area, a pig sty, a manioc field, and the warehouse where our clothing was stored. The unit hospital and the lake were across the road from the camp.

During the first part of our detention in the North, from 1976–1979, our relatives were not allowed to visit us. The only exception was for one of the informers within our group. The cadres had very strict instructions to check all of our correspondence. Letters to our families had to be very short. We were prohibited from using foreign words or indicating where we had been sent. Even so, we tried to inform our families by tricks, and in the end, almost all of them had figured out where we were. I wrote that I had met a friend of our family. Since this man was a native of Yen Bai, my wife realized where I was. To reach us, families had to use an APO code and number. All incoming and outgoing mail had to have these numbers. We were all subject to very strict censorship, and most of us were scolded because of the contents of the letters that came from our families. Sometimes, the cadres misread what had been written, and would punish the prisoners for statements that their wives had never made.

Daily life in the North meant facing one more enemy, the cold. We were accustomed to heat, not the freezing cold we encountered at 3,500 meters. In the morning, our hands were frozen. When we had lived in the South, we had collected sandbags left by the Americans. We preferred these over the Vietnamese bags because the American bags were made of nylon thread, from which we could make many things. We would take apart the threads one by one and join them to make one long thread. We would twist two or three threads together to make a stronger one. With these, we made hammocks and shoulder bags. All of these we brought up north in order to remake into those precious things that kept us warm: gloves, undershirts, and cap covers for our ears.

In the North, we were issued Vietnamese-style pajamas for prisoners. These were dark blue with a white stripe, a ridiculous-looking clown's cloth that made us easy to recognize if we tried to escape. Although they did not fit, it was against regulations to change them. We did so anyway. The pajamas also lacked pockets, for these too were forbidden. But we needed pockets for our private things, the photos of relatives, letters, and money. We made hidden pockets.

Whenever we went to or returned from the fields, we were subject to body checks, so we made our pockets in very secret places, under the bottom of trousers, or right behind the neck. My secret pocket was ridiculous. My wife sent me a package. In it was a Western suit for winter. It even included a vest and waistcoat. For weeks and weeks my fellow inmates ridiculed me about that suit. "She forgot the necktie! Maybe she realizes you are in the middle of Hanoi, where the suit will fit your environment! Oh, you are going to be released soon, so your wife prepared you with such clothing."

But she was not so naive. There was something in the waistcoat. Later I found a very lovely letter and some money hidden in the back, and this helped me really quite a lot. Later on, when I was in my next phase of detention in Nghe An [Central Vietnam], I gave the full suit to the Senior Public Security Captain who was also my cadre and the deputy of the camp. Because of this I got his sympathy, enjoyed his favor, and finally was released.

Although I was allowed to keep that suit, I was not such an idiot that I would wear it in the jungle. I only wore it when I was around the camp.

The cold prevented us from bathing. The water from high mountain streams was like ice. Some prisoners never took a bath during the whole winter. We got lice, which caused itching and scabies. Because we slept so close to each other, almost everybody had it. Most of the elder officers had horrible lung diseases. To avoid their bad breathing, I would lie with my head at their feet. This angered the other prisoners, who uttered acid remarks, but I didn't care. A few others also slept in this reversed way and like me were condemned as eccentric.

The daily routine of the North differed from that in the South. Here we were required to address the cadres only as "Brother Cadre," without forms of respect that had been used in the South. In the North, we had political study only rarely, maybe once every month or two. The routine of the day was hard labor, for everybody, with no exception. From 1976 to 1978, we ate black-wheat, a small grain used for feeding animals and sent to Vietnam as aid. The first year, we received it in the form of flour, but from 1977 to 1979 only as unprocessed grain. We had to cook it a very long time, and even then the husk remained quite tough. For the older people, whose teeth had been destroyed by malnutrition, it was very difficult to eat. We had to crush the grain in improvised mortars and pestles. The hardest year was 1978–1979, because we had just started producing our own crops but at that time had only manioc and corn. We had no potato or sweet potato. The cold, the bad food, the lice, the hard labor, the *nostalgia*, the harsh words from the cadres and young guards: all of these destroyed us and killed us slowly day by day. Over time, we changed, as shown by our insolent reactions to our usurpers.

Usually we were up at 6:00 A.M., awakened by the hitting of the rim of a vehicle. After 20 minutes of required calisthenic exercises, and a roll call, we went to work. Often the assignments had been given to us the night before. Each cadre as well as each guard had a quota of a certain number of kilos of vegetables per month that had to be filled under his direction. We worked until noon, then ate lunch consisting of one piece of boiled black fodder-grain cake. Sometimes we had manioc, but it is poisonous. First we had to peel back the skin and when we did that, almost half of the white was thrown away already. In principle each prisoner received one and a half kilos of manioc per day. But after peeling and cooking, only half of that was edible. Sometimes we brought manioc that was too old; it was like a piece of wood, no longer edible. To be fair, we divided the manioc into as many parts as there were people in the unit. We selected the pieces by lot. The unlucky ones who got the old manioc went hungry for that meal.

Around 2:00 P.M., if we had spare tobacco or cigarettes, we did an exchange. Those who were addicted would abstain from a meal to pay for the smoking. When we had corn, we were all the time hungry, for it was the worst. The edible part was about one fourth of its total weight. Corn that was too young had nothing on it to eat. So we had to eat everything on it except the leaves. We even ate the corn cobs. This was hard for older men such as me with poor teeth.

At meals like this, I saw men weeping. At such times, I thought of our life in happier times and our present condition. Then I would recite two lines from Nguyen Du's *Tale of Kieu* that expressed our changes of fortune.

> Why before brocade?
> Why now fading like a flower on the road?

Usually we missed at least one day of meals per week, but I had a strategic reserve coming from my family.

In order to prevent other people from stealing our extra supplies, we kept one man from our unit at home to guard our things. We were allowed to do this. He would clean up and receive new daily food rations and drinking water. We took turns doing this. During the days, our things were safe; at night, we used to put our food supply under our heads as pillows.

Even during this period of misfortune, we sometimes discovered the romantic side of life. Life was very hard in North Vietnam, but the scenery was quite spectacular. I used to recite classical verses as a diversion from our real misery.

A couple of others also recited verses, some prisoners sang, but most of the inmates cared only about looking for some herb, something edible that they could grab at the first view along the road and pop into their mouths.

One day, we went out to work near the district headquarters of Yen Binh and met two groups of prisoners who had been sent to this area in the early 1950s. The first group consisted of the Catholic natives of Quynh Luu District in Nghe An Province in Central Vietnam. In 1953, these people revolted against the Communists. After their revolt was crushed, those suspected of inciting and participating in the revolt were sent to the North, where they will remain for the rest of their days. (See Hoang Van Chi 1964: 224–225, 228.)

The second group consisted of Vietnamese soldiers of the French Army who were exiled to this remote part of the country right after the partition of 1954. They were so naive that they did not go south when they had the chance. They too will never go home. Both of these groups have now intermarried with the Tay people. Other captured soldiers of the French Foreign Legion were not repatriated after 1954. They were forced to remain in North Vietnam, where many married Vietnamese women. Not until 1975 was an arrangement made that allowed them to return to their native country.

After talking with these two groups of prisoners, I concluded unhappily that we, too, had been exiled to the far North forever; we also would never be allowed to return. I became quite depressed.

In 1979, because of the border clash between the Vietnamese and Chinese, our fate was changed. The Communists quickly moved us down from that area. The Vietnamese-French soldiers and the Quynh Luu Catholics remained because they were too few and dispersed to be a threat.

Once, during a political study session, we were required to discuss the elites of Vietnamese society. One man, usually very taciturn, told a story about a Vietnamese painter who won an international prize for one of his works. It depicted just one human buttock, skinny, wrinkled, and bony, over which had grown a cobweb. He explained that the Vietnamese are so hungry that they do not defecate for days on end; this allowed the cobweb to be spun over the buttock. For this he won the first prize. As this colonel spoke, not a trace of emotion showed on his face. We nearly laughed to death when we heard the story. Such ridicule helped to keep up our spirits; we had no other means of defense.

As prisoners, we had to observe four major holidays for the Communists. On three of them, we were granted one day off, and the favor of eating rice. Except for these holidays, we never saw a grain of rice. On the lunar New Year, we were given three days off. This was a big, well-organized festival. We were given a big, live buffalo, one or two pigs, enough rice for one day, and some sticky rice for traditional rice cakes; also some green bean for a special dish.

All of us were very happy and longed for this occasion and the big meal it brought. We also organized theatrical shows, singing accompanied by our handmade musical instruments, sports games, and the traditional writing on long hanging wall papers. We gave a written speech to the cadres, organized a procession, and most important reinforced the kitchen crew. The volunteers to the kitchen expected to be able to steal some extra buffalo meat, pork, salt, and rice. A team was selected to kill the buffalo; surely they stole some meat at that time. They stripped the meat from the bones and threw the bones in a garbage pit in the kitchen. Right on the third day of the festival, many people returned to the kitchen and dug the bones out of the pit to strip and eat the last pieces of meat still remaining on the bone. The meat was rotten; flies and larvae were all over it. Still, dozens of men gnawed at the bones and scraps of meat, and also ate the rotten vegetables and leaves. This was the sight of the festival.

Two times I almost died, and when a prisoner was close to death, the camp officials sometimes released them. One time, in 1978, the cause was a very small phosphorus-covered centipede, which glowed at night. Chickens are fond of eating the centipedes, and when a chicken is killed, the centipedes are fond of feeding on chicken. If we eat a chicken that has eaten centipedes, we become poisoned.

I had stored some of my dinner food to be used for breakfast. A centipede crawled all over it, leaving its phosphorus poison behind. Then it came to my sleeping place and crawled onto my back, inside my shirt. That day, I took my breakfast as usual, then went to work. Two hours later, I suddenly felt violently sick to my stomach. I could not bear it anymore, so I asked the cadre permission to go back to my quarters. I was crying; then I fell into a coma, which lasted until 9:00 P.M. Our unit leader was so bad that he did not bother to inform our cadre. I felt I was going to die, so I called a friend of mine in the unit and made a final statement to be told to my family about my death. At that time I didn't realize that I had been poisoned by the centipede.

That evening by chance the medic male nurse passed by our quarters. The inmates called him in to look at me. He could not figure out what was wrong. He gave me a sedative and scolded, "You are pretending to be sick. You should respect the sleep of others!" With the sedative I slept.

The next morning, I felt something itching on my back. It became more and more painful. I asked the inmates to look at it. They all concluded that I had been attacked by the poisonous centipede, whose phosphorus had destroyed part of my skin. At that point I realized that the centipede must have poisoned my breakfast. My health deteriorated seriously after that, so I was sent to the medical committee which examined those prisoners who were eligible for being released. They put my name on the list for release, citing reasons of ill health. Not long after that, an informer falsely denounced me as a CIA agent in order to gain special privileges from the cadres, and my name was taken off the roster.

My second close call with death came when a young man passing by threw me a handful of a fruit similar to a fig. Although edible, it is somehow dangerous because of its high degree of acidity. When it rolled my way, it was very precious. To have extra food during the day! I didn't hesitate. I ate it. The problem is that since 1960 I have had a duodenal ulcer; overconsumption of this fruit led my stomach to hemorrhage. The next day, just as I stepped away from a latrine out in the fields, I collapsed. The prisoners carried me back to camp. For the second time within a short period, I was close to death. I had already been removed from the list of people to be released. During this second illness, I remained off that list.

[See also Chapters 19, 20, 22, 32, and 33.]

CHAPTER 22

Harshest Incarceration:
1979–1981

NARRATOR 12: EX-ARVN COLONEL

This chapter tells of the colonel's worst ordeals, both physical and spiritual, which led to deep depression and two attempts at suicide.

Camp Number Six, Nghe An Province, Central Highlands

When the Vietnamese Communists foresaw their clash with the Chinese, they quickly evacuated all of the reeducation camps along the northern border. Because I had been denounced as a CIA agent, I was classified as among those who were most dangerous, and I was in the first group of prisoners to be moved to Nghe An Province in the Central Highlands. Ironically, the very informer who had falsely denounced me was also sent south with my group. Of the men in my northern camp, only a dozen or so made the trip with me; the other 300 men sent with us were from other camps. We were sent to many places before making the long journey to Nghe An by truck.

We were taken to Camp Number Six, located in an arid mountain area near the Laotian border. This camp had been a French prison for the detention of Vietnamese revolutionaries. During the time of Communist rule, the prison had been used to house civilian criminals. Now they converted the prison into a detention center for South Vietnamese officers of the old regime. The criminals were moved next to us to a site where a new jail was built of light materials such as wood and bamboo. The civilian criminals were much better off than we were because we were put in the old buildings of brick, stone, and iron, which in summer kept the heat in, and in winter retained the chill. It was both terribly hot and cold. We were further depressed and terrified when we found that our guards were from the Public Security Agency, for they are brutal, like the KGB of the Soviet Union.

We were locked in small rooms in which we were so crowded that there was not enough sleeping space for everyone at once. We had to build platforms to stack people for sleeping. About 80 or 90 people would be locked into a room six meters wide and about twice that long. In rooms that measured 8 by 24 meters, the Communists put 150 to 200 men. Our own clothes and blankets were not enough to keep us warm, and we had nothing else. We made our own extra clothing with U.S.A. sandbags. That helped us quite a bit.

To add to our misery, we found that fish were swimming in the well we used for drinking water. This revealed that the well was polluted, since the fish had found an underground channel leading from the nearby lake into which we drained the waste from our latrines. That was our only source of drinking water during our entire internment.

We were organized into units of 80 to 100 men, controlled by a company leader selected from the prisoners. Our company leader, a former intelligence officer, was a brutal man who flattered the Communists and denounced everybody. The prisoners threatened to kill him by putting a long nail in his ear while he was asleep. Although they did not follow through with this, they did throw his slippers in the latrine box, and his hat in the human waste pit. Right at the field where we worked, two inmates of our company once beat him, with the approval of all of us.

In Nghe An, prisoners were punished by being put in a small cell with no light, where they remained for 10 days or more with one leg chained, with half the food ration, and with all correspondence and family packages denied. Two Catholic priests were put in these isolation cells in 1979. When I left in 1981, they still were in there.

For beating our own company leader and informer, the two men were put in the cells for 15 days. One of the men was a writer and former director of military television in South Vietnam. Shortly after his release from the cell, he cut a vein in his wrist, poured his blood into a cup, and suddenly threw it into the face of the great informer, our company leader. This was a great insult. All of us were taken by surprise and quite afraid. At first, we thought that the company leader was wounded and bleeding. He himself was so terrified that he rushed to the small window with iron bars to call the guards for help. Again the writer was sent to the isolation cell. The next day, every one of us was furious at the company leader, who now was isolated all by himself: we ignored him, turned our backs on him, and would not speak to him. We avoided looking at him, even though he had the full support of the head instructor [of a group in a reeducation camp], a man of the Public Security Agency.

The senior captain, a man named Luyen, was strong, brutal, and shrewd, with much experience in dealing with prisoners. Because he was a fat man with a big face, we called him "Flat Basket Face," along with a term of disrespect. When our company leader informed him of this, the senior captain became furious. Most of the time Flat Basket Face punished the whole company. He hated us to such a degree that he made us work even on Sundays. This was hard agricultural labor, in which we cultivated rice, sweet potatoes, corn, peanuts, and bean, all this in a region considered to be the poorest in Vietnam.

We have a Vietnamese expression, "Dogs eat pebbles; chickens eat salt." With any pieces of earth available, we tilled the soil. The whole year, the earth had no time for rest, for after we harvested rice, we harvested sweet potatoes, then peanuts, and so on. The land is so arid that the people are very tough, but strangely enough, the women of this area are really beautiful. Ho Chi Minh came from here, as did many famous men of our country. Camp Number Six was located at Xa Thanh My village in Huyen Thanh Chuong District.

Flat Basket Face considered us to be his personal enemies. Not only on Sunday, but every day he worked us hard. We went to the fields earlier than other units; we returned later than anyone else. The usual working hours were from 7:00 A.M. to noon and 2:00 to 5:00 P.M. The work was not easy. We had no machines; even buffalo or oxen were unable to do the work. We had men replacing animals as tractors for plowing. The soil was so dry and poor that fertilizers were needed for each crop. The only fertilizer available was human and cattle waste.

Because of his animosity towards us, Flat Basket Face forced us to use our hands to carry these human wastes, still fresh, to fertilize the fields. We tried to use two pieces of wood or bamboo to pick up the waste and spread it, but he prohibited that. We had to use our bare hands. Some of the prisoners put on rubber gloves sent to them by their families; he made them take the gloves off. He was happy to get revenge on us.

Since we were forced to return from the fields later than anyone else, the guards who accompanied us were in a hurry to get home. Most of the time they refused to let us bathe at the pond or wash our hands. According to regulations, we were supposed to bathe twice a week, but as a punishment, Flat Basket Face refused to let us do so. Despite this, strange as it may seem, we rarely had skin infections.

The worst of all was that when we got back to our quarters, the jailer on duty would rush us into our cell and lock it quickly, for he was in a hurry to go to his family. Our hands remained dirty with human waste. We had to eat like this.

When we realized that we weren't allowed to wash our hands, we tried to rub our hands on the road or on scented leaves as we walked back to camp. We hoped to eliminate the bad smell of human waste. As we stopped to scoop dirt and leaves, we became spread out. The guards shouted at the stragglers to move along. For one week we were not allowed to wash our hands. During that time, we tried to get water from the rice fields to wash. In our cell, we had stored a little water for drinking and brushing our teeth. It was not enough for bathing.

After a week, we gave up resistance against Flat Basket Face and our company leader. When we flattered them, they let us wash again. Then another incident occurred. Over and over incidents would develop, and we would be punished by having our food supply cut, our correspondence held up, or we would be put in solitary cells. According to regulations, prisoners were not supposed to be beaten, but in rare cases, this too happened. One day in 1980, we heard a rumor that Flat Basket Face was retiring. We made a feast of the occasion. His successor was a 20-year-old private of the Public Security Agency. His name was Son, which in Sino-Vietnamese means "Mountain." The nickname we gave him was "Seven Mountains." This was a trick to divert him so that he did not realize we were talking about him. We would say, "When we work, Seven Mountains comes from far away." Eventually, our informer told him about this.

Seven Mountains was so young compared to us. We considered him in status as we would our own sons: it was unworthy to deal with him. In doing this, we made a mistake and created a new and brutal enemy. Sometimes we were able to manipulate him, but at other times, he treated us badly, and sometimes even gave us beatings.

One time, we were ordered to select peanuts for future planting. Seven Mountains watched us closely so that we would not steal and eat the peanuts. One of the prisoners stole some and was caught by Seven Mountains, who started to criticize him. The prisoner responded by shouting back loudly and pulling out his shirt in an insolent manner to show that he had hidden nothing. Seven Mountains lost face in our presence. He thought for a while, then ordered the prisoner to go to his office, located some 50 meters away. We listened to the sounds of beating and shouting. When the prisoner returned, his face was bruised. We were upset by the incident.

The prisoners who were treated most brutally were the criminals: thieves, brigands, murderers, and government officials who had been caught mismanaging funds. Although they were isolated from us in the jail area, we worked side by side with them in the fields. They knew how to plow the land, so we took orders from them and got advice, since we were unskilled labor. Mostly they duped and cheated us. They'd promise to help sell our clothing, watches, and rings, but then they just swindled us. Some of them were always unfriendly, but others faked friendliness to make a profit off of us.

One time, a number of the criminal prisoners stole some of our clothes in the field and were caught wearing them. For this, the cadre and guard beat them with rifle butts until they got tired. One of the criminals fainted after being kneed and kicked in the stomach and smashed with rifle butts on his shoulders and head. This was the first time we had seen that sort of beating, since we political prisoners were not supposed to be beaten.

The cultivation of rice did not benefit us, for we could not eat it uncooked. The vital thing to do when we stole food was to eat it immediately, to fight hunger. We preferred to cultivate corn, manioc, sweet potatoes, peanuts, and beans, for then we had a chance to steal food.

The cadres and guards had had long experience in dealing with prisoners. Because they knew that the loss in these kinds of crops was heavy, they developed many preventive measures. Peanuts were considered high quality crops. To prevent insects, particularly crickets, from destroying the seeds, the Communists put the peanuts in a concentrated DDT solution. This impeded both insects and prisoners. The peanuts mixed in this concentrated solution smelled very strong. The peanuts were brought out and distributed to prisoners only very late in order to avoid the loss. Can you imagine—we, the educated officers who can realize how much danger the DDT solution is, nevertheless ate those peanuts raw, covered with DDT. But we did not become ill. There was an unexpected effect: the DDT killed all of our intestinal worms! So it helped! To fight the hunger and to kill the worms.

I remained there a long time, but I did not see any adverse effects on the prisoners, none at all. We joked about this, "All kinds of diseases are afraid of Communism!" We stole the peanuts and ate them raw, reducing our immediate hunger. Others, more careful, took the peanuts back to camp, soaked them in pure water for a time, and then fried them before eating. This was perilous. If a prisoner was caught with stolen crops, he would be beaten by the guard, forced to write a self-criticism, or sometimes put in solitary confinement.

No one thought of escape. There was no way. To the west was Laos, also under Vietnamese Communism. To the east, an escaping prisoner would have to ford rivers before reaching the grand road.

Along the way, he would meet a hostile local population. Nghe An had been the cradle of revolution for centuries and centuries. We do speak Vietnamese, but our accent was of the South, which betrayed us very easily to those people who speak the central accent.

The harvesting of peanuts was really a feast for us. There was a kind of fresh peanut, not yet dry, which smelled good for eating. We also liked to steal beans; because they were not mixed with DDT, we could eat them safely. With sweet potatoes, we could eat both the vegetable and its young leaves. Although the guards watched us to prevent theft, the prisoners stole about 10 percent of the crop. We had watchers too, looking out for the guards.

Corn was also ideal. We had the right to choose the best ones, which meant the medium young ones. We also ate some kind of corn milk which was raw but delicious, juicy, and very nourishing. But with corn, we had the problem of hiding the traces, the leaves, the cob, and the husk. Some of the prisoners were very negligent in leaving traces. They unintentionally denounced not only themselves but all of us.

At harvest time, we tried to give some of the crop to the civilian population, although these were serious violations for the Communists. A row of workers would take off the whole plant of corn. Another team would collect it and put it in one spot. A third team would separate the corn from the plant. Others would collect the corn and take it back home. But instead of taking the corn from the plant, we would leave some hidden underneath a mound of husks and then we'd signal to the civilians to pick it up after we had left. I would pretend to go to the latrine in order to talk with the local people, or I'd scratch my head, with my thumb pointing backwards, indicating where the food was hidden. Central Vietnam is an extremely poor region, and people are hungry. Whenever there was a harvest, poor people stood by to watch until we got all of our crop. Then they would collect what we had left.

Because of this, the civilian people became friendlier to us. They helped us buy food and other things from outside. Some of the prisoners exchanged clothes for food. Those who traded with the local people often lived quite well. Sometimes I stole peanuts and sweet potatoes, but I never traded directly with the local people. I was too afraid of being caught and punished. When I wished to trade, I gave my clothes to another inmate, who did the transactions for a commission. The civilians did not denounce us because they hated the Public Security Agents.

The crops stolen but not consumed right in the field were brought back home. The prisoners would hide them in many places on their bodies. Some wrapped the plants compactly in a piece of cloth and hid the packet in their buttocks. Others had shirts with double linings. They would have a hole somewhere which led into the lining. Usually when we went to the field, we were permitted to carry a container of drinking water. Some of the prisoners drank just half of the water. After wrapping the stolen crops in nylon, they placed them at the bottom of the container. If the guards checked, the container appeared to be simply full of drinking water. Some men tried to carry food in under a hat.

A number of people were caught, but many were willing to take the risk. Some were very smart; when caught, by using sweet words they tried to persuade the guards to ignore the incident. And sometimes the guards or cadres did that. The North Vietnamese soldiers were more moved by our words; their mission was fighting, not guarding prisoners, so if we kept talking and pleading with them, at last we would succeed. But the guards of the Public Security Agency were trained to work with prisoners, and they did not have a heart. They were unmoved by our words. They were used to giving brutal beatings to the criminal prisoners. They were usually pretty well educated, they knew their mission, and they could not be reached by sweet words.

Attempts at Suicide

At this time, I became so depressed that I tried to kill myself. I made two attempts. I was sick with a duodenal ulcer. When I had too much worry and hard labor, my ulcer returned. All the medicine my family had sent me had been confiscated. The ulcer was very painful and bothersome, particularly at sunset time. I was completely exhausted, thirsty, tired, and sunburned from the daily work. In 1975 I had entered the camps weighing 75 kilograms; by 1980 I was down to about half of that, around 40 kilos.

During my whole military career I had been a diplomat, enjoying good food, good drink, good wine. I had become very fat. Now in 1980, at the age of 53, I was starving with the worst of food. The metabolism of my body underwent a brisk change to which it could not adapt. I became extremely ill, tired, and depressed. I would recite those two verses of Nguyen Du which described how our lives may be transformed: earlier like rich brocade, later like a discarded flower.

Most important at this time, each prisoner was assigned a definite quota of work to be finished by one way or another. Otherwise he received collective criticism and even punishment. Others were strong enough to make a dike; it had to be the length of an arm span, made of mud. I could not do it in time, so I would be criticized by the inmates, who had to wait until I finished. The official condemnation would come later, at the weekly self-criticism meeting held on Saturday night. This lasted indefinitely, depending on the problems discussed.

Personally, I am rather self- or inward-turning, very sensitive about my self-respect, so this hurt me seriously, the fact that I was holding everyone else back. Some of the younger inmates were very insolent: "When you eat, you can eat the same amount as me, and now you work. I can complete my portion of the work; why can't you finish yours?"

This was very hurtful to my self-esteem, my self-respect. Also, my ulcer hurt me almost all winter. The brisk change of season affected it. The more it was cold, the more I had the sickness. To add to this, I had the constant worry that there was no hope of getting out of prison. All of this led me to the final choice of ending my life, the sooner the better.

I told no one of my decision. First I tried to store some chloroquinine, a strong antimalarial drug. I hoped to kill myself with an overdose of this. But during an unexpected inspection, my stock was seized. These were medicines sent to me in the family gift package, but as always happened, from time to time they would be discovered and confiscated. But then I managed to have my wife bring me more medicine, for she came twice to visit me.

The first time she came, I was brought to the guest house for visitors, located within the camp. We sat across a table. Other visitors and prisoners were there. We spent a lot of time just weeping, we were so moved. We were given 20 minutes by the guest house noncommissioned officer. He was very rich, thanks to bribery and bonuses. By giving him money, visitors could stay longer with the prisoners. My wife stayed two nights in the guest house, the first night when she arrived, and the night prior to her departure.

At that first meeting, in the middle of 1980, she told me how our two sons had fled the country. I told her about my health and my needs, and asked her to bring chloroquinine when she next saw me. But most of the time we were so emotional we forgot to talk about everything.

About four months later, she made a second, unexpected visit to me which caught me by surprise. This visit lasted about half an hour. She handed me the chloroquinine but then burst into tears as she informed me that our two sons had been captured in their attempt to escape. Both were in Con Son Jail, a remote island used for isolating criminals and political detainees. This was very hurtful. I feared that my sons would die and my family would have no more heirs. My wife was very angry with me. She reminded me that in 1975 she had implored me by telephone to let her and the children escape in advance of me, but I had preferred that we escape together. My plan for our escape had failed. Whenever a bad event occurred to our family, she had the same criticizing behavior towards me.

After hearing this, I was completely depressed. I tried to take my own life with the new dose of chloroquinine, but I just got sick. The company leader reported this, and I was taken to the dispensary. No one knew what was wrong with me because no one was qualified. I remained in the dispensary only a few days because it was so uncomfortable. The food for patients was very much less than for those who worked. In the dispensary I was alone, with no one to help me as in our own unit quarters. So I returned to the unit.

I got a second amount of chloroquinine from my friend who in protest had cut his vein. I complained about fever. This was malaria country, so he gave me some medicine. He did not realize that I intended to take my life with it.

As I had done the first time, I took all of the medicine. I got vertigo, but that's all. I did not go to the dispensary; I preferred to stay in the barracks.

At last some friends gave me a philosophy of life. They knew that I was depressed. I kept a notebook about the Buddhist philosophy of life. The remarks I wrote on Buddhist philosophy helped me through this period. I have this notebook today, since my wife sent it to me when I had escaped to Thailand.

The man who had cut his vein helped me most. He too wrote a book, a technical one dealing with photography. He often asked me to give my opinion of his book. Since he remains a prisoner, I am sure it will be seized and taken from him.

He was a smart man with a French education. He was on the list of South Vietnamese authors condemned by the new regime. The two of us were the only people in the company who were interested in literature and spiritual thinking rather than just seeking food. He did not grab food. By that time, his daughter was in Canada; she was rich enough to supply his family in Vietnam with money, and they sent him all kinds of food, clothing, and medicine. When we were in the fields, we worked closely together, and that's where we talked. We also spoke at night. I was in the upper platform right above him. We would exchange gifts of food that we received from our families. During the time he was cut off from receiving packages because of his beating the company leader and throwing blood on him, I shared my food with him.

The number of visits a person received from relatives depended on how much money his family had. We could not pay for a visit every month, but others were able to do so. My wife figured out a way to visit as many times as she liked. When she went to the North, she would take goods from the South and sell them. When she returned, she sold goods from the North. In this way, she paid both for her expenses and for my things. She was very good at business. When I returned from the camp, I found that she had set up a successful business exchanging diamonds, jade, and money. She had to be an expert to determine the quality of diamonds. She made many trips between Saigon and Hanoi, but she visited me only twice, so that she did not draw the attention of the Communists to her.

Relatives could bring prisoners unlimited amounts of things, but to reach us they had to travel by bicycle. This limited the size of packages. A rich family would bring in a convoy of bicycles. Usually we received sugar, cigarettes, cake, sweets, salty food, dry fish, dry meat ready to eat, roasted peanuts, fried beans, roasted rice, cooked dry flour, fish sauce, and candies. Supplies like this might last us for three months. Money and medicines, both prohibited items, often were hidden in the foods.

I think that the American prisoners of war were treated better than we were. The Communists were very smart, well trained, and briefed about their behavior to Americans who were placed in the Central Prison in Hanoi. They were treated well. While the Americans were threatened and treated badly by the countryside people outside of Hanoi, once in the "Hanoi Hilton" they were fondled compared to us, not because the Vietnamese Communists are humanitarian, but to please and ease American public opinion, and to look for some money. But for us, outside of the little help our families gave, there was no one to take up our cause, no hope at all that we would ever be released. And many of the inmates I knew are still living out their lives in reeducation camps.

Early in 1981, I suffered from appendicitis. I underwent a surgical operation done by a noncommissioned officer Vietnamese surgeon. I was given anesthesia, but the bad hygienic conditions of the operation caused complications of diarrhea that lasted about five days. Each day I went to the latrine 20 or more times. Finally I could not walk any more. They continued to give me antibiotics. The more I got, the more diarrhea I got, until someone explained that the antibiotic killed the organisms which create fermentation in the intestine, and this creates diarrhea. Then they stopped all antibiotics. A few days later I recovered, but I was completely dehydrated and exhausted. At that time, the lunar New Year, an amnesty was declared, and I was released, apparently because I was so ill. I had not expected this, so I wondered again about those two verses of Nguyen Du: inexplicably, my fate had reversed again.

[See also Chapters 19, 20, 21, 32, and 33.]

CHAPTER 23

Ten Indochinese Days: 1975-1978

NARRATOR 13: EX-ARVN CAPTAIN

"I want people to know what happened to us when America abandoned us to the Communists, what it is like to live under Communism, not as idealized in books, but as people actually live it. Americans should hear how our freedoms were taken away, how we were sent off to reeducation camps, starved, put in metal connex boxes for punishment, overworked with excessive labor, and allowed to die without adequate medical treatment. I remember the horrible screams of prisoners as their gangrenous limbs were sawed off without anesthesia. We must never forget the names of those who resisted reeducation at great personal risk of torture or execution. That's why I want to tell you about the three years I spent in Communist reeducation camps."

As he spoke, Captain Hung looked at me intently; his deep-set eyes spoke of suffering; his thin frame and enormously thick spectacles conveyed an impression of frailty. But the hard line of his thin lips revealed his determination to survive the camps and escape from Vietnam.

We were sipping jasmine tea, sitting at a table in the back room of a Vietnamese Buddhist pagoda located in a West Coast city. Captain Hung spoke excellent English, learned during extensive job training since his arrival in America as a boat person in 1980. Because jobs in his field were scarce, he was unemployed at the time we met, and so he spent his time, as did many other young men, helping out with repairs and maintenance of *the pagoda. When he heard that I was seeking to interview a survivor of a reeducation camp, he offered to tell me of his experiences.*

"I hate Communists," he said. "When I was six years old, the Communists came to our house in Hanoi, killed my father, and took away our property. My mother died of grief a year later. I never forgot that, so in 1954, when the opportunity came, I left for the South; I was fifteen years old. The rest of the family, my sisters, remained in the ancestral village of my father. Not only Americans, but many South Vietnamese were completely fooled by the Communists. Because I was from the North, I knew the Communists well; I realized the danger if they won. That's why I fought them to the end."

He spoke in a blunt uncompromising manner that at first made me uncomfortable; I was not used to hearing such polar contrasts and extremist views. Captain Hung could find nothing good or even neutral to say about the Communists, except possibly that they had dedication and stubborn will. "They are liars," he said; "that's how they operate. And they are corrupt, far more than the South Vietnamese ever were."

I wanted to understand why he, like so many other Vietnamese-Americans, spoke of Communism with such vehemence. That his father, a wealthy contractor, had been killed by the Communists, came as no surprise, nor did his personal reaction. But as I listened to his story, I came to see in it not the individual sufferings of one man, but the despair of a people who witnessed the fall of their nation, the destruction of their way of life.

Except for the murder of his father, Captain Hung's childhood memories were pleasant, and they helped to sustain him during the dark years of his detention in reeducation camps. In Hanoi, he lived in a two-story brick house that was painted yellow. He remembers eating well: rice, pork, chicken, lots of fish, and fresh vegetables. Although they were Buddhists, his father sent him to a Catholic school so that he would learn French. Soon after that, his father was killed; then his mother died, and Captain Hung's life changed.

He was reared by his paternal aunt, a widow who brought him back by steamboat and bus to the ancestral village of his father, in the heart of the Red River Delta. She showed him a book about the history of his family and told him how his grandfather and great-grandfather had served as high officers for the emperor in Hue. He adjusted to the rhythms of this rice-growing village, where people used peanut-oil lamps for light and thatch *for cooking fuel. Most people lived in mud and thatch houses; his family was one of four or five that had brick or stone houses.*

Captain Hung's schooling took place in one of the three humble Buddhist pagodas of the village. After school, he and the other boys played with homemade toys: marbles chipped from stones and smoothed on cement, a soccer ball or volleyball made from the bladder of a freshly killed pig, dried, inflated, and wrapped with dry banana leaves and string made from the dry trunk of a banana tree.

Captain Hung especially recalled the two harvest seasons, May-June and October-November. At this time, people worked extremely hard. Farm wage laborers would arise about 4:00 A.M., eat, leave for the fields by 5:00, and work straight through until 10:00, when they would take a 15-minute break. The owners of the lands on which they worked would bring them tea, handmade molasses candy, and betel for chewing, and at noon would bring them lunch consisting of rice, fish, vegetables, small crab, and crab soup. About 6:00 P.M. the men would tie the bundles of paddy they had harvested, hoist about 300 pounds on shoulder carriers, and bring them back to the threshing yards in the village, after which the owners fed them an evening meal of rice and fish. Later, the workers would drag a stone cylinder wheel around in a circle over the paddy to separate the straw from the grain. The workers preferred to be paid in cash, but usually received grain. "People lived modestly and simply," Captain Hung said, his face softening. "The work was hard, but we lived in a rich rice-growing area and had enough food to eat."

He fled to the South in 1954. He joined the armed forces, received special language and intelligence training in the United States, and worked alongside an American marine unit throughout his military career. After the fall of South Vietnam, Captain Hung, along with thousands of other officers of the ARVN, reported as ordered for what they were told would be ten days of reeducation training. Later, when they realized that this announcement had been a ruse to get them into harsh labor camps, "ten Indochinese days" became an ironic expression that referred to their being held for many years.

Because he was of lower rank, and presumably of lesser risk than higher officers, Captain Hung was sent to the less harsh labor camps of South Vietnam, where he remained for three years before he was released. Captain Hung's story is notable for its account of the resistance of prisoners to

*Communist reeducation. Resistance activities were probably more frequent
among the younger officers, who tended to be more hot-headed than their
older superiors and who were in the more accessible southern camps, where,
if they escaped, they would not immediately stand out as outsiders.*

*Captain Hung expressed great contempt for his Communist captors, but
even greater resentment at the way his own commanding officers abandoned
their men during the fall of Saigon. After his release from the camps, he
wandered through the streets of Saigon for several months. He described
that time under Communist rule as one of pervasive scarcity, corruption,
and demoralization of society. He escaped from Vietnam by boat. A
nephew and niece on a different boat disappeared, and Captain Hung as-
sumes that they are among the thousands of fleeing boat people who died
on the seas.*

*During a four-month period from November 1981 through February
1982, Captain Hung and I met some nine times for about 16 hours to record
his life history. In March, he accepted a job in the area of his training, and
is now outwardly a successful tax-paying wage earner and family man.
But those three years of horror linger in his memories. He does not want
them to be forgotten, for in his view they remind us of what the reunification of Vietnam really meant.*

"Fight Until Your Last Drop of Blood!"

On the morning of April 23, 1975, as the Communists were
closing in, my general ordered me and other officers to assemble
our men for a big meeting. This was to be his final, stirring speech.

"You men have to stay in this spot to fight the Communists,"
he said. "Unite to fight! Don't divide; don't separate!" He swore at
some of the officers who had already run away, including one of his
trusted colonels. He shouted, "Don't run! Fight! Use your weapons! Fight until your last drop of blood!"

Then he ran away and left us to our fate. He betrayed us; he
broke his promise and flew off to America. I know where he now
lives. A man like that, I hate him. He is like our President Thieu,
who also abandoned his people.

That's the way the war was in Vietnam. The high-ranking officers told us to fight, but they never did. Why, they didn't even plan

the fighting: all of the organization, the plans of attack, were written by our captains who gave the orders to their lieutenants. The high-ranking officers signed the plans and took credit for it. On April 30, I was in Saigon, where I was stationed. We knew the end was near. President Thieu had already run away, so we expected to hear Duong Van Minh, the Interim President of Vietnam, make an announcement. We waited; we wondered: would he tell us to fight on or to surrender? Around 10:30 A.M. the announcement came. He told every soldier to drop his weapons and go home. There would be no more fighting. We should welcome the Communists. Many people cried, and some committed suicide. I heard later that five of our generals killed themselves. They were men of honor, and we will remember them always.

A few weeks later, I reported for reeducation. I was sent to Ka Tum, in the Tay Ninh area of South Vietnam, very close to the border of Cambodia.

Starvation, Torture, and Death

During the first year, each prisoner in our reeducation camp was given a monthly ration of 16 kilograms of uncooked rice, along with vegetables, fish, and a small amount of meat. In the second year, our ration of rice was cut to 12 kilos. For rice they substituted flour, corn, and a coarse grain that is fed to horses and pigs. We had to cultivate our own vegetables. By that second year, we were better organized and planted kitchen gardens. But the funny thing is, if we grew more vegetables, they cut our rations; if we grew fewer vegetables, they gave us larger rations.

I remember one day when a prisoner went to the jungle, killed a huge snake six meters long, and dragged it back to camp. All of the men in Platoon B had a good meal that night. I was not part of that group, but I lived very close to them. At the end of the month, the Communist financial officer called the leader of Platoon B to his office and said, "For the next two months, Platoon B will get less dry fish and vegetables. You've had too much meat this month."

"What meat?" asked the platoon leader.

"Snake meat."

The platoon leader replied, "We caught it in the jungle."

"The meat belonged to the government," said the official.

From then on, if any prisoner caught something, he ate it in the jungle, or he cut it up, sneaked back to camp with it, and ate it without letting the Communists know.

Each morning when we passed through the bamboo gate on our way to jungle work, we had to report to the sentry, telling him how many of us were going out to work, to what unit we belonged, and what our work assignments were for that day. We were not allowed to use the word "comrade" to the guard, but had to call him "Elder Brother." He used the same term for us. When returning through the gate, we had again to tell the sentry how many prisoners were with us, even if we had just gone out and come back. Prisoners who were carrying things might go back and forth ten times, and each time the first man in line would report to the sentry. The rest of us had to stand there, no matter how heavy a load we carried. We could neither put it down nor proceed until the guard gave us permission. To punish us, some guards forced us to stand for long periods. Any prisoner who walked through and reported without slowing down was punished.

Every day a few of us out of the group of 800 were made to stand for over an hour. This happened to me 20 times. During these punishments, prisoners fainted from exhaustion, for it was easier to carry wood while walking than to stand with it. Some of the men had made many trips, and often had carried a single load for over an hour. They were tired and would forget to stop for the sentry perched high atop a tower. Then they were made to stand still and hold that load for one or two hours. At that point, they collapsed. This never happened to me, but about 30 men in my unit of 200 fainted, particularly in the second year, when they were starving and weak. When that happened, the sentry would give us permission to carry the men into camp, then return and bring in their wood, in addition to our own loads. The sentries were low in rank; this was their only opportunity to punish us. The sentries from the North were harder on us than those from the South.

As the days went on, our standard of living became worse and worse; many prisoners died. In my group of 30, two men died; some groups had more and some had less who died. The causes were first that we were forced to do very heavy work while receiving very little food. We quickly became exhausted; we deteriorated fast. Second, many people had dysentery. Third, because of diet deficiencies, particularly lack of meat and milk, many people developed rheumatism and other crippling and paralyzing diseases that looked like polio. Finally, although we had doctors, we had no medicines and no surgery room. The amputation of limbs was done with a handsaw, without anesthesia. I know of six prisoners in our battalion who had their limbs taken off in this way. Several of them died from infections. (For a Viet Cong surgeon's report of performing amputations without anesthesia during the war to save Viet Cong soldiers, of whom 50 percent survived, see Mangold and Penycate 1985: 189.)

The reason they lost their limbs in the first place was infection. While working in the jungle, they would get a slight injury. Because we had no medicines, infections developed: pustules grew, the infection spread until the arm or leg was full of gangrenous pus. Then the limb had to go. The prisoner was put in sick bay. Inside a mosquito net they cut off his limb, applying the only medicine they had, hot water. The patients cried loudly because there was nothing to stop their enormous pain. Everyone in the camp heard their terrible screams. Then their stumps became infected, and they died. Because we were often switched from one group to another, I did not see all six of these men die, but others told me what happened to them. We knew when someone had died because we had to wrap a mat around the corpse and bury it. In the second year, we made wooden coffins for those who died.

In that first year, Ngo Nghia, a former first lieutenant of a parachute troop, was sentenced to die for killing a Communist soldier while trying to escape from the camp. I was forced to witness his execution. He was 26 years old. Since that time, a lot of people in the U.S.A. have collected money for his widow.

Because we were moved around so much, we often didn't know what happened to those who resisted. Often they would disappear at night, never to be seen again.

But I do remember one incident that happened during my third year as a prisoner. A French radio-television representative came to visit the camp, along with seven or eight other people. To prepare for this, two days earlier the Communists told a 21-year-old second lieutenant, a former student at the University of Saigon, to deliver a speech for the TV crew. The Communists wrote the speech for him: "We prisoners have been treated very well; we have been given good food and shelter and have received good lessons to study. All of us former ARVN soldiers recognize that we are guilty, and that we made too many mistakes against the People. We thank the Communists for coming to our country to liberate South Vietnam."

Instead of reciting these prepared words, he gave his own speech, written with the help of his friends, which contradicted everything that the Communists wanted him to say: "We are treated badly; we have no medicine and not enough food. We are forced to do heavy, exhausting labor."

When the Communists heard this, they called out, "Who is still CIA among you?" As soon as the reporters left the camp, the Communists beat that lieutenant for a long time. Then they handed him a prepared confession. He tore it into pieces.

That was the last we ever saw of him. The following day, one of the reporters came back to the camp and asked to see the lieutenant. The guards said, "He is not here anymore; he's gone."

Each day, each man assigned to wood cutting was supposed to cut down one tree and bring back one log 4½ meters in length and 23 centimeters in diameter. No man could carry that heavy weight, so the Communists explained, "We don't ask you to carry it by yourself. We ask six of you to cut down one tree, carry it to camp, return to the jungle, and get the rest: one tree for each man."

Sometimes we worked until midnight, for if we didn't finish, we were put in the connex. Depending on the seriousness of the offense, we'd be kept there for one day, three days, sometimes over a week. Each day we received a small amount of water and one-half of a meal. Before they'd let us out, the Communists would force us to sign a confession and promise to do better in the future.

I was put in there three times for three days each. I just sat there with the others who were being punished and thought about the corruption and cowardice of our former generals and president, who had left us behind. There wasn't enough food; I was starving, and my head began to ache. I became dirty, itchy, and like the others in the connex I developed rashes, since there was no water with which to bathe. There was a small hole in the connex, through which friends handed us a can to use for urinating. Also, they would bring us little bits of food, which they would hand through the hole. Each time they came, they were accompanied by a Communist guard, who would not let them talk with us. In the connex we had no blankets, and we got very cold. We also were covered with mosquito bites; we were itching all the time, and we frequently became ill. What made the connex terrible for us was that it was so bitterly cold in the cold season, and so unbearably hot in the summer. We dreaded the cruel torture of the connex.

Resistance and Escapes

Despite our fear of punishment, many of us resisted the Communists as best we could. Some people composed songs making fun of them. At night, we sang these songs softly. Other people claimed to be sick and unable to work, which was their way of not cooperating with the Communists. Others deliberately injured themselves, but in doing this they risked being thrown in the connex.

We also resisted the Communists by sabotaging their orders while appearing to follow them. Once they ordered us to cut a tree 4 meters long and 25 centimeters in diameter. We did exactly what they asked for, except that the tree we cut was so crooked that it could not be used.

"Why didn't you cut a straight one?" they demanded.

We replied with a joke, "Sir, this is the Year of the Snake, so all the trees in the jungle are bent. That's why we cannot find a straight one."

Some of the guards laughed at this, but others became quite angry. They shouted, "Get a straight tree tomorrow, not one but two trees!"

We did the same with bamboo. They told us to cut straight bamboo; we cut curved ones. We couldn't be open in our resistance, but step by step we did our best to disrupt their plans.

Our greatest success came when they ordered us to build them a headquarters and meeting house. We did our best to make as many mistakes as possible. Since we had no nails, we had to fit bamboo dowels into beams made of logs. For these dowels, we used broken or very weak bamboo. The beauty of this was that our intentional error was not visible. The whole building stood; it appeared to be stable. But two or three days later, a big wind blew and the house suddenly collapsed, killing one Communist lieutenant and one Communist soldier, and injuring one prisoner who was unlucky enough to be called in to clean the house. That was the only time I saw a success like that. We felt very good about it. We had no weapons, but we used our brains against them.

The Communists were really angry: "Next time, if you don't build carefully, you will be killed!" But they did not actually kill anyone for these mistakes.

Among us were a couple of cowards who obeyed whatever the Communists told them. We saw them out of the corners of our eyes; we did not like those men, for they sometimes informed on us. If I suspected a man of informing on us, I would avoid him.

There is something else we did very secretly, so that these informers would not turn us in. In the second year, relatives visited many of the prisoners, although not me, because all of my relatives were in the North. These visitors brought food, which helped the prisoners stay alive, but they also smuggled in some American books, including *The Godfather*, *Gone with the Wind*, some James Bond novels, and even *The Pentagon Papers*. The men who visited us were searched, but not the women; they hid the books in their clothes. We read *The Pentagon Papers* secretly to learn about our war. Only a few of us could read English; most of them were doctors. I could read English since I had lived for a year in America. We tore the book into little parts, read small portions, and exchanged them with trusted prisoners. We were never caught, and the Communists never realized we had them, although from time to time they staged impromptu searches for prohibited goods. We stored our book fragments in nylon bags buried in the firewood pile or under the thatch roof.

In the camps, our physical condition deteriorated. The lucky ones, about 60 percent, simply got thinner and thinner, weaker and weaker, and sick. About 30–40 percent of the prisoners became much more ill, with rheumatism, paralysis, or worse. Our legs became so small that you could see skin and bone only, no flesh. Of course we suffered from vitamin deficiencies; that's what our camp doctor said. After two years in the reeducation camp, I had shrunk from 140 pounds to 90 pounds, and after only one year my hair became gray. I think it happened because I thought too much. I kept remembering the mistake I had made when I decided not to escape from my country. I had believed the Communist lie that North and South would be reconciled.

The Communists promised us that we would be released. In the first year, we believed them. When we weren't, and life became very hard, we realized that the Communists had broken their promise. They had told us to bring supplies to last for ten days. After two years, not a single person had been released. We thought of only one thing, escape.

Actually, quite a few prisoners escaped, sometimes as many as 30 at a time. One night in 1978 the battalion commander told us that 50 men from our unit of 800 had escaped that week. In other weeks, only three or four people would escape, usually at night or in the early morning. They'd wait for their connections, then go. Sometimes we knew this, but also that we couldn't go at that time. So we'd say goodbye.

If caught escaping, prisoners were put in a connex box or in a bamboo house surrounded with barbed wire. In the house they had to sleep on a wet dirt floor, with no blanket or clothes, and their food ration was cut in half. The metal roof made it very hot when the weather was hot, and extremely cold when the weather was cold. Two men from my unit died from exposure in this house, and my friends told me of another 30 men whose deaths they could document. I think the number who died was more than that.

Not only did we work, but we also were forced to receive instruction from the Communists. They presented these in ten lessons, which were very stupid, but they taught them as if they were correct. During the lessons we just sat and listened to them talk. The lessons might take eight hours in a day, with a couple of hours of discussion at night. After the lessons had finished, we might get a week full of discussion in our own groups.

Sometimes the Communists stayed with us during the discussions; at other times we were alone, but then we had to keep minutes of our discussion. We did not take this stuff seriously. While making it sound believable, we actually made it as ridiculous as possible, since the Communist who read it usually was not well educated.

We resisted the discussion lessons too. The Communists instructed us to clap our hands when the instructor completed a paragraph. At the end of the lesson, we were supposed to clap much louder. Some of the lessons they gave us we didn't want to hear; we wanted to leave, but they forced us to listen. Sometimes, when we thought we had stayed too long but were still in the middle of a lesson, we'd clap our hands too long. The instructor thought he was doing a good job, but we were signaling to ourselves that we wanted to leave. We'd clap too much at the end of each paragraph. We also resisted by claiming to be sick on the day of the lesson. On those days, suddenly the sick bay would be filled.

Even so, we were forced to listen to these lessons, and then to discuss what they told us to discuss. Once, they told us that the Americans and the former regime had been cruel, and we were told to talk about that. We tried to use very good words to show how cruel the Americans were to bring bombs, cannons, and tanks to kill the Vietnamese people. ARVN troops went through the countryside raping women, killing chickens and pigs, using chemicals to burn a lot of trees. We used very strong words, but in our hearts, we thought differently. We could not say what we really thought. All the time, we said, "Yes, yes, yes."

"Do you love Ho Chi Minh?"

"Yes, yes, yes."

"Do you hate Thieu?"

"Yes, yes, yes."

When we were alone, we thought otherwise. But we also thought, "The Communists are stupid, yet they defeated us."

A lot of Vietnamese believed that we lost because the Americans withdrew their military aid to us in 1975. We also lost because of corruption in Vietnam. But the big thing was the American decision not to supply money for arms. Until then, we had believed that we could resist. When we heard the news in March 1975 that the U.S. Senate had voted not to give us aid, everybody was down. Still, lots of troops, not the highest, but from major down to private, wanted to continue the fight. Lots of Vietnamese thought that the Americans would return to liberate them, especially after the news of Communist cruelties became known. I never believed that. Instead, I figured that we had been betrayed and abandoned. I wondered if we had been victims of a U.S.A.-China agreement, that as a trade-off we would be divided up and given to China. Or perhaps Vietnam was a pawn in an international chess game: "I get one piece if you get another." As we suffered through the Communist lessons, I pondered sadly how such a turn of events could have come to pass.

Father Pedicab

I was moved around a lot. When I was in Unit B-13, Camp C-1, I met four Catholic priests. Three of them, all former army chaplains, were strongly against Communism. The fourth, Father Hoang Van Thien, originally had advocated compromising with the Communists. During his first few weeks in prison, he had been very calm and quiet, for he believed them when they told him that he and other prisoners would be released after ten days of reeducation. After four months in jail, however, when no one had been released, he came to hate the Communists. To show his resistance, he put cardboard signs on himself. On the front panel, he wrote the word "Papillon," a reference to the famous book by that name as well as an indication of his intent to escape. The Communists did not realize what the sign meant. On his back panel, he put the words, "Prisoner at hard labor." The Communists were furious when they saw this, but they did not kill him because he was not violent. He was like Gandhi.

Every day, from eleven-thirty to two, our lunch and rest hour, he would put on his signs, carry an iron digging stick to the backyard near our sleeping quarters, and dig some holes to plant vegetables. The ground was very hard, full of gravel and cement, but day after day, through sun and rain, he was out there working. He never wore a hat or shirt; he soon became very dark and skinny.

Whenever we had lessons and discussions, he would never say anything, but alone with me he talked about himself. We became

good friends. In our country, we have a three-wheel bicycle pedicab. Before the Communists came, he used to drive a pedicab in
the city of Hue, and he donated his earnings to the poor people.
That's why people called him Father Pedicab. He was not the only
priest to do this sort of thing. In Saigon, Father Phan Khac Tu was
known as Father Garbage Collector because he donated his earnings
as a garbage collector to the Catholics and the very poor.

Father Pedicab was about 36 years old and wore very thick
glasses. He was thin and tall, about five feet six inches, with dark
brown skin and a large, high forehead. His father and mother were
Catholic. They wanted him to become a priest, and he had wanted
that ever since he was 10 or 11 years old. He could speak good
French and Spanish. He had spent seven years in Belgium studying
in a seminary to become a Father. As a priest, he had no family;
instead, he had devoted his life to a search for peace.

One day I asked him, "Why did you become Father Pedicab?"

He replied, "Because I saw the way the government acted, not
bringing our people to be happy and with peace, but bringing corruption. I did not like these unfair conditions. I wanted to do something good for our people. But I know I'm only one small element
in society. I know what I did is like putting salt in the ocean."

Then he quoted a proverb, "The little crab forms balls of sand
[to carry] from [the beach of] the China Sea, but tires itself out for
nothing." Then he added, "That's like me; what I do is not useful,
but I do it."

Another time, he said to me, "I don't want to get any favor from
the Communists. If I had asked one of my friends, maybe I would
not have gone to jail. But I want to share with other South Vietnamese the suffering of our people." He told me that he wanted to
see what had happened in jail. That's why he was a very quiet
prisoner.

In January 1976, after a group discussion with the Communist
representative, he finally spoke out. "You told us to bring food and
clothes for ten days. Why do we still stay here now? You told us
that this is a reeducation camp. We came here to study. So when
does the class start, and when is it over? Tell me exactly the day and
the time."

The Communist leader did not answer his question. Three days later, Father Pedicab and the other three priests were transferred, and we did not hear about them as long as we were in the camps. I had known Father Pedicab for about six months. Not until I was released in 1978 did I hear any further word about him. I met a priest in Saigon who told me that Father Pedicab had been sent to the North, but he didn't say where. All he said was, "Father Pedicab is very weak."

I remember Father Pedicab's last words as he received the orders to be relocated. "I would like all of you to use my vegetables, and when you use them, do not forget the poor Father. I will pray for you."

He must have known he would be taken away, for the night before, the last time I was alone with him, he reminisced again about his life's direction and also that of the Vietnamese people. "My parents had only one child, me. Every Vietnamese wants to have their son married and have children to continue the family line. My father knew that, but still wanted me to become a priest. His lineage was offered to God, to serve God and our people. Even though I am a Catholic, I have read a lot of books about Buddhism and other religions. I don't mind when I eat Buddhist meals [those offered to ancestors]. If they ask me to eat, I am happy to do it."

Then he returned to a theme we had discussed often, why the South Vietnamese had lost to the Communist North. "I myself don't believe that we were defeated by the Communists," he said. "The victory was not won on the battlefield but in the arena of propaganda. Ours was not good; we failed to show the world that we fought for the right cause. The Communists had the right kind of people as foreign spokesmen; we didn't."

He concluded, "I think that this is our destiny. The circle, the wheel, it has to turn. When it turns at this point, we have to collapse, but the wheel never stops. It keeps on turning."

The next morning he was gone.

Altogether, I was moved to five different camps in South Vietnam. In the first two years, I was in three camps in Tay Ninh Province. In my third and last year, I was in two camps in the Phuoc Long area. The earlier camps were much more difficult. By the time we were in the last two camps, I think that the Communists had the policy to release us. We got more food, so that we didn't look so starved. No fence surrounded us, and we easily met other civilians who were not in the camps.

And then one day I was suddenly released without warning.

CHAPTER 24

Buddhism Under Communism: 1975-1978

NARRATOR 5: NORTH VIETNAMESE
BUDDHIST NUN

In the view of the Buddhist nun, the Communists proclaim that they allow religious freedom, while in fact they undermine it. She describes how the Communists denounced Buddhist monks, disrupted religious traditions, and constricted religious and social freedoms.

The Closing of the Orphanage

Fifteen days after the fall of Saigon, the Communists sent four people to visit the orphanage that I ran. First they asked me questions about my activities, the financial situation of the orphanage, and about all of the property belonging to the orphanage. They addressed me not with terms of respect, but as "Elder Sister," which was less respectful.

One month later, they sent five men to mix with the children and ask them questions: "Are you satisfied?" They tried to find if the children were unhappy with me, if I had anything to hide, if I had exploited them. They needed evidence to accuse me and evict me. Then the men made an inventory of all the items in the warehouse, and from that time took over control of the orphanage. They let me stay, but would not let me do anything. They kept the key; I became just an employee without any authority. I was not even allowed to speak with the children.

The Communists would not allow me to hold a ceremony on the anniversary of the death of the Buddha, nor to preach at gatherings. Twice they did let me invite a senior monk to give a talk. The first time was about three months after I was relieved of authority; the second was one week later. On a third occasion, the Communist with the key did not show up to unlock the pagoda. The monk and the audience waited outside for a half-hour, and then returned home.

The man with the key appeared long after. I asked him, "Where were you?"

He replied, "I was down over there."

I said, "This is Thursday, and the monk came. Why didn't you open the door?"

He did not respond.

When I complained to the Director of Social Services, who supervises all orphanages, he agreed to let a monk come and preach, provided that he submit his text in advance for approval, that those who attend leave their names and addresses, and other restrictions. People would be afraid to leave their names. It was impossible, so I canceled the talk.

This is typical of how the Communists treated us. They claimed that they respected religious freedom and that they did not forbid religion, but in hidden ways they disrupted and prevented religious gatherings and worship.

Soon after, the Communists separated the children according to age, and moved many of them out gradually to other orphanages in the countryside. They removed the food from our warehouse. Then they moved out the machinery for making bags and ampules. We had used these machines for earning income to make the orphanage economically self-sufficient. The Communists offered to hire me as an employee to continue to run the machines. I refused, saying that the government has few resources, and it should spend its money for others. My actual reason was that I did not want to be ensnared in their trap, under their control, and subject to their orders. I wanted to remain free.

Monks Denounced

One day I was told to attend a ward meeting. When I arrived, a Communist official handed me a piece of paper and said, "We brought you here to denounce the six senior monks we have arrested. Write your opinions!" He did not address me by my title as a Buddhist nun, but in a more familiar, less respectful way.

I hesitated, but a monk near me wrote, "Buddhist monks contribute to the well-being of society."

After reading it, the Communist official said, "No! Write it to accuse the *traitors* who have been arrested!"

The monk wrote another general statement. "Be calm. The government will only punish those who commit crimes and reward those who meet government goals." This monk wouldn't betray his teacher, who was one of the six arrested monks.

Then the Communists brought in their agents who claimed to represent various groups: a woman's association, Catholics, and a Buddhist association. One after another they stood up and said, "Those monks are traitors. They have plotted revolution against the government. Punish them!"

For their third and final step, the Communists handed around a people's petition, prepared in advance, which enumerated all types of wrongdoing the accused traitors were said to have made. Then the officials asked, "Do all the people agree?" Everybody at the meeting automatically raised their hands. "Then sign the petition!"

My heart was beating wildly. I feared that the Communists would insist that the first and most important signature be that of the monk whom they had ordered to write the denunciation. If he signed first, he would betray not only Buddhism, but his own teacher, who was like his father. If he refused to sign, he would break up the meeting and himself be condemned. But the Communists asked an old man to sign first. He was said to represent senior citizens. Next, they asked a representative of veterans. The monk was placed tenth. This is how the petition received its signatures.

In this atmosphere, the Vietnamese Communists declare that they allow freedom of religion, while in fact they discourage it.

They encourage sons to denounce fathers, students to accuse teachers, and novices to betray their monks. This is very difficult. If you press the trigger of a gun, at least you kill someone fast. But this other way is a slow death, much more terrible. After three years of living under Communist rule, I realized that they intended to destroy religion. It was then that I decided to escape.

The majority of those who escape do so not to improve their economic or material life but because life in their homeland has become unbearable. They spend a fortune to escape, even though life for most of them is not easier in America. They come here for freedom. They wanted to stay in Vietnam, to help rebuild the country after years of war, but they were not accepted.

Whenever people visited me, they complained about the Communist invasion of their privacy. They were especially upset that nobody could trust anybody, for Communist agents were everywhere in disguise. The agents would say something critical about the government, and if you agreed, they would report you. If they went to your home and saw you talking with another person, they would immediately separate you and ask you both to write on a piece of paper what topic you had discussed, and turn you in if your reports were in disagreement. So whenever we began a conversation, we first agreed on a fictitious subject that we would describe if we were forced to report it. If Communists suddenly appeared, we would switch to that topic. Parents dared not talk to their own children, for the next day the children might involuntarily reveal something to their friends at school. Even husbands and wives became wary of one another.

I had lost all freedom. I could not talk. I could not circulate freely. This was no life at all.

[See also Chapters 7, 30, and 38.]

CHAPTER 25

Escape from Ban Me Thuot: 1975–1978

NARRATOR 6: CENTRAL VIETNAMESE FISHERMAN / BUSINESSMAN

The narrator describes his flight, along with other civilians, from the advancing North Vietnamese Army during their final victorious campaign. (For other accounts of what happened and attempts to explain the Communist success, see Elliott 1980, Harrison 1983, Karnow 1983, Pike 1986, Snepp 1978, Tran Van Don 1978, and Van Tien Dung 1977.) Mr. Liem also describes conditions of life under Communist rule, and the reasons he chose to escape from Vietnam. (For conflicting accounts of economic and social conditions under Vietnamese Communism, see Doan Van Toai and Chanoff 1986, Duiker 1981, Gough 1978, Nguyen Long 1981, Nguyen Tien Hung 1977, Nguyen Van Canh 1983, Scholl-Latour 1985, and Truong Nhu Tang 1985.)

I remember when the Communists came in. My family was living in Duc Lap District [in the Central Highlands] when they attacked in March 1975 and took the town of Ban Me Thuot in that district. That was the first major location occupied by the Communists [in their final offensive]. It was on a Sunday morning, so my brother and my family prepared to go to church. Then we heard artillery bombardment. My brother said, "That's our fire, not the Communists."

I climbed up a tree to see. It was a continuous Communist bombardment. I told my family and wife that it was the Communists. We must prepare to leave. Hundreds and thousands of mortars fired on that district.

I saw even trucks thrown out from the ground; also bodies from the bombardment were strewn all over. I saw very clearly thousands. I saw the Nationalists: for every five shots they fired, the Communists shot hundreds or thousands. Everything caught on fire. They stopped the Nationalists.

Lots of people were afraid. They ran out of their houses to see what would happen. Each carried a small amount [to take with them], but they didn't know where to go. They went in the direction of Ban Me Thuot.

Duc Lap was occupied by the Communists, so people ran away to Ban Me Thuot. They thought they would be safe there. But just a few miles from Duc Lap, they were stopped by the Communists.

On the way to Ban Me Thuot, just in front of us, a young couple were blown to bits. They were the first to be killed in the bombardment. The rest of us were stopped on the road by the Communists. Although they took care of our wounded and gave us food, we were terrified of them. People threw away everything, even their watches. Those with clean shirts made them dirty because they were so afraid of the Communists.

In the beginning, the Communists showed us, not dangerous, but gentle behavior. They said, "We just execute our orders from our superiors, but we have yellow skin and red blood just like you."

So we went back home. There, however, we heard that the Communists would cut off the heads of the men. We didn't want that, especially in front of our wives and children, so we young men escaped to the forest and hid. Better to die in the forest than lose our heads in front of our loved ones.

Now we had a choice, to return to Ban Me Thuot, in the mountains, or to go towards the coast. But when we went deep inside the forest, we got lost. On the first day, nine of us had only one cup of rice. For the next nine days, we had no food. Since we were starving, we decided that we might as well die on the road. We walked until we reached a road. After a while, a Communist truck came by. Then a Honda motorcycle passed us. No one bothered us. Then we realized that maybe people had freedom, so they could use the Honda; maybe the fears of beheading were based on rumor. After we walked about two kilometers, the Honda came back, and I saw that one of the men on the motorcycle was my nephew. He had been looking for us. He said, "No one is getting killed; the Communists did not cut off any heads. You should come home."

We returned home and found that in those first days we had freedom to resume our business. The Communists gave difficulties to people who had worked for the previous government. The rest of us were free to do what we had been doing.

During the first year of liberation, everything seemed good. After that, life became harder and harder.

Five months after liberation, the Communists came to me and said, "You come from the coast. Go back home."

Another said, "If you know how to work as a fisherman, do it; if you stay here [in the highlands], you don't have much chance to succeed."

I had been away from our fishing village for many years. I had worked as a farmer and small businessman; I had also been in the Nationalist Army for a number of years. I no longer knew how to do fishing. Even so, we moved back to the coast.

For the first year, we worked for other fishermen. In the second year, we earned enough money to buy a boat, a small sampan that could travel on the sea.

Already at that time, I had decided to escape from Vietnam. From the day of liberation to the day I left, it was three years. Life under the Communists was so hard compared with before. Every three to six months, the Communists would do an inventory of everything in our houses. People owned these things, but the government controlled it. In that sense, it belonged to the Party and the nation. The reason why I, my family, and other people decided to escape from Vietnam was that we didn't own anything at all.

Food prices increased. It became hard to get work, and finally we could not find work. We could not freely buy rice. Everything belonged to the government cooperative. Under their control, even rice became scarce. A person had to have a ticket to buy everything.

Each family had a ration ticket book for rice, meat, milk, things like that. When a person went to the government cooperative, they gave him some rice and took the ration ticket. They gave the buyer what they had, but they did not have everything. We were authorized to buy up to a certain limit, but it was not enough for us. That's the reason we had to buy outside the cooperative, on the black market. Because we had insufficient rice, we had to buy other things outside, such as corn and manioc. Still, it was not enough, so we had to add water and make soups of rice. That made people dissatisfied. That's why we and many others turned to unlawful or black-market behavior. (See Duiker 1983 for a brief discussion of Vietnam's economic crises after 1975.)

[See also Chapters 8 and 37.]

CHAPTER 26

Communist Intimidation of Schoolboys: 1975-1979

NARRATOR 8: SOUTH VIETNAMESE YOUNG POET

This chapter presents a youth's view of Communism, and how he and others resisted it with ridicule and the printing of clandestine pamphlets. They escaped from Vietnam when their activities were about to be uncovered.

I was 13 years old when the Communists came in 1975. Before that, I knew nothing about the Communists. I lived under their rule until 1979.

Every Thursday, our weekly work day, I would plant sweet potatoes and manioc. Did I like this? Of course not. Hard work. Also, every month or two we had to clean and sweep the streets. We also had military training in which we learned to fire a rifle. At first we drilled with wooden weapons, but when I reached the age of 16, we used real rifles.

I was afraid of the Communists because if a person had a loose tongue, he would be arrested and be sent to jail. I had a friend who was two years younger than me. At the age of 14, he went to an Independence Day meeting organized by the Communists, in which people had to recite slogans for Uncle Ho: "Great Uncle Ho! Long Life Uncle Ho!" Instead of reciting that, my friend reversed the phrase in a way that altered the meaning to "easily duped by prostitutes." That's what he was heard singing, "Uncle Ho is easily duped by prostitutes! Long Life Uncle Ho!" For this he received six months in prison.

We used to change the words to songs or add additional lines. We were told to sing, "Who loves Uncle Ho Chi Minh more than do young children?" We were supposed to repeat that line a second time. Instead, we sang, "Who loves to eat bread and another rice cake more than young children?" The meaning of this was that young children now go hungry.

We used to sing, "Uncle Ho, even though very old, is still cheerful." Then we'd add, "Uncle Ho, even though very old, still likes to play around with girls."

Sometimes we'd sing, "Oh, my beloved country, I love you forever!" Then we'd sing, "Oh, my beloved country, eating manioc I suffer too much!" Manioc is the worst of foods, but that is what we have to eat under Communist rule.

Some people in America like the Communists. That's because they never experienced the hardship or bad treatment under the Communists. After 1975 people in Vietnam hated the Communists. Some of them supported the Communists and gave them food and rice during their fight against the South Vietnamese government. Now they regret it. They realize that it was like feeding a lion cub who, when it grows up, eats those who fed it.

Before 1975 the Communists mostly were deep in the jungle, so we saw little of them. I never saw Communists in my village until they won. There was not much fighting, but sometimes Communists attacked the village and killed South Vietnamese soldiers. But it's hard to remember because there was not much of this. During the war, my brother-in-law became an interpreter for the Americans who stayed on our island. When he was with the Americans, he'd see films and eat chocolate. The Americans acted normal; my brother-in-law did not see anything strange or any bad behavior from Americans.

Like my brother-in-law, my father supported the South Vietnamese government. My father was an employee of the district, so when the Communists came, he lost his job. He hated the Communists, and he wanted to get out. I knew this even though my parents never talked in front of me and never talked politics to us children. But they did say to me that they did not want me to become a soldier and die [in the fighting against the Khmer Rouge in Cambodia]; they wanted me to escape instead. When I told them that I wanted to go on the boat, my father gave my mother some gold to give to me, but I refused to take it. I knew they needed the money to survive.

But soon I had no choice; I had to escape. I and 20 other friends wrote leaflets calling on the people to stand and fight the Communists. I hate the Communists, and this was a way for me to ventilate my hate. I didn't know if it would bring in any result or make any sense. But I wanted to do it, even though we were afraid that we would be caught, tortured, and put in prison. To disguise ourselves, we who were right-handed wrote with our left hands.

In the school, all the teachers were Communists. The children who attended were from families of farmers and fishermen. Those who came from the families of former civil servants, even if they were very bright, were prohibited from going on to college because of the association of their parents with the former government. Those who completed high school were drafted into the army and had no further opportunities for education. I didn't want to be drafted. I saw it happen to others, and I figured it would happen to me. I wanted a choice. What I saw was no freedom; my future was to be drafted into the army and then be killed. Lots of my friends were in the army, although I do not know how many died. My uncle, who was drafted, was killed in Cambodia. His body was sent back to his family.

One day the principal of the high school called me and one of my friends to his office. Both of us had been making the leaflets. The principal said, "You are reactionaries! Traitors!" Although he had no proof, I was scared. I suspected that they might arrest me. Then he said, "I know that those who have distributed the leaflets are students at this school." He did not specify names; he used general terms, and I think he was guessing. But why take a chance? I stopped doing the leaflets for one and a half years.

Then one day, another friend, not very close, asked me, "Did you make leaflets against the Communists and distribute them?" I was astonished that he asked this.

About this time, my friend who had been called into the principal's office with me said, "We've got to get out of here. We've got to get to America. I've got an uncle in Chicago who can help us. Let's get out."

I agreed. I trusted him, for I had known him since we were babies. Also, my friend started this conversation first; then I responded and went along.

My friend organized the trip. It was only at the last minute he told me and invited me to come along. He stole a boat belonging to a woman who was about 60 years old. The people of our island hated her because she was tricky, untrustworthy. She organized an escape trip, got people to pay her gold, and then she kept it. None of the persons could complain because they were doing something illegal and would go to jail if caught. So we chose to steal her boat, and on the third attempt, 16 of us made good our escape. All of the boys except me were 14 years old; I was two years older.

[See also Chapters 10 and 40.]

CHAPTER 27

Visits to a Reeducation Camp: 1975-1981

NARRATOR 11: SOUTH VIETNAMESE SCHOOLTEACHER

Ba Tam was a victim of both sides of the war. Her husband was shot by the French. Her sons were taken away by the Communists to reeducation camps, and one of them died in attempting to flee from Vietnam. Most accounts of these camps have been by the prisoners; in this chapter, a mother describes how she visited one of her imprisoned sons.

The French caused me much trouble in my life; they were responsible for the murder of my husband in 1946. Yet they also helped me. I think they were basically good people. Because of the military situation, they did what they had to, they shot my husband. But when they saw my situation as a widow, they helped me get employment and provided free housing for me at the school where I taught.

My children grew up without a father. I was their sole means of support. I taught in a school; to earn extra money, I sewed dresses, and I spent the money on my children: on food, private lessons, clothing, books, and medicines when they were ill.

So everything was all right. We had an easy life. Two of my sons joined the military. My daughter won a scholarship to America in

1962, left Vietnam, and never returned. My youngest son, a university graduate, took a position in banking.

By the time I retired, the Americans were in Vietnam. Their behavior was all right. While they were here, the country had economic prosperity. Rich people became even more successful, but even for people of modest or low income, like me, life was good. We lived well. Some of the poor Vietnamese girls sacrificed themselves by working in the bars, making friends with Americans to earn dollars. Those who followed the traditional customs disliked those girls who sold themselves at the bar; they were considered not respectable. Still, life was much better than what followed when the Communists took over.

In 1975, when the Viet Cong [Editor's note: She uses this term to refer to the Communist government] came to control the South, the people at first thought it was a nice thing. They greeted them happily, pleasantly. For about a month, life remained the same; we went to the market as usual.

Then in June of 1975, the Viet Cong ordered all high officials, employees of the old government, and military officers to turn themselves in to go and study politics for one month. If they went, nothing would happen to them; if they refused, they would be arrested and imprisoned. Some of the men who reported have never been returned.

All three of my sons went, my two eldest for four years, and my youngest for six years. He was taken to a harsh camp in the very north of Vietnam. Soon after, I lost all of my retirement that I had saved up for so many years. I spent it in order to eat. Simply to get food, I sold my jewelry and household things. The Communists devalued our currency, and they confiscated money, jewelry, and gold that people held in banks. Since I had very little money, the Communists returned most of my money to me. But people became unemployed and hungry. They began to hate the Communists and to seek ways to escape. My daughter in America sent me gifts. I sold them to help my youngest son who was in a reeducation camp. My two eldest sons received help and food from their wives.

When my sons were sent off to reeducation camps, I heard nothing from them for one and a half years, and I thought they were dead. Then I received a letter from my youngest son saying that I would be allowed to visit him. He wrote, "They have treated me very nicely, during the time I have been in the Long Khanh Camp. The daily activities are easier here than in other places. After a year they transferred me to Gia Rai Camp in Eastern Xuan Loc, South Vietnam. They do not have enough water here, just dirty water from the mud."

I visited him at that camp two times. I had to present a permit issued by the V.C. [Viet Cong] and sent to me by my son. I met him at a place outside the camp, and I was given 30 minutes to talk with him. Because my son had asthma, he had lighter work than others, who cut trees. To help him survive, I brought him 10 kilograms of noodles, rice, preserved meat, dried shrimp, salt, and lemon grass. That was all I could afford to buy.

He was very happy to see me. Many prisoners were malnourished; they lacked vitamin C, and some were unable to walk. Most of them, including my son, were very skinny because they did not have enough food to eat. I wanted to cry, but the officials had warned me that if I did, my son would be forced to miss a meal. The V.C. staff remained in the room with us.

The third time I went to see my son, the officials told me that he had been transferred to the North: by ship to Haiphong harbor, by train past Hanoi, and finally by truck to Lao Cai, next to China. Later I found out that the prisoners selected for this journey had been handcuffed together to prevent them from escaping.

During the year that my son remained in Lao Cai, he was not allowed to write home. The camp itself was one of the nicest, since it was set up to show overseas visitors who wanted to see the condition of the camps. When China and Vietnam had their border conflict, my son and the other prisoners were transferred to other camps.

In September 1979, three months after he had been transferred to Vinh Phu Camp, I received a letter from him along with a visitor's permit. In the letter he said that he suffered from beriberi and asthma. It took me seven months to prepare for this trip to the North. I bought flour, sugar, dried shrimp, Vietnamese sausage, and rice. I filled out a short application for permission to visit him. I said that I wanted to see him because of his illnesses. The officials were very polite, but slow. I waited; they did not issue the permit. Later I found out why: they were corrupt; they expected me to give them some extra money. Instead of doing this, I asked a friend with some connections to tell these officials to issue the permit. One month later they did.

The ticket seller at the train station also wanted a bribe. One of my friends paid a little extra and bought the ticket for me; without the bribe I would have had to stand in line for up to ten days. The trains were very crowded; there was no room unless you bribed the ticket seller.

I traveled to the North with two friends. We did not dare to go alone for fear that we would be mugged or have our goods stolen. I know many older people who lost everything, particularly at night when thieves took advantage of the crowding and the darkness. We guarded our luggage closely. Despite the difficulties of the long journey, I was happy inside because I was going to see my son. Although food was sold on the train, I brought fruits and water with me.

To reach Hanoi, we traveled for three days and nights. I remained overnight with a relative and bought some condensed milk and butter on the black market. We traveled overnight to another station. From there, we walked to a ferry boat on the Red River; our luggage was carried by cart. After a three-hour trip by boat, we alighted and walked about six kilometers to the visitor's house, located some distance from the camp. It was quite cold; there was not enough room for everybody, and not enough blankets or beds.

The next morning, the prisoners were led to the visitor's house. When we saw our loved ones, we were happy, but when we saw their physical condition, we started to cry. The soldiers waved their rifles at us and warned us to stop. We were given one to two hours to see our relatives, depending on their behavior in the camp. We were allowed to hug and touch them. We spoke softly, but did not dare to say much because we were being watched. The only thing my son said was that I should bring him as much food as possible. On the way back home, we cried a lot.

In 1981, after six years in reeducation camps, my youngest son was released. Only then did he tell me about life in the camp. Each morning he received two pieces of sweet potato for breakfast. The prisoners had to cultivate fields or cut down trees. Some of them cultivated vegetables, not for the prisoners, but only for the staff. The worksite for prisoners was five or six kilometers from the camp, and at the worksite they received Russian cake made of flour. Sometimes prisoners stole vegetables because they were starving. Sometimes they ate manioc, although this was very dangerous, for if they ate too much, their skin would swell and turn yellow. Dinner consisted of one bowl of rice with salt. Once a week they were given political lessons. On Sundays, they did not go out for daily work, but stayed home and did their own cooking.

Because of the way we have been treated by the Communists, many people have tried to escape from Vietnam. Even though they have a high risk of dying along the way, they dare to try an escape. In 1980 my first son escaped; he disappeared and has not been heard from since. We now assume that he is dead. My other sons remain in Vietnam, but want to leave, using the Orderly Departure Program, but it is a long process. My case took four and a half years.

[See also Chapters 13 and 41.]

PART V

Flight to Freedom

Introduction

The ordeals and plight of Vietnam's boat people have been the subject of numerous books, newspaper and magazine articles, and documentary films. For many of these people, including several of the narrators in this book, flight from Vietnam was not their first, but their second, refugee experience. In 1954, during a period in which people were given the opportunity to move either to the North or to the South, countless thousands of North Vietnamese, mainly but not exclusively Catholics, fled to the South. Many brought with them harsh stories of persecution and terrorism, including the murder of members of their family.

Since 1975, well over one million Indochinese refugees have fled from their homelands; most are Vietnamese (Wain 1981: 6). The ordeals of many boat people have been terrifying; at least 10 percent of those who attempted escape have drowned, died of starvation or dehydration, or been killed by Thai pirates (Wain 1981: 83). Many Vietnamese women have been raped and some kidnapped by pirates (Grant 1979; Nhat, Duong, and Vu 1981; Wain 1981: 70–73). Many victims or witnesses who survived these horrors, especially women and young children, have been psychologically devastated by their experiences. Others have been able to pick up the pieces and have proceeded to adjust, with varying degrees of success, to their new lives in America.

The ordeals of these refugees do not end with the completion of their harrowing escapes. Most of the narrators had to adjust to living in refugee camps for varying lengths of time. These camps varied in the harshness of living conditions and also in the treatment of refugees by camp guards and officials (see Knudsen 1983, 1986, 1988). Part V includes three narratives of refugee camp life that illustrate some of these differences. What all three accounts have in common is a description of how ordinary social behaviors and etiquette deteriorated. For those who are not resettled easily or quickly, the refugee camps can be a devastating experience, as people find themselves in a limbo situation, unable to be placed, but also unable to return to Vietnam (see also Bousquet 1987: 34–53). It is under these trying circumstances that personal character and the formative experiences of childhood affected the ways in which the narrators coped with unsettling new situations.

CHAPTER 28

Despair in a Refugee Camp: 1975

NARRATOR 2: SOUTH VIETNAMESE ELDERLY RURAL WOMAN

Ba That provides a vivid account of the chaotic final days of the Republic of South Vietnam, the escape of her family from Vietnam, their voyage to Guam, and their stay in the refugee camp. Especially noteworthy is her description of how the refugees abandoned conventional civility, particularly towards elders, and how she and her husband suffered because of this.

Escape from Vietnam

In 1975, I began to worry what I would do if the Viet Cong entered Saigon. My two sons who were in the military told me that they would flee, whether or not my husband and I went along. We looked for a way to escape and didn't know where to go. I was afraid of the Viet Cong a lot; I would take a risk to leave Vietnam. It did not matter to me where we went as long as we left. My husband was very upset and unhappy about the invasion of the Communists. He became apathetic, indecisive, and depressed.

At that time, I withdrew all our money from the bank, sold our chickens, and used all of the money to buy a small boat. My sons bought food and oil for the trip. They wrote a letter to another brother of theirs who lived a few miles away and asked him to return home.

My eldest son drove off in his car without us. He went to our boat. I was so sad. We had to get to the boat by ourselves. At 10:00 A.M. I walked with my two daughters to the Y Bridge, which got its name from its shape. On the street I saw a navy man carrying a bag. He followed me. Criminals had been released from the jails and were all over the streets. Near the police station, there were lots of Honda motorcycles that belonged to the police. I saw lots of men come over with guns, shoot the locks, and take all the Hondas. I did not know at that time who was who. They had lots of jeeps without gasoline that were scattered all over the streets. I saw men trying to push them. The navy man who followed me asked me where I was going. I replied, "I'm going to my son's house."

He said, "All the big boats have already left. I have a small boat hidden someplace. Could you let me sit at your son's house for a while?"

I said, "I don't know."

My daughter ran ahead to my son's house, but nobody was there except a servant woman, who said that my son's family had already left. She didn't know where they had gone. Now she was waiting for her husband, who was a Viet Cong. This was the first time that the servant had revealed the secret of her husband. My daughter was scared; she ran out and told me before we entered the house. We turned around, caught a Lambretta taxi [a small, three-wheeled vehicle], and headed back to my husband's sister's house.

When we arrived home, I ran upstairs. I was afraid my sons would leave me behind too. I picked up my packed bag and asked my husband, "Where are your clothes?"

He was sick; he didn't care. He just pointed and said, "It's there." His bag was empty; he hadn't packed anything.

I picked up his empty bag. I hurried my youngest daughter, "Go! Go!" My husband went downstairs to chat with his sister and his nephew. I threw some clothes in his bag along with his tooth-brush, hurried downstairs, handed him the bag, and said, "We must leave."

He replied, "I don't know where to go." Later I found that he took out his toothbrush without my noticing it.

I put all of the bags in the taxi while my husband waited. He did not want to leave. He was ill, sad, depressed. He did not want to talk to anybody. His sister also refused to go. She cried when we left.

The taxi man asked for more money, since he was carrying more stuff. My daughter paid him and said, "Okay, but now you have to go faster." I remember at the time that we were suffering; we didn't know where to go, just vaguely. When we arrived at the Ong Dong Bridge, we found that the Viet Cong already controlled it.

When he saw this, the taxi man said, "I'm afraid to pass the bridge."

My daughter said, "Go ahead, it's all right."

"Okay," he said and drove slowly across the bridge. We went down the hill and over to a small road. We drove a long way down that road looking for the place where our boat sat. All along the way, the Viet Cong displayed lots of flags.

My husband was scared. He said, "Return home."

My daughter told the driver, "No, we cannot return home; we must go."

My husband turned to me and ordered, "Let's go home, let's go home."

I said, "Okay, you can go home, but I'll continue."

He stayed with me. Not far from where our boat was hidden, we saw three small girls standing on the roof of a house displaying Viet Cong flags. They called out to me, "Madam, it's already a peaceful time; where do you have to go?"

I told them, "I have to find my children to return home."

We continued down the road, crossed a small bridge, and stopped. Two of my sons were waiting for us by the barge, ready to go. My daughter-in-law had paid one million piasters to the owner of the barge, a businesswoman who used to sell sweet drinks to people along the riverside.

Finally we left. When we arrived at the gate at the mouth of the river, I was so happy. We transferred to another barge, and it took us out to sea, but not far from the shore. At night we reached a Vietnamese Navy ship near the Saigon River. As people climbed aboard the high sides of the ship, we heard shots and explosions on shore. I was among the last to board. I was pulled up while the ship separated from the barge. I was scared, but not much. We went down into the hold. On the first day, we received no food and we were starving. I just drank one cup of cold water.

By evening I was exhausted. It was crowded. My son told me to sit down and lean against a very big chimney. I was hungry, and so tired I could not lift up my arms. My daughter went over to a woman who was preparing condensed milk for someone. That woman gave my daughter a little of the milk for me. When I sipped it, I felt comfortable.

My husband did not do anything. He was barefoot because he had left his slippers on the barge. Now he just sat next to me; he did not care what we were doing, and he did not listen to me. He used to argue with me, but now he was silent. I did not know what kind of sickness he had.

When I arrived on the ship, I was happy, but also sad because I was thirsty and starving. Then my husband kept silent. He was depressed. It was so crowded that we had no place to stand or even sleep. We sat or squatted on the floor in the hold, with our knees up, with everyone around us. I feared I could not live with the other Vietnamese people on board. They threatened us and yelled at us; they would not let us lie down. Even the military men were very impolite, and so were the Chinese-Vietnamese. So I worried.

The next afternoon, the men of the ship started to cook rice and serve us. We received plain rice, nothing else. My granddaughter went into the kitchen and got some salt and bean curd sauce for us. That night, the boat overflowed with water and the sailors called us to bail out the boat.

At nighttime, we tried to sleep; we placed shoes next to us as a border. Because the shoes were dirty, it would keep people away so that they would not sleep too close to us. Every time I went to step down to go to the restroom, people would curse me out and refuse to let me by. The group slept in a circle, but the older people were pushed in the center by the younger people, who were very strong and impolite. This made it easy for those on the outside of the circle to go to the restroom, but the older people had no narrow space to pass through. When I tried to push my way through the circle, they said, "This is my path, where we stay! Too much trouble! Why do you always have to go?"

"Let me go just a little bit," I replied.

"Liar! Stay there!"

I took a long time waiting. I would stay there, hold on. I would not eat or drink so that I didn't have to go a lot. They were very cruel people. They cursed me insolently, very bad curses, and they did this even to the mother of one of the doctors. They invaded her space. She told them to move back to their own space, and they cursed her for this. What these people would do was to take spaces for ten people even though they were only a group of five, so others suffered and got upset.

I did meet three men who were polite. Once my daughter called me. They said to me that if I were to go away for a while, my daughter should save the space for me; otherwise it would be taken. They helped to reserve the space for me. After a while, my daughter-in-law called me to go below the deck. It was hot, but I stayed there most of the time during the trip.

My grandchildren, I felt so sorry for them. They did not have anything to eat. In the morning, they always vomited. Some former police officers tried to help them and gave them some cooked food.

For three days we remained on that boat. During that time, we had no water to drink; also, we lost our suitcase which contained medicines and some jewelry. I assume someone took it.

On that third day, another Vietnamese ship appeared. It did not have too many people aboard, so we were told to transfer, and then we could get water from them. It was easier to cross over to that boat because there was a bridge. Then we found that we had been cheated: they had no water. It was hot, and we were thirsty.

Once aboard that ship, the men were forced to go down into the hold and pull all the materials out to make a tent to cover the ship. Because it was a warship, it had no cover. My children had lost their shoes in the ocean, so their feet were burned. Also, they suffered from thirst. On that ship, we had a place to sleep, but the stronger people invaded the cleaner area near the front of the ship. Those of us who were weaker were pushed to unclean places where dirt fell, along with water from the rains. When the water dripped, we had to suffer because we could not move elsewhere. We had to accept that.

The next day, an American ship approached and gave us some water, but even then we did not have enough to drink. When we asked for more water, just a small amount the size of a condensed milk can, the Vietnamese authorities sometimes gave us a little, and sometimes they didn't. They even took the can away, so we had to search for a plastic bag to hold water. This too they took away without giving us water.

On the ship, people were divided into groups: the pilots, the navy, the civilians. Each group had a representative. When the American ship sent over food such as cases of apples, canned food, and water, these representatives took them, including the canned meat. All we got was the sauce from the can.

We remained on that Vietnamese ship for three days. On the last day, around midnight, the American ship approached again and gave us some more food supplies. A Vietnamese lady who spoke English told the people on the American boat, "Give food to each family, not to the Vietnamese ship captain, because he will just keep the food for himself." The Americans did that; they made a list and gave food to each family. On that day for the first time we got something besides plain rice. The Americans told us to pull down our Vietnamese flag and put up an American one.

I was very sad. I lay down and did not want to eat. My children were very happy. They received food after they filled out a list. The children called me up to get some food, but I said, "You go ahead and eat; I don't want to." They kept calling. I said, "I'll eat tomorrow morning." My husband ate, for he was starving.

At 9:00 A.M. on the seventh day, we arrived in the Philippines. They allowed us in because we flew an American flag and were led by American ships. After going through several checkpoints, we were searched twice all over our bodies. Then we waited to be transferred to an American ship. Now we had lots of water, so we washed clothes, and the children bathed.

Around 3:00 P.M. we were transferred to American ships. We were supposed to walk across a very big bridge. On either side of us stood American soldiers. They told us to withdraw all the knives and scissors if we had any, and they told us to throw away all medicines. Instead of walking across the bridge, the Vietnamese people competed, *pushed* each other to get across first. They even shoved the priests! The people of North and Central Vietnam are *strange*. They said their ship arrived first so they should go first. The American soldiers saw me, an old woman, carrying a big bag of clothes. They held my hand and pulled me up; they even carried the children.

For seven days we remained on the American ship. Here we had a place to lie down. The Vietnamese ex-soldiers, pilots, and the Chinese-Vietnamese had to stay around the border of the ship. The floor on the ship was like the surface of a table. All of the refugees were authorized to stay on the platform floor. To go to the restroom, we had to go downstairs to another area. But if a person was in the middle of a floor, it was very difficult to get out because of the large numbers of people all over the floor. Again people cursed one another. So the former soldiers and the Chinese-Vietnamese pushed us weaker people in the center of the floor, while they remained on the borders.

If I had to go to the restroom, they'd insult me by saying, "This old woman, too much of a disturbance." Because of this, I went to the restroom only once a day. Then I would insist that they give me a small pathway. But once we went down, they would not let us get back up. And if I insisted on returning, they'd scream loudly, "This old woman is very undisciplined! She wants to go back and forth!"

So I held it inside me. One night around 9:00 P.M., I called down to my eldest son, who stood on the lower deck, "Son, I want to go and urinate; how can I go?"

He begged people to let me pass through, "Please let my mother go down." But it was dark; I didn't see well enough to find my way. My son begged them to help. I don't know why, but someone was so polite; they used a flashlight to show me the way.

I could not walk in the dark; I had to crawl like a baby. When I saw that the way was so difficult, I said to my son, "Well, that's okay, I can wait until morning."

He replied, "No, Mother, you cannot wait; go." So people let me go. Little by little I crawled down. My son waited for me to go down and come up again.

The next morning, my son's wife came up, called me to go and stay with them on the lower level.

Guam

After seven days we reached Guam. I was so happy; so was everybody else. I remember, it was dawn; people screamed out in excitement, "We have arrived! We have arrived!" That morning, we went ashore slowly.

We went to the immigration office. I just waited for them to finish the paperwork. I didn't know what was happening.

We went onto a bus which took us to the camp. But it was a tent. Soldiers let us sleep on military cots. I stayed in Tent Number 40 with my family.

Once we arrived, I became really sad. I thought about my sons who had split up in order to escape from Vietnam. I did not know what had happened to them.

At noon I went to the dining room to ask for food. I was hungry, but happy that they had food for me. There was rice, vegetables, a piece of chicken, and fruit cocktail for dessert. The food was put on paper plates, and we ate with plastic spoons. We would stand in line and be served. I brought some back to the tent for my husband, who had fallen asleep. During the first few days, the Vietnamese volunteered to work at the dining room, where they served food. But they often did not give us enough rice, only one spoonful when we needed two. If we did not have enough to eat, we had to go back and ask for more. There was also a faucet of water for drinking.

My daughter-in-law heard that there was a page area used for families to search for missing relatives. When we checked there, we found that my two sons had put in a search for us and their other relatives.

For bathing, we used the common bathroom. All of the women, young and old, had to take baths together. It was funny, for we never did this in Vietnam. Some of the women hesitated. They kept their pants on while they bathed. We had great difficulty. The girls were embarrassed, because this was really strange. We waited until nighttime to take our baths.

Vietnamese people who did not have enough education would steal and fight with others in the camp. The refugees in the camp included not only captains, lieutenants, and generals, but lots of ordinary people, government employees, businessmen, and even pedicab drivers. At night when people were asleep the uneducated people would enter tents, use a flashlight, and search for things they wanted to take.

Although we had tents, blankets, and good food, what made the camp so difficult was the lack of discipline. The stronger people would simply go into the tents of others and take things. There were not enough American soldiers to guard the camp. We had an electric light in our tent. At night my sons used to take off for another tent where they could get some leftover cooked soup. Usually they would not return until after 11:00 P.M. Remaining in our tent were just me, my husband, and our two daughters.

In the next tent were lots of men about 30 to 40 years of age. I had a radio, and they saw it. Whenever my children would go to take a bath, they'd give me their purses and watches to keep because I didn't go anywhere. I'd just stay in the tent and sew clothes.

One night, my husband, my two daughters, and I were sleeping in the tent. A man unzipped the tent flap, entered, used the flashlight, and searched for things. My daughter was sleeping near the edge of the tent; I was sleeping near the center. Suddenly my daughter saw him and let out a scream of fright. "Mister, you've gone into the wrong tent!" He was not afraid, but continued to search with the flashlight. She screamed again. Finally he left, fearing that the American guards might find him. My husband once saw an American guard chasing someone who came into our area. My husband was afraid, so he closed our tent.

Usually I would stand in line during meal times. We had nothing to do all day but stand there, and you could not believe how long that line became, over 100 yards. It took two hours of standing in line, sometimes while it was raining, to get a meal. While in line we'd chat with one another. And we heard some people say, "Getting in line to receive a meal is very disappointing. I want to go back to Vietnam."

Others would reply, "No, don't go back! There's very great suffering there!"

Standing and waiting in line for long periods was very difficult. But it did not matter, I did not worry because I had food to eat.

The morning meal included rice left from the night before, bacon, fried eggs, canned meat, and a vegetable such as salad or something else depending on what they had left over. The noon meal consisted of hot rice, hot thick soup, hot vegetable, fish, eggs, and sometimes fruit cocktail.

After lunch, I'd go and get some water; sometimes I'd wash clothes or take a bath. The Protestant people had a tent where they gave away thread. My daughter would ask them for thread, and sometimes material, but she often was so slow that they had already given most of it out. They had sewing machines that we could use. My daughter-in-law had brought a small pair of scissors in her cosmetic box. When my daughter brought back cloth, I would make shorts for my children.

Sometimes there was distribution of secondhand clothes, soap, or materials. I was disappointed because I'd still have to get in line a long time to get those. Outside, the Vietnamese guarded that place; they did not let us in because we were pushing each other. It was crowded, so my children usually sat outside under a tree. Sometimes when our turn came, everything was gone.

There was no organization of the Vietnamese in the camp. We were strangers to each other. Even the people in the nearby tents were strangers. We did know one family who were friendly and whose children were polite. Others remained unknown and not friendly.

My children didn't know what to do, how to spend their time. In the morning, they would just wait around; then at noon they would wait in line for that meal. They had to remain in line; they could not take food for others unless those people were ill.

When I left Vietnam, I was very sad, but when I boarded the American ship I was happy because I knew we had left and were not going to die. I was waiting to meet my two sons who had escaped by airplane. One had gone ahead to America; the other was waiting for us in Guam. After waiting night after night, our names were finally called, and all of our family who were in the camp went to the United States together.

[See also Chapters 4, 18, and 35.]

CHAPTER 29

Better to Die at Sea Than to Remain: 1975-1976

NARRATOR 4: CENTRAL VIETNAMESE TEACHER

Phuong Hoang explains why he decided to escape from Vietnam, tells how he prepared secretly for one year, and describes his 1,500-kilometer sea voyage to the Philippines.

A Year Under Communist Rule

In my town, there were only low Communist soldiers, not officers. If people made them angry, the soldiers would kill them and go on. I saw this happen in the market. A soldier grabbed hold of a man and said, "Two days ago you sold me a watch, and it doesn't work. That's wrong. I'll kill you for that." He raised his gun.

The women in the market cried and pleaded with the soldier, "That man did not know the watch was bad; he bought it from someone else and just sold it to you."

The soldier pushed them aside, shot the man, and left. We lived in an area like that; it's not right at all to kill people just because someone feels like it.

When the American soldiers were in our town, they did not act this way. Sometimes on holidays they drank a lot and sang loudly, but that was all right; they were good. They'd walk around the town, and say hello to people; we liked them. Our own soldiers also had good discipline, and good weapons, unlike the Communists, so I could not understand how we lost so quickly. The Communists did not know anything about modern life. What they had was good propaganda, a lie.

Within a few days, the Communists came to every house and searched them. They were quite bewildered and uneasy at what they saw. "What's this?" they asked, pointing to our ceiling fan and our electric lights. When I turned on the fan, they ducked. One young man decided that it was a machine to cut off the heads of prisoners.

"Don't you know?" I asked. "Haven't you ever seen one?"

"Never." When they were small children, they had been picked up and taken to the jungle, where they had been taught how to fight. That's all they knew. They had no understanding of the city. "What's that?" they asked, pointing to the television set. I told them about it, explaining that it was like a movie, but not a real movie. When they saw the toilet bowl, they wanted to know what we wash in it. They were so young and strange. They wore a peculiar uniform; they talked in a funny way, and they expressed very different opinions and ideas. When they talked to us, they used words we did not understand; their customs were unfamiliar to us. They had never seen a watch. They assumed that our floor was made of mud, so after drinking some tea, they poured the rest on our tile floor. To their amazement, the liquid was not absorbed.

The Communists required us to make an inventory of the items in my house, along with the names and family histories of my relatives, including grandparents and parents. One week later, they called us again and made us do it all over again, exactly the same way. The shops also were inventoried. Some people prepared false lists that did not include all of their items. When the Communists caught them, they tied their hands behind their back with electrical cord, and led them away. They never returned. The shops were sealed with a sign saying that these people had lied by not accurately listing their goods. I knew many people who disappeared like that. Other shops closed after the Communists took over because people could not pay the taxes assigned to them. The owners tried to sell their shops, but no one would buy. It was terrible. Vietnam had always grown large quantities of rice; under the Communists, farmers had no profit incentive to grow rice; yields declined, as did quantities of rice available to us. To survive, we had to turn to the very expensive black market.

Two months after the Communists inventoried my house, I was forced to attend reeducation sessions each day for one month. There the Communists said that with a rifle they shot down B-52 planes. One South Vietnamese man laughed and said, "I cannot believe this. A B-52 flies so high that a rifle cannot shoot that far."

You know what happened? The next day that man had disappeared. When we saw this, we worried about our own situation.

Each day we had to listen to them boast and lie, "Our army is so courageous, so powerful, we beat the American people! We beat the South Vietnamese Army! Life in South Vietnam is fictitious; the prosperity of South Vietnam is fictitious!" Day after day they repeated the same thing. We could not live with that, so after a while I said to a teacher who was a friend of mine that we had to find some way to get out of Vietnam. This was very difficult, because the Communists were watching us at all times. It would take us about a year of careful preparation before we dared to attempt an escape.

If we wanted to visit a friend a few kilometers away, we needed a special pass. To get it, we had to answer questions: "Why do you want to visit your friend? What subject will you discuss with him, and for how long?" It was terrible. When two people talked together, the Communists would come by and ask, "What did you talk about with that person? Tell me."

This was the most terrible aspect of the Communist government; we could not talk together because every time, they would ask, "What did you talk about? Was it against the government?" They were always listening to overhear us.

One day, a neighbor of mine passed by a large photo of Ho Chi Minh pasted to a door of a cinema near my house. I heard him say loudly, "I see him this day; it's a bad day for me because I have seen his photo." Two hours later, he was ordered to report to a government office; he was never seen again. Soon after, his family moved to another place.

By now life had changed a lot. I could not trust anybody, even my wife or children, for inadvertently they might say something that could incriminate us. When my children came back from school, they told me that their teacher asked them, "What did you eat at dinner? Did you have chicken or pork? Did you have a lot of it? What are your father's opinions about our government? Does he like it or dislike it?"

My children were old enough so that I told them, "Never listen to those teachers; when they ask, just say that you don't know."

Education had now become nothing: no English, no French, just the history of Ho Chi Minh and General Giap, and work in the gardens, that's all. I was angry when I heard my children say, "Today I'm going to school, not with books, but with a hoe."

One day, the Communists told every family to put a photo of Ho Chi Minh in the center of their sitting room. We did this, but when we closed the door, my wife took down the photo and threw it on the floor, saying, "That kind of people, that man killed lots of people, made people poor, and gave many hardships to us. Now there is no work."

I said, "Don't say that; maybe someone will hear you and take you to jail."

But she was so angry at the Communists that she frequently threw the photo on the floor, and I'd have to tell her many times to be careful of her behavior. "That's only a photo. They ask us to hang it up, like the Catholics put up a picture of Jesus. Put it back. Maybe when the children go to school, the teacher will ask them and they will say how you treated the picture. And then they'll take you to jail."

My wife was always unhappy under Communist rule. Every day she'd say, "We don't know about our future."

I'd reply, "Don't say that. We know not to ask about the future."

For one year we lived like this. We learned that all the promises of the Communists were lies. They talked one way and did another. They claimed that all people would be equal, not too rich or too poor. Everyone would plant rice, and it would be divided with the poor. All houses would be divided equally. There would be no more unemployment. And there would be freedom: people would be able to go anywhere and do what they liked. It took only a few days to find out that everything they said turned out to be the opposite of what life would be like under their rule.

I could have worked for the Communists, but I did not want to. I hated them, for I remembered how in years past the Viet Minh had killed villagers who worked for the French. The French selected old villagers to be chiefs. This was an obligation. At night the Communists in the form of the Viet Minh would call these people outside, kill them, and leave them on the street with anti-French signs on their chests. They were savage. I remembered how they killed my uncle for the "crime" of selling a bunch of bananas to a French soldier. They forced him to dig a hole in the ground; then they hit him on the head with the shovel and tossed his body in the hole, just because he sold one bunch of bananas. I remembered how they fired mortars into schools and cinemas. I thought about the estimated two million people who had been killed in the 30 years of war with the Communists. They claimed to have liberated us from a bad government; instead, they had enslaved us.

Escape

Not long after I had completed my month of reeducation, a former student of mine came to my house and asked if I wanted to escape from Vietnam. He said that lots of students wanted to flee, and he mentioned several whom I knew. I replied, "No, this is my home, and I am happy here." I didn't trust him; I thought he might be an agent for the Communists. A couple of months later, he returned and asked again. This time, I thought that maybe we could trust him. I asked my friend, the teacher, what to do. We invited that young man to a restaurant, and while we gave him food and drink, we investigated his mind.

The student said, "I have a fisherman's permit that allows me to take a boat out to sea." This was quite valuable, for the Communists controlled the seashore to prevent escapes. City people were not allowed to walk along the coast, and boats were not allowed to pass from the river into the sea without a valid permit. And people who wished to buy or sell their boats also needed a permit from the Office of Marine Products.

My friend and I bought a boat, 12½ by 3½ meters, for 35 million piasters in pre-Communist currency, a lot of money. We paid both the seller and the Office of Marine Products. Our payment was half in money and half in gold. In addition, we paid another 3 million piasters for fishing nets. Instead of staying at home, I could now go out fishing.

Although we had a boat, we did not know how to navigate. Neither we nor the student with the fishing permit had ever done anything like this. We did not even know how to anchor the boat. I thought I had found a good place to anchor the boat. The tide came up, then receded, and the boat ended up on its side. For six hours it remained, until we hired some workers to put the boat right side up. That cost us another 30,000 pre-Communist piasters.

Around three in the afternoon, the fishermen would go out to fish. They would stop at a Communist checkpost located just before the river emptied into the sea. After showing their permits, the fishermen would proceed to the open sea. If their permits had expired, they could be sent to jail; that happened to one of my friends. My son, my friend, and I also pretended to go out to fish. The problem was that our fishing net was too big and heavy for the three of us. We caught hardly any fish.

Our real purpose was to learn how to navigate. Once out at sea, with no mountains or landmarks, how could we tell north from south, east from west? We needed a compass, but at first we could not find one. A person caught buying a compass would be thrown in jail because the authorities assumed that such a person was trying to escape. We studied the stars in the night sky. I found that there was a kind of star cluster in the west. I didn't know its name, but I recognized the shape of the stars. Every night I would look for it. Finally I also took the chance and bought a small Japanese pocket compass. I still have that compass. I worked with it until I learned to use it. I also found an old tattered map of Southeast Asia that had been published in a newspaper. I measured the angle to the east that I needed to follow; then I measured the distance from my home town to Manila, the intended destination for my escape: it was about 1,500 kilometers [900 miles]. I drew a bigger map which I put in my boat.

For one year, I learned and practiced navigation, changing oil, and fixing the diesel engine. I also bought small quantities of fuel, a gallon at a time, and sometimes only a liter or a quart so that I did not attract attention. Had I bought large quantities, the authorities would have noticed, asked me what I used it for, and might have taken me to jail. I spent a lot of money on fuel. Then I would transfer it from metal cans to plastic containers that would not be corroded by sea water. To transport them, I hired a pedicab driver, paying him 100 piasters, two or three times the usual price. I would follow on my bicycle, but never too close, so that if the Communists stopped the driver, they would not catch me. Then I paid a young woman some 50 piasters to carry the diesel cans out to my boat. This, too, was two or three times more than the usual price. In that way, they would like me and work quickly.

In the afternoon, my friend and I would go out in the boat and remain on the sea overnight. Our aim was to transfer some of the diesel fuel in small cans to a larger tank, originally taken from a truck, that we had transported and hidden between rocks and covered with grass and leaves on an island nearby. Usually the Communists were on the lookout for people carrying a lot of fuel, water, and food, signs of an intended escape. Those people they put in jail. Since we carried only small quantities at any one time, the Communists did not suspect us when they searched us. At first the large tank gave off a hollow sound, but as we filled it, the sound changed.

In the meantime, we had problems with the large fishing net and with fishing at night. Usually we went fishing with about eight people. Our method was to string a large circle of about 20 bright gasoline lanterns mounted on floats. The diameter of that circle was about 50 meters. The lights would attract the fish. To check that the fish had been drawn towards the lights, a fisherman would swim slowly and silently around the circle. If there were enough fish, a second fisherman using a float would swim around the circle of lights pulling a rope to which was attached an enormous, heavy net, which contained a small pocket.

Then six fishermen in the boat would pull in the two sides of the net; the closer it came to the boat, the quicker they pulled so that the fish could not jump out. The fish became caught both in the small pocket and the wider net.

When there was moonlight, the lanterns were not bright enough to attract the fish, and we could not use the net. If we could not use the net and bring back fish, we would not be allowed out. We'd try to go to the far side of the many islands off the coast, but we were also afraid to do this in the dark. In June came big waves and rough sea. The authorities began to be suspicious of us. By this time, my permit to fish had expired. Each day at the checkpoint, I'd say, "Please let me go out for some fish for my family."

Each day, they'd say, "Okay, you can go out."

Then one day in August, the guards stopped me. They said, "Month after month you go out, but you bring back no fish. You don't look like a fisherman. What do you do? Do you have relatives in another country beyond Vietnam?"

"No," I lied. "I had a little fish which I salted already." I am not surprised that they questioned me. I looked and behaved differently from fishermen. In appearance their skin was much darker, tanned from years of outdoor work. I tried to darken my skin by splashing with sea water and drying myself in the sun. I ended up red and burned, not tanned like the fishermen. They didn't cross their legs when they sat; they liked to bathe by diving into the sea; they cooked in ways that were different; they were hard to make friends with; and they had different customs.

I think the officials realized that I was not what I claimed. "You cannot go out there unless you have a permit," they said. "Let us see your papers."

I replied, "I have applied for a permit at the Office of Marine Products. Please let me go out this afternoon only. I just need to catch fish to feed my family. If by tomorrow I don't have a permit, then okay, I'll stay home." I knew that I would have to leave the next day. Because I was not a fisherman, I could not get a renewal of the permit.

I took the boat out, anchored it near the island, and returned to shore in a small bamboo raft about three feet wide.

The following day, Sunday, August 8, 1976, at eight in the morning, my friend and I led our families to the small raft. We were dressed in swimming suits, nothing else. It appeared that our little group was going out to swim, fish, and have some fun. At that moment, neither my wife nor my four teenage children had any idea that this was to be their last day in Vietnam. I had told no one in my family of my plans, not even my son who sometimes went with me out on the boat, for I feared that by accident they might say something that could betray us.

The raft held only a couple of people. I made several trips back and forth between the shore and the island until all 19 people were on the larger boat. As they climbed aboard, I said, "We are leaving our country. Get into the boat quickly and lie down so that you are not seen. If the patrols spot you they will shoot us."

They were surprised; they had had no warning; they had carried nothing with them. Everything had been left behind, including their clothes. On the boat, I had stored water in diesel cans and some special dry food that contained vitamins. I expected to supplement our food by fishing along the way.

I turned over the engine, accelerated, and fled as fast as we could away from a shore that we would never see again. For two hours we went at full speed. At that point I figured we probably were safe, since the Communists used patrol boats that were no faster than ours. None of the passengers in the boat said anything. They were too seasick.

For three days and four nights we traveled eastward. On the journey, we did not talk. I spent my time fishing and bailing out water. Along the way, we passed several ships. We called to be rescued, but they did not stop. On that fourth night, when we were within 100 kilometers of Manila, the sea became quite rough; it was terrible, with huge waves battering us. We would have died had we not been saved by an Italian oil tanker traveling between South Korea and Saudi Arabia. Not only did the captain save us, he also attached and pulled along our boat. Later we were able to sell it in Saudi Arabia; we received $3,000 in U.S. currency.

The captain of that tanker was formerly from East Germany. He picked us up because he realized that, as he had done years before, we were fleeing from Communist oppression. He offered to put us ashore in a free country. For two days we anchored in Singapore while he tried to get permission for us to land; Singapore refused. We traveled to Saudi Arabia, where we remained for two weeks while the ship was loading oil. The other family that had escaped with us had relatives in Canada. At that point, the Canadian government accepted them. My family remained on the ship. We went to Madagascar, South Africa, Angola, then up to Spain, into the Mediterranean Sea to North Africa, and finally to North Italy. Our journey took two and a half months. In Italy the International Rescue Committee processed our application, and ten days later we flew to the United States to begin a new life in an unfamiliar land.

Some people from my town had fled before the Communists arrived in 1975. As far as I know, my family was only the fourth to escape once the Communists took over. Later, many others would escape. But when we set out on our journey, we had no idea what would happen to us or what country would allow us to land. All we knew was that we had to get out, even at the risk of losing our lives. We were very lucky to have been saved by that captain. Looking back on it now, our sea voyage, with only a toy compass to guide us, was very dangerous. Still, it would have been better to die at sea than to live another day under Communist rule.

[See also Chapters 6 and 36.]

CHAPTER 30

People at Their Worst:
1978-1979

NARRATOR 5: NORTH VIETNAMESE
BUDDHIST NUN

The Communist take-over of South Vietnam in 1975 and the consequent suppression of religious and personal freedoms prompted the nun to flee the country. Under Communism, although her activities were curtailed, her identity remained unchallenged. As a Buddhist nun who could attract followers, she was feared as a potential source of dissent. As a refugee, however, she found herself to be considered powerless and worthless. Her social role changed from respected teacher to displaced boat person.

In Vietnam, the nun's image of herself had been reinforced by prevailing cultural values and practices, and by the society of monks and nuns of which she was a part. While she faced uncertainty regarding her success in spiritual development, the general direction of her quest was clear. As a refugee, she and others faced serious threats to their identities. Their status, the social importance they had had in Vietnam, was denied by fellow refugees as well as by refugee-camp guards. Frequently she heard people say, "All people are equal here; everybody is out for himself." She rightly comments that this was the most trying time of her life, when uncertainty and the potential for disintegration were at their greatest.

Becoming a Refugee

We escaped at twilight on August 19, 1978, with perhaps 150 or 200 people in our small boat. We were so crowded that we were cramped. While I sat on a barrel of water, with my knees bunched up, the girl who accompanied me sat on the floor, with no place to stretch her legs.

As we pulled away from shore, I thought, "Destiny, I have no control over it; what will be will be."

That first night, everybody was very tense. We all worried that the Communist officials, whom we had bribed to let us escape, would now report us. Some people became seasick; others prayed that we would escape. Soon the children fell asleep, while the rest of us sat quietly. No one ate that night, but from time to time people drank water.

Throughout the next day, we remained obsessed with the fear of being caught before we reached international waters. Our minds were not free to think of anything else—except the children: they asked for oranges. People now ate, those who had brought food with them. The others were out of luck. I had not brought food, but the captain of the boat shared his provisions with me and the girl.

Because we slept crowded on the boat for several days, we soon recognized who was good and who was bad. We could not move around the boat, but we could turn around in one place. From time to time, high waves swept over the boat, drenching us if we were outside. Those on the inside were suffocating with insufficient air. People didn't know or care whether the person next to them lived or died. Maybe they were too tired, maybe they concentrated on their prayers, or had a lot of problems on their minds, but the way they sat conveyed the message "Don't bother me."

On the second day, the boat reached international waters; now we worried about not seeing any commercial boats that might pick us up. Since we had no nautical map or compass, we feared that we might be lost.

On the third day, the boat owner and captain told us that for the past day we had been going in the wrong direction, and he didn't know exactly where we were. Now we began to panic. People complained, "We're lost, the boat is lost!" Some people talked of the dreams they had had the night before. Particularly disturbing were the dreams about owls, and those in which one person got others to follow him. Both of these are signs of death. Night birds, especially the owl, are considered inauspicious and are greatly disliked by the Vietnamese people. If someone in a family is seriously ill and at midnight an owl sings, the family says that the person will die. We have an expression, "Wicked like the owl."

On the fourth day, some 30 or 40 ships passed us without stopping. Now we were really scared. Some people made large S.O.S. letters with cloth while others burned cloth to attract attention. Unlike the first day, the people were noisier now. They talked about the boats that passed us by, the fish they saw in the water, or the fact that we were lost and going in the wrong direction.

We felt that our situation was hopeless, that we would die. The passengers blamed the boat owner: "He did not know anything. We trusted him and he is incapable, and now we are lost. He took us to sea and dumped us." Others complained about the boats that passed us by: "They are inhuman." Most of these complaints were from women, but the men also spoke harshly: "I told the captain what to do, but he didn't listen, so look at us now." Whoever spoke tried to show that he was right and the others wrong.

Near the end of this day, a Thai fishing boat approached us. One of their people asked in English what had happened to us. Through an interpreter, our captain explained that we had lost our way. He asked that we be allowed to board their boat. The Thais offered some fuel, along with cigarettes and drinking water.

We took the 5-gallon containers of water. People stood around waiting to drink that water. There was only one cup. I stood next to the container and asked for the cup. A man gave it to a family who were his friends; then they gave it to other friends. Since I did not belong to any group, I was ignored. The container was emptied; then the next. Still, no one gave me water, but passed the cup to others.

In the meantime, after our captain pleaded with them, the Thais let two-thirds of our people transfer to their boat. Now began a mad scramble; those who understood the offer rushed over without consideration of women or children. Families were divided. I lost track of the girl who was traveling with me. It was everybody for himself. I ended up in the Thai boat, where we could circulate freely. The Thais provided food.

A woman of our group washed her handkerchief and put down her bar of soap. I picked it up and asked, "Could I use it?"

She replied angrily, "Why do you use my soap?" I put it down silently.

After another two days and a night, the Thai captain told us that we were close to Malaysia. He told us to return to our boat, and he showed us the direction to the shore. Early the next morning, we arrived, but we were immediately stopped by a patrol boat. We found that we were near Kuching, Borneo. The patrol guards searched us, then forced us to wait all day at the mouth of a river. During the search, my religious vestments and books were found, so people discovered I was a nun. Before that, they had not known; I had disguised myself as a layperson by wearing a wig and ordinary clothes.

That day, the children played, but everybody else became agitated. They talked a lot without making any sense. As they bumped against each other in the cramped quarters, they fell into irritable arguments, "Why did you touch me!" The children ran back and forth, making the boat tip; parents called to them to be quiet.

A Malaysian came by and gave us a message written by Vietnamese refugees in the nearby camp. It warned us that the Malaysians would tow our boat out to sea and send us away unless we destroyed the boat. The owner's brother made a big hole in the boat. When the owner started the engine, water rushed in and the boat collapsed. People jumped into the water, which was only about four feet deep, and waded to shore.

The authorities took us to a stable for cows, and we remained there for four days. The Red Cross provided rice and cooking utensils.

I felt humiliated because they put us in an abandoned stable along the river, a place for cows and animals. The officials were not hospitable. I felt rejected. This was the time of most suffering for me.

Life in a Refugee Camp

One morning, we were taken to a large barge and sent down the river on a journey that lasted about an hour. When we arrived at our destination, we were both surprised and discouraged. We had expected something better. We had left a country in which we had lived in brick houses; now we were put in makeshift huts of palm-tree leaves and bamboo. We slept on the floor and in some cases in the open air. The next day, the Red Cross brought some tents.

We were desperate; we never imagined that we would live in such an unbelievable place, surrounded by barbed wire, prevented from leaving or entering by armed guards. Every four days they gave us rice, but it lasted us only three days. We had to adjust to this low ration. Sometimes we received canned fish and meat. I did not eat these, but for others these items were important. Not until four months later did the people of the camp receive fresh meat and vegetables, given twice a week. Probably they changed the contractor.

Once a week a medical doctor visited our small clinic, but for the most part we were not ill, outside of occasional headaches.

But we had to stay too long in one place with no exercise. Life was monotonous. We had nothing to do. We had the same food every day. We had no water for bathing, just for drinking, so we swam in the sea. A lot of people had scabies, and they were both-ered a great deal by mosquitoes, since only a few people had mos-quito nets. At first, two or three people would crawl under one net together. In order to maximize their use, people threw the nets over tables: one person would sleep on top, the other below. Later, more nets were given out, and as people left the camp, they gave their nets to others.

At first the Red Cross was involved in transmitting mail. After three months, when they refused to do it, the police took over this task, but they told us that for the purposes of control, we would be allowed to write letters only in English or Chinese, not Viet-namese. This was another humiliation for us, but even worse, we had a hard time sending out mail. Sometimes a few guards would take out the mail. In return for this, we hired them to buy things in the market, and we let them overcharge us and make a profit. We knew they were poor and needed the extra income.

I had carried a small address book with me from Vietnam. Immediately upon arriving in the camp, I wrote to the Catholic charity organization that I knew from the time I had lived in West Germany for five years. I told them that I needed a watch and a radio. They promptly sent me about $500. When I received it, I decided not to buy things, but save the money. I wrote also to a family in Washington, D.C., and asked them to forward a message to some monks in the United States. Within three weeks, the monks had sent me $200 and the offer to sponsor me and anyone else who sent them papers.

Before the money and letter arrived, people did not treat me well. I had brought no money with me from Vietnam. After arriving in the camp, I borrowed a small sum from a woman. Later, the girl who had accompanied me from Vietnam asked me for some fruit. I told her, "There is a very good lady who lent me a little money; ask her for a little more."

The woman spoke harshly to the girl, "This is the second time you want to borrow!"

Now that I had money in my hand and a sponsor who would help others, suddenly people came to me for help. The woman who had once refused to give me a piece of soap now was enthusiastic, warm, and friendly to me. Suddenly, too, everybody claimed to be Buddhists, as were their fathers. Whenever they had some vegetables or extra food, they gave it to me. The person who had refused me water and had completely ignored me now gave me warm and polite greetings. She often brought me gifts. "We just offer you," she would say, using respectful words.

When we had transferred to the Thai boat, people had looked down at me in a strange way and said, "Why should she get on the Thai boat? Why her? She should stay with her master." They thought that I was the servant of the boat owner. These same people now inquired about my health with a great show of interest, "Did you sleep well last night? How do you feel today?"

From the ordinary point of view, the behavior of those people was not good. But from the religious, the Buddhist point of view, what they did is normal. People just act or behave according to their interests, what they see as beneficial for themselves. People don't judge a person in their true value or depth, but judge just appearance. If a person is introduced to you as of low status, you may treat him as of less value than if you thought he were of higher status. Not long ago, I was a religious leader with high status in Vietnam, the director of an orphanage. Suddenly, I was brought down to earth, I had nothing. In good times, it is very easy to adjust with the situation; you can gradually move up or down. But when the move is sudden, it becomes very difficult.

In these circumstances, I had to struggle to show my real personality. In the refugee camp, everybody had lost their former positions and their constraints. The refugees said, "All people act alike. Everybody is the same. If you strip the uniform off a colonel and a private, they are the same." But I disagree. It depends on one's true personality. I am different in the quality of my person. I show care to people, all people. I do not run after power. Some people if hungry simply grab food. If you really care, even if you are hungry, you still look and give the food to a person weaker than you.

Experience has taught me a lesson that if someone is in need, we have to share with them. Times may change, but don't act nasty. Be nice, be helpful to everyone in all cases. According to the Buddha, charity should be done according to the following principle: ignore the giver, ignore the receiver, ignore the quality [value] of the gift. If you want to help me, just do it, but without attaching value to the gift.

Each day we would hear an announcement of people who would leave the camp. One day, the Red Cross announced my name as one who had been accepted for the United States. Perhaps if that had happened after only a couple of months in the camp, I would have been excited. But by the time it came, after I had been there for one year, I felt no excitement. I knew it would happen. I left the next day for a transit camp. After a few days for health screening, I boarded a plane for America. When I landed, I was met by the monk who had sponsored me. He took me back to his pagoda, where I remained for nine months.

[See also Chapters 7, 24, and 38.]

CHAPTER 31

Perilous Journey: 1979

Collected and written by Joseph D. Gosha
Edited by James M. Freeman

NARRATOR 14: YOUNG SURVIVOR
OF A MASSACRE

In 1982 Joseph D. Gosha suggested that I include in this book a life story told him by Mr. Hieu, then a 16-year-old high school student. The story was of a harrowing 26-day boat journey across the South China Sea. Along the way, the refugees faced hunger and thirst, a massacre, and demoralization and despair as ship after ship passed them by. Conventional etiquette and social controls deteriorated, but somehow the passengers of the boat forced sufficient cooperation among themselves to enable them to survive until they were finally rescued. Mr. Hieu was 14 years old at the time he made this journey.

Many of the persons who narrated their life stories to me had escaped by boat from Vietnam, and I have included some brief selections from their accounts. I decided to add Mr. Hieu's account as well because it contains three compelling features of special significance. The first is Mr. Hieu's brief but moving description of his family in Vietnam and the sacrifice they made to enable him to escape. The second is Mr. Hieu's recollection of his emotional states during his escape. The third is his description of the massacre. The attacks of Thai pirates on Vietnamese boat people have been well publicized; so too have the attacks by Communist Vietnamese patrol boats. Less well known is what has happened to boat people such as Mr. Hieu who inadvertently landed on islands controlled by the Communist Vietnamese. Independent confirmation of Mr. Hieu's account comes from

Narrator 12, the ex-ARVN colonel, who survived a similar experience in his flight to freedom (see Chapter 33).

After arriving in the United States, Mr. Hieu attended high school; upon graduation he joined one of the branches of the armed forces. His adjustment to America is successful. Still, he will always carry with him the memories not only of his perilous journey, but of the family that he left in Vietnam, whom he probably will never see again.

Escape

My name is Hieu, and [in 1982] I am a 16-year-old junior in high school. I came to this country in 1980 from Vietnam. My family consisted of 23 persons: my father, mother, and their 10 children, and the 11 children of my deceased uncle [his father's elder brother] and aunt.

We were one big happy, though noisy, group. At mealtime, my mother called us by sounding a loud buzzer that could be heard not only through the house, but all over the neighborhood. Since we always ate at the same time, some of our neighbors would schedule their activities according to the sound of that buzzer.

Almost every weekend we'd go to the beach. Along with friends and neighbors, we would pile into the back of my father's big truck, which he used in his business. My oldest brother drove, while my father and mother drove their friends in my father's car.

Holidays were wonderful times for our family, especially the New Year, which was the most important festival of the year. At that time people throw off the old and embrace the new; they pay off their old debts, if they can, as a means of looking forward to new prosperity. They try to forgive and forget old grievances with neighbors and acquaintances, and make resolutions to live better in the coming year.

Our family, like most others, would celebrate the Vietnamese New Year for three whole days. On the first day of the New Year, my father followed the ancient custom of "lucky money." He'd give each and every member of the family a generous gift of cash. One year, my father called us together in the living room, told us of his financial setbacks during the past year, said that he expected things to get worse, not better, and that, because of this, our lives would be changed during the coming year. But when we opened our gifts, we found them to be as generous as before. We all understood and appreciated his sacrifice.

Less than six months after I came to America, I heard that my father had died on October 12, 1980. I miss my father very much; I loved him, and he loved me. I had hoped he would live to see the day when I had really achieved success in my new life here in America; this would have made him very proud.

One week after my father died, but before we knew of his death, my brother, sister, and I, all of whom had escaped together, received a letter he wrote to us from Vietnam. He described his youth in Vietnam, when he was quite poor and on his own. He told how he worked his way up to become a successful businessman, and he discussed our futures in America. He cautioned us not to be overwhelmed by the new society around us, wished us success and happiness, and urged us to study hard and think carefully before making any important decisions.

When I think of his advice, I know that it is good; I wish he were still alive to guide me further along my way.

In 1975, when the Communists first "liberated" South Vietnam, my father chose not to leave. He also did not want anyone in his family to leave. Peace had finally arrived in Vietnam after 30 years of war and revolution. Despite Communist control, my father hoped that we could live a satisfying life in the countryside, so we moved from Saigon to a small village about 100 kilometers away.

At first, my father's assets were intact, and this enabled us to enjoy life and avoid difficulties created by the Communists. As time went by, my father's assets were either used up or confiscated; our life became more difficult as the Communists controlled more aspects of our lives more closely. We were no longer allowed to be in control of our daily lives. We no longer had freedom of speech. People watched everything we did and reported it to the Communist officials. We were denied the choice of how to make our living. After confiscating our property, they changed currency, so that our old money became worthless. They sent thousands and thousands of people to prison, reeducation camps, and new economic zones, where people were forced to eke out an existence in the middle of the jungle. And on top of everything, there were shortages everywhere, especially of food and medicine.

By 1978 my father, like almost everybody else except the elderly and the few people who were Communists, sought ways to get members of his family out of the country. But by that time we no longer had enough money for all of us to leave.

In the last two months of 1978, when I had just turned 13, my father arranged for me to travel with a family friend to Saigon via small riverboat. In this way, I gained some experience on the water. Then in early 1979 my father helped another friend buy a small fishing boat. I helped this friend take care of the boat and learn more about it. Three times a week for three months, we took the boat out to sea and did some fishing. This was to convince the Communist river patrols that we were serious fishermen. Our true purpose was to prepare ourselves to escape. The patrols became accustomed to our boat, and when we did leave for good, they did not stop or question us.

On the night of June 12, 1979, I was sleeping on the boat, as I often did, when my older brother came to tell me to go right home because my father wanted to talk with me. When I arrived, my mother, brother, and sister were sitting in the backyard, illuminated by the light of a large full moon. My mother told me to pull up a chair and join them. Then she told me that I would be leaving Vietnam the next day. At first I was taken aback. I could not say anything. Before that moment, I had been really excited about leaving; I knew what my father intended for me, but not when. Now that the day had come, I could not believe it.

I now understand what that day was to mean to me, though at the time it did not cross my mind. Now that I have left, I fully realize that my family, home, and country probably are behind me forever. That is a source of sadness that is with me always.

The next morning, I went to say good-bye to my best friend, who lived two and a half miles from me. I found that he had already left for work. His mother asked me to carry her on my bicycle to her daughter's house. When we arrived, we found a terrible commotion: her daughter had just committed suicide with an overdose of drugs. Her husband had been put in jail for trying to escape from Vietnam. She became depressed because she had no money to bribe the jail officials to release him, so she took her life.

Because of this tragedy, I was delayed in returning home. Suddenly I realized that I was late for the most important appointment of my life. I rode home as fast as possible to find my father pacing outside the house, extremely agitated.

He shouted at me, "On a day as important as this, you're goofing off as always! If you had been any later, you would have missed your chance to leave Vietnam, probably your last chance!"

He was so angry he wanted to hit me, but he could not because he knew that this was the last time he would ever see me. My mother gave me a tender slap on the back and told me to get going. I'm sure she wanted to hug me, and I wanted to hug both my mother and father, but I couldn't because there were a lot of people on the street. To this day I deeply regret not having the chance to really say good-bye to them.

On board the small fishing boat, which was to be my home for almost a month, I found five other people: my father's friend, who organized the escape and served as captain, his son and daughter, a young man who served as copilot, and a young mechanic. We intended to pick up two more groups of people at a prearranged rendezvous point about 30 minutes away.

We arrived at the rendezvous point an hour late and set our boat to make a wide circle of the area. A small riverboat pulled up beside us. While moving past us, men from that boat discreetly handed us bags of rice, sugar, lemons, and dried fish, which we quickly stowed below deck. The whole operation took only a few minutes; then, to avert suspicion, the other boat pulled off in the opposite direction.

By this time, we sighted our first group of fellow travelers; they were hiding behind the bushes along the shoreline. The Communist security forces carefully patrol all of the shorelines and river banks near the sea; they become suspicious any time they see groups of people enter these areas, especially if they do not appear to be working. Others who live and work along the shoreline also try to discover those who are escaping so that they can extort money and gold from them in return for not reporting them.

Because we saw so much activity along the shoreline and on the river, we threw out our nets and pretended to be fishing. Meanwhile, our compatriots on the shore settled back for what proved to be a long wait.

Around 1:00 A.M. I awakened to find that ten people from shore, including my older brother and younger sister, had swum out to the boat, carrying the vital cans of gas and water with them. I heard our captain arguing with a couple of other men about whether or not to wait for the second group of 15 people, including the captain's wife and daughter, as well as a trained navigator. Finally the captain announced that we would leave without them, since to escape we had to be some distance from the coastline before dawn. For the captain, separation from his wife and daughter was inevitable; better that it be caused by miles of ocean than by Communist prison walls.

Later, in the refugee camp, we found out that the missing party had been captured by the Communist patrols. They never would have joined us no matter how long we had waited.

The captain and his assistant remained on deck pretending to be deep-water fishermen, while the rest of us waited below deck in silence. The 14 of us below nearly burst the hold of our tiny boat, 29 by 9½ feet. How could we have breathed had we been joined by an additional 15 people?

When I awoke the next morning, the mountains of Vietnam were still visible behind us. The captain told us to remain below deck. That afternoon, the captain called down to tell us to come up on deck; we were beyond the range of the Communist patrol boats. What a relief his words were, for we had spent more than half a day in that tiny, suffocating hold.

Ordeal at Sea

On the first day, the sea was extraordinarily calm, smooth as glass and sparkling. One of us exclaimed that even a 5-foot boat could make the passage on water this calm. We had all heard stories about the ravages of the South China Sea, how many Vietnamese seeking freedom had disappeared on the sea. One of my sisters is among them. She left without telling us in 1977. We have not heard from her since, and we assume she is dead.

Out of a large piece of canvas, we made a makeshift sail that also served as a large S.O.S. sign. For masts, we used two long sturdy pieces of wood from the boat's decorative masthead.

For two days, the weather stayed calm and the sea peaceful. We made good progress. Unfortunately, we did not know where we were going. The only instrument we had was a land compass. Our captain tried his best to keep us going in a direction that would bring us to friendly shores.

In those first two days, we saw many boats, some close and some far. Often we called for help, but none responded. I am convinced that most of these ships noticed us but were unwilling to take on the responsibility of rescuing us.

On the third evening, we saw two large cruise ships, ablaze with bright lights. We moved in their direction to seek assistance. Through the portholes on one of them we could see people dancing. But when we called out, the ships moved away. The next morning, we encountered another large ship, which also deliberately avoided us.

Our first few days had been relatively smooth, thanks to the tranquil seas. Nobody had become terribly ill. Our biggest problem was dealing with the disappointment of being pointedly ignored by ships that could have assisted us.

By the fourth day our captain was worried. Our fuel was low; so was our food and water, for half of our supplies had been lost when the third group had been captured. Our captain knew that we would have to find land quickly or perish of hunger or thirst.

Near evening, we spotted seagulls, a sign that we must be near land. We followed them for a day and a half. At sunrise on the sixth day, we sighted two islands. Because of the fog surrounding, we couldn't make out details, but one seemed to be covered with trees, while the other seemed open. We chose the island that seemed to have little cover so that we could see more clearly any danger that might exist.

Not until we had almost landed on the island could we make out the shapes of people and a fairly large structure that appeared to be a lookout tower. I later learned that it had been built during the Vietnam war by the U.S. Army. Our captain realized that we were probably about to be caught by the Communists. Despite this, he moved forward, since we had little food, water, or fuel.

Suddenly shots rang out, hitting the prow of the boat, shattering splinters of wood, sending smoke into the air. A young man behind the prow jumped up, ran back, and dove behind the engine compartment, which rose about three feet above the deck. The roof of the engine compartment served as the floor for a totally open, but covered, half-cabin above.

I had been sitting on the roof of that cabin when the shooting started. I quickly crawled back and rolled off onto the deck below. Remaining in the cabin were three children: the son and daughter of the captain and my sister.

The next shots ripped into the cabin. The captain's daughter was hit in the neck and died almost instantly. Someone told the captain. Though shots were whizzing around everywhere, he jumped up into the cabin, picked up her body, climbed down to the deck, and carried his daughter to the front of the boat to show the gunmen that they had hit someone. Apparently he hoped that this would get them to stop shooting. He was hit by a rain of bullets and fell dead.

The next shots hit the engine compartment as well as the engine itself and ricocheted in every direction. A young man in the hold in front of the engine compartment peeked out and was hit in the back as he sought safety. I had looked out at the same moment and saw him fall and scream. With me forever are his screams and the sight of his flesh being ripped apart.

I was halfway out from behind the engine compartment, still crouching next to the tiny strip of deck between the engine compartment and the bow of the boat. I never felt any physical pain, but when I looked down I saw that I was lying in blood. Whatever entered the side of my upper thigh is still there today.

While lying there, I saw five people swimming from the island to the boat. The first one climbed over the side and asked me to help him start the engine. I told him I would not help him lead us further into the trap. For some reason the shooting had died down, so I assumed that these swimmers would be the death of us all.

Another one of our passengers, a former ARVN major, talked with the swimmer; then the major started the engine and moved us away from the island. For 20 minutes the boat moved; then the engine died, empty of fuel. We were out of rifle range, and the Communists did not come after us.

All of us were in a state of shock. Only the presence of the five newcomers kept us from being paralyzed with inactivity. We listened as they told us of the terrifying events that had occurred during the hours before we had reached the island. In retrospect, by telling their tale of inhumanity, they made it easier for the rest of us to understand and cope with our situation.

I do not know all the details of that grisly day, for as time wore on, the five survivors became less willing to talk or recall those events. Only one of the five lives in the United States, and he now refuses to discuss the event.

They had left the coastal city of Nha Trang, in Central Vietnam, in a wooden fishing boat that carried 120 refugees. Their journey was uneventful until they reached the fateful fog-shrouded island around 3:00 A.M. As they moved closer, they spotted the watch towers but saw no light or activity. Then they heard voices shouting in English. Because they thought they had discovered Americans, they made their way to the island and ran their boat aground on a sandbar. Since the water was quite shallow, some of the younger men went over the side to try to dislodge the boat. Others helped women, children, and elderly men over the side and through the surf to the nearby shore. By now, half of the passengers were huddled on the beach.

Suddenly, brilliant beams of light flashed and focused on the beach. At the same time, a great number of Vietnamese Communist soldiers with automatic rifles stepped out into the light and surrounded the people on the beach. Those in the water turned back to the boat and frantically tried to free it from the sandbar.

The Communist soldiers ordered the refugees on shore to form a line stretching across the beach. These unarmed people were crying and pleading with their captors not to hurt them or abuse them, but to send them back to Vietnam and its prisons. The soldiers shouted for order, then ordered a spokesman for the prisoners to step forward. The leader of the soldiers said he would speak with his commander to determine the fate of the prisoners. He walked away from the beach.

Not long after, two huge explosions shattered the boat, direct hits from shells fired fore and aft. Bodies, blood, wood, and metal flew in the air. When they heard the explosions, the prisoners on the beach panicked. As they dashed for the water or for cover away from the beach, the soldiers opened fire on them. Very few survived.

The few people in the water not killed or wounded by the initial blasts swam away from the island. As they clung to debris from the boat, the soldiers picked them off one by one. The struggle was continuous and exhausting. The surf aided the soldiers by carrying their targets back towards shore and in range of the rifles.

About three hours after the shooting began, our boat approached the island. At first we heard no shots; indeed, the first ones we heard were those that ripped into our boat and killed the captain's daughter. For about 30 minutes after that, the Communists continued shooting. We saw people running along the beach, and we saw them shot down in their tracks. I cannot describe the horror, the tremendous frustration I felt. It was like being in the middle of a war with no weapons, with absolutely no way to fight back. I knew that the people running on the beach had no hope. They could only run until surely they must die. I wished I had an atomic bomb to blast the island from the face of the earth.

The shooting stopped, replaced by an eerie silence. Then we saw the young men swimming out to our boat. The last of them to scramble aboard had a small piece of wood embedded in the side of his forehead.

Later, in the refugee camp in Japan, we found that the five young men were not the only survivors. Eight other young men beat the tide and swam to the other small island three or four miles away. It belongs to the Republic of the Philippines. These men are now resettled throughout the world.

Approximately 120 refugees began that journey; 13 survived that slaughter: no women, children, middle-aged or elderly adults.

With our fuel gone on the sixth day, we drifted aimlessly for another 20 days and nights, totally vulnerable to the sea around us. Never in my life will I forget those 20 days and nights. It's hard to speak of them, sometimes, but they are seared in my memory forever.

For the next 16 days, we saw no other indication of human life, no sign of the world outside our boat. During that period, I came not to care whether the world, or life, continued. Usually I slept in the upper cabin; every time I awakened, I saw the ceiling of that cabin; I realized where I was and was shaken to the depths of my being by a feeling of tremendous despair. Often I simply wanted to lapse back into the unconsciousness of sleep.

We all thought we would die. With absolutely no control over our destiny, what hope did we have?

Our resignation and despair put all of us in a trancelike state. In our stupor, the boredom was unbearable. The stress of this led us to lose control of ourselves. In Vietnamese society, polite speech and actions are very important. There is a proper place for everyone in the social order. But on our little boat, that social order often seemed as if it had never existed. We were out of control. If an adult bumped into me, I'd swear at him, just like everyone else on board. All of us were experiencing a kind of hell, and it was nearly impossible to break out of ourselves and reach out to one another.

I could not control myself; I realized I was crazy. Sometimes I cried. At other times I wanted to cry but didn't because crying was too damn tiresome and exhausting, too. The same with laughing: it just did not matter.

Sometimes I needed to scream. When the pain, the anger, the sadness, the hunger came to be too much to bear, I'd scream as long and loud as I could. I screamed for all of us, and because I wanted everyone, everywhere to notice: *Why me?* Sometimes I could not even scream but only surrendered to the boredom, the utter lethargy of my circumstances.

I also prayed. On the third day after we escaped from the island of death, we finally released the bodies of the captain and his daughter into the sea. They were wrapped in nylon rain tarps. We had hoped to reach some small island, or any land, so that we could give them a decent burial. As our own situation became more uncertain, we realized that the chances of finding land were incredibly slim. At that point, we decided to bury them at sea. We prayed silently for them, and for ourselves.

Four days later, we had one more burial at sea: the other young man who had been shot. During the first five days of our journey, he had said absolutely nothing and had kept totally to himself. Everyone on board realized that he had had no experience with the sea. He bore his seasickness and misery very poorly. His face was drawn and pale. I had this strange feeling that looking into his eyes was looking into the eyes of a devil. Because he made me uncomfortable, I avoided him.

After he was shot, he talked all day and night, to anyone who would listen, about his family and his life in Vietnam. Then he became weaker, finally delirious. He continued to talk when no one was listening.

What bothered me most was when he called for me by name. We were extremely short of water. Because of his injuries, he was thirsty and begged for water continuously. He would call each of us by name asking for water. After three or four attempts, he would switch to another name. He never quit. The oldest man on our boat took over the responsibility for him and helped him whenever he could.

On the morning of our tenth day at sea, I awoke to the sound of that old man asking for help to push the young man's dead body into the water.

The day our gas ran out, we had with us ten quarts of uncooked rice, five gallons of water, and just over a pound of sugar: no charcoal for cooking, no cooking oil, salt, pepper, or fish sauce. Morbid as it might sound, we were more concerned that we had more people aboard than we could feed adequately. Although two of our number had died and a third was dying, we also had picked up another five people. We had no idea how long our meager supplies would have to last. We were fully aware that we might drift on the high seas forever without ever coming to land or being helped by ships.

Thank God for rain and raincoats. Even though squalls are a deadly danger for small fishing boats in the ocean, the rains that came proved to be our salvation.

For the first five days of our journey, the skies had been clear, the sea calm. Finally we saw rain pouring from clouds in the distance. As the rain came towards us, we used our rain ponchos to catch some five gallons of rainwater and refill our water cans. Four times during our 26-day journey we received rain. The second time, we collected 2½ gallons of water. The third time, however, the rain continued nonstop for two days. Our water cans filled; now we worried about the damage that this storm might bring us.

The storm brought strong, terribly cold winds. Our boat was strong enough to withstand the waves, but the cold was almost impossible to bear. The rain, too, was cold, and we had no protection: no warm clothing, no fully enclosed areas of the ship to shelter us. We all huddled, miserable, in the half-open cabin and engine compartment, trying to gain warmth from each other. On the morning of the third day, the rain stopped, and the sun returned to comfort us with its warmth.

Before this third rain, we had rationed our water strictly. I was always thirsty. I'll never forget what that thirst was like. One night I could not sleep, and I could not stand it any longer. I was in the very back of the boat, while our water was stored near the front. I had to sneak some water for myself, despite our ration plan. To do this, I'd have to find a way to the front of the boat other than going through the cabin. Otherwise, I'd surely be caught.

The cabin stretched above the engine compartment from one side of the boat to the other, with only a very narrow area on either side. I climbed onto the railing on top of the bow, hugged the wall of the cabin, and slowly made my way forward. The waves were rocking the boat. Had I slipped and fallen, I would not have survived. Then I had to return the same way; I don't think anyone saw me.

Twice a day for 15 days, 16 of us shared a bowl of rice. Each of us would barely get one mouthful a day. When we were lucky, we had fish with our meals. Since the bottom of our boat was covered with barnacles, fish swam around to feed on them. We used the barnacles to catch fish. On some days we caught enough to have a small, if boring, feast; on other days we caught none. We had no way of preserving the fish we caught, so we had to eat them then and there.

While we had line to use for fishing, we had no hooks. One ingenious member of our group solved this by making hooks from steel wire found inside our boat's radio.

We had a rule on board: anyone who did not work did not eat. One of my jobs was fishing. One morning, I lay down, weak from hunger. My brother called me to get up, but I did not move. He called me again. This time I got up, prepared a line, and dropped it over the side of the boat. Within ten minutes, I had pulled in a big, fat fish. I went to the other side of the boat. Minutes later, I had pulled in another one as big and fat as the first.

We cooked our meals over a wood fire, made from the chopped pieces of a heavy wooden beam that stretched across the front of the cabin. We took turns chopping at this beam: with a sharp knife it was possible within five minutes to cut a piece big enough to make the fire.

Another of our jobs was bailing out the water. The adults took turns doing this. The waves were always sending water into the boat. During our two-day squall, the waves were so high that water flew into the semi-elevated cabin. Whenever the water in the boat got too high, two or three of the adults would start bailing.

One evening at about dusk, high waves brought a number of small squid over into a corner of the boat. Two young men were so hungry that they picked them up and ate them raw.

Our hunger was consuming. Often we could think of nothing except food. During that time, I mentally kicked myself countless times for not having a last big meal with my family. My regret was not that I lost a special occasion, but rather that I hadn't consumed the food. It sounds crazy, since that meal wouldn't have done anything to alleviate my hunger out on the ocean. But that was the thought that really preoccupied me during those days.

One of my few pleasures on that boat was sitting and listening to one of my fellow passengers, a man from Saigon, talk about food. He was a terrific storyteller and well acquainted with all of the culinary pleasures of that city. Each night, I'd ask him to tell me about food: ordinary meals as well as special holiday feasts. Somehow, listening to him, and also remembering some of my favorite dishes, provided a real joy that made hunger easier to bear. The oldest man in our group did not agree. He'd yell at the storyteller to shut up, or at least talk about something else.

On the evening of our twenty-first day out at sea, we cooked our last minuscule ration of rice. The significance of this did not go unnoticed. From then on until we were rescued, found land, or died, we'd be eating fish only.

For 16 days after we had escaped from the island of death, we saw no sign of the outside world. Once we spotted mountains far off on the horizon, but without gas we were unable to approach them. The waves moved us in the opposite direction. Finally on the twenty-second day we saw another boat. I cannot describe the joy we felt upon seeing that *other boat*. Our entire universe had been the ocean around us. We hoisted our huge S.O.S. sign and made as much noise as we could. The boat came quite close but never stopped. Our disappointment was tremendous.

That same night, when we saw two huge aircraft carriers, we became more hopeful. We grabbed all of the flammable materials we thought we could spare and built a fire in one of the larger water barrels. We kept the fire going all night; we were sure we would be noticed and assisted. That night, I watched three airplanes take off from the deck of one of the ships. In the morning, with the coming of clear light, the ships were nowhere in sight. Heartbreaking disappointment again!

Over the next two days we saw ships and boats too numerous to count. Apparently we had drifted into a major shipping lane. Every time we spotted a new boat, the children and adolescents on board stood on top of the cabin, made noise, waved our sign, and did whatever they could do to attract attention. The adults hoped that somebody would have pity on the helpless children.

There was nothing I hated more than climbing on top of the cabin to wave for help. At first, I had as much anticipation as anyone else, but it didn't take long for me to realize that our task was a hopeless one. Boats passed right by us, so close that we saw people on their decks. They chose not to see us. Most avoided us pointedly.

It was a tremendous struggle to drag myself up each time a new boat was sighted. Regardless of how much I wanted to have hope, and wanted to be helped, I thought that these people had nothing in common with us. After all, our own countrymen, the Communists on the island of death, set out to murder us, so why shouldn't these foreigners leave us to die on the sea?

On the twenty-sixth day, we came into the view of a large

freighter flying a Japanese flag. The ship crossed our path, went ahead a short distance, then doubled back and crossed our path from the other direction. It turned around one more time, but then, instead of crossing our path, it headed directly towards us. We were stunned. Would they help us? When they came within hailing distance, someone threw a rope down to us. With tumultuous joy, we fell all over one another, laughing and crying. Our days without hope had ended.

We had to wait for quite some time before we were allowed to board the freighter, and it was several days before we finally reached land. But shortly after we climbed the rope ladder or were carried up on a suspended gangplank, an event occurred that I will never forget. Crewmen from the freighter went over to our boat and cut holes into its hull. We stood and watched silently. That fishing boat had represented a time and events in our lives that had a significance beyond compare. Now it looked small and far away as it sank to the bottom of the ocean.

CHAPTER 32

Bien Hoa Jail: 1981

NARRATOR 12: EX-ARVN COLONEL

The colonel and two of his sons were caught attempting to flee Vietnam; for this they were placed in an overcrowded civilian jail. Because he was eventually given assignments that took him throughout the jail, he met many prisoners, including a Jesuit priest who had spent five of his six years in jail shackled in solitary confinement.

When I returned home from six years in reeducation camps, I was told that each Saturday morning I must report to the ward office with a written account of my activities during the past week.

For four weeks I observed these regulations obediently, but I found that I could not stand it. Besides reporting every weekend, I had to put up with many visits of the Public Security Agent of my street. He looked for me too many times during the week, and bothered me too much. He was very modest, a Southerner, and very polite with me, but younger than my youngest son. I had to spend too much time playing host to him, offering him tea, our best cigarettes; it was too much.

In early May, I decided to flee the country with my two sons. In 1980 they had been caught and imprisoned for attempting to escape from Vietnam, but had been released after five months. They had no desire to remain another day in Vietnam. We went to Ca Mau, the southernmost part of Vietnam. We put down half of our fare to escape, some nine taels of gold, more than nine ounces.

For this trip, we carried three or four shirts and a pair of trousers, but no food or water, since the organizers of the escape had promised to provide them. They warned us not to carry provisions, since this would attract the attention of the Communists.

Around 5:00 A.M. about 100 of us got into a big riverboat, and we started towards the sea. Just as we were about to leave the mouth of the river, we heard the firing of small arms. A small boat came aside and someone ordered us to come over to the riverside. We waited for almost 24 hours. The next morning, around 2:00 A.M., the guards searched each of us. About two hours later, I noticed that my younger son had secretly fled. He had pretended to go to the latrine, but kept going. An hour later, I heard a lot of shots fired very close, and people screaming. I was terrified that my son had been shot. A few moments later, the guards dragged back three young men, but with relief I saw that none were my son.

An hour after that, the women and children of our boat pointed to a strange sight; they laughed, but also expressed fear. A tall man covered entirely with mud walked towards them with his hands up. A Communist soldier marched behind him, shoving the muzzle of his rifle into the prisoner's back. Barking dogs followed. The prisoner was my 24-year-old son. While others laughed, I looked on terrified. The soldier ordered my son to go to the river and wash off the mud, which covered him up to his eyes. When the women and children had seen him like this, they had thought he was a ghost.

After he washed, the soldiers tied my son's hands behind his back around a tree. I could not keep away my tears. Around 10:00 A.M. the sun was very high already. He was exhausted, and the sun beat down on him. Water ran out of his nose and mouth. The women saw this and were so moved that they implored the cadre in charge to permit me to give him a hat. The cadre instead ordered others to carry my son to the shade. By that time he had collapsed. He had a very deep cut on his toes. I and my older son helped the younger one to lie down in a house nearby. Everyone rushed in to help. A nurse said, "The shop next door sells some alcohol; it is necessary to get some to clean his wound."

Late that afternoon, all the passengers of the boat were moved to the district prison without exception: women and children went along too. The prison actually consisted of two buffalo stables, one for the men, and the other for the women and children, very uncomfortable because of the rain and the mosquitoes.

Most prisoners moved quickly, but my two sons and I were stragglers. What a sight we made. All three of us were nearsighted. One son could not walk; he had lost his glasses and could not see. He carried his younger brother on his back. My eyesight, though terrible, was better than theirs, so I led them, limping along the banks of the paddy fields, to the stables. For being admitted to prison, we had paid nine taels of pure gold; the Chinese organizer of this disaster escaped.

For two months we remained in that prison. My wife visited us not only to provide us with rice, but to figure out how to get us released. The prison was much more crowded than the reeducation camps, and we had to lie in mud. Around 50 men were put in a room that measured 5 by 18 meters. Since there was not enough room to lie down, we built a small platform. The room for women and children was slightly larger, but also small.

We did not have enough mosquito nets. No work was required of us, and those with money could manage to get food from the outside. Otherwise the inmates did not have enough food. They received only some rice and salt, along with dirty canal water, which people used for cooking, bathing, and going to the latrine.

Although the Chinese organizer of our escape had fled, the Public Security Agent whom he had bribed to allow us to escape had been caught. He was a very rich man, but he was also in jail. My wife and other women went to this man's house and threatened to denounce his wife. Fearing this, that woman bribed officials to get me released. It took two months. My wounded son, who looked like he was 18 years old, told officials he was a student, and they released him. I told officials that I was a photographer and so they released me. There was no trial. My oldest son remained in jail for another three months. Early one morning, he escaped. He had been in Con Dao prison for five months, now in Ca Mau prison for three months. With this ended my first attempt to escape. In all, I made six attempts before I finally succeeded.

On my third attempt, I was caught but released soon afterwards. When I was caught on my fourth try, I was put in jail in Bien Hoa for nine months. That was truly horrible, a living *nightmare*. The Bien Hoa facility is one of no less than 30 reeducation camps and prisons that are found in Dong Nai Province.

Bien Hoa prison, also known as Reeducation Camp Number Five, formerly was for female prisoners under the Republic of Vietnam. It was built with money from the United States Agency for International Development (USAID) and is located on the outskirts of Bien Hoa city. The concrete flat roof of the wards is low, roughly seven feet high inside. Each ward is about 7 by 21 meters in size; originally it was furnished with 25 to 30 wooden beds for inmates. Windows and doors were covered with iron bars, and the doors were left unlocked except at night. The female inmates were allowed to walk around the inside yard of the quadrangle jail.

Because of the great increase of prisoners in the new Communist regime, the jail housed both males and females along with their children. Some wards contained 80 to 100 political detainees and criminals. I was put in such a room. No longer were there beds; everyone had to sleep on the concrete floor in three rows, like sardines in a can.

Never in all of my prison experiences have I experienced such a terrible detention as in the Bien Hoa jail. The crowding into small rooms and the oppressive heat from the low ceilings and from the animal heat of the inmates made this a suffocating horror, especially at night. Between 6:00 P.M. and 7:00 A.M. the iron doors were shut, and we were locked in that narrow space. The iron door had no opening, no bars. For 13 hours we would lie low on the floor; we breathed not oxygen, but carbon dioxide exhaled from the inmates lying next to us, much too close to us, and we became intoxicated! And we also got the worst scabies! Everybody busied himself with thinking about the barred door, thinking about how to save a place to get some fresh air when we heard the clanking of the jailer's bundle of keys as he fumbled to find the appropriate key to this double-locked ward.

In my early days in the prison, I mistook the jailer's behavior for contempt or even fear of the prisoners. Every morning, the jailer would swiftly put himself behind the door when he opened it. Later I realized that he hid himself there to avoid the blow of hot, suffocating human stench which was thrown out with the opening of the door. The low concrete roof absorbed the heat of the sun during the day and discharged it at night, along with the heat emanating from 100 human bodies. During the summer days in this tropical country, the inmates were confined in a virtual gas chamber.

Because of the shortage of food, the feeding of inmates was the worst possible: rice of lower quality and, when that ran out, dried corn. These were served with a little salted vegetable soup. With this sort of food and in these living conditions, inmates were kept alive at the lowest rate, well below cattle and pets. To spare the administration the feeding of the inmates, the officials authorized the families of the prisoners to visit them and bring them food once or twice a month depending on their detention status. Those who were pending release and were eligible to do daily labor could receive two visits.

For the first few months, I remained in this jail cell permanently without getting out, except for interrogation. Officials would call to ask me my identification and then to discuss the fact of my being caught on another of my boat escape attempts. In fact, my elder son, now in Canada, had taken a different route to get to the same boat. He had succeeded while I had failed and been sent to jail, again with no trial. For those who try to flee the country, there is no trial, just jail.

I feared that I was not safe in the jail. Whenever I heard the iron door of the jail cell creak open I felt sick; I shuddered with fear. A newcomer, a captured boat person sent to jail, might be pushed into the cell, recognize my true identity, and denounce me to the Communists. The officials had no idea who I was. I had given them a false identity. They did not know that I was an ex-reeducation camp prisoner who had evaded reporting weekly to the PSA office. So on top of all the horrors of the cell, I was constantly threatened by the fear of being discovered and also the nagging mental doubt that this time my wife could do nothing to liberate me.

In this prison, we were jailed along with many kinds of detainees. Most of them were criminals: murderers, robbers, rapists, and delinquents. This added to our misery, for the criminals would threaten us for food, money, tobacco, and clothes. We feared they would use force; also, they knew the Communist cadres better than we did, and they had a good relationship with them. We feared that the criminals would denounce us falsely any time that they liked. Our best policy was to be modest and to comply to their will; we gave them what they demanded. The next largest group was boat people. Finally, there was a small group of political prisoners. At its highest point, the Bien Hoa prison held some 1,500 detainees. These included 20 Catholic priests and 10 Buddhist monks, most of them captured boat persons.

The prisoner who had been detained longest in a cell was Le Ba Dung, a Jesuit priest. After 1975, Brother Dung found no more reason to stay under the Communist regime, so late in that year, he attempted to escape by boat from Vung Tau. He was caught carrying a briefcase full of documents that, he told me, were politically unfavorable for the new regime. Because of that, he had been accused of being a CIA agent and was sent to the Bien Hoa jail.

Most of the boat people were released after a short time, no more than one year. The exceptions were the Buddhist monks and the Catholic priests. In particular, priests do not have a chance to be released once they are detained because they are considered by the Marxist-Leninist regime to be like a narcotic poison.

Brother Dung had been in jail since 1975. For five years he was kept in solitary confinement with one of his legs shackled. For five years he was unable to stand up; he could only sit or lie down on a wooden board. He defecated and urinated in a container which another inmate would clean out every day under the supervision of a guard. Twice a day a half-ration of food was shoved through a small hole. Family supplies and visits were completely forbidden. Under these conditions, Brother Dung lost any notion of time. Imprisonment like this was reserved for those indefinite-term prisoners condemned for high treason, but without a trial or verdict. Most of these prisoners were Catholic priests.

In 1980, Brother Dung became seriously ill, so he was taken to the prison dispensary, and later transferred to Ward Number Seven, where I met him. At that time, he was unable to walk, partly because of his illness and partly because of his long confinement in chains. The years of isolation without speaking to anyone also changed his mentality. He was like a savage restive to society, and he was considered the principal troublemaker of the ward. He was against the other old Catholic priest who was in Ward Number Seven. I was the only one with whom he had sympathy. Even so, I tried to avoid talking with the priests too long or frequently lest informers in the ward take me for a camouflaged priest. Later I found that Brother Dung was released in 1982 as part of an amnesty.

In the fourth month, I was transferred to Ward Number One. This is a ward for inmates pending release. There I was ordered to sweep the rectangular yards of this section of the jail twice a day and to cook extra private food for all the inmates of that ward. Because of this job, I was able to go around and see many places and people in the prison. This was interesting indeed, but it also was a great threat for me; now there were more inmates in other cells who might recognize me from my former social life and denounce me unintentionally.

In fact, one person did recognize me. He tried to remind me where we had met. I said falsely, "Oh yes, I remember you. We met in prison once before!" Anyway it was mandatory that I do this work, so the only way to minimize the danger was to keep my eyes hidden most of the time under a traditional conical palm-leaf hat used by countryside farmers. On the hat I painted a half-serious, half-joking note in large characters, "Silent Mouth," and I kept dumb to most of the questions of the inmates. In South Vietnam, there is a sect of Buddhist monks who beg for food but never respond to comments or questions. So people recognized my behavior.

My wife again tried to get in touch with the right people to bribe them. After nine months she succeeded, and I was released on the eve of Christmas. However there was no way I could go home. For over a year, I had been delinquent in reporting weekly to the PSA office, so I had to remain in hiding. I would remain for a few days or weeks at the house of a friend, then move on to the house of another, all the time looking for an opportunity to escape once more.

[See also Chapters 19, 20, 21, 22, and 33.]

CHAPTER 33

Brutality in a Thai Refugee Camp: 1982

NARRATOR 12: EX-ARVN COLONEL

Conditions vary greatly in different refugee camps and at different times within the same camp (Knudsen 1983, 1986, 1988). During the period that the colonel was in the Sikhiu Camp in Thailand, refugees were not allowed to leave. Morale was low, for the prospects of resettlement to a third country seemed remote. According to the narrator, camp guards and officials often beat the refugees and skimmed off rations that were intended for refugee consumption. The colonel claims that his treatment in this camp was no better than in the Vietnamese reeducation camps in which he had been incarcerated.

The months and years that people spent in refugee camps were particularly hard; many of the narrators I interviewed told of feeling in a state of limbo, unable to return to Vietnam, uncertain about the future, demoralized as their length of stay in the camp extended, and worried that their actions in the camp might prevent them from being selected for resettlement elsewhere (see also Knudsen 1983: 171–173). After six years in Vietnamese Communist reeducation camps and jails, the additional confinement in Sikhiu Refugee Camp was a deep shock for this narrator. As an ex-officer in the Army of the Republic of Vietnam who had won an American military decoration, he was dismayed to find that American officials did not act quickly to secure his release. In the end, release came only as a result of the intervention of a Vietnamese friend who lived in the United States, and an American official stationed in Thailand.

Escape from Vietnam

During my detention in Bien Hoa prison, I met a Chinese man. The two of us planned that when we got out of the prison we would escape together to Thailand through Cambodia. At the last moment he gave up his plan, and his younger brother replaced him.

Although this was a dangerous journey, it was very easy for Vietnamese to travel in Cambodia during this time, since the Vietnamese Army occupied the country. Younger men might be checked by the Public Security Agency, but older Vietnamese were allowed to pass. There were many ways to travel. The most dangerous was by road, since a person could be stopped at many checkpoints. To get through, a person had to have official orders or papers. It was possible to get fictitious papers, but costly. An easier way to travel was to take a boat. Many tradesmen went up and down the Mekong River to trade in Phnom Penh. We could mingle with them.

In mid-May 1982 we went upriver to Phnom Penh, where we stayed for two weeks at the house of relatives of the Chinese man. From there, we drove a tiny Volkswagen down to Sihanoukville, on the southwest coast of Cambodia. This was the most dangerous part of the trip; we had two flat tires on the way, and no spare. We were almost caught by the Communist Vietnamese soldiers who maintained the security of the road. When we arrived at the wharf, we encountered another crisis. The boat my family had paid for was less than six meters long and had an old, tiny outboard engine. Six of us were to travel in this small boat. We could not turn back. That night, very late, we embarked. We crossed the sea along the Cambodian coast.

Early the next morning, a tempest hit us. It rained so heavily that the boatman was forced to land at the nearest island. There we spent five days waiting out the bad weather. Every time we tried to send our boat back into the water, big waves threw it back and hurled us onto sharp rocks. Every one of us was injured. On the sixth day, we rolled our boat over bamboo trunks around the island where it was sheltered from the wind. On our journey, I found the skull and tibia of a man. By superstition, I gathered these remains and made a prayer for the soul of the lost man. Early the next day, we lowered the boat into the sea and proceeded on our voyage. In the morning, we encountered a minor storm, but we managed to endure. Late that afternoon, we came to an island. The boatman said that this was Thai territory, but just as we were about to land, we saw far away two North Vietnamese soldiers in green jungle uniforms. Quickly we pushed out to sea again. They fired at us. Happily they only had small arms, and their range was too short. We tried to get away as fast as possible, but the wind and waves pushed our boat closer to shore. They continued firing, and one bullet hit and immobilized our engine. The soldiers kept firing at us. I don't know why, but as if by magic, a tiny fishing boat appeared, inside of which were an old man, an old woman, and a child. We waved our hands and signaled our plea to be rescued. The Thai fishing boat moved alongside us, dropped anchor, which our boatman gripped, and pulled us in the direction of the West. Within five minutes we were on Thai shores, where we saw Thai navy men playing volleyball. The fishing boat left. I went directly over to the navy people and addressed them in Thai, which I speak, "We wish to be hosted." They took us to their headquarters for investigation, then called the border police. They interrogated us a second time and gave us all a body check.

We were taken to the district police headquarters, where we were detained in a jail with bars. By chance, some International Red Cross people came to visit two other Vietnamese who were about to leave for a Western country. I spoke to the Red Cross people in French, and on my behalf they contacted a representative of the United Nations High Commission for Refugees (UNHCR). Later I learned that refugees arriving in Thailand who were unknown to any refugee or helping organization usually were secretly cast off to sea again.

Sikhiu Refugee Detention Camp, Thailand

I was sent to Sikhiu, a large detention camp that housed some 7,000 Vietnamese refugees. They are kept there indefinitely. I remained there for over six months. Shortly after I arrived there, I wrote a letter to the U.S. Defense Attaché in Bangkok informing him of my situation and asking them to get the Thai authorities to release me and give me political asylum. In my letter I pointed out not only my past cooperation with U.S. forces in Vietnam, but also that I had received two U.S. military decorations. My request was never answered. The U.S. Embassy in Thailand also did not answer my letters. Then I wrote to a U.S. Catholic priest who helped refugees. I again explained my situation and requested that he help. He, too, did not respond.

While I waited for his reply, I found myself again in a prison camp, and one which was no better than the border camp in which I had stayed in North Vietnam. We were deprived of everything. The Thais treated us as prisoners rather than refugees. Those who violated camp regulations were beaten inhumanly. They would tie a man's hands behind his back tight on a pole and then beat him on the back with a rattan pole. The number of times depended on the severity of the crime. For fighting, a man would receive 20 or more lashes. Then his head would be shaved, and he would be sent to the prison inside our camp. I saw this happen almost every week. Men were beaten even more severely for drinking alcohol; they were beaten for trying to get outside the fence to buy and exchange with Thai natives. Those who gambled for money received 10 to 15 lashes with rattan and were sent to the jail for periods ranging from one week to indefinitely. In all, I saw 20 beatings.

In principle, a refugee in the camp was under the protection and assistance of the UNHCR. That meant that we were supposed to receive food (worth five dollars a day per person), clothes, medicine, and lodging. In fact, all of the aid from the United Nations had to go through the Thais. By the time it came to us, almost nothing was left except for some rice and a few vegetables, barely enough to survive on. Fish and meat were almost nonexistent. If we distributed to each individual an equal portion of our daily ration, each individual would have received just one scale of fish or one bone of meat. The food had been stolen by the food supplier, a Thai man who had to pay a large bonus to the camp commander so that the commander could get his profit too. In addition, the people who worked in the kitchen also stole the food; they were Vietnamese refugees. In order for everybody to have something to eat, we reached a common agreement: a family would eat meat once a week; on the other six days they would not. The meat was so little that it could not be divided among all.

When my son in Canada and friends heard that I was in Sikhiu Camp, they sent me money. This enabled me to obtain food other than that distributed by the United Nations. A single man in the camp had a very inconvenient time. It took so long waiting for U.N. food. I preferred to use my time for other, more significant work.

We had other problems. Thai officials in the camp were involved in the exchange of things with the refugees. All the things sold to the refugees in camp were double the normal price outside. The Thai deputy commander of the camp was well known for raping two Vietnamese women and for beating people most ferociously, including women who stole things. Although complaints were made to the Thai commander, he did not respond. He was too busy with his business dealings, and from time to time he also beat refugees. Another deputy commander killed a young refugee in his twenties. He was one of the most brutal in the camp and did many of the beatings. The mother of the boy who was killed made an official complaint, and the matter is now under investigation.

There was quite a lot of stealing in camp; also gambling, drinking, and prostitution among the Vietnamese themselves. The Thais were also involved as consumers. Sikhiu Refugee Camp was a community that was rotten. The reason is that the people were so poor, so denigrated, so discouraged by their unknown and uncertain future that they abandoned themselves to vices. Even the intellectuals, the educated, I am very sad to say this, had no more morality. Everyone took advantage of any good opportunity that happened to him to exploit to the detriment of others. There was no law in this community. Everyone thought he was the center of the universe.

I did my best in the field of education. At first, I faced many enemies everywhere who tried to destroy my plan. In the end, I succeeded, thanks to the collaboration of a handful of young men who trusted in me and helped. I also had the assistance of the UNHCR, the camp commander, and some other humanitarian agencies. Some Thai people were helpful and sympathetic. The

UNHCR representative was a Thai. Another helpful person was a Thai woman deputy commander. She was a young, dynamic newcomer who was disinterested in corrupt business.

I organized a school of some 2,000 students ranging in age from 5 to 15, and I recruited about 100 teachers. No school had existed in the camp before this time. The camp had been started in 1979, and up to this point there had been no exit. No one brought in as a refugee had been permitted to leave. We set up the school in September 1982.

In addition to being the dean of this educational institution, I also was the leader of the Resistance Movement in the camp. I had some correspondence with one of the leaders of that movement, which was supposed to be the spearhead for resistance against the Communist government in Vietnam.

After six months in the camp, a Vietnamese friend and an American official in Thailand intervened to secure my release from Sikhiu, in return for my helping the American debrief deserters from the North Vietnamese Army who had escaped through Cambodia. As far as I know, I was the first refugee allowed to leave that camp. I was sent to the Cambodian-Thai border to conduct the debriefings. There I learned that the Resistance Movement was largely fictitious and unreal, so I withdrew my involvement with it. I found that the base camp of the Resistance Movement was not in Vietnam, as their followers pretended, but somewhere on the border between Thailand and Laos. I also discovered that they had lied about imaginary exploits and victories, which they reported to the Vietnamese magazines and newspapers abroad. I judged that it would be harmful to my own name to be involved with them, since they had received much money and material support from the Vietnamese refugee communities abroad, as well as from some foreign organizations.

When I worked for the Americans, I interviewed many North Vietnamese army deserters. These young men fled to Thailand by boat and walked overland through Cambodia. Through them, I was able to find out a true picture of Vietnamese activities in Cambodia both for and against the Vietnamese Communist regime. I also interviewed some Cambodians and came to understand their thinking and their resistance against the so-called liberation of the country by the Vietnamese Communists. I do not think the Cambodians will be able to recover their independence because of the disinterest their intellectuals have shown in the survival of their nation. I have spoken with many of their intelligentsia; they are discouraged, split among themselves, and do not have the endurance of the Vietnamese people.

Like many civilians throughout Vietnam, the Vietnamese Army deserters have no more confidence in their regime. Even high-ranking cadres still in the government consider themselves betrayed by the regime of which they are a part. They see this in the desperate situation of the economy, and in the corruption, which is worse than anything we can imagine, far worse than anything done in the previous regime. Even if he could be resurrected, the deified Ho Chi Minh could not change this situation unless the whole country were to be liberated from Communism. For the moment, it is really a ripe time for Northerners as well as Southerners, cadres as well as civilians, to have a tangible comparison of the reality and the viability of Communism with other systems in today's modern world.

When I think of all the events in which I have been involved, from the overthrow of Ngo Dinh Diem to my life in Communist reeducation camps, I realize that there are two aspects of the Vietnamese character which help to explain what has happened to us. The first is the extremism of Vietnamese behavior, seen in the activities of competing groups and political parties that refuse to compromise. The second is the failure of the Vietnamese to work together, due to their excessive individuality. The Chinese have had enormous influence on the Vietnamese, but they differ from us in these two crucial traits. The Chinese have had the ability to pull things together and to cooperate; also they have had the ability to follow the principle of moderation. We do neither, and those are the two flaws of the Vietnamese character.

[See also Chapters 19, 20, 21, 22, and 32.]

America: Heartache Beneath Success

Introduction

Part VI includes narratives from first-wave refugees who arrived in 1975, several boat people who escaped after 1975, an Orderly Departure Program immigrant, and a Chinese-Vietnamese refugee who was expelled from Vietnam against his will. In age they range from 18 to 80. Their experiences are quite diverse; they and their relatives reveal varying strategies and different levels of success and failure in adjusting to America. (For accounts and analyses of Vietnamese refugee adjustments between 1975 and 1980, see Finan 1980, Kelly 1977, Liu 1979, Montero 1979, and Stopp and Nguyen M. Hung 1979; the best single source on more recent adjustments is Owan 1985.)

Those who have had the most difficult time are older women; they tend not to be well educated or trained for occupations in America; they speak little or no English; they are uneasy about leaving their houses; they dislike American food; they encounter difficulties with their more highly acculturated children; they are quite lonely; and they dream of returning to their homeland—not as it is, but as it was before 1975. The older men see themselves as confronting many of the same problems, but they are not quite as isolated because of their education. Several of the chapters in Part VI illustrate these problems.

The Buddhist nun's account highlights some of the adjustment difficulties that people typically have when they arrive in America without relatives. Others who encounter difficulties are men and women who are unable to find employment or whose jobs in America are lower in status than those they had held in Vietnam. Loneliness is a problem for most refugees, but especially for those who have arrived in America without family. In his poetry, the young poet dwells on this theme: he sees himself as a "wild animal" separated from his social setting; he asks why he should continue to live.

Not all families have made successful transitions, even if they seem outwardly to have done so. The narrative of the elderly civil servant highlights such a situation: the sons of the family are successful in education and employment, in the health professions and in the electronics industry. At the same time, the bonds of their family have been shattered. To the outside world, they are a stunning success story; within the family, their success is a hollow mockery. The parents see themselves as being abandoned; the children view their parents as old-fashioned disciplinarians who meddle excessively in their lives.

Successful adjustments seem more likely to occur where family bonds and obligations remain strong but where people within those families allow for some flexibility to deal with a changed social environment in America. Historically, Vietnamese society has been dynamic and changing. Those Vietnamese who recognize this are better prepared to adjust to new situations than those who idealize Vietnamese institutions as unchanging. An example is the family of Narrator 6, where the children seem to be given greater freedom than they would have had in Vietnam, but are still under firm parental control and direction in such areas as education, career preparation, and social behavior. Once the children have mastered English, their very success in school may be a result of not taking on American values and habits of study but of retaining the discipline expected of them in traditional Vietnamese school environments.

Strong religious faith also has helped some of the narrators cope with stresses of adjustment. The nun, who draws on traditions of Buddhism, displays an extreme example of such faith. A Catholic example is the family of Narrator 6: they continue to pray daily;

the head of the family gives God the credit for his personal character, his ability to work hard and to have a strong motivation to succeed.

Other narrators also exhibit an extraordinary will to survive and to overcome obstacles that might disrupt their lives and overwhelm them. Virtually every narrator had confronted serious crises or hardships in Vietnam: loss of parents during childhood, loss of spouse, extreme poverty, extreme competition in school, loss of jobs, destruction of one's home, relocation, political repression. To survive these, they had to be flexible and resourceful. They also had an enormous commitment to support their relatives in need, and this is also seen throughout the narratives.

Whatever their success, every narrator retains that remote dream that Huu Nguyen has spoken of, to strive to return to a homeland, knowing full well that the dream is so difficult to achieve. That dream is tied to the image of an idealized family, harmonious and cooperative, and to a country in which social behaviors are "at ease," where people feel comfortable. Such an environment exists neither in contemporary Communist Vietnam nor in America. For the Vietnamese of America, their culture is not disintegrating; it is changing. But what will be lost is the remembered culture of a homeland as it existed in decades past. There lies the heartache.

CHAPTER 34

I Will Die Lonely and Abandoned: 1975-1985

NARRATOR I: ELDERLY SOUTH VIETNAMESE CIVIL SERVANT

This chapter provides a glimpse of the anguish of a Vietnamese elder whose children no longer obey him. Significantly, his family problems began not in America, but in Vietnam, when one of his older sons secretly married a woman without consulting his parents. This narrator, as well as others, says that the behavior of the eldest son is the most crucial, for he sets the example that his younger siblings will follow. This family's story suggests that we should be cautious in attributing personal and family crises solely to the refugee experience, since it is probable that many problems originated earlier in Vietnam and then were exacerbated in America.

The narrator also describes his attempts to get to know his neighbors in America, and several instances in which cultural misunderstandings occur and he and his wife are treated rudely.

We Study to Forget

When my family first came to America in 1975, we lived in a small town, where people were quite friendly, and where people protected us and took care of us, and where the children of the town were friendly with ours. Later, because our children wanted to be with other Vietnamese, we moved to a big city, where our life is quite different. I find that I am afraid of people. Every time I go somewhere, I worry that someone will break into my house and steal things. Also, the neighbors here do not want to associate with us; they are not friendly. And the city is so big! It has so many cars, so many streets, that it is kind of scary. I do not know American people here, as I did in the small town. I feel isolated.

For five years I rented a house in one area of the city. During that time I never found out the names of the families that lived on the right or left of me. All I knew was that on the right lived Mexican-Americans; on the left lived blacks. They never came to my house or spoke to me; I just knew them by sight, and we'd say hello to one another.

When I first came here, my neighbor on the right had a big dog that used to come into my yard. I was afraid of it. I knocked on their front door to ask them to deal with the dog.

The wife said, "Do you have any question?"

I replied, "I have been here over one year, and I would like to come in and become acquainted with you and your husband."

"Good, come in," she said.

"The purpose of my visit is to tell you something. Your dog has come to my backyard, and we are afraid of it, so please fix the fence between us. Only as neighbors I would like to be good friends with you."

"Good, I'd like to be your friend, too."

I asked, "How long have you been here? Where do you work now?"

And she asked me, "Where do you come from?"

I said, "We are refugees from Saigon. We first went to another state in America; later we came here."

She replied, "We, too, came from that part of America about two years ago."

After that, she and her husband never came to our house. From time to time I met them in front of the house when they went to work, and we greeted each other.

On the other side of us, the children of the black American family twice threw plastic bags with dead mice between our house and the fence. I did not see them do this, but I assumed it. We did not complain to their parents, since it was only a matter of children. We kept silent. After three years they moved away, and the house was bought by a Mexican-American family with four children. Both the husband and the wife worked; they left home early in the morning, and returned late at night, so I rarely met them.

One Sunday morning, I met the man in front of the house. He said, "Hello," and spoke to me in English. I told him that I was a refugee, and that I did not talk fluent English from the time I was here. I had tried to learn English and some Spanish. He showed some sympathy to me.

In the summer, his family visited Mexico for one and a half months. When he returned, I went over to see him and said, "During the time you were away, it was quiet here. But now many children play with your kids, and they disturb me too much. They throw stones at my car and scratch the roof." I wanted him to help me by telling the older children to stop that sort of thing.

He answered in a loud and angry voice, "Are they my children?"

I could not explain more. I said, "I don't know which children are scratching the car."

He shouted, "I don't know anything about it."

Less than an hour later, five children came to my driveway and threw a tennis ball against my car. My wife opened the door, and the children ran away and laughed loudly. One of his boys climbed on the tree in front of his house and pointed to the other children, "Here they are!" That Mexican-American man was there, but he said nothing.

I called my wife over and spoke softly. "Be quiet; if you continue to open the door, they will disturb you more." From that time on my wife and I were quiet when the children came to disturb us. They did it four or five times. And once a number of boys and girls from another block played, bouncing a tennis ball off our garage door. They did that only to our house.

Even though the Mexican-American man and I had that argument, we get along okay. All the family is nice, even the children. My granddaughter plays with them, and they like one another very much. They play inside and outside my house and theirs. Each morning the girl of that man knocks at our door and calls my granddaughter to go to school with her.

Sometimes I meet the mother-in-law of that man, and I try to speak Spanish with her, since that is the only language she knows.

She is from Mexico. She likes it when I speak with her. She is friendly. We talk about where we have come from, how many children she has, where she is going; she often walks to the stores.

One time, as I was walking home from the bus stop, two black American children 12 or 13 years old ran up to me and barred the way. I slid to the left; they moved to their right to block me. I slid to the right, so they moved to their left. They laughed. I was angry, but I said nothing. Finally I walked through them. One of them ran after me and slapped me on the back. I said nothing; maybe they thought I did not speak English. They knew that I was a refugee, so they teased me.

Many times Mexican-American boys around the ages of 13 to 15 would enter my backyard during the day while my wife was gardening. I would be at the kitchen table looking out at the yard. I'd hear them say, "She's in the backyard." I'd open the back door and meet them by the corner of the yard.

"What are you doing in this yard? Why do you always disturb us? I'm going to call the police."

"No English! No English!" they'd say. They attempted to tease my wife thinking she did not speak English.

We know other Vietnamese refugees who have difficulties with neighbors. A couple whom we know have been beaten up three times by black Americans while walking home from the bus. As a result of this, the woman said to me, "We are moving. We cannot stay in that area." She also was discouraging her relatives from applying to come to America.

One time, the children of my niece were beaten up by black children. My niece's husband talked to one of the black parents about this. The father became very angry. "I'll beat you too!" So my niece and her husband were very afraid. They sold their house and moved to another city.

We have seen the bad behavior of people, but many people are very friendly. Once I was able to speak English better, I met many good people, particularly at the college where I took language classes.

If I did not occupy myself in study, I would think about what I lost in my country, and it makes me really depressed. Many young people ask me, "You are so old; why do you continue to go to school?" They think it's not good to study. Many refugees are like me. It is hard to study because we do not remember, but we study to forget the past.

I did not have a lot of property in Vietnam, but what I miss most is my house, the one I constructed in the city where we lived. From time to time I receive letters from friends still in Vietnam saying, "I passed by your house and your fruit trees, and it was sad to see. Now the revolutionary government uses your house as a warehouse." The Communists announced that I had worked for the Americans, was therefore a member of the CIA, and would never return. Everything was taken out of my house. One of my sons who had not yet escaped had attempted suicide. I was depressed when I heard all of these things.

Although people in the small towns are friendlier, I like to live in the big city in America because we meet Vietnamese people. We can easily buy Oriental food; we also have met some people whom we knew in Vietnam. We talk to one another on the telephone, exchange information about what is happening in Vietnam, and discuss how to bring our relatives to America.

One of the surprising things for Vietnamese people is the way the Americans act when they go to a restaurant. After the meal is over, each person pays separately! Sometimes Americans invite Vietnamese to go with them to a restaurant, then split the bill. For us, this is a shock. The Vietnamese think that Americans are not intimate friends; they don't like one another. When a person invites friends to a restaurant, we believe that the responsibility for paying the bill should go to the person who issued the invitation. Potluck dinners are very strange for us Vietnamese, but we are learning to do it and like it.

I like the American custom of sharing. It prevents a misuse of friendship. We have a term for this, "eating free." This occurs when a person continually lets his friends pay without returning the favor.

Back when I was a primary-school teacher in the early 1940s, the staff from time to time would stop at a coffee shop. We noticed that everyone took turns paying except the principal of our school. Just before we got the bill, he would ask the waiter for some expensive French cigarettes and a match. He was the only one who smoked;

we simply paid the bill, and when we left, he would put the remaining cigarettes in his pocket. He did this for many years. Among ourselves we talked about this, but we never complained because he was our boss. I like the American custom of sharing better!

One time, I invited my American tutor here in the city to have some coffee with me, and I paid. A couple of days later she invited me, saying, "I owe you one coffee." She insisted. We don't have that kind of thing in Vietnam. We share, but we do it because we want to.

Undisciplined Children

The behavior of Vietnamese children in America is just beginning to change to the American direction. In Vietnam, children must listen to their parents and must not argue against them. They see the freedom of teenagers here, so they tend to imitate them. One of my good friends from Vietnam is really disturbed by the behavior of his five children here. One day, they did something wrong, I don't know what, but he got so mad! He threatened them with a kitchen knife. His wife called the police. Later, the man complained to me and other friends, "In Vietnam, my children listened to me, but over here they are not afraid of me anymore. They call the police." He was depressed.

With my family, too, my children, and their children, do not obey strictly. One of my sons has children who disobey and argue against him. He is afraid that they have too much freedom going to school; they associate too freely with girls, and they might run away together. So my son prohibited his sons from using the telephone, and as a result there is much disappointment in that family.

These things are very difficult, and I don't know what to do because of the loss of traditional custom. Other people also complain that their children living in the United States imitate the new life and distort our old Vietnamese ways. They have freedom to be promiscuous. I know that in Vietnam some girls are not good, too. But because of the strict control of the parents, that really helped the children. Both boys and girls need to be controlled. If boys have lots of freedom, if they are let loose, that is not good. They will do anything they want, pay no respect to their parents, lie to them, and fool around while pretending to take money for school.

When I was young, I did not have a father, but I listened to my mother. She told me to go to town; I couldn't do anything besides that. I listened to her. Every year I tried to study and go back home after the semester was over.

Girls here have parents who cannot control them. They will grow up and marry anyone they want. Our old way was good in Vietnam, but it won't work here. My eldest son has two daughters about 15 and 20 years of age who told their father that he is too strict. They wanted to move out and live with their friends. My son consulted a counselor, saying, "My daughters are really stubborn ones. What shall I do?"

The counselor, an American female teacher, said, "You cannot beat your children in America; that is against the law. Since the eldest daughter wants to move out, let her go; you cannot do anything about it. The other one is too young and cannot go. Try to control her, but not the older one."

I agree that if the eldest child is out of control, we have to let him or her go, but often I do not think it is good. Such a child is inexperienced and will make many mistakes. With regard to the Confucian rule, a girl should never escape the control of her parents until she gets married. Over here, females are as free as males.

In my college class, a young German woman asked me, "According to the customs of Vietnam, boys and girls are not allowed to kiss publicly, in front of everybody. But here it happens everywhere. What do you think of that?"

I felt embarrassed! In Vietnam, it would be the couples who would be embarrassed. If they were talking in an intimate way and I passed them by, they would look in different directions, the boy to the right, the girl to the left. A woman who kissed publicly lost the respect of young men; they would call her a prostitute and would refuse to marry her. But here in America, I saw boys and girls all over the place, holding hands and kissing.

Then the German woman asked, "What do you prefer, the American custom or the Vietnamese custom?"

I replied, "I like it here!"

She laughed.

Many people say that the difficulties with the Vietnamese family are a result of living in America, but that is not entirely true. Even in Vietnam, our children did not always follow our wishes.

In Vietnam we try to select a wife for our son who relates well to the family, so the selection should be done very carefully. In America, it is not the same way. Here children are very free; they marry whomever they choose, and they don't pay attention to what their parents say.

That happened to me in Vietnam. I had a friend who wanted to marry one of his daughters with one of my older sons. On the eve of the lunar New Year, that man and his wife brought gifts to us, so I had to do the same in turn. But my son kept silent. He took a girl in Saigon city, married her, and had two children by her. He misled me. Although he had been married for a long time, he never told me. He just kept quiet and avoided our attempts to arrange his wedding. Finally in 1968 my wife told him, "If you will not have a wedding, I will delay the wedding of your younger sister because the elder must marry first."

His mother was absent when he told me the truth. "I already have a wife. Not only that, but we already have two girls." It was a real embarrassment. The wife we had selected for him was well educated; the woman he took for a wife had a very low education. My wife and I were very upset, for our son had made us lose face. On the eve of the New Year, I had to go for the last time to my friend's house and offer him the last gift and confess that my son had already become married behind my back. I got so mad that I said to my son, "From now on, I never want to see you again! Please leave the family forever!" For about four years I did not see him.

In 1975, like us, my son and his family escaped by boat to the United States. He now lives in another part of the country, where he has a successful professional career. He and his family have visited us only once, when we lived in another state.

The behavior of this son affected our next two sons and several of our other children. His behavior was the key, because he set a bad example for the others. In Vietnam, when I mentioned how displeased my wife and I were about his choosing a girl whom we had never known, my next two sons would reply, "We are now adults. Why are you worried about who our wives might be? Let us be free about that matter." From that time, my wife and I connived to choose the right girls for them.

One day the second son roared up to our house in his Honda motorcycle accompanied by a girl sitting in back. "This is my friend," he said to his mother. He said nothing to me. My wife was silent. The woman came to the sitting room and stayed there alone. No one chatted with her. After an hour my son left with her. We never saw her again.

The third son also refused to listen to his mother. He knew many girls. And he refused the offer of a marriage set up for him by one of our relatives. One day in 1973 he came to us and said he wanted to marry a girl he had met in Saigon. We did not know that girl, but he insisted many times. He said he loved her and she loved him; no matter what, they would be married. So I consulted a fortune-teller who lived in my hamlet.

After reading the fortune-telling book, that man said, "The couple are not well matched. Their ages are against each other. Their future life will not be good."

I told my son what the fortune-teller had told me, and he in turn told his prospective father-in-law. That man, however, was a Christian who did not believe in fortune-telling. He said, "It's okay; I agree to marry my girl to you." He didn't care about bad fortune; he didn't care that the parents had not arranged the wedding, as long as his daughter had a husband. So I could not do anything else. We did not organize a big wedding; we just went through the formality.

The fortune-teller was right; it has not worked out well. In America, they live in the same city as we do, but we have no contact with them at all. We do not even know their telephone number or address.

A fourth son also does not obey us. He was for a while involved with a girlfriend of his own choice of whom the family was a troublemaker. We fear that he will follow the direction of his eldest brother.

Our eldest daughter married a man whom we did not think was a good match. Her husband has now left her.

Still another son, who lives at home with us and has seen all this, says, "You, Father and Mother, are always serious. After my wedding we will live apart."

Another of our daughters is married happily and has a small child. We gave her complete freedom to choose her husband here in America. I do not know much about her husband's behavior, but I gave permission, first, because she wanted him; second, because her brothers and sisters accepted him; and finally, because we also liked him when he came to visit us. We also write frequently to his parents in Vietnam. That marriage has worked out well. Even so, when I think back on it, I do not have any happy memories of our children.

In Vietnam, if a son refused to obey his parents, they might throw him out and say that he should never see them again. When they died, he would not be allowed to come back for the ceremonies, nor would he be allowed to wear symbols of mourning. In any family, most children are obedient, but I know many people who have been disowned. Sometimes parents relent when it is a son they have dismissed; for girls, disobedience is unforgivable.

These rules were strictly enforced in Vietnam. In America, the problem is that we emphasize control of children, while Americans emphasize their freedom. One of my wife's sisters-in-law in Saigon had a son who brought home a girl whom he said he wanted to marry. It is very peculiar for a bride to visit the groom's house before the groom visits the bride's house. The groom should do some sort of service of help to her family; we call it "groom's work." [This was found in the past in the countryside, where the economy was agricultural.]

Even after the engagement, the future bride is not allowed to visit the future groom's house. In fact, in embarrassment, she often avoids him when he visits her house. My wife's sister-in-law was quite offended, and so she replied with a big insult, "What an ill-bred girl she is! The boy is not yet a groom, but already she makes herself like a bride." Perhaps had her son not brought that girl to the house in violation of the custom, his mother might have relented, but she was so angry she refused to hold a wedding for him.

Parents will not be able to hold back the changes that are happening. In America, girls will select their own husbands. Among my friends, the majority now do that, including my own youngest daughter.

In the old days in Vietnam, the behavior not only of unmarried girls, but of wives, was carefully controlled. In 1941, when I was a teacher in a village school, a matter came to the attention of the district chief. A woman caught her husband sleeping with another man's wife. To punish them, the district chief told the two lovers to walk one behind the other around the market of the town carrying a large drum suspended by poles. A policeman accompanied them. As they walked, the man called out, "I'm not sleeping with my wife; I'm sleeping with another man's wife. The district chief forces me to beat this drum." The woman called out, "I'm not sleeping with my husband; I'm sleeping with another woman's husband. The district chief forces me to beat this drum."

This was to humiliate the two people, for after they were released, the story went all around the district. The reputations of their families were destroyed. It would create very bad effects on the next two to three generations. People remember this matter and will remind each other and laugh. Their children will have a harder time getting married, because people remember the bad personalities of the two lovers.

Many times I go to the gatherings of the Vietnamese elderly people. Most of the time, I hear them talking about the good behavior of the Vietnamese children. They talk of the piety of their children and the good behavior of their married children. Sometimes I felt bad; my family has had a rough time, while these people bragged that everything was going well.

Then I took a trip to Hawaii with other Vietnamese people, most of them women. When they discussed their sons, daughters, and daughters-in-law, it was very different: bad behavior, how wives cheated on their husbands, how children disobeyed and showed no respect, how they told their parents not to interfere in their lives because it's none of their business, how they said that they had a higher regard for their spouse than their parents. When I heard all that, I did not feel so bad.

In America, there is nothing to hold our family together. In this city alone, my family numbers some 16 people spanning three generations: we live in several different locations in the city. We also have others of our family living elsewhere in America. Even so, we have nothing to look forward to. If I returned to Vietnam, the Communists would put me in a reeducation camp, which would kill me. But here in America, my wife and I will die a lonely death, abandoned by our children.

[See also Chapters 3, 14, and 16.]

CHAPTER 35

I Cannot Learn English: 1975-1984

NARRATOR 2: SOUTH VIETNAMESE ELDERLY RURAL WOMAN

Ba That describes problems of adjustment in America that are faced by many elderly Vietnamese women. Her major problem is her lack of knowledge of English and her inability to learn it. She speaks of other problems, including difficulties with her children, and then tells of her wish to return to live in the Vietnamese countryside.

First Adjustments in America

Church people, our sponsor, and my sixth son came to pick us up at a bus station and took us to our sponsor's house. It was located in a small town in a southern state. The sponsor was very polite. My son had said that when we came over here, we might enjoy living in this big house. The sponsor saved two bedrooms for us. Every day I cooked. In the morning while my daughter went to work, I took care of her infant daughter. I also would clean the house, which was big. At noon we all would eat together with our sponsor. In the afternoon I would cook for our children. That's how we started our days.

After a few days, our sponsor saw that my husband was depressed, so she asked him if he would like to plant some things in the garden. I had lots to do, while he had nothing, and he was so sad. She got someone to plow a part of her backyard so that my husband could grow cucumbers, squash, carrots, and radishes. He began to work in the garden; so did I. When I had free time I planted onions, garlic, and corn. For two months we lived in that house.

Then our sponsor rented us a two-bedroom townhouse that was close to her home. Because a church member owned it, the rent was low, only $60 a month. The church provided everything for us: pots, bowls, dishes, a small washing machine, curtains, sheets, blankets, beds: all of our needs were met. One man from the church also offered us an electric stove and a refrigerator. The minister of the church and his son also helped us move and showed me how to use appliances that were new to me, such as the washing machine and the electric stove. The market was close by, so my husband would ride there on his bicycle and bring back food. Around noon, I would visit my sponsor's house to work on the garden we had started. We also started a garden in our new house, and we grew some very large squash.

When we visited our sponsor, she always offered us some food, like watermelon. Other church members would give us leftover cookies and other food. My sponsor bought us a gas lawn mower, and this enabled my youngest son to cut grass to earn money while attending school. We remained in that house for two years. My sponsor's sister-in-law also hired my son to work in her large garden. Nothing unusual happened during those two years. We met lots of Americans, mostly church members, who would visit us every Sunday. They included a doctor, lawyers, teachers, plantation owners, and others. They offered us a lot of stuff.

The Americans are much nicer than the Vietnamese. No Vietnamese would have fed us like that, treating us just like sisters and brothers. We are strange to them, but they helped us. That's very nice; that's precious. Even so, after one year, we decided to leave. The reason was that our daughters and sons were leaving to work in another state. They told us to follow them so that we could all be together and they could take care of us. They said it was not right to let the church people help us all the time. Also, the weather was warmer in their new location; there was no snow.

One of the reasons my children left was the school. Most of the students were white, so it was hard to study. Also, since the town was small, there was no university, only a high school.

The first persons to leave were my daughter, her husband, and their daughter. Then another daughter left because her sisters and brothers told her that she could get better training and jobs elsewhere. These two daughters had worked in a shoe factory and saved some money, which they gave to us when they left.

During this time, the minister, our sponsor, and the people in the church told us to stay with them and buy a new house. Our children disagreed, so we did not let the church people know for a long time. Finally we told our sponsor that we planned to move to the West Coast. She burst into tears. She was so sad; she begged us not to leave. The church people also tried to persuade us to stay. We said we didn't have the money to buy a house, $50,000 to $75,000. They said not to worry about that. They had an architect draw up a house plan for only $5. Then the people kept asking us whether we wanted it or not. In the meantime, our children hurried us up to move, so we told our sponsor our decision, and they had to accept.

At that time, my husband did not know English well, and I still do not, so we didn't understand very well. But off we went to a different state, using a car that my daughter left behind for us. The trip took three days and two nights.

A Second Adjustment

I regret that we moved. I wanted to stay there. My children insisted that we move. Now I would like to go back, but my children are here, so I cannot. I prefer to live in the countryside, as we first did when we came to America, and not in a city as we do now. It is like Vietnam. I didn't want to leave Vietnam, but all of my children were gone; I'm old, and they have to take care of me. So I had to follow them. That's what I did again in America.

The main problem that I have in America is that I don't know how to speak English. Second, if I wanted to go somewhere, I cannot. I would have to use a car, but I cannot drive. If I use the bus, I am afraid that I will become lost.

I have lots of barriers. If I have to fill out papers, I cannot. I also am unable to answer the phone. I know how to take down phone numbers, just a little, not much. If I'm sick accidentally, I don't know what to do because we are always home by ourselves, my husband and I. In Vietnam, we had relatives nearby, and if something happened, they would get together. I'm kind of sad because over here relatives are too far away from us. If people speak a little, I can understand only a very little, not a lot.

My children take care of me like usual. I have a hot temper; I always yell at them if they do something wrong. I see that children do not obey me as much as when they were in Vietnam. It's sad sometimes; it creates anger. When I lived in Vietnam, it was different. My children were young at that time. We took care of them so they obeyed us more. They were afraid of us and respected us more.

Here we need them more; they don't need us.

In Vietnam, if I wanted to go to the market, I just picked up a basket and went. I didn't need anybody to take us. Over here, I have to wait until the [children] take us. If they don't go, we don't go. This makes me feel sad, yes.

Here in America, I just remain. I don't change my traditional ways; I still keep them. My children have adapted to American customs in hair styles and dress. While I was on the island of Guam, I heard women say, "Now most Vietnamese women in the U.S.A. will become men [dress like men]." And that is true; they dress according to what the people here do, except older women like me, who keep our old ways. The older women don't change much, and most of the older men don't change either.

We see big differences in food given to babies. In Vietnam, we did not have baby food. Mothers nursed their babies or gave them condensed milk or powdered milk or cow milk. Children here get used to American food. Our granddaughter eats hamburgers and canned food, but she will not touch Vietnamese food. She is unable to eat. She tastes only a teaspoonful; then she sits there and looks. So her mother buys her hamburgers. For breakfast she eats cereals, bread, milk, and noodles. When she was young, she ate Vietnamese food, but only a little. She likes bread. Once in a while I cook rice chicken soup; she will eat only the rice, nothing more. Now she can eat imperial rolls and fried rice, but will not touch regular rice.

Once in a while we just force her to eat it. Her mother still feeds her rice, even though she's now 11 years old. I hear that other Vietnamese children are the same.

Me, I cannot eat American food. No hamburgers. I cannot eat butter or cheese, not even beef, ham, or milk. I can eat some American cake, but no cookies; they are too sweet. But my husband, he can eat anything. As for me, I eat lots of chicken with lots of salt and lemon crust, and I barbecue them. I eat roast pork, eggs, chicken curry, chicken rice soup, duck rice soup, boiled vegetables such as squash, fried vegetables, fried fish, and potato. I eat a lot of the American vegetables because we have the same kinds in Vietnam; fruits too.

If it were peaceful, I would live in Vietnam. I would live in the countryside because I have property and fields near the river, also a big garden with lots of fruits such as jackfruit and banana. I'd go back and live there. I'd make my living selling rice paper or chicken and pigs. It's more of a comfortable life.

Over here, for older people, we receive money from the government; if not, we would die of starvation because we are older and don't know what to do. In Vietnam, we have less fear of survival, but over here, I'm afraid that when I get older I'll have to go into a nursing home to stay there, because all of my children are working. My husband and I have to stay home ourselves, all alone. Now I am fine and can stay home, but later what will happen? Old age here is scary.

Children over here don't take care of their parents. In Vietnam, if poor, a person lived with his children; if rich, with only one child, possibly the youngest. Life was much more comfortable if rich because children and grandchildren would take care of you.

In America, every time we want to go somewhere, we have to wait for our children to take us. If we want to visit relatives, we don't know what to do. In Vietnam, we could travel around much more easily.

In Vietnam, a person would build a house. Children would want to remain in that house. Even if they went away for some reason, they would want to be close by at the time of the death of the parent, and they themselves would want to be buried near their ancestors. Rich people preserve a piece of property on which to bury the family members; it's a grave property. From the twenty-third to the thirtieth day of the new year, children must visit the graves of their ancestors.

In Vietnam we had a house. Once in a while our children came back to visit. Our youngest remained in the family, while those who lived close by would see us often. Here in America, that's not so. Two of my sons I never see. I don't even know my grandchildren, how tall they are.

The difference is that over here children do not obey their parents; in Vietnam, they obeyed us more. Over here, whenever we say something, they like to argue about it. My husband and I dislike this. If our children want something and we don't like it, they will not listen to us. Things we consider to be right they consider wrong. Like a wife they select whom we don't like. They argue with us, against it, saying that it's right for them and that they will take the responsibility for it. They claim it's their *right* and that we don't have the right to tell them what to do. It is just like we are strangers; they won't let us interfere. One of my sons has a girl-friend. She came to visit him several times. Each time she ignored my family, just walked in and did not say hello, sat down on the sofa and faced the window. I assume she came from Central Vietnam because she didn't talk to us. I assume that every time she came here she must have called my son first because I see that my son always waits at the door to greet her at the first ring. After conversation with her, they take off.

Sometimes I get really upset. I talk to him. He argues with me. It's his selection, his way; it depends on him; parents don't have the right; nobody has the right; this is his right. Not only does he tell us this, but he wrote me a letter like that.

Once I talked to my younger son. I told him that when a son marries, the family must like the marriage to have happiness. If the family does not like your wife, it's very complicated, less happy. So when getting married, let your parents choose for you the right one so that when your wife bears children, they will look very nice. But if she's ugly, she'll give birth to ugly children.

My son replied, "You're too old-fashioned. Parents-in-law must be equal to your own parents to satisfy you. The wife's parents must be suitable or equal to your own family. My wife will stay with me; she won't stay with you parents. Therefore there is no need to select to suit you."

This sort of behavior is found among the educated younger children, who consider themselves to be higher in evolution, less old-fashioned. Even in Vietnam, this began, and they have continued this trend here in America. In Vietnam, I had lots of grand-daughters-in-law. They dared not behave like this girlfriend of my youngest son. In Vietnam, they respected us a lot; not here. What has happened to me has also happened to others. My niece found that her daughters-in-law behave like that, with disrespect. So her children are like my children.

What makes me most upset is when I talk to my children and they argue. Then I am very sad. I told my children that I do not say anything now, but that they should not disturb me. I told them, whoever they marry, whenever they come to my house, they should not disturb me. If I am disturbed, I will curse them, and they will have to carry bad things forever. "I don't want to see your faces. Do not disturb me." So they know and they don't come. Our children do not keep the old traditions. They live apart from one another.

No matter what might happen, no matter where we would have landed or stayed, we had to leave Vietnam, not only for America, but for anywhere. If my husband had remained in Vietnam, the Communists would have arrested and killed him. Therefore we had to go. We left everything behind.

[See also Chapters 4, 18, and 28.]

CHAPTER 36

We Cannot Walk in Our Neighborhood: 1976–1982

NARRATOR 4: CENTRAL
VIETNAMESE TEACHER

This narrator too speaks of the many difficulties he and his wife face in adjusting to American life-styles. His wife speaks no English and remains at home, unhappy and lonely; he works at a low-paying job, which in status is far below that which he had held in Vietnam. When walking down the street, both of them are harassed by youths who shout out insults as they pass by in cars. They see the future of their children as bright, but their own as bleak.

My family arrived in America in October 1976. At that time I spoke a little English; my wife spoke none. I had not had any intention of coming to America, but since I had a relative here, the International Rescue Committee contacted the American Embassy, and we were brought into this country.

I remember our first misunderstanding. We saw lots of people waving to each other in greeting. My wife said, "Oh, how do they know us like a friend, that they're calling us to go over to them?" For us, the gesture signified "Come here."

We were sent to a place in the South where the people were quite friendly, but the climate was too cold for us in the winter, and much too hot in the summer. There were mosquitoes and flies all over. It was not pleasant.

Although white people were friendly with us, we saw discrimination against blacks. I asked a black friend to go with me while I visited a friend. When he saw that I was about to enter the house of a white man, he said, "I'll stay outside and wait."

"Why not go inside?" I asked.

He replied, "My mother told me not to go to white people."

I tried one more time. I took a white man to a black man's house. The white man wouldn't go in. "Why?" I asked.

"My mother told me not to visit black people."

One day I went to the store and selected lots of oranges, apples, and vegetables. I had only ten dollars in my pocket. The girl at the checkout counter added up the cost of the items and said, "You owe fifteen dollars."

I replied, "I've only got ten, so I'll put back some oranges. Give me ten dollars' worth. Tomorrow I'll buy more."

A black woman standing behind me said, "Let him get everything; I'll pay the rest for him."

That was the first time something like that happened; I'll never forget it.

On another occasion, when I had moved to another state, an old man saw me buy a hamburger but nothing else at a hamburger stand. He asked, "Why did you buy only a hamburger, and nothing to drink?"

I replied, "I don't have enough money, only a little over a dollar."

The old man said, "I'll buy another hamburger for you."

"No, no," I said. "It's too much for me."

He bought me another hamburger and some orange juice. We sat down and ate together.

Some people are good, but others are not friendly. Where we live now, we cannot ride a bicycle, for young people shout loudly as they drive by in cars. I don't care what they say, but they startle me when they drive right behind me, pass me close by, on the narrow road, and then shout in my ear.

Sometimes my wife and I walk along the sidewalk. Even that we cannot do, for the young people shout out at us as they drive by. My wife feels bad when she hears this; she does not want to go out. I care about that. I say to her, "Let's drive to the park; then we can walk there." But walking nearby is better because we do not need a car.

My wife often feels so lonely here in America because she cannot walk near her home, for she is afraid that people will shout at her. She has friends around here, but if she wishes to visit them, she asks me to accompany her. So her behavior in America is quite different from how she lived in Vietnam, where she'd leave the house alone two, three, or four times a day, visiting the market, her parents, and her friends. She used to walk a lot and enjoyed it very much; now she fears to do it. I don't know, the old people in America are very nice, but young people are rude and destructive. At the rear of my apartment stands a large wheeled garbage bin. It is real dirty and has a bad smell that attracts lots of flies. Many people also go there to drink beer and smoke cigarettes. The manager of the apartment put up a sign to keep out of private property; still, two to three carloads of dirty young people with long hair gather around the garbage bin; they make so much noise, even at night. Often they are drunk. They throw cans and empty bottles on the roof; the clatter is terrible. Even though the manager calls the police, these people often return. And they end the evening by urinating on the fence.

Although some other Vietnamese people live near here, we do not see them often. They work all day, eat, sleep, watch television, but don't go out much except to work. Like my wife, they have stopped walking in the neighborhood because the youths shout at them. In Vietnam, the old people used to walk a lot, stopping along the way at restaurants, where they would meet friends, talk, and drink coffee. Sometimes they would go fishing or swimming, and at other times they would visit friends. All of that is gone for them in America, and it is no longer possible in Vietnam either.

My wife says, "I feel so lonely when you and the children are away from the house." She stays home and cooks and does housework. The children too are lonely. I tell them to take the car and visit friends, but they say, "That's a waste of gas and money." They understand our situation, that with my low-paying job, which may stop at any moment, we do not have enough money to support us. A couple of my children attend one of the colleges nearby; I drive them there before going to work, and I pick them up after work.

But my wife remains alone all day. For companionship, I bought her two birds in a large cage. From time to time, one of the birds sings. Because she has poor eyesight, my wife cannot watch television. Her days are long. I work five days a week. On those days, I am tired. All I want to do is relax, eat, drink, and go to sleep. On the weekends, I take her to the market, and we go to the laundromat. Sometimes we write letters to our relatives and friends. But our life is a lonely one in America. That's why lots of old people want to return to Vietnam. Religion here won't help them; that's only for a few hours on Sunday. People still remain lonely. They dream of fighting the Communists, throwing them out, and returning to live out their days peacefully in their homeland. But this is only a dream.

Sometimes my friends call me on the telephone. We talk about our lives here and what other people are doing. We sometimes invite one another to come by and take some food. This is different from Vietnam, where we used to just arrive at the door of our friend, and they'd invite us in. We'd say, "We've got some food ready; why don't you stay and have some." We'd travel around a lot and visit friends, more than here in America. We'd help our friends get jobs, and we'd share room, clothes, food. A friend might stay with us for months; we don't care about that. During holidays, maybe four or five people will come by and stay. That's how we do it.

For my wife, adjustment in America is very hard. For me and my children, adjustment is not that difficult. I had some experience in dealing with Westerners before I left Vietnam. My children are young enough to adapt to new customs. Within three days of our arrival in America, I had enrolled them in school; within four months, they were speaking English.

Somewhat difficult for us was learning to cope with American food, which contains too much salt and sugar, and very peculiar seasoning. We dislike it, and I still eat mostly Vietnamese-style food. At my place of work, I eat food that I have taken from home. My daughters have learned to tolerate American food, but prefer Vietnamese.

Also hard for us is the speaking of English. Often we can read well, but because of our pronunciation people think we are not well educated. We find it quite difficult to ask for information over the telephone, so we may drive 20 or 30 miles to get the information. Yesterday, I tried to call a pet shop where I had bought two finches. I said to the man, "The mother bird has laid five eggs, but after they hatched, she kicked them out of her nest area, and they died. What should I do to prevent that?"

The man at the pet shop said, "Sorry, I cannot understand what you said."

I asked an American friend to call for me. He received the information and relayed it to me.

That's not the only language problem. One morning I was cleaning our floor with a vacuum cleaner that made a lot of noise. The people who live below us pounded on the ceiling with something. They were angry, I guess. I went next door to an American lady and asked her to explain to the people below that I was cleaning with a vacuum cleaner. She did that, and the people said it was okay.

In 1979, I enrolled in a technical training institute where I received nine months of instruction. I started out in one field, but a friend persuaded me to try another. It turned out I had quite a bit of skill for it, so my counselor at the institute let me switch. After completing my training, I went out to look for work. My friend, who was younger, was hired immediately; I had more difficulty, for when people saw that I was in my fifties, they were not anxious to hire me. After two months, one company offered me a job. The man who hired me said, "Take five dollars an hour."

I replied, "No, six."

"Okay," the man said. "I'll hire you."

In Vietnam, a man of my age would have retired. I would have been able to support my family to the end of my life. But not in America. I tell my children to work hard, because I will not be able to help them forever; one day they will be on their own. I have no security of any kind here; I must keep working as long as I have a job, and it might end at any moment.

I liked my job in Vietnam much more. I talked with people of a higher class, and people treated me with respect. I had three months of paid summer vacation every year. The status of my job in Vietnam was much higher than the factory labor I do here. That is very difficult, not only for me, but for many other Vietnamese men. We have lost our country. We are making a new life in another country. We don't care about our second life in a new country, that we are lower in status. Even though it is difficult, many of us are happy because our children have a chance here. I'm at the end of my life; I'm happy simply to sacrifice for my children. I'll take any job to help them. I do know some Vietnamese people who are unable to adjust to the loss of their status.

I am happy that I was able to change my life and start a new job in America. At least I showed I could make the adjustment. But if you ask me what life is like for me here in America, I have to tell you: Terrible! I say that because all the money I get from my new job is gone. Almost all of it goes for rent, which is increased too much. We have no money for heating. In the winter, we keep warm by wrapping blankets around ourselves, and we cover the windows with sheets. We can buy a blanket for seven dollars and use it for a year. We have no need for heat. We never use our big oven, but boil all of our food to keep down the costs. For food, we don't pay too much. If food increases in price, we decrease how much we eat. If rent increases, there is no way to decrease. Rent is a major problem for us. I have some health coverage at my place of work, but it is so inadequate that when I am ill, I try to avoid doctors and hospitals because they are so expensive. I use home remedies; my wife uses herbal medicines. That's why we are able to survive on so much less than other Americans.

I often wonder what will happen to my family. The future of my children is bright, for they work hard and have talent. They know they must work hard, for I will not be able to help them much longer. The work I do requires good hand-and-eye coordination. One day I will lose that. What will happen to me then? Sometimes I worry about my future; at other times I don't care.

[See also Chapters 6 and 29.]

CHAPTER 37

God Made Me a Hard-Working Man: 1978-1983

NARRATOR 6: CENTRAL VIETNAMESE FISHERMAN / BUSINESSMAN

By contrast with some of the other narrators in this book, this narrator reveals a success story in progress. He tells how he built up a thriving business, even though he has little education and limited English skills. He gets along very well with his neighbors, who are from many different ethnic groups. His children are successful in school and are adjusting well to their new environment. His one concern about America is that laws in this country make it difficult to educate and rear children according to Vietnamese customs.

"I Am Happy in America"

On our third attempt, my wife, children, and I escaped by boat from Vietnam and arrived in Hong Kong, where we remained for three months. Then my brother, who came to America in 1975, sponsored us, and we arrived in America in 1978.

We stayed with my brother and his family for five months. Neither I nor anyone in our family spoke any English before our arrival in America. I realized that I must study to communicate. Even though my brother was in one place, I decided to move to the West Coast. For nine months we lived in one town, where my children went to school. My wife and I also attended school to learn English. Although we received public assistance, we were always short each month by $20, $30, or even $40. If the situation continued like this, we'd have no money for clothes for the family. Even then, what we bought were old clothes that cost 20 or 25 cents apiece.

We made a visit to one of my sisters who lived in a small city that was surrounded by a lot of farmland. I saw that many of the people worked as farmers. I thought, "Maybe it's better for us to move here because I am used to working hard. God made me a hard-working man."

In 1980 we moved to that farming town. As soon as we arrived, I started to grow vegetables in the small backyard of the house we rented. In the meantime, I also worked as a farm laborer. We earned $35 to $45 a day, and that made me feel at ease. During the day I worked outside; in the evening I worked in my backyard. We began to sell what we grew, and from this we earned $200 a month. We liked to have our portion of land to do something, but we did not have enough money to buy.

We received help from the Public Housing Authority. The new house we moved into has four bedrooms. Each month we pay $50. The rest [probably $400–$450] is paid for by the government. The owner who rents us the house likes me very much because we keep the house very clean. Last Christmas, the owner gave our family a gift of $50. I moved all of the fruit trees from the old to the new house, and also planted a larger garden of vegetables and herbs. We have very good relations with our neighbors. They like us very much. They hire us to work on their backyards. That's the reason our income has increased. I grew too much to sell only to our neighbors. I needed to find a market.

One day I went to the farmer's market. I didn't know how to do it. I brought my vegetables there but they chased me away. [He had no permit.] The second time I went back, they chased me away again. But that time I asked, "Can you help me so I can sell vegetables like other people?"

That man told me, "Okay, you come with me; I'll show you how."

He gave me an application form, his business card, and an appointment. He explained to me during the appointment how I should do it and what kind of product I should have. He told me, "I want to come and see your garden, if it fulfills the requirements."

I agreed. He came down to inspect everything and wrote down on a piece of paper all the vegetables I grew. Then he gave me a permit. I brought my vegetables to the market, and nobody chased me any more. We earned some more money.

Now that we had additional income, we reported to Social Services. If I make above $100, they reduce public assistance from $40 to $50. If I make above $200 a month, they reduce from $100 to $200 a month. By doing so, by earning my own money, I feel better than if I do nothing.

After two years of this, we can save some [a lot]. Then we decided to have a fish truck. I borrowed some from my brother because it costs $4,000 to $5,000 to have a fish truck. During my work as a fish merchant our income was better. Since I always report what I earn, the Department of Social Services reduced our cash assistance. My family has eight people. In the past we received $900 a month. Then last summer, they reduced assistance to $500, and last month they dropped it to only $14. Later, if we make a little bit more, we won't receive any help from the Department of Social Services. My wife and I don't want to stay doing nothing.

I am very happy in America for three reasons. First, I am very proud that I can do many things that other people could not do. Even though I do not know English very well, I did not bother anyone in dealing with paperwork or with translations. I myself did everything. I am very pleased by that. My English is not fluent, but when I speak with American people, they understand me, even though my grammar is not very good.

Second, I am at ease about living in America. Americans treat Vietnamese very well. I suppose if Americans had to live in Vietnam as refugees, the Vietnamese would not help them as much as the Americans helped me. We are very happy to live in America. I have received letters from Vietnamese refugees living in other countries. I am able to compare my life with theirs. Life in the United States is much better than in other countries of the Free World.

Third, what I like most is *freedom*, to move, to do business, and the freedom to work. I have freedom for myself, to work, to live, freedom to do everything you want. You can apply for a job or you can do a small business. You can apply for a license for a small business with no difficulties, no obstacles.

Although in America we live with everything free, to move, to do business, we still have the need to return to Vietnam one day. This is our dream. In Vietnam, before the Communists came, we had a sentimental life, more [mentally] comfortable and cozy, more joyful. To go out on the street, in the market in Vietnam, makes us more comfortable in our minds, spiritually.

Here in America, we have all the material comforts, very good. But the joy and sentiment are not like we had in Vietnam. There, when we went out from the home, we laughed, we jumped. And we had many relatives and friends to come to see us at home. Here in America, I only know what goes on in my home; my neighbor knows only what goes on in his home. We have a saying, "One knows only one's home." In America, when we go to work, we go in our cars. When we return, we leave our cars and enter our homes [and do not meet neighbors]. We do not need to know what goes on in the houses of our neighbors. That's why we do not have the kind of being at ease that we knew in Vietnam.

Everything is very smooth for us in America, and we have quickly adapted to our new life here. Every place we live, Americans have been our neighbors. This is our fourth home. When we left our previous place, our neighbors cried, for they liked us very much. We used to visit one another and exchange gifts at Christmas. When we came to this place, two or three neighbors came to see us. Since that day, they like us. Thanks to God, I have that thing, that kind of nature.

This morning, one of my neighbors came to our house. He and his family were leaving home for a month. They gave us the keys to their house, and we will watch it while they are away.

Another neighbor, an American Indian, also likes us very much. When he and his family went to the Philippines, we watched their house. When they came home, they gave us a gift bought in the Philippines. They know we are good people, so they trust us. I drove them to the airport and brought their car back home. When they returned, I picked them up at the airport. So we have a very good friendship. I'm friendly with the Vietnamese too. Because I am a businessman, all my customers are friends. I know that some people do not like the Vietnamese, but I have not been affected by this.

I think we are successful in America, and so are my brothers and sisters who are here. When my brother came to America, he did not receive any assistance at all. As soon as they got to America, that family started to work, so they needed no help. That brother sponsored my family to come to America. He told me, "You should not receive public assistance; you should go to work."

But when I came here, I was not healthy. I moved to a healthier climate, studied English, and got ready to work. My brother and sister-in-law have worked ever since they came here in 1975. They bought a big boat, they bought a house, and they have already paid off the mortgage.

When my sister came to America, she did as I am doing now. She and her family grew vegetables. Now they have two Vietnamese grocery stores and are the most successful Vietnamese refugees in their area. They live in the South, where they just bought a good house for $40,000, which is a lot in their area.

Another sister lives in the same town as I do. She and her husband are old, but their children are doing very well too. So four of my mother's children are now in America; four remain in Vietnam.

To live in America means that our life has changed. In Vietnam my family was very poor. We had to work very hard. We didn't have enough food or clothes. Under the Communist regime we were not free to do anything. If we made more than we needed, then the rest belonged to the revolutionary government. They did not want us to become rich. We needed to use old clothes. If we had new clothes, that's not good under the new regime because it showed that we had the capitalistic spirit.

My family living in America has everything complete and happy, and a new chance. I hope that my children become new people. My daughter in the eighth grade is the smartest of my children; she always gets A's. My youngest boy, who is eight years old, always is first in math in his class. My two oldest sons are not so good, but are above average and are preparing for electronics careers.

Cultural Differences

But the children are different here in America when compared with Vietnam. There is this big difference. Children growing up in Vietnam are afraid of their parents. Even when they marry, they still have respect and fear of their parents. In America, when they become 18, they lose their fear. They depend on the law of the land and go out of the house.

The one most difficult problem is the American law, and the American way to educate children. This is a big obstacle for the Vietnamese family. In Vietnam, in educating our children, if we cannot get success telling them what to do, we would punish them with a beating. By doing so, they would become good people. Here we cannot beat the children. That's the reason there's a big obstacle for us. When a child doesn't want to study, but likes to play with friends, if they want to smoke marijuana, when they do such bad things and parents tell them not to do so, the first, second, and third time, if they still don't listen, then parents *put them on the floor and beat them.* By doing so, this is the best way to prevent them from doing bad things, to get them to become good people. But here we cannot do that.

In my opinion, the Vietnamese have a lot of bad children because of American law, which is not like Vietnamese law. There are so many Vietnamese teenagers who came to America and who became not good people because of American law. When parents beat the child, the police come and arrest the parent. In the Vietnamese view, this is *the most dangerous and difficult obstacle.*

This is the *one most important thing* I want Americans to realize about the Vietnamese. The problem with educating and rearing the children is difficult because of American law. There's a second important point. Vietnamese life is not like American life. The Vietnamese have *villages, neighbors, and sentiment.* The father-child and mother-child relationship lasts forever, until the parents are very old. Children have the duty to take care of their parents. When the children were young, parents had the duty to raise and educate them. When the parents are old, duty is reversed: children take care of the parents. This is not like in America, where adult children

leave the home, and old parents go to the nursing home. I'd like
Americans to know that. I have met and talked with a lot of old
American people. They have said to me, "When we become old,
we [husband and wife] live together. When we become sick, nobody knows. When the postman comes, makes a surprise visit,
only then does someone know we are sick. Sometimes our children
aren't close by, or they live in a different state."

I ask the old people, "Do your children give you money?"

They reply, "No." These children do not think very much about
their parents. This is very different from Vietnam; when children
are married, they stay at home. When the parents become old, the
children are together and take care of them.

But there are good lessons to be learned in America, such as
public sanitation. That is what I have learned from America. At
home, everything is arranged orderly and clean. Also, my American friends say what they think. This is different from what a Vietnamese would do. The American way, that's what I want my children to do. When we have one, we say "one." When we have two,
we say "two." If that is a cow, we say it is a cow; if it's a goat, we
say it's a goat. Vietnamese can learn this from Americans. I don't
want to say what Americans can learn from the Vietnamese.

There are other changes in our life from our days in Vietnam.
At the end of the lunar year, we had our New Year celebration. It
was two to ten times bigger than in America. They were happy
joyful days. Now here in America, we celebrate for only one or
two days because of the American work schedule.

Work in America, Nostalgia for Vietnam

Because of the work I do, I don't have any specific schedule.
Mine is a free career; it's possible on Monday this week I do one
thing, but on the next Monday I may do something else. Usually
on Friday I go with the truck to a seacoast town where I buy fish.
On Saturday, my wife and children help me to sell fish in the
market. When we finish, about noon, we take the truck home and
clean it.

Beside that, my wife and I take care of the backyard, watering,
adding fertilizer, cutting our own vegetables, which we do on

Wednesday. On Thursday and Friday, we cut those vegetables we can keep for two or three days. We cannot wait until the last day, because we would not have enough time. My children help my wife and me when they finish school. They either cut the vegetables or put them together so we can sell them on Saturday at the farmer's market. These are the kinds of things I do every week. So I'm free only on Sunday and sometimes on Monday too. My very busy day is Saturday, our family business day.

When we first moved here, a Vietnamese Catholic priest told me to help the community. At that time, I was less busy, so I helped as a member of the Vietnamese community parish council. Nowadays I don't have time to attend mass every day, only on Sunday. But we pray every day, with a short prayer in the morning, and ten rosaries each night before going to bed.

Some people have been involved with the Vietnamese Resistance Movement to drive the Communists out of Vietnam. I haven't participated in any organization. I'm neither a politician nor a highly educated man. There are many organizations for Resistance. I went to a few meetings, but I didn't know which organization I should join. I'm in the middle. I'll wait until a very strong one develops; then I'll join. Before, I did contribute some money, but that is nothing. It's like a grain of sand in the desert. I cannot leave my work, so I contribute a little from my money.

Of course, we must love our land, our country where we were born, where we have our own parents, where we have the tombs of our ancestors. The fact that we had to leave our country was something against our will. When we left our country, we turned our heads and cried. And after many years of living in America, we still remember our country.

One day, if the Free World can do something to bring freedom back to Vietnam so that everyone can go back, that would be a very precious thing. Just because we have a comfortable life in America, we'll not forget our country. We pray and hope that one day Vietnam will cease to be a Communist regime so that we can return to our country, to see again the tombs of our ancestors, to see our brothers and sisters. I still have a lot of relatives living in Vietnam. My family and my wife's family consist of 400 to 500 people. Only one-fourth of those are in America. We four brothers and sisters are in America, but that's nothing. The big family, the rest of our relatives, are still in Vietnam. In our homeland, when we had ceremonies to remember our ancestors, 100 people gathered together.

I still remember Vietnam a lot; my mother remains there. Even if my mother were here, I would remember my village where I spent my childhood. I still remember the small road, the trees in the village where I grew up. Vietnam is forever in my mind.

[See also Chapters 8 and 25.]

CHAPTER 38

They Tell Me Their Troubles: 1979–1984

NARRATOR 5: NORTH VIETNAMESE BUDDHIST NUN

Social, family, and religious patterns that were maintained in Vietnam are rapidly changing in the new American environment. The Buddhist nun's description of this provides insights into the dilemmas faced by Vietnamese people attempting to adjust. Though some Vietnamese Buddhist monks, faced with problems of survival in America, have abandoned their monastic activities, the nun has not. Her solution to this newest, most unpredictable, and most complex change in her life has been to provide a haven of Vietnamese culture where lonely refugees can retreat to rekindle old memories, maintain cultural traditions, and feel comfortable for a while before returning to the pressures of American life. The services provided by the nun are by no means traditional; they are themselves adjustments to a strange new environment. The nun's activities reflect her remarkable flexibility in adjustments that does not diminish her steadfast identity and commitment to seek what she calls "permanence, not the impermanence of this world."

Why Vietnamese Are Not at Ease

In February, around the Vietnamese New Year, the Vietnamese of a midwestern city invited me to visit them. I went there for four days and performed religious ceremonies for them. They had a pagoda, but no full-time religious person, so they were happy to have me there. Most of them had come to America in 1975, and most now had jobs at the automobile plant. At first they had encountered many difficulties in this foreign land, but through much effort they had overcome them. Now they had secure jobs, money, and the ability to provide material needs. Nevertheless, the people who were 30 years and older did not feel satisfied, they did not feel comfortable. They said that if they could return peacefully to their country, they would. Their children do not wish to go back, nor to learn Vietnamese, for they have no attachment, no memories of Vietnam as do the older people.

For the elders, life is unbearable because it is not the way life used to be. Here they just work every day without being "at ease." "In our country," they said, "when we return home from work, we have friends, neighbors, sentimentality, the family, the environment: we feel secure, we feel relaxed physically and emotionally. In Vietnam, you work, but you also can ask to take off a couple of days. If you do that in America, you will be fired. Here you have to work, have to eat, have to run; you must, you have no choice."

We Vietnamese have grown up and lived in a period of continuous war for over a century, ever since the French came to our country. I, too, was uprooted and forced to move many times because of war. That's why I and many others never had long-range plans. We lived day by day. One government after another rose and fell, with no continuity. Family life, too, was not consistent. First it was based on Buddhism, then on Confucianism; when the French arrived, we turned to the French, then the Japanese. When the Americans came, we learned American ways.

Despite all of this, we have an absence of pressure in Vietnam that you do not have here. In America, we are never free of pressure, never free of worrying. There is permanent pressure here because you don't feel "at ease." That's why you cannot enjoy life.

The concept of "at ease" does not mean not doing anything at all. You may work very hard day and night, but you enjoy working, you have an enjoyment of life, and a sense of security. So it means, "free of worry," or rather, we may still worry, but we feel relaxed. If someone tells you how to do something, makes you do it his way, then you do not feel "at ease," but when you do a task freely, when it is not another person's assignment, then it is "at ease." In that sense, the term means "comfortable," and that is what is lacking in America. People frequently say, "Life is not comfortable."

Now you can understand why people have left Vietnam after the Communists took over. What exists there now is not Vietnamese; it is a Russian import. It is inconceivable that "at ease" could exist when people control your life day and night, when your neighbors watch you, and your children spy on you, when you are controlled by the rationing of your food, by restrictions on your travel, and by prohibitions on what you are allowed to say. If we had felt "at ease" in Vietnam, we would not have passed through death as boat people to come here. We came to America not for material gain but for freedom.

We have another important belief, that of suffering. The Buddhists believe that you suffer if you do not have a cause or purpose. But if you believe, as do the Buddhists, that "nothing is permanent," that you are born, grow up, and die, then you see nothing abnormal when someone in your family dies, so why suffer? If something wrong happens, again there is no need to suffer if you believe in the Buddha-teaching of causality. If bad happens to me, I realize that maybe I did a sin in an earlier existence. If good comes my way, I am not overjoyed, because that may just be a reward for my earlier good behavior in another life. So to understand is not to be too happy or unhappy.

There is also no need to feel hopeless. If we suffer, we can correct the cause of that suffering. We can redeem ourselves; we have that chance, for we are solely responsible for our acts. Nobody can save us but ourselves. The Buddha is like a medical doctor who can show us the way but cannot save us if we choose not to take the medicine.

These ideas have been very important for the refugees who have lived under Communism and who are trying to adjust to America. One man whom I know spent three years in a Communist reeducation camp. It just happened, and he had to accept it. Not only did he not feel miserable or suffer, he felt satisfied because he had the opportunity to share suffering with other people. Suffering or enjoyment, it depends on our state of mind, how we conceive it.

Here, too, when refugees arrive in America, they experience a lot of hardship. If they sit down and think about their past, they suffer, they worry, and it does them no good. They destroy themselves after two or three years. Regret destroys the self. If they temporarily forget, not forever, and look forward to the future, they will not feel so bad. For example, unemployment is universal, but it is temporary. If you are unemployed, spend less money, manage, survive, until you can find employment.

Some people are in really dire need. When I find this out, I call on people to help. We do not have any organization to do that. Rather, we do it for each case as it comes up. I just help them personally. I prefer that; I believe that it is not good to have an organization. I do not want to be under the influence of others. If someone is in need, I do not want to have to ask permission of a group to help that person. I decide right there, and if I cannot do it alone, then I ask others.

That's why this pagoda was founded. Three to four months after my trip to the midwestern city, a group of people, mostly women, requested that I establish a pagoda for them in their city. To show respect to the monk who had sponsored me, I told the people to ask him. He agreed to their request.

I rented a house on a corner, next to an elementary school, so only one family lives next to us. When we have large ceremonies, we use the school auditorium next door. Our one neighbor is very friendly. When he saw that I did not have a lawn mower, he came over and mowed my lawn. Later I bought a lawn mower. If I want to plant something in the yard, he offers to help me. From time to time I borrow implements from him. The landlord also is a good person. He is not Vietnamese, but he often brings his friends and relatives to see the pagoda. I pay him the monthly rent in cash which comes from donations.

We have no regulations. Those who worship and wish to give donations do so. Those who wish to help in other ways do so. Everybody is treated the same. Those who come to worship are completely free; nobody asks anybody anything. We have no president or organization, no fighting between factions. Even for big or great ceremonies, we have no organization. People come, they help as they will, spontaneously. Women know in advance what to expect. After talking to each other, they make informal, casual arrangements on what foods to bring.

The pagoda has grown by word of mouth. I did not advertise much because the pagoda is too small. If too many people come to our ceremonies, we will be too crowded, and the neighbors might complain.

I had been in foreign countries, so I knew the importance of retaining one's native language. When I established the pagoda, the first thing I thought of was starting language classes for children. I asked several of the parents to bring children for the classes. At first, only a few did so, but they did not see it as important. They had to drive their children here on the weekends, an additional burden.

The first classes began two weeks after the pagoda opened. Only four or five children attended, sometimes only two. In the summer vacation time, we offered classes from 1:00 to 4:00 P.M. on Monday through Thursday. People gradually learned of the classes, taught by volunteers, heard they were free, and realized the need. Now during the school year we have six classes totaling 75 students ranging in age from five to middle teens. They meet on Sundays from 10:00 to 12:00 A.M., have lunch provided free by the pagoda; then from 1:00 to 3:00 P.M. they participate in activities which we call the Buddhist family. It's like scouts.

In the Buddhist family activities we teach a three-word motto: compassion (to others); knowledge (to determine needs); and involvement (acting courageously based on knowledge). If you have no compassion, you will not treat others well; without knowledge you are blind; but without involvement, your knowledge is useless. Knowledge without action is useless; you cannot just sit.

That is what I taught my children in the orphanage in Saigon. We lived in the spirit of those three words. And I try to teach the same things here. The older children can understand about Buddhism; the younger ones cannot, but they can follow these simple words each day. I want them to help others, to bring a cup of water to a child who is sick, to share a piece of cake, to help with chores, always with this spirit. When they get into arguments, I try to resolve them by reminding the children of those three words. If they have jealousies, I explain that they lack involvement; if they have rancor, I point out that they lack knowledge. In this way, I show them that events of their everyday lives revolve around these three words, all of which are concerned with helping people, sharing.

The children study Buddhist teaching, they play games, and they learn camping skills and handicrafts. At the end of the lunar year, we have a big event for the children. They give musical performances and receive prizes, while their parents prepare a feast. Rather than hire professional singers, I prefer to encourage the children to perform and to make their own costumes and props so that they develop confidence in themselves.

For adults, however, we have the main altar where they can worship. On it we have many images that are designed to remind us of Buddhist teachings. These include representations of the Sleeping Buddha, who reaches Nirvana, and of the Bodhisattva Kuan Yin [or Quan The Am; see Chapter 12], who helps those in distress.

Also at the altar, we have fortune sticks. These are of Chinese influence. Some people who are doubtful of their ability to make a decision pray to the Buddha to give them some guidance; they think it helps to select a stick. It has a number. They consult a paper with that number on it. The paper contains a Vietnamese poem, written in Chinese characters, with explanations in Vietnamese, providing guidance on how to behave. The fortune paper might tell you to be satisfied with what you have, or to start new activities on particular days. But the main thing is that it tells you to do good things.

The fortune sticks do not belong in a Buddhist pagoda, but we have to satisfy the needs of people. The sticks are used mainly by women, particularly old women. Whenever they come here, they look for and use the fortune sticks. If we didn't carry them, they'd go to another pagoda. Sometimes young men in distress turn to the sticks. And even some Catholics and other Christians come here to use them.

People in great distress depend not on fortune sticks, but on Kuan Yin. She is part of the Mahayana tradition. Some people say they have received miracles from her.

I have had a miracle of Kuan Yin. Usually I dry my clothes at the laundry, but on this day, for the first time, I decided to dry clothes on a line outside the pagoda. Suddenly, I saw a fire in the house next door. I intended to call the fire department, but the fire was too close, so I put a hose of water on it, called a boy nearby, and he and others put out the fire. If we hadn't, the pagoda would have burned. When the landlord heard of this, he said the pagoda had been saved by the Buddha.

Many people come to the pagoda, where they remain for two to three hours. They have many things in their hearts. They talk to me, and I speak to them about the Buddha teachings, to set their minds at rest. In a sense this is like counseling therapy, and it clarifies and helps them to deal with their problems, marital and economic, as well as those of loneliness.

Buddhists come here for help because they feel at home here. Everything looks like their home in Vietnam, the atmosphere, the furniture. Furthermore, things here are informal and not expensive, so they are not too removed from their own experience.

Some people come here to meet others. When they see old people here, it reminds them of their parents in Vietnam. When they see young people, it reminds them of their younger brothers and sisters in Vietnam. They see the figure that they miss and compare them with the letters from their own people, and that makes them feel better. They eat vegetable dishes like those prepared by their mothers in Vietnam. This relieves them. At the pagoda they don't have to face an actual reality in this country. Some people say that the sound of the bell lightens their sorrow. By coming here, their memories are revived. When they lived in Vietnam, they heard their mothers reciting the canon, but they never paid attention. Now they visit the pagoda and appreciate its value.

Many young adults in the ages of 20 to 25 have no family in this country. They are very lonely. Often they come by themselves to the pagoda. I cook for them. I provide some family for them, like a sister figure. If they need something and I have the possibility, I help to show them that somebody cares about them, pays attention to them.

People visit me with two different types of problems. The first is that of specific crises such as bad news at home, illnesses, or the need for specific services such as dealing with various agencies, or performing ceremonies at funerals or at the anniversaries of deceased family members.

The second kind of problem involves people who want to talk. Usually they do not go directly to the point because their problem cannot be expressed in an explicit way. First they go to the main shrine to worship. Many of them consult the fortune sticks. Then they bring them to me and ask me what it means. I select the paper, read the poem, and explain it to them. When that person sees the relationship between the explanation of the poem and their personal problems, they volunteer more detail.

At first, they don't say anything in particular. Normally they wait until nobody else is here before they volunteer more information. Sometimes they come back two or three times but just talk indirectly, "My family has some problems; I'd like to talk with the master; since she's busy, I'll come back." It is not good manners to go directly to the point. To warm up the conversation, I use all the information people have told me, for example, how much rent people pay. I use all the clichés to encourage them to talk about themselves and their difficulties: the weather; how many relatives are in Vietnam and how many in America; if married, how many children there are; and so on.

I see that people have problems, so I try to give them the time. Most of their problems involve their adjustment in this country. For example, a relative comes to live with a family, but the family does not know how to tell the relative to share costs. Not to tell is bad, but telling directly also is bad. Sometimes children don't want to go to school, or they want to get married, or they want to live separately from the family. Parents worry about this because they fear the children are not mature enough, but also because it involves extra costs. Some of the elderly people complain that they are made to baby-sit over weekends; they do not want to do this, but they do not know how to say no. This is made more difficult because the children never say to their parents that they are going out for fun, only that they need to go out.

The problem for the elderly is that they want to go to the pagoda, but they depend totally on their children, who are reluctant to take them. So the elderly are unhappy. In Vietnam they were not dependent on their children; they used taxis, pedicabs, or they rode with friends, but here that is impossible.

People also complain about the difficulties they have with the English language and their difficulties in getting jobs. They never mention discrimination, but they frequently complain about the stress of living in America, running all the time, with no time to relax physically and mentally. There is too much to do in learning how to survive and not enough time to do it.

They wake up early, work all day, return home tired, then get up early the next day. So do Americans, but Americans do not have to learn a new language at the same time. This is a continual task and a continual strain. People are very insecure. In Vietnam, a person could depend on parents and relatives, and so not go hungry. Here if you do not do everything yourself, you go hungry. People also send much of their earnings back to Vietnam. Two days of average American wages enables a family to live for three months in Vietnam. If one's brother is in a concentration camp and his wife and children are starving, how can a person not send them money? Previously in Vietnam, people didn't have those worries; a person could earn and easily support a family of ten.

On occasion, young men come here who say they want to become monks. Often they are sad and lonely; rarely do they show any strength or determination. If they believe that they want to live the religious life, I explain to them that at the monastery where they will be sent for their training, the path will be very difficult to follow: one meal a day, very isolated, and cold, so they may feel even more lonely. And they will not be able to communicate easily with the monks because most of them are English-speaking Americans. The young men are often too enthusiastic, I think, and also of volatile temperament, showing excessive determination, and then losing heart. Very few people here have the even temper and perseverance to live successfully in the religious life. You cannot be successful if you want to run away from ordinary life because you are lonely.

Sometimes people talk to me about some injustice they have endured. I usually tell them to forget it, not pursue it, or they will simply become more personally involved, but nothing will come of it. Everything is unjust. Instead of using their time for more useful activities, they will be wasting it on a lost cause. Injustice is greater now than it used to be because now that society is modernized, injustice is much wider. Missiles can kill many more people than do spears.

A lot of people complain that they are suffering and that they do not want to live. In one month, for example, ten people told me that they were considering suicide, and three people attempted it. I try to convince people that life is precious, and that others suffer much more. Often the complaints are not really serious, such as when an old lady said to me that she wanted to die because her children didn't treat her as well as in Vietnam.

The quarrels in her family follow a cycle. Her children did not treat her well; now the grandchildren treat the children badly. The grandson says he doesn't want to recognize his parents anymore. The old lady says, "See, the cause and the effect!" She moved to the pagoda for a while and lived here, and her 27-year-old grandson said, "Since you have left, I too have not gone back home."

When they live in American society, the behavior of the children changes. They do not have a connection with their country, and the old teachings and customs disintegrate, for there is nothing to hold them together. Furthermore, every day people work hard under pressure; they are tense, fatigued. They have no time to think of how to act, behave, treat parents. The old woman suffers because she stays home all day long, so has no means of communication outside, no one to take her outside. She is isolated, a recluse, as are most of the older women and men.

One old man told me that fortunately he has one grandchild, so he has the means to communicate. If not, he would become mute, remaining home alone, while his son works all day. When his son returns home at 6:00 P.M., he eats dinner, reads the newspaper, and goes to bed.

Although old people like that are depressed, they are not the ones who attempt to take their lives; mostly it is younger men and women in their middle twenties and early thirties, people who have no family and who have felt lonely; they have had no one with whom to talk. In Vietnam, it was much easier. They mixed with their countrymen. But here people feel isolated. They have no support. Life has no meaning. Whether they die today or later makes no difference. To prolong life is simply to prolong suffering.

In Vietnam, we have had some unhappy and frustrated people, but at least when they came home, they saw their parents and relatives, who made them forget all unhappiness and also made them feel some responsibility to their family. In Vietnam, if a person commits suicide, he hurts his family a great deal. People say that the family is very unfortunate, that they must have committed a sin in the past, so now they are paying that debt. People who commit suicide or have mental health problems are viewed as people guilty of religious sins in the past, so now the family must pay the price. This is a great stigma to the family.

But in America, people do not have any connection, they do not hurt anybody, so they feel free to commit suicide.

A Vietnamese woman married to a Mexican-American came to complain about her long-standing marital and family problems, that her husband acted polite to his work partners, but rude at home.

Because this was a personal family problem, I would not make any comments about what is right and wrong. Instead, I tried to explain to her about the role of women. "As women," I said to her, "we cannot expect to be getting our way all the time. We should show some abnegation, some flexibility. If the husband is angry and will not pay attention to the wife's illness, the wife must accept that. Maybe it is fate, and we cannot escape that."

I advise not only women, but also men to show abnegation. I advised this woman to look at the bright side of her husband, for example, that he brings in a check, gives it to her, lets her handle the financial aspects of the household. If the man shows nice behavior with his co-workers, but not with his wife, perhaps it's her fate that she got that kind of husband. If he does not show love and affection to his child, then the child will follow his mother.

Many Vietnamese complain of headaches. They work very hard in their jobs, then return home to find a peaceful time to relax, but receive a letter from Vietnam, and it's always bad news, followed by a request for money and gifts, or just complaints of the miserable life, arrests, harassment, and jailing of relatives. Often the people cannot solve the problems mentioned, such as requests for $500, or relatives who are stuck for years in refugee camps, or even undisciplined, uncontrollable children. So they get headaches. They are unable to sleep.

Insomnia is widespread among the Vietnamese. If they tell a doctor, he tells them to see a psychiatrist or a counselor. When they go to these people, they find that they receive advice that is not related to their problems.

In some families, husbands have become quite uncontrollable in their anger and hit their children until they bleed. In one case, the husband would refuse to talk to the wife if she tried to interfere or if she would talk back to him. For two weeks or more, he would talk through the children to communicate with her. The more silent he became, the more she talked to him trying to get him to respond. When he could no longer stand it, he left for a friend's house.

In Vietnam, it's much easier. When a woman raises her voice and tries to dominate her husband, he goes out to see friends and they may go to the movies or theater. You might stay with the friend for a few days, until the wife has to go looking for you and beg you to return. The children can go to school by themselves, so the absence of their father does not disrupt their routines.

In America, it's much more difficult; first, because friends are not as close here; second, because housing is much more restricted, and there may be no room for a friend; and finally, because if an angry husband is late for work, he is fired. So there is a lot of pressure in the United States that Vietnamese didn't feel back home. There is no safety valve. In Vietnam, after the husband has stayed away for a few days, his parents and relatives can intervene; they can take his side so he doesn't lose face, and they can mediate for him. A wife's parents would tell her to go to her husband and that helps her to save face. She says to him, "My parents ordered me to ask you to come back."

But in America, there are no parents, and no place to go.

One time, a lady with two small children under three years of age came to the pagoda, worshiped, and threw the fortune sticks. I asked her why.

She said, "I plan to move away."

Again I asked her why.

She replied, "I came here with two children. I live with another family, but they are not helpful. I don't have transportation, a car. I plan to move away."

I asked, "You want to move to another state, but whom will you live with?"

She said, "I know someone."

I said, "Here you have good weather, better than other states. Adjustment will be difficult. With whom will you live?"

"A man. I was engaged to him before 1975. After 1975 he left, and he is married now. After he went, I married another person, and I have two children. In the refugee camp, my husband met another woman and abandoned me and the children. That man in the other state has invited me to come there and be with him, even though he's married to another."

When I heard this, I feared that the woman would be putting on make-up, looking for another man, and she might neglect her children. I felt that she was unstable, and that if she went there, the man would be emotionally divided in two and could not support all of them. There she would have to live alone, with no money, and lots of troubles. She'd have to get a job. Here she has friends. The only thing I advised was, "Don't go; you'll destroy happiness."

The woman replied, "You are like my mother; I listen to you."

She has to baby-sit her two children, so maybe she can baby-sit other children and make some money. When she came to the pagoda and looked at the fortune sticks, I knew she was lonely and isolated. I said, "Now you have a pagoda. You can stay here." She stayed through the afternoon because she had nothing to do at home and she's not happy there, sharing it with other people. Living together with people who are not your relatives has problems, mostly that the children fight or are noisy, or that they have too many visitors, or the children mess up the house and won't clean it. The television may be on all day loudly. The days become long. The old people have a different character. They complain about small things; they are meticulous; they criticize and don't let things go. Living together is quite difficult. All of this is a consequence of the problem of divided families, some in Vietnam, some in America.

Even if families are later united, there may be problems. I heard today about a lady who had come to the United States with her child while her husband remained in Vietnam. He just arrived in America to find that his wife went to work every day, drove the car, took the child to the baby-sitter, and he simply stayed home, feeling neglected that his wife did not pay attention to him. Sometimes she returns home in a bad mood, so he suffers a lot. When she comes home with an unpleasant attitude, he suspects that she has a boyfriend. He lives in hell, and he wants to leave for another country.

A woman came by who complained that her American husband didn't love her. Yet he had learned Vietnamese, sent their children to Vietnamese language lessons, and took them to the pagoda. So I said to her, "Your husband shows he loves you by learning your language and raising your children in your tradition." We see that people always complain, and their complaints range from the truly serious to the banal.

Particularly when people are suffering, they often misunderstand the Buddhist view of events. They expect that an immediate cause will produce an immediate effect, so they wonder, "Why did I receive unfortunate results when I did good?"

Such a view distorts Buddhism. For an orange seed to grow into a tree, you need many causes: soil, sun, rain. The effect may be different at different times. We have to pay attention to different circumstances. When we were boat people, our seat on the boat was considered a good place to sit; when we reached shore, we no longer found the boat seat comfortable. In the refugee camp, we used small sticks with which to eat our rice. They were very precious to us, as were empty cans. But when we arrived in the United States, do we use those things? Life in the refugee camp was better than in Vietnam, but who is satisfied with the camp? We expected to go to another country and have a better life. So too, this life is a false and temporary life, not a true life. If we would like to elevate ourselves to a higher one, we must still depend on our false life, our body.

Buddhism aims at something higher, but people distort that by saying our goal is disinterest. Not so, for our goal is to go for something that is permanent. So if we live here, we cannot do simply nothing. We should do something. The next 20, 30, or 40 years, we act, then we die. If we do nothing, it's just a waste of our life. We should do something, try to help, sacrifice our time because we believe that we can help. If we use our time just to enjoy, that's a waste. If we see a person is hungry, we should give him cake to satisfy his hunger, but it is not good enough if we do not also teach him to avoid sins, not to steal, but to earn the food.

We try to elevate ourselves over and above all the normal passions: anger, selfish stupidity, and greed. If we let our emotions disturb us, we are never happy, never elevated. So according to Buddhism, we must ignore all those passions, get rid of all passion and desire.

The person who achieves this is happy, enlightened. Such a person does not regret this work, is ready to enter another world. This person is very rare, for he is close to being a Buddha.

My master knew in advance that she would die. She told her followers who had come to see her to return in one week to see her die. They did not believe her, did not take her statements literally. One week later, she asked to be cleaned for death. After hot water was boiled and herbs were thrown in to make a scent, she died.

Permanence Through Change: Influence of the Master

In earlier Buddhist periods, many people became enlightened, but in our present era, of one million persons, not even one will gain enlightenment. I am not discouraged to see others fail, but am discouraged about myself. If you say something flattering, I am happy; if you criticize, I am sad. I become discouraged when I cannot control my emotions. I try to convince myself like the Buddha had done thousands of years ago that the body is just temporary, that nothing lasts, that nothing is durable, all is temporary. The more we realize that, the more we can neutralize every passion, not become angry, overjoyed, or jealous. It is like food: it's delicious, we appreciate it, but after two or three hours of digesting it, do we dare to touch it? Three hours earlier we took very good care of it. If someone takes some of it, and we have one piece less, we feel bad. But three hours later, who wants it?

One time, I lost $50 I was given for being at a wedding. I was in a hurry; I bought some tofu, and on the way back, I lost the money. I felt bad. But a few hours before, that money belonged to another person; it wasn't mine. When they contributed it, I didn't expect it, and yet one hour later when I lost it, I felt bad. I try to get rid of attachments like this, but this happened. I felt unable to control my feeling. And that is my main concern.

The most important influence on my life was my master, the Reverend Dam Soan. My master always advised me to do everything; she was the best. My master was a woman, but her knowledge was very wide; she knew almost everything. She always said, "Be modest, even though you do something. Don't be pretentious. If you don't keep modest, if you are haughty, people will dislike you, and it will be very difficult to succeed. You will not be able to do anything wisely. If you don't have a correct point of view, if you are no longer impartial, you will think you are superior, and you won't respect the ideas of others. You will feel that your own ideas are better than everybody else's. Then other people will hate you."

We know that sometimes a person has good ideas, sometimes bad. Sometimes an illiterate person has better ideas than a learned person. So my master emphasized that we should not think our ideas are better.

My master also taught that we should not establish close relationships with others because then you begin to depend on them. She stated that we should not depend on anybody, but rather just keep open with everybody, be concerned about everybody. If you develop a close relationship with anyone, then another person hates you and becomes unhappy. I personally am not caught into anything. *I am free.*

When I was about 17, I developed a special friendship with a nun in her early twenties. If a person is just a usual friend, you don't develop deep emotional attachments. Because our friendship became very close, we developed *resentment*. If I don't know you well, I don't care, and I don't develop resentment. But if you are my close friend, I pay special attention to how you react to me. That happened with us.

The master recognized that, saw the backfire of a close friendship, so she told us to stay apart. If we would be distant, we wouldn't develop like this. If you have a special affection, you cannot share with all; if you have $100 and give it to one, you cannot share it with others. If you choose one person as a close friend, you ignore the others, even if they try to treat you nicely.

We treat everybody with the same standard, not too close and not too far. If you are too close one day and too far the next, that person will become jealous and will develop hatred. The next time, he is your enemy. That's why we try to develop equal distance between all.

My master taught us to help people as long as we live, that we live to help others, not to enjoy life, not to drink, not to be involved in the pleasures of the world. "Do something useful," she said. "Don't just let time pass."

Once in Vietnam, after the Communists had taken over, I went to visit a nun. About halfway there, I saw a lot of people collecting wood, splitting it, tying it, and selling it. I thought, "They work very hard to make a living, they suffer, while I go to visit someone." I continued my visit, but I was not happy. I just didn't feel right wasting time.

So in conclusion, don't depend, don't be emotionally attached to others. Do everything the right way; don't be haughty, but modest. I try to follow that, but sometimes it is difficult to control. Even if one tries, it is impossible. But you cannot wait until you are perfectly successful. I follow my master, who said, "Start to do something; don't wait until you have all the necessary means. Just do it."

My master was of medium stature, not thin, not fat. I am very proud of her, that she was of good appearance, not abnormal. Her spiritual, intellectual power, her knowledge and activity were superior to others. *I prefer to say no less than others rather than superior.* That's an example, like a mirror reflected. There are two things, one physical, the other spiritual. She was a mirror-mold [exemplary] person.

Her voice was soft, mild. She was not impulsive, but calm. Her speech was like that. Even though her speech was soft, her rules were very strict. She did not want attachment. I used to think that her way was too strict, but I now realize that hers was the logical way to act.

I thought that my master required us to just work without enjoyment. But from the teaching of my master, now I have achieved something, that people love me and show me consideration and respect. If I led a free life, maybe we would not sit today to talk. I did not tell this story to intend to expose something that is good. It comes naturally. My working spirit, my way of life leads to this.

When I think about my master, I feel very grateful. I benefited a lot from her teaching; she helped my personal growth and my achievement of becoming a *person spiritually successful in all respects*. Parents raise their children with the expectation that they become successful. I am very happy, very lucky to have had a master like that. Had I met another master in a different situation, I might not be here today.

[See also Chapters 7, 24, and 30.]

CHAPTER 39

I Want to Live Without Trouble: 1980–1984

NARRATOR 3: NORTH VIETNAMESE CHINESE-VIETNAMESE ELDER

The narrator describes how, because he was Chinese-Vietnamese, the Communists intimidated him until, unwillingly, he left Vietnam. He then comments on what he sees as the strengths and weaknesses of America. Despite his avowed rejection of Communism, his remarks reveal the extent to which he was influenced by living under Communist rule for over two decades. Many refugees would disagree strongly with his statements about the Vietnamese in America.

During the time of French rule, those of us who were Chinese were set apart from others. People were afraid that when the Chinese gained wealth, they'd send it back to China. As a Chinese, I was considered a foreigner, and I carried Chinese papers. Because of this, when I was in high school, I was exempt from entrance exams and could enter the high school.

When the Communists took over, our position at first was good because China was considered close friends with North Vietnam. They praised China, and so the Chinese participated in all activities from 1954 to around 1960 or 1962. As a minority group, the Chinese had privileges reserved for them, such as entrance into the university without high grades.

The treatment of the Chinese depended on how friendly Vietnam and China were at any moment. When war broke out between China and Vietnam, we were asked to leave. I was expelled because I allowed a relative to stay in my house illegally, that is, I failed to report to the proper authorities that someone had come to live in my house. For this, my neighbors distrusted me. Actually, I was not expelled by any official document. Rather, they used my relative's visit as a pretext to put pressure on me, with veiled and indirect threats. The Administrative Committee of the Ward invited me to meet with them. The Public Security Agent explained, "For your protection against the Chinese aggression, we have to bring you to another place in the countryside." When I came back home, the Public Security Agent came to my house and asked, "Do you have any relatives in Hong Kong? You should leave."

After that, I understood that I could no longer stay on in Hanoi. I said, "I am poor; I have no relatives in Hong Kong."

The Public Security Agent said, "See if you can sell anything, even the door, but not the house, to give you the money to go."

The house was very big; that's why they didn't want to let us sell it. We were very bewildered. We were now old. I had no career except my government job. How could we survive? I didn't actually want to go, but so many of our relatives had left already, and that gave me a very good impetus, urged me to go.

I had lived all of my life around Hanoi; I had never been to other provinces, never to South Vietnam. Many of my friends and relatives never thought I would go; they were quite surprised when I left for Hong Kong. My wife's sister, resident in America for six months, sponsored us, and three months later, we arrived in the United States.

When I lived in North Vietnam, even though I was not hungry, the food was meager. Even though I had money, I couldn't buy much food. My entire monthly salary was not enough to cover our food needs. For a North Vietnamese arriving in America, it is really paradise; we can buy food so easily, so cheaply! I live on public assistance. President Reagan wants to cut our aid. I don't think his cuts will affect us much, and I accept them because of his big efforts to resist the Communists. That's on the physical life, the material life.

I have talked with many Vietnamese, and they say that even

though they have a good material life, their sentimental life is not good, not relaxed, not at ease. Those Vietnamese who are less than 30 years of age will be integrated into American society. Those people who are 30 to 50 years old and those over 50 still miss their old society; they cannot fully integrate. If 50 years later the two cultures can be integrated, then the people will feel more at home. Once people live here, they must have an American soul. When people think of becoming a United States citizen, they think of the benefits, the jobs, the travel abroad. They never think, for example, of patriotism, of attachment or devotion to their adopted country. But if they think only of benefits, what will they do if there is aggression against the United States? Will they stand and fight for their country, or will they run away?

If you don't have a good foundation, no ideals, no attachment, then you won't die for your country. The majority of Vietnamese are like that now. They are not devoted to America. I think that America should create those kinds of people who will fight for their country. That should be the criterion for education in America.

The bad thing about America is that there is too much freedom. Americans think only about the maximization of profit, what they can do that will benefit themselves. There is too much individualism and freedom of one group at the expense of others, with little concern for the common good. Every community thinks of itself too much, not of the country, so people can sell secrets to the Russians just for money, for profit.

Some U.S. Congressmen proposed measures to lessen accidents on the highways, but other Congressmen and lobbyists opposed this because it affects capitalists. If a proposal for the good of everybody affects their profits, companies lobby or buy off the Congressmen.

Because of the division between legislative, judicial, and executive branches, the president is always affected. Every time he wants to make a decision he is controlled and hindered; he has to consult with the legislative branch and he cannot make quick and good decisions. The presidential term is only four years. How can all of the projects or plans be carried out in such a short time? Leaders can have a long-range view on many matters, maybe 20 years, but their term is too short to carry it out.

Because of too much freedom, Americans are so *careless* about so many things. When they go out on the streets, they do not wear shirts, or dresses; some use the flag for shorts and for trousers. But the flag is symbolic of the country.

Many people who stretch their legs on the bus don't leave room for other people. Some women put handbags on the seats and don't let others sit down. I use the bus often; I see such disregard for people.

On American Independence Day, not many houses hang out flags. People are individualistic, and even neighbors do not know one another's names. One night, an old American man was robbed near my house; his wallet was taken, but no one seemed to care. Passersby watched as the man was dragged into the bushes and robbed. They did nothing.

Another point of too much freedom: Americans do not have many children, and the trend to remain single is on the rise. In my view, a superpower should have as many people as possible to be strong. Compare the populations of other superpowers; many are populous; many countries are really scared about the population of China.

If the Constitution could be changed and not too much freedom were allowed, I think America would be better off. For example, freedom of the press is excessive. If they would try to help and say something good about the government instead of criticizing it, they could not be exploited by the Russians, who use these negatives in their propaganda.

In the American educational system, both technology and human relations and values should be given equal emphasis. Family values, such as relationships between grandparents, parents, and children, should be introduced into the educational system. Too much emphasis is put on technology to the neglect of humans, so that when people grow up, they only think of money and profits at the expense of everything else. That's all they know.

I have tried to be humble. I've been here only a short time, but the things I've told you are really big. People think too much about themselves. They are too selfish, too individualistic.

There's much that's good in America. In their deeds, Americans are energetic and great; they do great things. When I came here to live, I found in my contacts with Americans that they were honest. If a teacher doesn't know something, he doesn't pretend; instead, he says he doesn't know. When I was in high school, I took a philosophy class in which the teacher made a mistake. He stated the wrong century in which Auguste Compte was born. A student discovered that. The teacher, in trying to cover this up, said, "There are two Auguste Comptes." What I like about Americans is that they admit they don't know.

Vietnamese refugees in the United States are very much anti-Communist. They try to identify those who show some sympathy with Communism. It is not accidental that in the last two years [1982–1984] two people [elsewhere in America] have been murdered, for they openly praised the Communist regime. When a respected professor wrote an article in which he referred to Ho Chi Minh as "Uncle Ho," people got very angry: "He's not our uncle; he destroyed the country."

Once I met some South Vietnamese military officers who said, "I hate Americans. Because of American policy we lost and have to suffer here."

I replied, "You should not complain about this because America should put the interests of its own 200 million people first, above those of South Vietnam's 20 million. All Vietnamese suffered, not just you." They became quite angry at my remarks. Because I come from the North, people believe I sympathize with the Communists. This makes it difficult to live, and now I'm very cautious. I'm old now; I don't want to have trouble, just to live in peace. My family heredity is that people do not live long. I don't want to do anything to affect my life. I just want to live a few more years.

[See also Chapters 5, 15, and 17.]

CHAPTER 40

Victim of a Youth Gang
Stabbing: 1981-1982

NARRATOR 8: SOUTH VIETNAMESE
YOUNG POET

Some refugees, such as Narrator 6, appear to get along very well with people of many different ethnic groups in America. Others, such as Narrators 4, 1, and 7, have had a much more difficult time, and they also relate incidents of anti-Asian and antirefugee backlash directed against themselves, their relatives, or their friends (on attitudes towards Vietnamese refugees, see Baer 1982, and Starr and Roberts 1981). I decided to interview the narrator of this chapter in part because he had just been stabbed by a gang of boys who told him to return to his country. He describes the incident and his reactions to it. He also presents poems that describe his loneliness in America.

Lonely in America

I came to America by U.S. Air Force plane, along with 300 to 400 others. Although most of the travelers were Lao and Cambodian, one was my old friend whom I had known from the island. We had escaped on the same boat, we had been in the same camp, and now we traveled to America on the same plane. We would end up living in the same city. He's not in the eighth grade. He lists his age as 15, although he's actually 17.

This was my first ride in a plane. It was wonderful to me. We could hear music, or we could smoke. If we were hungry, we called the serving man, "Hey, give me something to eat." I didn't eat anything because my heart was beating so hard. I was worrying, what is my future? My attitude was mixed: joy, yet sadness; happy to be out of danger, but worried about my future. A bus took us to a motel, where my brother-in-law met me. He had escaped from Vietnam in 1978.

For the first three days, I just ate and slept. After two weeks, my brother-in-law took me to the high school near where we lived. An official gave me a paper with rules, which my brother translated: no drinking, smoking, or fighting. A student had to wear shoes and must dress properly. Girls could not expose themselves. Then they gave me a test. I found the math to be easy arithmetic that I had learned as a child, simple algebra, trigonometry, and geometry. The reading and writing test was very difficult.

I thought it was wonderful to attend that high school because many Vietnamese students were there. I was happy. In fact, I saw many of my old friends from the island: the children of fishermen and farmers who had never gone to school. In Vietnam they had been very poor. In America they were good students trying hard to study, while I was lazier.

My classes consisted of English as a second language and an introduction to electronics, in which we learned how to solder, we learned Ohm's law, and we learned about capacitors. When in Vietnam, I never had a chance to learn about such things. Now I could do it and receive useful training that was the equivalent of learning to be an electronics assembler. In addition to taking an easy algebra course, I took physical education, in which we played volleyball, which I liked best of all the sports. Most of the Vietnamese boys liked soccer best.

I would attend school from 8:00 A.M. to around 2:30 P.M. Then I would return home. It took me more than an hour to walk, so I usually took the bus. I would wake up around 7:00 A.M. and drink some coffee but not otherwise eat at home in the morning. I ate breakfast at school: two pieces of bread, some cheese, and milk. I'd eat that during a ten-minute break at midmorning. After school, I went home, did some homework, played basketball in the yard, sometimes played the guitar, and watched television.

At home, we took turns making dinner: chicken, hamburgers, vegetables, bread. Five of us lived together in a two-bedroom apartment: my brother-in-law, his 18-year-old cousin, two older cousins of mine, and me. All of us came from the island, along with many hundreds of other people who now live here. At least 20 students from my island were attending my high school.

One day, I was walking home from school when I heard someone speak behind me, "Hey man, hey bitch, get out of America, man!"

"Okay, okay, okay," I said. I didn't want to fight.

"You are a dog!"

"Okay, I'm a dog."

Still, the four Mexican-American boys surrounded me and pulled out their knives. I was scared until the fight began. I fought with my hands and I kicked. I took three knives away from them, but the fourth boy stabbed me in the head. Then I ran, with the blood streaming down, and three of them ran after me.

Suddenly an old white man came out of his home. "Hey, man, stop fighting," he said. "There's so many people against one." The Mexican-American boys ran away, and the old man took me to his home. There was much bleeding; I felt the hurt after the fighting, and then I felt scared. He gave me a towel with warm water to wash off the blood; then he called the police.

When the police came, he told them what had happened. They wanted to take me home, but I was scared of them. I don't want to be involved with the police. They were helpful; they asked, "What happened? Is there anybody at your home?"

I said, "There's a man with whom I share a room; maybe he's home."

No one was at home. I called another Vietnamese friend, a former classmate of mine at the high school, who now has a job. He had once hurt his hand and had had to go to the emergency room of the hospital. He took me to the emergency room. After one hour, a doctor took me into a room and told me to lie down. After that, I don't know what happened. I was in there about an hour. I suffered from shock a little bit. The doctor put some stitches in my head, and he asked me how it happened. I told him. The people at the hospital were very helpful. I was not afraid of them. There were many emergency cases that day, so we had to wait. After I was done, I stayed overnight at my friend's house. At my own home, there was nobody there to help me, since they were working at night. But my friend's mother and family helped.

She asked in a criticizing way, "Why were you involved in a fight? Why did this happen? If you avoided it, this wouldn't have happened to you."

I replied, "No, I was forced to fight. I did not start the fight. Then your son saw my head and took me to the hospital."

I did feel angry after the fight, but I am not angry now. When it first happened, I said, "I want revenge." But I don't want revenge now. It's a foolish thing.

In December [1981] we celebrated the death anniversary of the father of one of my roommates. This man had died ten years ago. For his anniversary, my roommate prepared offerings of soup, egg roll, steamed pork, beef mixed with cabbage, and rice noodles to be eaten with the egg rolls. We put everything on the table, and stood in front of the altar with bowed heads and the palms of our hands placed together. My roommate said, "This offering today is given on the day that marks your death. We invite you to come. We have a small feast for you that comes from our heart." When the candles and incense were lit, all other activities and noise stopped; we observed a solemn moment. To do this ceremony is to fulfill our duty. After the offering, we invited friends to eat the food. Fifteen of our friends also brought food, and we shared a feast.

Afterwards, we talked about school and studies, moving to other parts of America, and comparisons of life in other states. We realized that there were many training programs in our city where we could learn job skills, but since there were many Vietnamese here, we spoke Vietnamese and did not learn English.

My life is different in America. When I lived in Vietnam, I never stayed home. I'd leave to study, or I would go to the river or shore to swim or fish. I liked to fish on the sea, around the many small islands near my home. Out on a small boat, I'd use a pole to catch big fish of 30–40 pounds. For bait I'd use a small fish through which I'd stick a hook. I would zigzag the pole in the water as the boat moved. This attracted the larger fish. When I caught them, I'd take them home and my mother would cook them for dinner. Here

I never go fishing. Sometimes I go to the beach area, but I only walk around.

In January of 1982, my father sent me a telegram informing me that my sister had left Vietnam. The telegram was in the form of a secret message. It said, "Your sister has gone to Saigon." I knew this meant that she had left Vietnam.

Since then I have waited. I will sponsor her. I have two sisters. When I got the telegram I didn't know which sister had escaped, the younger one or the older one whose husband already lives in this city. If my older sister escaped, her husband will take care of her; if it is the younger, I'll have to quit school and give up my education to support her. I'll have to do anything to support her. I think it's the younger sister who escaped.

Once a month I write home. Every three or four months my family writes to me. My father says that I should try to study, try to establish my future. Now that my sister is coming, I plan to get a job before she arrives; then I can send money to her [in the refugee camp]. Then I can also rent a house for her. I know that when she arrives, she can apply for refugee assistance. This might take several months or a year before she can get here. A brother has a responsibility to his sister, for her future. This is a far better thing to do. Now I must help my sister; I can always go back to school.

Poems of Loneliness

In Vietnam I am a poet, but here I cannot do it because I do not have enough English. Here in America, I have written about 100 poems in Vietnamese, but I cannot translate them. I write these poems for my girlfriend. I show them also to my close friends. It is hard to write poems; I am the only one who does this. My friends do not. Sometimes my friends borrow my poems and recite them to their girlfriends. Many of my friends play the guitar. So do I. But I also write the lyrics to songs. A Chinese-Vietnamese friend of mine, who knows notes and plays the piano, writes the music.

I started writing poems when I was 13 years old. I saw my elder brother writing poems, I looked at what he did, and I felt real good. So I started writing poetry. The writer must follow the form of the poetry [rules of rhyming, intonation, and tonal rhythms].

The poems I write always are about my country, my school, and my friends. I'm also writing a novel, which describes when I left my country for America. How the life is there and here in America. I call the novel "The Sorrowful Hero." That's me. I have not told my social worker about my poems. That's my secret; this is my thinking.

When I feel sad and lonely, I write poems or I play the guitar. I play only when I feel sorrow. I learned in America, and sometimes I play with six friends. We'd like to form a band, but we do not have enough money for equipment.

It is very hard to leave your country. We are a people, we have a spirit; it is very hard to leave. When I think of this, I write poems. Often I remember my island home, and I write about it.

[Poems translated by Huu Dinh Nguyen]

THE SOUND OF THE ISLAND

For thousands of years I have stood here, unperturbed,
Defying the winds and waves, the storms and rains.
Years and months I spend playing with the sea waves,
And with the Islanders intoxicated by Nature's fragrance.

Ngàn năm ta vẫn đứng trơ đây
Sóng gió, giông mưa có sá gì
Năm, tháng ta đùa cùng sóng biển
Cùng người dân đảo thắm hương say.

Sometimes I think of how the Communists have changed my island. I write about that too.

HOMELAND IN SHACKLES

My homeland then, battered by tens of thousands of waves,
Still playfully stood up against the ocean's fury.
Defying the storms, braving the waves.
Fleet after fleet of boats still departed for the open sea,
While rows and rows of coconut trees, casting long, green shadows
    on the water,
Stood bathed in gentle breezes.
Our people, neither arrogant nor tricky,
Used to live unconcerned, enjoying days of happiness.
My homeland then knew no competition and rivalry.

Nursing no hatred, bearing no grudge against anyone.
It lived peacefully and happily, surrounded by long stretches of
    sand as pure and white as its people's sentiments.
But on a harsh sunny day,
Cruel waves swept through my beloved island,
Sweeping away lovely shapes and shadows.
Taking their place were shackles and tears.
And the sounds of hatred and sobbing resounded everywhere.
Once again, fleet after fleet of boats, leaving behind
    the homeland and everything else, took to the sea,
In quest of freedom and hopes.

Quê tôi đó với vạn làn sóng vỗ
Vẫn vui đùa cùng cuồng nộ đại dương
Từng đoàn ghe dù bão tố vẫn coi thường
Vẫn tiến bước, kiên cường cùng sóng nước
Hàng dừa xanh bóng in dài xanh mướt
Đứng hòa mình cùng làn gió nhẹ đưa
Người dân tôi không kiêu ngạo, lọc lừa
Sống bình thản với chuỗi ngày hạnh phúc
Quê tôi đó không tranh đua, chen chúc
Không oán hờn, không uất hận những ai
Sống êm vui giữa dãy cát trắng dài
Cát trong trắng như tình người trong trắng
Nhưng một hôm vào một ngày rực nắng
Sóng bạo tàn cuốn hải đảo thân yêu
Cuốn trôi đi những bóng dáng yêu kiều
Thay vào đó gông cùm cùng nước mắt
Khắp nơi vang căm hờn và tiếng nấc
Từng đoàn ghe lại lần lượt kéo nhau đi
Bỏ quê hương, bỏ tất cả những gì
Để tìm đến Tự do và Hy vọng . . .

I wonder what has happened to my family and to my friends,
and I think of my homeland far away.

I MISS YOU, O VIETNAM

When the autumn afternoon came and the autumn breeze gently blew,
I gazed in astonishment at the leaves of grass swaying slowly.
And gloomily I recalled the good old time
Which was being shut off and gradually wiped out from my
    subconscious.

I don't know whether my homeland is still existing.
With grief, I see months and days passing,
I miss you, O Vietnam, where repose generations of my ancestors.
I miss my small village stretching out amidst the ocean.
Where is my family now? I wonder,
And the old school, when the classes begin,
Are the doe-eyed children still there or already gone?
Some of my friends are probably still in the South,
The others sent to the North.
Tell me, my dear, is homecoming day still too remote?
And there is no more fond and pleasant memory.
O my homeland! Why are you still far away from me?

Chiều thu đến, gió thu hiu hiu thổi
Ngơ ngác nhìn những ngọn cỏ nhẹ đưa
Ta thẫn thờ ôn lại thuở vàng xưa
Đang khép kín, xóa dần trong tiềm thức
Quê hương ta nay còn hay đã mất
Ta đau buồn nhìn những tháng ngày qua
Nhớ Việt nam, ôi dòng máu ông cha
Nhớ quê nhỏ vươn mình trong biển cả
Người dân ta đang miệt mài vất vả
Gia đình ta chẳng biết đã về đâu
Ngôi trường xưa, khi giờ học bắt đầu
Những cặp mắt nai vàng còn hay mất?
Bạn bè ta người phương Nam, hướng Bắc
Ngày hồi hương xa lắm phải không em?
Giờ còn đâu những kỷ niệm êm đềm
Quê hương hỡi? Sao còn xa xôi mãi?

Sometimes I get frustrated when I try to do my homework. One
of my poems describes how I feel at that time.

FRUSTRATED AT MATH

X and X, Y and Y, what a bore,
And there is that logarithm, which one really needs the strength of
   a water buffalo to tackle.
Sin and sin, cos and cos, I have had enough just looking at them.
Why did anyone create these goddamned devils which make me
   stay up all night long?
Come on, fella, please cut some of it off,
And spare me a headache.

X, X, Y, Y, nghĩ phát rầu
Thằng logarit quả sức trâu
Sin, sin, cos, cos nhìn đà ngán
Mấy cha toán học nghĩ quá ngầu
Chế chi loại quỷ trời đánh đó
Khiến cho ta thức suốt đêm thâu
Thôi cha giảm bớt giùm đôi chút
Cho kẻ học sinh khỏi nhức đầu.

I am lonely; I live in a strange land, and I have no direction like
I did in Vietnam. I have no friends, no family, no lover. I am alone
with my dreams, and I write about that too.

I AM JUST AN ANIMAL GOING ASTRAY

No scholar with towering talents and golden rhetoric,
I am just an animal going astray,
Living day by day in a strange land.
Having surmounted untold trials,
I still dare not embark on an adventure of love.
A shimmering light and the moon are my friends.
Sitting alone, I plucked at my guitar,
Making each note ring like a loving word
Each sound an affectionate whisper.
My lover! Please open the gate of Paradise,
To end my lonely nights of sorrows, forever.

Tôi không phải là một nhà bác học
Có tài cao với văn ngọc lời vàng
Tôi chỉ là một loài thú đi hoang
Sống lây lất hoang đàng trên đất khách
Tôi vượt qua với muôn vàn thử thách
Với tình yêu tôi chả dám xông pha
Đêm hắt hiu bầu bạn với trăng tà
Ngồi đơn lẻ cung đàn tôi run phiếm
Mỗi nốt nhạc là mỗi lời âu yếm
Mỗi âm thanh là mỗi tiếng yêu đương
Người yêu ơi! Hãy mở cửa thiên đường
Cho đêm vắng vấn vương không còn nữa

When I think of how lonely I am in America, I wonder why I
am here, what I have to live for. And my poems speak of my
unhappiness.

WHY AM I IN THIS WORLD?

Some cans of beer scattered on the table,
Slowly I nibbled some pieces of dried meat,
And nipped some bitter liquid.
It was already dawn, but in my stupor,
I thought it was still dark.
"Why am I in this world?" I wondered.
"Why should I continue to live,
When I have neither a country nor a home
And when I had only 'liquid' and 'smoke' [beer and cigarettes] as
    friend?
Why am I in this world at all?" I wondered.

Lóc nhóc trên bàn những hộp "bia"
Lai rai ta nhấp miếng thịt khià
Nhâm nhi vào đã vài men đắng
Gật gù trời sáng ngỡ còn khuya

Ta nghĩ sao đời lại có ta?
Sống chi không nước lại không nhà
Bạn ta là "nước" cùng "mây khói"
Ta nghĩ sao đời lại có ta.

I remember crying twice in my life. The first time was when my
father hit me. The second time was when I left my country.

[See also Chapters 10 and 26.]

CHAPTER 41

My Daughter Neglects Me: 1984

NARRATOR 11: SOUTH VIETNAMESE SCHOOLTEACHER

Although she had been in America less than one month, Ba Tam had already become disillusioned about life with her daughter's family. She was particularly concerned with her enforced idleness, her inability to travel about, and her feelings of loneliness and neglect. Her solution was a shocking departure from the adjustments of the other narrators in this book.

I tried to get out of Vietnam since 1975. Because my daughter lived in America, I hoped to be able to leave, but the soldiers at the American Embassy refused to let me board the airplane. From that time on, my daughter tried to get me out. Because I am old, the Viet Cong did not make any difficulties for me. They give a hard time only to the young people and to big families.

My daughter says that she does not mind helping me with food, but she is afraid for my health. She cannot afford to pay for my health coverage, and I do not qualify for Medicare, since I am not a refugee, but an immigrant who came to America under the Orderly Departure Program.

I was happy! America! It is just like heaven! Because people live here in *freedom*. You can go anywhere. You can live richer. Over here I see people go by in cars, but in Vietnam people ride bicycles and are poor.

I remember that when I first came here, I could not recognize my daughter, whom I had not seen since 1962, but she recognized me, even though I was old and very skinny. Because of the difference in hours, it took me about a week to adjust to night and day in America.

I also got used to American food; I can eat American food! My daughter cooks American food, and she and her Vietnamese husband live and eat like Americans: salad, canned food, barbecued chicken, no soup.

I'm sad, though, because my daughter's children speak only English. Also, at my daughter's house, I do nothing. My daughter won't let me do anything because she thinks everything is strange for me. She tells me to rest. But I cannot stay doing nothing. My daughter does not let me cook; she does the cooking, and I water the garden. I help them clean house after eating. On Saturday my daughter turns to the Vietnamese broadcast because she thinks that I am sad. I regret I don't know how to speak English. I can speak French, and I *will* learn how to speak English.

In Vietnam, every family, even Christians, must have an altar to worship ancestors, and the Buddha too. But not here in America. I never see any houses with altars here.

My religion is Buddhism. I went to pagodas all the time. In Vietnam, we have monks who preach Buddhist religion on Sundays and formal days, and I went to the pagoda at those times. I've not yet visited a pagoda in America.

I notice that Vietnamese people in America don't go to the pagoda a lot because they live far away. They rarely have free time. I miss not going to the pagoda because I have just arrived here. In Vietnam I used the bus to visit friends and the pagoda. It's cheaper. Over here, my children must go to work. They don't have time to drive me. This is my major concern; I am *very sad*. In Vietnam, we went by pedicab or Lambretta, the three-wheel cycle, which could carry several people. We moved around a lot, either with these vehicles or by walking. Over here in America, I can walk only a couple of kilometers; then I get tired.

In Vietnam, under the Communists, people like me who were over the working age of 60 could wander freely all about the town. Nobody bothered us; no one created trouble as long as we didn't involve ourselves in politics. It was easy for us to travel. I went all over, sometimes to coffee shops, sometimes to big restaurants. At first these were reserved only for the Viet Cong, but later they let in everyone. The prices were cheap. My friends and I would buy beer, cola, orange, and sweet cakes, sometimes even ice cream.

In Vietnam, in a village, from one end to another, everybody knows each other. Even in the city where I lived, we knew each other and visited one another. If I was sick, my friends visited me, and I did the same for them. I would see my friends at the market. When I think of that, I miss not having people I know nearby. It's very sad. Over here I live at home, and I cannot go anywhere. In Vietnam, if I felt sad, I'd go to visit my friends, my fellow "sisters."

Older Vietnamese people who come to America write letters back home. They don't have work or jobs to do, even though they are active people, so it is sad for them. Because there are lots of cars here, they do not walk. My daughter warns me that I may be run over by cars, so I am afraid to walk. In Vietnam, we went to the pagoda or to friends; here we stay at home. I want to find something to do, but cannot find anything suitable. I am very sad, and I have nowhere to go.

[Editor's note: In 1986, Ba Tam moved out of her daughter's house to a town several hundred miles away. At the age of 76, she has decided to live out her remaining days, not with her family, but with several elderly friends who, like herself, embody a life-style and values no longer shared with the generation of their adult Vietnamese children.]

[See also Chapters 13 and 27.]

PART VII

Interpretations

CHAPTER 42

Implications for Biography

This book is an outgrowth of a perspective and a style of research that I have developed over the past 25 years. As a graduate student in anthropology at Harvard in the late 1950s and early 1960s, I was taught that the aim of research was the development of an objective and universal social science. But when I went to India and lived and did research in a Hindu temple village for three and a half years, I found that my professors had not adequately prepared me for the moral and human confrontations that I faced. When I began to work with Untouchables in India, I found that the issues of their lives could not be separated from basic concerns of human rights, for the concept of "Untouchable" was not morally neutral. While social scientists were writing forgettable tracts about status emulation among Untouchables, in which the actual people were largely lost in the abstractions of social science, these same people were being subjected to the horrors of object-lesson violence inflicted on them by higher castes who wished to keep them subservient: being burned alive, having eyes gouged or hands and feet cut off, women raped, houses leveled, and people beaten. The last occurred in the village in which I lived. I realized that in a population of over 100 million Untouchables, despite all that had been written about them, there were no accounts by illiterate Untouchables describing their personal experiences in their own words and in their own terms.

I set about, therefore, to collect and publish the life history of an illiterate Untouchable (Freeman 1979). I thought that what would make a maximum impact was not my words, but those of an Untouchable himself. My aim was to convey one compelling theme, what invidious injustice can do to people, how it affects their outlook, and the cost, in psychological and social terms, of this injustice. In this way I hoped to articulate the plight of previously "invisible" people.

Hearts of Sorrow also has an overriding theme that touches on issues of human rights: the Vietnamese refugee experience. This book has traced how the fall of Vietnam to the Communists influenced the lives of ordinary Vietnamese people who have come to America, and the ways in which they themselves view their experiences. The key to understanding their responses to adversity and to adjustments in America is examination of the cultural and personal values which they developed and elaborated through their lives. As this book has shown, the great diversity of their adjustments and their often contradictory views are reminders that we should not make hasty judgments about Vietnamese views and character.

Epistemological Implications

My studies in India and my more recent research with the Vietnamese call attention to four epistemological issues that are central to the study of biography.

First, the creation of a narrated life story, elicited by the promptings of an investigator and affected by translations and editing, cannot help but be a rearrangement of the raw data of a narrator's original account. Clearly I have done this in *Hearts of Sorrow*; the life-story accounts are the collaborative result of narrators, researcher-interpreters, and myself. This does not prevent the final result from being a faithful portrait of some features of the narrator. The contributions of an investigator who collects and edits life stories can be compared with those of the photographic artist who produces a portrait of his subject by controlling the lighting and background in his studio and modifying the composition of the portrait in the darkroom by selective cropping. Life stories, too, are consciously staged and directed—both by the investigator and the narrator.

Even though a life story might take a different shape if it were collected by a different person at a different time, the narrator can nevertheless remain recognizable, just as he would if he were to sit for a portrait by two different photographic artists with their own distinctive styles. Karsh's portrait of Churchill, while instantly recognizable as a Karsh photograph, is nevertheless a portrait of Churchill and not of Karsh (see Freeman 1979: 392).

Second, the relationship between narrator and investigator compels us to recognize that we are part of the subject we study, a point that has been made in many contemporary studies, as well as some earlier ones (Clifford 1983; Clifford and Marcus 1986; Crapanzano 1980, 1986; Devereux 1967; Freeman 1979; Freeman and Krantz 1980; Geertz 1988; Langness and Frank 1981; Marcus and Fischer 1986; Rabinow 1977; Shostak 1983; Titon 1980). In asking people to tell me the story of their lives, I was not observing a pre-existing social reality. Neither the Indian Untouchable nor the Vietnamese rural woman whom I interviewed had any idea what a life story was, and certainly neither would have related theirs had I not prompted them. My interviews involved the creation of a whole new body of data that previously did not exist. An extensive life story of this sort is the joint production of two or more persons with the right combination of personalities, interests, and biases, who happen to come together at the right time and place for creating the life story. By its nature, such a life story involves the *creation* of the very data that are analyzed. These life stories of Vietnamese-Americans came into being, not as an integral or historical part of the cultures of the narrators, but because an American outside investigator provoked and guided their creation. Many Vietnamese-Americans were initially shy about telling their stories because they did not wish to appear to brag about themselves and in some cases considered disclosure of family events to be best left unsaid. Others did reveal many aspects of their personal lives that they wished to have included in the published accounts. The resulting narratives are both American and Vietnamese; they translate accounts of Vietnamese life-styles into an American idiom.

Third, the study of collaborative biographies that involve narrators and investigators calls into question conventional ideas about objectivity in the social sciences. For years, descriptions of events in anthropology and other social sciences often occurred *as if* the investigator were an invisible cloud hovering over an event.

This convention of reporting can be likened to the conventions of Western theater, where spectators and actors agree to accept the fiction that the action on stage occurs in a room with three walls, with the fourth wall removed, so that the audience, separated from the stage, can look in. As recent developments in theater show, changing the space between audience and participants changes the relationships between them (Roose-Evans 1970; Schechner 1973). Similarly, collaborative biography heralds a shift of convention, from viewing the relationship between observer and observed as a scaffolding separable from content, to the view that the relationship is inseparable from content.

Finally, this shift compels us to question the universal applicability of Occam's principle, often called the Law of Parsimony, which states that it is *"vain to do with more what can be done with fewer,"* in other words, that entities must not be multiplied beyond necessity. "What is needed," says mathematician Karl Menger, "is a counterpart to the Law of Parsimony—so to speak, a Law against Miserliness—stipulating that *entities must not be reduced to the point of inadequacy*, and, more generally, that *it is vain to try to do with fewer what requires more*" (Menger 1960: 415; see also Maurer 1978). What is original about Menger's formulation is his use of the metaphor of a prism, which resolves conceptual mixtures into the spectra of their meanings, much as a beam of light passing through the prism is separated into colors of the spectrum (Menger 1960: 416).

Although Menger applies his principle of the prism to mathematical functions, it is also appropriate for the study of collaborative biographies: they require an *expansion* rather than a contraction of complexity in order to describe the phenomena adequately. This becomes evident when we recognize that the investigator's role in the creation of a collaborative biography is not an interference with the data, but rather an integral part of it, indeed *is* the data.

Moral Implications

Not only my actions as an investigator, but the moral implications of my research are inseparable from the research itself. Research does not occur in a vacuum, but in a social and cultural environment. Both researchers and human subjects of study have values which I see not as external interferences but as central aspects of any research. Descriptions of enforced starvation in reeducation camps are hardly neutral; neither are accounts of Communist persecution of Catholics and Buddhists, or descriptions of how some generals and other high officers of the defeated Army of the Republic of Vietnam abandoned their men in the field, or how the Americans did this to their Vietnamese counterparts. Both I and the narrators who discussed these topics see them as matters of human and moral significance. When the elderly Chinese-Vietnamese gentleman from Hanoi spent some 20 hours describing to me his experiences of living under Communist rule from 1954 to 1980, he did it for a reason: he wanted Americans to realize how ordinary people adjusted to Communism, what it did to them psychologically, and why the worldview of the Communists enabled them to withstand the American challenge. By contrast, the elderly South Vietnamese civil servant, who narrated, for over 106 hours in the course of a year and a half, the story of his life, was less concerned with convincing me about political matters; those he took for granted. He wanted me to learn about and appreciate a way of life that no longer exists. The Buddhist nun who devoted more than 60 hours of her time to narrating her life story was concerned that Americans come to understand the Buddhist way of life and its role in helping many Vietnamese people adjust in America. The narrators in *Hearts of Sorrow* are not neutral; all have a message. The narrators hope that their life stories will have an impact on people's lives.

Furthermore, my relationships with various narrators all have moral implications. In my earlier project in which I collected the life history of an Untouchable in India, I confronted moral problems that I have never been able to resolve satisfactorily. My interviews with the Untouchable took place in the context of our unequal relationship and his oppression by his countrymen and countrywomen. I could alter neither of these. We were friends, in a distant way, but not equals. I was a wealthy and powerful outsider of high status, he was not, and neither of us could forget that. I was eliciting information in his native language to translate into English for an English-speaking audience, reflecting a relationship of cultural dominance and subordination that some researchers label "colonialist." I felt uneasy about our relationship, but the Untouchable made it clear that any attempt on my part to treat him as an equal would be mere pretense in light of the larger setting of social inequality, poverty, and degradation in which he lived. Even with the wider context, I was beset with doubts. As a foreign researcher offended by atrocities inflicted on Untouchables, I nevertheless felt unsure of what justification I had to deliberately intervene in the internal affairs of a host country that had graciously allowed me to live and conduct studies within its borders (see Freeman 1984).

I now realize that I am not against intervention, but rather its use when I have little or no control over the outcomes of my direct actions, as in the case of Untouchables in India. I prefer a more focused intervention, in which I see a possibility of accomplishing what I set out to do. As a consequence of this, my research has taken the turn of meeting the expressed needs of various communities. Responding to a request by the Lao Iu Mien people of San Jose, California, I codesigned and codirected, with social worker Huu Nguyen, a federally funded English training, job training, and job placement project for the Iu Mien, Hmong, and Lowland Lao peoples of Santa Clara county. A distinctive feature of the project was its participatory character: representatives of each group were involved in decision making, including the hiring of personnel; moreover, the project was designed so that the students themselves could take over tasks such as social adjustment services and job placement, in other words, become self-sufficient both in employment and in the delivery of services to their own people (Freeman, Nguyen, and Hartsell 1985).

This book is another example of participatory research. In responding to the stated concerns of many Vietnamese-Americans, I designed a collaborative biographies project to enable them to express their own views of their life experiences, in their terms, edited by me in consultation with them and the researcher-interpreters. Although we had our idiosyncratic motivations, we also shared an explicitly stated common goal, and the narratives were shaped by us with that in mind.

The final result is very much a product of the time in which it was written. The narrators had limited or no skills in written English; however, they wanted their life stories to be published in English for an audience wider than Vietnamese-speaking people. I served, therefore, as a transitional mediator between two cultures; in coming years, Vietnamese-American writers can be expected to express themselves eloquently without the need for cultural translators.

The participatory style of the research in this book contrasts with previous asymmetrical American and Vietnamese relationships. America, a contributor to the destabilization of Indochina, has emphasized how Americans suffered in the Indochina wars, but has overlooked the sufferings of the Indochinese, just as it ignored their views during the war years. Finally, an important aspect of the project is that the biographies will also be published in Vietnamese (see also Freeman 1985a, 1985b).

In creating this book, I aimed to document the lives of ordinary people, many of whom acted in extraordinary ways when confronted with great crises. From the stories of these "invisible" people, we may gain insights about well-known events from perspectives that previously had been overlooked. Furthermore, I intended that this research would result in tangible benefits for the community of people that was the subject of study. For the narrators and other Vietnamese-Americans, this book is both a "salvage ethnography" and an attempt to set the record straight. The life stories presented in this book document a heritage, much of which is rapidly changing. By coming to understand and appreciate the varieties of perspectives and life-styles represented by the narrators, by realizing how Vietnamese-Americans view themselves, we may be able to dispel some of the stereotypes about them, and avoid misunderstandings and conflicts. These accounts provide a depth of detail of refugee viewpoints, needs, and concerns that might be of use to federally and privately funded service-provider agencies that aim to serve the immediate survival needs of refugees. Finally, these stories call attention to successful adjustment strategies in America that other Americans might have overlooked.

The Editor's Role

If I could have interviewed Albert Einstein, the reader might wish to know something of my own perspectives, but legitimately could expect that I would not share center stage in this interview, since the subject of the interview has a distinctive and important contribution that transcends my perspective. Indeed, the focus on our interactions might very well obscure this contribution.

Similarly, if a narrator is directly involved in a momentous historical event or sequence of events, such as the collapse of Vietnam, the appropriate emphasis might be the effects of that event on the narrator rather than my interaction and dialogue with that person. An excessive emphasis on the latter might lead us to lose sight of the larger historical event. The two emphases point to different levels of magnification through which an individual's life is revealed.

While I tell something of my own background and perspectives, and describe some of my interactions and dialogues with the narrators and researcher-interpreters, the appropriate focus of this book is the effect of a traumatic historical event on their lives. I am preparing portions of the full texts as dialogues for publication elsewhere, with additional discussion of the editing process (on my personal background, see Freeman 1979: 393–396). Appropriateness depends, as common sense suggests, on the subject and on the aim of the investigator: the biography of a refugee from Vietnam requires coverage that goes far beyond that of narrator and investigator relationships (see also Marcus and Fischer 1986: 42, 68, 78).

Implications for Cultural Dialogue and Critique

All too often, studies of refugees focus on the one-sided view of how newcomers adjust to American life. This book has attempted to convey more than that. It provides multivocal views and commentaries on Vietnam and on America. We see how Vietnamese-Americans view their own cultural background and some of the formative events in the contemporary history of their native land. We also see how they react to the people and customs of America.

By documenting the refugee experience in this way, the narratives in *Hearts of Sorrow* highlight a dual critique. On the one hand, Americans might reflect on Vietnamese-American views of America, its economic opportunities, and its social limitations. Perhaps never before in American history have so many refugees succeeded economically so fast and so well. Some of the adaptive patterns of Vietnamese-Americans, particularly those stressing consensus, familial cooperation, and self-help, may have been overlooked by Americans seeking to improve their own economic and social predicaments. Americans might think also about the Vietnamese-American critiques of political freedom, discipline, and friendship. Furthermore, Americans might reflect in new ways on their role in the Vietnam war and their present relations with the Socialist Republic of Vietnam, based on the alternative perspectives offered by Vietnamese-Americans.

On the other hand, Vietnamese-Americans, as a consequence of their resettlement, are now learning American strategies of economic and social survival and are reflecting upon themselves and their life-styles in ways that previously they had not recognized. Their customs and outlook have been challenged in their new setting; the political and social leaders of the older generation have been largely discredited or at least bypassed. Some anti-Communist resistance groups have been accused of fraud and have lost most of their followers. Both Catholic and Buddhist factions within their religions have fragmented these religious groups. The old-country idealized roles of females, children, and elders have been challenged as traditional social controls are loosening. Many Vietnamese-Americans have been confronted with antirefugee backlash, occasionally violent, in which the attackers question the right of refugees to stay in America, use its resources, and take jobs. Vietnamese-Americans find that their customs and previously unquestioned beliefs are often misunderstood; in the case of the corporal punishment of children, their custom violates American laws. Vietnamese-Americans are forced to reexamine their own assumptions about parental versus children's rights in light of this conflict.

For many people who were born in Vietnam, life in America, despite its positive features, also retains its heavy burdens: the necessity to adjust to a world that is not "at ease"; the memories of war, flight from oppression, and relatives left behind; the dream of returning to an idealized homeland that no longer exists. The successes of the Vietnamese-Americans are all the more remarkable when they are considered in light of what these people have endured.

The terrible tragedy of the refugees from Vietnam has, ironically, turned into America's good fortune, and I hope ultimately into theirs. I believe that America is much the better off for having brought the Vietnamese here, for they are an invigorating force that already has contributed much to America, and they have already prompted other Americans to reflect on the American experience in new ways.

Bibliography

Bibliography

The references listed are representative, not exhaustive. They range from anti-Communist writings to sympathetic apologies for the Socialist Republic of Vietnam. They may be compared with the refugee viewpoints presented in this book. The bibliography also includes selected references on refugee resettlement and some sources related to issues in biography.

Baer, Florence E. 1982. "Give me . . . your huddled masses: Anti-Vietnamese Refugee Lore and the 'Image of Limited Good.'" *Western Folklore*. Vol. 41, October, pp. 275–291.

Banerian, James, ed. 1984. *Losers Are Pirates*. Phoenix, Ariz.: Tieng Me Publications.

———, ed. and trans. 1986. *Vietnamese Short Stories: An Introduction*. Phoenix, Ariz.: Sphinx Publishing.

Bousquet, Gisele. 1987. "Living in a State of Limbo: A Case Study of Vietnamese Refugees in Hong Kong Camps." In *People in Upheaval*. Scott M. Morgan and Elizabeth Colson, eds. New York: Center for Migration Studies, pp. 34–53.

Butler, David. 1985. *The Fall of Saigon*. New York: Simon and Schuster.

Buttinger, Joseph. 1958. *The Smaller Dragon: A Political History of Vietnam*. New York: Praeger.

———. 1972. *A Dragon Defiant: A Short History of Vietnam*, 2 vols. New York: Praeger.

Clifford, James. 1983. "Power and Dialogue in Ethnography: Marcel Griaule's Initiation." In *Observers Observed*. George W. Stocking, ed. Madison, Wisc.: University of Wisconsin Press, pp. 121–156.

Clifford, James, and George E. Marcus, eds. 1986. *Writing Culture: The Poetics and Politics of Ethnography*. Berkeley, Calif.: University of California Press.

Condominas, George. 1977. *We Have Eaten the Forest*. New York: Hill and Wang. Orig. pub. 1957.

Crapanzano, Vincent. 1980. *Tuhami: Portrait of a Moroccan*. Chicago: University of Chicago Press.

———. 1986. *Waiting: The Whites of South Africa*. New York: Vintage. Orig. pub. 1985.

Devereux, George. 1967. *From Anxiety to Method in the Behavioral Sciences*. The Hague, Netherlands: Mouton and Co.

Doan Van Toai and David Chanoff. 1986. *The Vietnamese Gulag*. New York: Simon and Schuster.

Duiker, William. 1981. *The Communist Road to Power in Vietnam*. Boulder, Colo.: Westview Press.

———. 1983. *Vietnam: Nation in Revolution*. Boulder, Colo.: Westview Press.

Elliott, David, ed. 1980. *The Third Indochina Conflict*. Boulder, Colo.: Westview Press.

Finan, Christine. 1980. "A Community Affair: Occupational Assimilation of Vietnamese Refugees." *Journal of Refugee Resettlement*. Vol. 1, no. 1.

FitzGerald, Frances. 1973. *Fire in the Lake: The Vietnamese and Americans in Vietnam*. New York: Vintage. Orig. pub. Little, Brown, 1972.

Freeman, James M. 1979. *Untouchable: An Indian Life History*. Stanford, Calif.: Stanford University Press. Paperback ed., 1981.

———. 1984. "Knowledge, Compassion, and Involvement." *San Jose Studies*. Vol. 10, no. 2, pp. 15–30.

———. 1985a. "Indochinese Refugees Have Helped More Than Hurt America." *San Jose Business Journal*. Week of October 8, p. 5.

———. 1985b. "Indochina to Silicon Valley: Refugee Impacts and Prospects" [in Vietnamese, Linh C. Brown, trans.]. *Dan Toc*. No. 194, October 26, pp. 2–6.

———. 1986. "The Consciousness of Freedom of India's Untouchables." In *Social and Economic Development of India*. Dilip K. Basu and Richard Sisson, eds. New Delhi and Beverly Hills: Sage Publications, pp. 153–171.

———. 1987. "Turnings in the Life of a Vietnamese Buddhist Nun." In *Betwixt and Between: Patterns of Masculine and Feminine Initiation*. Louise

Carus Mahdi, Steven Foster, and Meredith Little, eds. La Salle, Ill.: Open Court, pp. 264–278.

———. 1988. "Vietnamese War Widow." *San Jose Studies*. Vol. 14, no. 2, Spring, pp. 59–70.

Freeman, James M., and David L. Krantz. 1980. "The Unfulfilled Promise of Life Histories." *Biography*. Vol. 3, no. 1, pp. 1–13.

Freeman, James M., Huu Nguyen, and Peggy Hartsell. 1985. "The Tribal Lao Training Project." *Cultural Survival Quarterly*. Vol. 9, no. 2, pp. 10–12.

Geertz, Clifford. 1988. *Works and Lives: The Anthropologist as Author*. Stanford, Calif.: Stanford University Press.

Gough, Kathleen. 1978. *Ten Times More Beautiful: The Rebuilding of Vietnam*. New York: Monthly Review Press.

Grant, Bruce. 1979. *The Boat People*. New York: Penguin.

Haines, David W., ed. 1985. *Refugees in the United States: A Reference Handbook*. Westport, Conn.: Greenwood Press.

Harrison, James Pinckney. 1983. *The Endless War: Vietnam's Struggle for Independence*. New York: McGraw-Hill. Orig. pub. 1982.

Hickey, Gerald C. 1964. *Village in Vietnam*. New Haven, Conn.: Yale University Press.

———. 1982. *Free in the Forest: Ethnohistory of the Vietnamese Central Highlands 1954–1976*. New Haven, Conn.: Yale University Press.

Hoang Van Chi. 1964. *From Colonialism to Communism*. New York: Praeger.

Huynh Quang Nhuong. 1982. *The Land I Lost*. New York: Harper & Row.

Huynh Sanh Thong, trans. 1973. *The Tale of Kieu* by Nguyen Du. New York: Random House.

———, trans. 1983. *The Tale of Kieu: A Bilingual Edition of Truyen Kieu* by Nguyen Du. New Haven, Conn.: Yale University Press.

Isaacs, Arnold. 1984. *Without Honor: Defeat in Vietnam and Cambodia*. New York: Vintage. Orig. pub. 1983.

Karnow, Stanley. 1983. *Vietnam: A History*. New York: Viking Press.

Kelly, Gail. 1977. *From Vietnam to America: A Chronicle of the Vietnamese Immigration to the United States*. Boulder, Colo.: Westview Press.

Knudsen, John Chr. 1983. *Boat People in Transit*. Bergen Studies in Social Anthropology 31: University of Bergen (Norway).

———. 1986. "Health Problems in the Refugee Career: Refugees from Vietnam via Transit Camps to Norway." In *Health and International Life-Courses*, by K. Ask, R. Gronhaug, A. Tesli, and J. Chr. Knudsen. Bergen Studies in Social Anthropology 37. University of Bergen (Norway), pp. 51–98.

———. 1988. *Vietnamese Survivors: Processes Involved in Refugee Coping and Adaptation*. The Migration Project, Department of Social Anthropology, University of Bergen.

Langness, L. L., and Gelya Frank. 1981. *Lives: An Anthropological Approach to Biography*. Novato, Calif.: Chandler and Sharp.

Liu, William. 1979. *Transition to Nowhere: Vietnamese Refugees in America*. Nashville and London: Charter House.

Loescher, Gil, and John A. Scanlon. 1986. *Calculated Kindness: Refugees and America's Half-Open Door, 1945–Present*. New York: Free Press.

Mangold, Tom, and John Penycate. 1985. *The Tunnels of Cu Chi*. New York: Random House.

Marcus, George E., and Michael M. J. Fischer. 1986. *Anthropology as Cultural Critique*. Chicago: University of Chicago Press.

Marr, David G. 1971. *Vietnamese Anticolonialism 1885–1925*. Berkeley, Calif.: University of California Press.

———. 1981. *Vietnamese Tradition on Trial 1920–1945*. Berkeley, Calif.: University of California Press.

Maurer, Armand. 1978. "Method in Ockham's Nominalism." *The Monist*. Vol. 61, no. 3, pp. 426–443.

Menger, Karl. 1960. "A Counterpart of Ockham's Razor in Pure and Applied Mathematics: Ontological Uses." *Synthese*. Vol. 12, no. 4, pp. 415–428.

Montero, Daniel. 1979. *Vietnamese Americans: Patterns of Resettlement and Socioeconomic Adaptation in the United States*. Boulder, Colo.: Westview Press.

Moore, Barrington, Jr. 1978. *Injustice: The Social Bases of Obedience and Revolt*. New York: M. E. Sharpe, Inc.

Narada Maha Thera. 1982. *The Buddha and His Teachings* [in Vietnamese]. Reprint of 1964 edition.

Ngo Vinh Long. 1973. *Before the Revolution: The Vietnamese Peasants Under the French*. Cambridge, Mass.: MIT Press.

Nguyen Du. *The Tale of Kieu*. [See Huynh Sanh Thong, trans.]

Nguyen Long, with Harry H. Kendall. 1981. *After Saigon Fell: Daily Life Under the Vietnamese Communists*. Berkeley, Calif.: Institute of East Asian Studies, University of California.

Nguyen Manh Hung. 1985. "Vietnamese." In *Refugees in the United States: A Reference Handbook*. David W. Haines, ed. Westport, Conn.: Greenwood Press, pp. 195–208.

Nguyen Ngoc Ngan and E. E. Richey. 1982. *The Will of Heaven: A Story of One Vietnamese and the End of His World*. New York: Dutton.

Nguyen Tien Hung. 1977. *Economic Development of Socialist Vietnam, 1955–80*. New York: Praeger.

Nguyen Van Canh, with Earle Cooper. 1983. *Vietnam Under Communism: 1975–1982*. Stanford, Calif.: Hoover Institution Press.

Nhat Tien, Duong Phuc, and Vu Thanh Thuy. 1981. *Pirates on the Gulf of Siam*. James Banerian, trans. San Diego, Calif.: Boat People S.O.S. Committee.

Nidorf, Jeanne F. 1985. "Mental Health and Refugee Youths: A Model for Diagnostic Training." In *Southeast Asian Mental Health: Treatment, Prevention, Services, Training, and Research*. Tom Choken Owan et al., eds. DHHS Publication No. (ADM) 85-1339: U.S. Department of Health and Human Services, pp. 391–429.

Oberdorfer, Don. 1984. *Tet!* New York: Da Capo Press. Orig. pub. 1971.

Owan, Tom Choken et al., eds. 1985. *Southeast Asian Mental Health: Treatment, Prevention, Services, Training, and Research*. DHHS Publication No. (ADM) 85-1339: U.S. Department of Health and Human Services.

Pike, Douglas. 1978. *History of Vietnamese Communism, 1925–1976*. Stanford, Calif.: Hoover Institution Press.

———. 1986. *PAVN: People's Army of Vietnam*. Novato, Calif.: Presidio Press.

Rabinow, Paul. 1977. *Reflections on Fieldwork in Morocco*. Berkeley, Calif.: University of California Press.

Refugee Reports. 1987. Washington, D.C.: American Council for Nationalities Service.

Roose-Evans, James. 1970. *Experimental Theatre: From Stanislavsky to Today*. New York: Avon.

Rumbaut, Ruben G. 1985. "Mental Health and the Refugee Experience: A Comparative Study of Southeast Asian Refugees." In *Southeast Asian Mental Health: Treatment, Prevention, Services, Training, and Research*. Tom Choken Owan et al., eds. DHHS Publication No. (ADM) 85-1339: U.S. Department of Health and Human Services, pp. 433–486.

Rumbaut, Ruben G., and Kenji Ima. September 1987. "The Adaptation of Southeast Asian Refugee Youth: A Comparative Study." Executive Summary. Final Report to the Office of Refugee Resettlement, Washington, D.C.

Sagan, Ginetta, and Stephen Denney. 1983. *Violations of Human Rights in the Socialist Republic of Vietnam, April 30, 1975–April 30, 1983*. Atherton, Calif.: Aurora Foundation.

Santoli, Al. 1985. *To Bear Any Burden*. New York: Dutton.

Schechner, Richard. 1973. *Environmental Theater*. New York: Hawthorne.

Scholl-Latour, Peter. 1985. *Death in the Rice Fields*. New York: Penguin Books. Orig. pub. 1979.

Shostak, Marjorie. 1983. *Nisa: The Life and Words of a !Kung Woman*. New York: Vintage. Orig. pub. 1981.

Snepp, Frank. 1978. *Decent Interval*. New York: Vintage. Orig. pub. 1977.

Starr, Paul, and Alden Roberts. 1981. "Attitudes Towards Indochinese Refugees: An Empirical Study." *Journal of Refugee Resettlement*. Vol. 1, no. 4, pp. 51–66.

Stopp, G. Harry, Jr., and Nguyen M. Hung, eds. 1979. *Proceedings of the First Annual Conference on Indochinese Refugees*. George Mason University, Fairfax, Va.

Terzani, Tiziano. 1976. *Giai Phong!* New York: St. Martin's Press.

Titon, Jeff Todd. 1980. "The Life Story." *Journal of American Folklore*. July–September, pp. 276–292.

Tran Van Dien. 1981. *The Childhood Memories of Vietnam*. Bilingual edition. Westminster, Calif.: NV Printing.

Tran Van Don. 1978. *Our Endless War*. San Rafael, Calif.: Presidio Press.

Truong Nhu Tang, with David Chanoff and Doan Van Toai. 1985. *A Vietcong Memoir*. New York: Harcourt Brace Jovanovich.

Van Tien Dung. 1977. *Our Great Spring Victory*. Don Luce, trans. New York: Monthly Review Press.

Wain, Barry. 1981. *The Refused: The Agony of the Indochinese Refugees*. New York: Simon and Schuster.

West, F. J., Jr. 1985. *The Village*. Madison, Wisc.: University of Wisconsin Press. Orig. pub. 1972.

Library of Congress Cataloging-in-Publication Data

Freeman, James M.
    Hearts of sorrow : Vietnamese-American lives / James M.
Freeman.
      p.   cm.
    Bibliography: p.
    ISBN 0-8047-1585-8 (alk. paper)
    1. Vietnamese Americans.   2. Refugees—United States.
3. Refugees—Vietnam.   I. Title.
E184.V53F74   1989
973'.049592—dc20   89-32115
                                         CIP